Fear of the Consequence of Failure

To Wendy,

it was fun while it lasted at QVS.

John Robinson

Fear of the Consequence of Failure

The story of a life in the Army of an ordinary person in the extraordinary world of Bomb Disposal

John Robinson

First Edition

ISBNs:
978-1-80541-425-4 (hardcover)
978-1-80541-300-4 (paperback)
978-1-80541-301-1 (eBook)

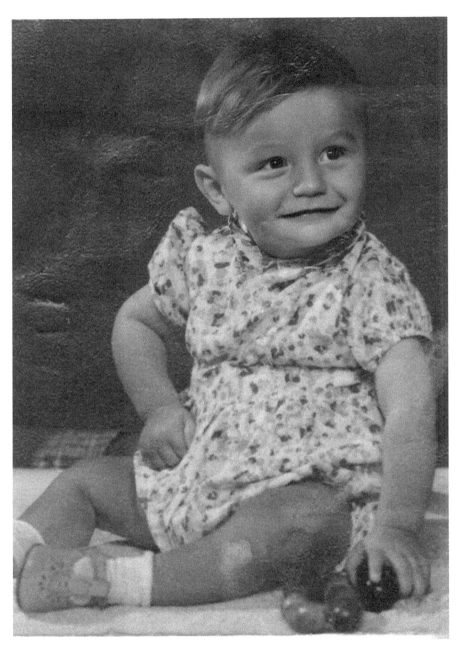

Yours Truly – Possibly the only time I was ever charming & charismatic.

Contents

Dedication

To my late wife, Christine Louise Robinson PhD
And
All EOD and Search Personnel, past, present, and future

This book is dedicated firstly to my late wife, Dr Christine Louise Robinson (nee Main). I use her academic title not from a wish to be highbrow but out of respect for her massive work ethic in becoming a Doctor of Philosophy whilst bringing up two sons, working and struggling to cope with terminal cancer. In year three of her first degree, Christine flagged, and an investigation revealed dyslexia so debilitating that she typically had to work three times harder than others to keep up. After support measures were put in place by Stirling University, Christine thrived, completing a master's degree before embarking on her PhD. Her chosen theme was research into homelessness among veterans.

We had married at Edinburgh Castle in 1984. She was by my side, tolerating my many nuances and coping alone whilst I was away from the marital home on frequent deployments. By the time we had been married for seven years, we had been apart for three of them. For my part, I was single-minded about my bomb disposal employment and was probably selfish in expecting her to manage.

Christine worked for the Army in Germany in the late 1980s, firstly in Rheindahlen Garrison where she was employed in G4 Estates. I was in Bessbrook Mill at the time, and in a memorable phone call, she let me know she was alright after a large car bomb detonated outside the Officers' Mess, not far from our home. Her sister, Audrey, was staying with her at the time and perhaps Prosecco could be blamed for them sleeping through the bang! What did annoy her was typing out reams of works service request forms for the many hundreds of broken windows needing the glass replaced.

Her next job was in the Families' Office of the 7th Signal Regiment in Herford. I had already deployed to the first Gulf War when elements of that regiment deployed, and Christine was the first point of contact in caring for their families.

After our two sons were born and I had left the Army, Christine wanted greater challenges and she completed a university access course before being admitted to Stirling University. After a BSc (Hons) in Environmental Geography, she was admitted to the Faculty of Social Sciences, gaining a master's degree in Housing and then a research PhD concerning homeless veterans. It was whilst researching for her PhD that she was diagnosed with Mucosal Melanoma, a very rare and aggressive cancer. She underwent life-changing surgery, but this was too late to prevent the cancer from spreading. Whilst undergoing debilitating treatments, she completed her PhD, worked in the Charity Sector, and was appointed a Research Fellow at Stirling University, successfully attracting a very large research grant aimed at helping veterans.

Christine succumbed to cancer on 15 January 2019, three weeks after her 59th birthday. If this book makes a profit, half of it will be donated to the charity Melanoma Action and Support Scotland (MASScot).

Christine in 2015 after her life-changing surgery

Secondly, this book is dedicated to all those who have served in the EOD and Search Roles, including Bleeps in the electronic search role. Bleeps and Sappers kept me and many others safe both in Belfast and South Armagh; Bleeps with their passive and active sweeps and Sappers conducting isolation and final approach route clearances. These were huge responsibilities thrust on their very young shoulders. For me, the Royal Engineers were always a reassuring if mischievous presence and I took it in my stride (literally) when Dutch, my Search Advisor (RESA), made a swansong bet with the Final Approach Man that he couldn't goad me into wading chest-deep along 100 metres of the rapidly flowing and very cold Forkhill River on the pretext that this was the safest route to reach a suspect device. Dutch had to pay up, but the grin on his face as I emerged with water gushing out of the bomb suit showed he didn't mind a bit! My Sappers were given a hard time by one of my superiors whilst supporting me in high-risk operations which was undeserved and could have destroyed the essential RE/RAOC working relationship. Fortunately, at our level, trust and mutual respect overcame the parochial hubris.

Above our level, there existed a Corps rivalry concerning who did what in bomb disposal and who did it best. It was, for me, the most embarrassing 'pissing contest' in town. Each Corps had its own respective bomb disposal role. It was as if the RAOC suspected the RE was trying to eclipse them and steal the vaunted terrorist bomb disposal role. There was no need for this paranoia. At the time, respective bomb disposal procedures, philosophies and doctrines were quite different. It was notable in the Gulf War that the officer commanding 49 EOD Squadron RE requested an RAOC Ammunition Technician warrant officer be embedded within his squadron to enhance the overall capability, efficiency and, most of all, safety for all concerned. I think he was pioneering in this approach. Since those times, the roles have merged somewhat and, who might make a safe and reliable EOD Operator is a matter of individual capability and not what cap badge sits in his or her hat. Yes, I said 'her'. Initially, the trade was only open to males, although I believe there was a temporary inclusion of females as ammunition examiners in the Second World War. In 1992, I was chuffed to see we had the first female on the ATO (Ammunition Technical Officer) Course at Shrivenham when I was the SAT. I think she did well, and she had to tolerate not a little chauvinism. Some readers may well know of whom I speak; suffice it to say, I thought she was the best 'man' on the course! The other half of any profits from this book will be donated to the Felix Fund. I have added the URLs to these charities below, along with their mission statements.

Melanoma Action and Support Scotland (MASScot):
https://www.masscot.org.uk
Melanoma Action and Support Scotland (MASScot) is Scotland's only skin cancer-specific charity. Formed in 2003, MASScot supports people who have been diagnosed with Melanoma and other skin cancers. We provide complementary support, counselling and therapy services for skin cancer patients and their families and carers. Melanoma is the fifth most common cancer amongst all age groups in Scotland. When it comes to those aged 15 to 34, it is the most common. As a result, since 2013, we have provided an educational resource in schools to warn young people of the dangers of overexposure to the sun.

The Felix Fund: https://www.felixfund.org.uk
Felix Fund – The Bomb Disposal Charity. Every day, bomb disposal and search personnel deal with highly pressured situations. This continued exposure to intense stress can have lasting effects, both physical and mental. Felix Fund aims to assist with the well-being of individuals

within the Explosive Ordnance Disposal (EOD) and Search Community across all British military.

Introduction and Foreword

Thank you for buying this book; or, if you borrowed it, please buy a copy anyway. The proceeds are going towards the welfare of EOD and Search personnel and their families for those killed, wounded or adversely affected in or by their actions, and to a worthy cancer charity. I've already gotten what I personally wanted out of writing this book. It has been a cathartic experience and I've left my family a record of this part of my life as I have regretted the very sad paucity of information concerning my grandfathers' service in the Great War. In tribute to their service, I would like to record that they were both wounded; one was gassed and suffered life-limiting damage to his lungs. The other suffered shrapnel wounds and, I suspect, PTSD. Coincidentally, in very different units, they were wounded and repatriated to recover at about the same time. I once saw a posed photograph of them, long since lost, taken in a photographer's parlour studio. One is seated in a woven peacock chair and the other standing slightly behind him. A faded drop serves as a background with Grecian trappings and a palm plant evident despite being threadbare. As a sign of the growing and uneven rates of economic and industrial attrition during the war, one grandfather is wearing a completely blue uniform and the other is in khaki but is wearing a blue armband. I believe the blue colour indicated hospital dress and their temporary non-combatant status as evacuated wounded soldiers. Each grandfather was entitled to the British War Medal and the Victory Medal, but these medals are sadly lost.

My father's father, Wilfred Robinson, was a lay Methodist preacher in peacetime. Dad was the youngest of five sons, but one was severely disabled. Grandad Wilfred would play the organ in the Methodist Chapel during services. He was in a minority of grown men in Southchurch who could read and write well, and, before the Great War, he was a warehouseman in the local Co-operative Society shop, before becoming involved in Life Assurance, much like his father George before him. After war service in the Light Infantry, however, he fell upon hard times and became unemployed but managed to make some money for subsistence by playing the piano in local pubs. Money being short led my father to chop up soapboxes for firewood and sell the bundles around the village. Years ago, I had seen an old, dog-eared photo in his album, and I asked him why a Charlie Chaplin lookalike had been to Southchurch. His reply was memorable and deeply saddening. The man was in fact a Means Test Inspector. As Grandad was unemployed, he had claimed the dole. In a somewhat brutal process by modern standards, the Inspector would call at a claimant's home to assess all sources of income and what assets could be sold off. The Inspector had just means-tested my grandfather. My father, who was probably about 7 years old, ran up to his father with an outstretched hand holding a few pennies, his takings for the morning's work which had been unusually fruitful. The Inspector pounced and counted the coppers in my father's hand and then docked the same daily amount from my grandfather's dole. The Inspector, doubtless pleased at reducing the claim, turned and left. My grandfather dragged Dad inside and thrashed him with his belt. My dad held no bitterness over this episode. He had been foolish to flaunt the money in front of a stranger; he was to blame, and he had to pay the price. My grandfather was never employed again except as a labourer in the Labour Corps during the Second World War. He was sent to Otterburn which was being developed as a range where he helped to lay the roads. He was to die in 1961, aged 71, whilst Dad was serving in Aden. In later years, I was employed at Otterburn, learning my craft on large-scale demolitions and providing technical cover on unit firings, unaware that my grandfather had helped to build the place years before.

Addendum: Towards the end of my finishing the first draft of this book, something quite amazing happened. I was contacted on Facebook and told that a silver war badge belonging to my grandfather, Wilfred Robinson, had been found in a field near Bishop Auckland. A journalist from the Northern Echo had publicised the find on behalf of a metal detectorist who was seeking to reunite the lost medal with the family. It got better. I had already tried my hand at researching both of my grandfathers using online resources, but Wilfred Robinson was something of a mystery. The family thought he had served in the Green Jackets. All I had to go on was that, and his name and years of birth and death; nothing else. The man who discovered the silver war badge was a Mr Mark McMullan and it transpired he was also something of a historian and he enjoyed linking special finds to people. I had never heard of the silver war badge. They were awarded to soldiers who had been invalided out of the service and were intended to be worn on the right breast of the holder's civilian jacket to signify the man had served his country. The badge was 33mm in diameter and around the periphery it read: + For King and Empire + Services Rendered. In the centre was King George V's cypher GRI, standing for Georgius, Rex, Imperator (meaning George, King and Emperor). More importantly, the obverse bore the engraved badge number of the holder and this badge number was unique to a medal roll in the National Archive. This led to Mark finding some of Wilfred Robinson's service history. He had enlisted on 25 October 1916, originally into the Yorkshire Regiment. He then transferred to the Corps of Hussars and was eventually transferred to the Dorset Regiment. He had two regimental numbers and had indeed been wounded. He was discharged on 16 September 1919. In terms of the bigger picture and the massive sacrifice of those who served in the Great War, his exploits are probably unremarkable but not to me and my family and so, after decades of ignorance, we now know something of his military service and that he did his duty. The photographs I have seen of his medal show the badge number as B306311 and very tellingly, it looks like the clasp pin had snapped which may explain how it came to be lost.

Badge No B306311 issued to 46705 Pte Wilfred Robinson. He served in the Yorkshire Regiment initially and then transferred to the Corps of Hussars before transferring to the Dorset Regiment. This badge had been lost near Bishop Auckland and was discovered in Coronation Field, Southchurch, by history hunter Mark McMullan in 2023.

Wilfred's parents, Mary and George Robinson and brother Sydney

My father's father, Wilfred Robinson, circa 1912

Mark McMullan's research and the subsequent publicity then led to another discovery; we had a second cousin alive and well in his seventies living just 10 miles away from my brother David in Coventry. The opportunity to meet him arose when I attended a 321 EOD Unit 50th anniversary reunion in early May 2023. This reunion had been planned to take place two years earlier but was postponed due to Covid. Our cousin turned out to be quite a character and he brought along his Victorian-era family Bible which contained a great many contemporary press clippings and notes about his family. It was a window into our shared past and many of the handwritten notes were written in a style identical to our own late mother's handwriting. There was no apparent reason for this but perhaps there was a common denominator in the form of a strict schoolteacher who might have enforced common standards of writing techniques.

My mother's father was a Master Joiner by the name of John William Sanderson. He had married Doris Acaster who originally came from Hull and had left that city on medical advice due to the pollution there. Together, they had ten children, but I believe one child died shortly after birth. He was fully employed for most of his life, outfitting shops, making coffins, large items of furniture, pit props and such like. In the Great War, he served in the Army Ordnance Corps as a Master Joiner and was allocated a platoon of Pioneers as labour support. They would tour the lines between lulls in battle to build, install and repair the woodwork used to shore up and line the deeper trenches. It was in this role that he was caught during an artillery exchange and exposed to mustard gas. It left him with a life-long debilitating cough. The family was relatively prosperous compared to most in the opencast mining community in Southchurch and they owned a part of a privately designed and built villa which still stands to this day on the banks of the Gaunless. This property passed out of Sanderson family ownership in the 1990s, a very sad loss to me, having spent so many happy, if brief stays there between Dad's postings. John Sanderson passed away when I was six months old. My grandmother passed away in 1986, aged 84, despite a prodigious smoking habit of between 20 to 40 fags a day - Capstan Full Strength and Woodbines in the old days and then filtered cigarettes in later life. Despite concerns for her health in youth and the enforced move away from city life, her lungs were in fine shape and the cause of death was an aspirin-induced stomach haemorrhage. She was a woman of small stature but huge character. She would never back down, was invariably firm, very patient and was a classic matriarch. As a child, I would watch entranced as she rocked back and forth in her rocking chair, knitting, watching TV, chatting to family and smoking all at the same time. It was unbelievable that she could smoke a cigarette all the way down to the end without taking it out of her mouth and then lift it from her lips and deposit it in the ashtray without any ash falling away. An enduring mystery; how the hell could she do that? The happiest memory for me was the whole family and most of the surrounding street watching the 1966 World Cup final live on TV in her living room. Even the winning goals failed to dislodge her fag ash!

My mother's father John William Sanderson
circa 1916

Doris Sanderson (nee Acaster) just after the Second War above left & the Acaster family during the Great War. Grandmother-to-be Doris is on the right in the back row. Dad and brother both serving soldiers. The family were boat people and Doris's own mother drowned in an accident. Her stepmother sits before her.

So sad, then, that it's all gone. Typical of their generation, there was no talk of the war; never. No sign of any medals. To research their war-time exploits would entail a large effort and doubtless some costs. This cannot be right; hence this book about me, written for my children and future generations. Another ambition is to publish this book which is no easy task. Any proceeds will be divided equally between my late wife's charity, Melanoma Action and Support Scotland (MASScot), and the Felix Fund. I hope this telling of my story proves to be interesting, funny at times and poignant.

This book covers the working life of an ordinary person who became immersed in somewhat extraordinary circumstances. The author is the eldest son of a sergeant in the Royal Army Ordnance Corps (RAOC). 22292337 Sergeant Ernest Robinson served initially as a National Serviceman in the late 1940s. Like most young men of his generation, Ernie was called up for National Service but was initially put into rehabilitation due to his very low body mass, typical of the poverty and malnutrition of his time. Placed on arduous duty rations of four meals a day and incessant physical training, he recovered to an acceptable physical standard for military service. On completing National Service, he met Betty, his wife-to-be. In Civvy Street, he had a range of unskilled jobs, most notably as an undertaker's assistant. This ended abruptly when he and a colleague dropped a coffin when trying to negotiate a bend on steep and narrow stairs in a house in Southchurch, which is near Bishop Auckland. The coffin tumbled, end over end, down the stairs before bursting open and ejecting the corpse into the street.

Road signs as you approach County Durham announce the County as 'The Land of the Prince Bishops' and Southchurch is more formally known as St Andrew's Auckland. In my frequent visits to Southchurch, I noted it was anything but princely. As an infant, Dad would take me to his father's house for a weekly bath in a tub in front of the fire. The water came from a communal pump and was 'heated' on the fire. By the time I was lowered into this scum-pot, made viscous by several previous bathers, it was tepid, and I probably emerged dirtier afterwards. Most of Southchurch was grindingly impoverished. A typical terraced house had an earth closet toilet outside (a nettie), shared with several other houses. There was no electricity, and the rooms were feebly illuminated by gas mantle lamps. Vermin thrived and all bedding was infested with bed bugs.

My father enlisted for Regular Service in September 1950. He and Mum were engaged by then and she accompanied him to the recruiting office where her spelling of the word 'scissors' in his aptitude test carried him over the threshold required to become an RAOC Storeman. As grim as military service could be in those days, the food was plentiful, accommodation was generally better than his family endured in

Southchurch and beer and fags were guaranteed. His first four years were spent unaccompanied in Egypt. He and Mum married later on in December 1950. I was the product of a spell of home leave during Christmas 1953. Siblings followed rapidly and I was to become the eldest of seven children.

Responsibility for my siblings came early for me. I have several recollections of note from my childhood experiences in Aden (present-day Yemen) and the districts of Ma'ala and Khormaksar. I was six years old when we flew to Aden by RAF Bristol Britannia. I had already attended several schools in the UK for very short periods and our first accommodation was in a flat in Ma'ala, along the main street. I attended the Chapel Hill Primary School in the mornings, and, in the afternoons, after the obligatory midday rest, I would play with Arab boys amongst the herds of goats that wandered all over the rugged terrain. I remember watching Arab boys at their Islamic schools (Madrasa), through their barred but glassless windows, as they chanted verses from the Holy Quran. The call of the faithful (Adhan) to prayer by the local Muezzin became a more evocative memory to me than Christian church bells.

On my seventh birthday, my parents took me out to an evening meal at a restaurant at Khormaksar airfield. They had got me a white suit and a black bow tie and my hair was slicked with Brylcreem for the occasion (yuk). About the same time, Dad took me on visits to tour the Ark Royal where I was taken up and down on the aircraft lift between the flight deck and cavernous hangar below. We visited a submarine moored offshore and a stool was found so I could play with the periscope.

Looking back, that time seemed like a rite of passage as I was now made more responsible for myself and my three siblings. At the age of seven, I would babysit them whilst my parents went to functions in the sergeants' mess. On the eve of my fifth sibling being born in Munster, Germany in 1964, I despaired of having so many sisters. To placate me, I was promised I could name the child if it was a boy. I always wanted a brother called David and so it was to be!

My lovely, lovely 'bruvva' David on a birthday treat in 2022

My birthday was too late in the academic year for me to start primary school until I was six. It turned out that the age difference between me and my next sibling, Sheenagh, was 11 months, so we went through school together in the same year. Teachers often assumed we were twins. Sheenagh almost became like the brother I longed for and we were often in scrapes with other kids where we supported each other. I recall with great sorrow how she was judged to be thick by teachers in Singapore and she was placed in the remedial section of our year. Sheenagh was not thick by any measure but in those days, if you weren't achieving grades in class commensurate with your peers, you would go into the 'one size fits all' remedial class; how different things are today. Sheenagh invariably showed great strength of character growing up and was the closest to me of all my sisters.

Between postings home and abroad, we would live at my maternal grandmother's house during Dad's embarkation/disembarkation leave. As children, we loved these episodes of fun. There was a small river (the Gaunless) which I almost invariably fell into during every visit. My cousins would then light a bonfire to dry me out before I had to go in as darkness fell. Usually, we didn't attend school there but, on one visit, I was captured by the School Inspector and made to attend Cockton Hill Primary School in Bishop Auckland. It was one of approximately twenty-two schools I was to attend growing up and I was mercilessly singled out for my 'posh' accent. This was a common theme whilst at local authority schools in the UK. The teachers often had little time for us as they knew we would be gone in a few weeks or months. I vividly recall one occasion in Geography when the teacher had us queue at his desk so he could imprint an outline stamp of the world into our exercise books. This was a prelude to a quiz where we had to name countries and capitals. I paused as he stamped my book

13

and he demanded to know why. I said it was amazing how the continents looked like pieces of a jigsaw puzzle that had been separated. He loudly rebuked me in front of the whole class for my whimsical imagination. The irony was that this was the year that the Plate Tectonic Theory was published.

The other kids could be awful. One morning, after a playground beating and being dunked in mud, I was singled out by my 'wicked witch' teacher and given the tawse for having dirty hands and feet. The next day, I got the same treatment for not wearing the regulation pumps in class and for using a paintbrush like a scrubbing brush. I was only there for a few days and was beaten three times. I started having nightmares and became withdrawn, preferring my own company. This also brought some danger; a large gang of feral Southchurch children caught me alone and I was pursued by them, becoming surrounded as I tried to escape across a large pipe over the River Gaunless. On this occasion, the biggest kids demanded that I say 'Winston Churchill' which I did, apparently passing the test to see if I was a Nazi. If I had pronounced the 'W' as a 'V', I would have suffered a worse beating than I actually got; it turned out they had heard we had lived in Germany. I don't think they knew the war was over!

Most of my schooling was in British Forces Education Service (BFES) schools overseas. This was, in my opinion, a much better experience than I had of UK local authority schools. In the BFES schools, the other kids' circumstances were generally the same as mine and our teachers understood why we were different. I excelled at English Language, Engineering Workshop Theory & Practice and woodwork. I had a deep-rooted fear of maths which has lasted all of my life. My last school was St John's Comprehensive in Singapore and this was to be the only school where I really thrived, enjoying nearly all of my subjects and a very patient maths teacher stretched my achievement from a CSE Grade 4 at the mock exam to a Grade 1 in the real exam. In all, I attended very many schools in England, Wales, Germany, Aden and Singapore, sometimes only for a matter of days between my dad's postings. On being interviewed on arrival at a new UK local authority school, a common feedback comment was that I must have a broad background. This was true but it was extremely shallow. In hindsight, the gross lack of continuity, the various syllabi I was subjected to, the bullying by other kids and the impatience of many of my teachers left their mark. I was a loner with little confidence. I had learned that early aggression and violence in socially challenging situations could defeat or deter the bullies but that increased my isolation. The worst of this was in a secondary school in Pembroke Dock. I was regularly punched, kicked and verbally abused. This was my first secondary school, and nowadays, the transition from primary schooling is quite carefully managed. My experience there was anything but. One day, I was at school in Bunde Primary and we were having lunch. A teacher came over and told me to finish up quickly and go to the headmaster's office. There I was told my family was moving back to the UK immediately and we were to be on a flight that evening. I lived right next to the school and ran home to find Mum frantically packing suitcases. We had known we were returning to the UK at some time in the near future but for some reason, unbeknown to me, we were being packed off that instant. Looking back, the sudden urgency and disruption didn't seem out of place to me at all; in fact, it was normal. Quite why a family of eight would be treated like that would be bizarre by modern-day standards. We caught the flight and when we landed in the UK, we went by train to Southchurch for a short stay before getting another train to Pembroke.

Me and my sister Sheenagh started at the Coronation Secondary School Pembroke in early September 1966. One day, it came to a head outside the boys' toilets. I was pinned against the wall and several boys took turns giving me bodychecks of the kind you would see in the popular Saturday afternoon TV professional wrestling shows. A big heavy kid charged towards me. The boys who were holding me against the wall flinched as he neared. I broke loose and ducked, and he head-butted the wall and stunned himself. In a red mist, I tore into the others as a playground chant of "fight, fight, fight" erupted and eventually, I was dragged off one of my erstwhile attackers by a teacher. After that, I was left well alone. My aversion to school led to truanting. The school had two campuses and we walked between them each day. I noticed that staff did not conduct a roll call on arrival. If anyone was noted as absent, there seemed to be an acceptance that they had a bona fide reason. At the time, I had volunteered for violin lessons. These were given one-on-one by an unpaid and lovely elderly lady. The times were varied to suit her availability, and this became my default excuse. The fear of being caught was easily eclipsed by the fear of the subjects, teachers and pupils I avoided whilst truanting. There was one exceptional teacher; my form tutor. I remember her outward-looking style of real-world teaching and coaching. Under her tutelage and mentoring, the terrible coal tip disaster in neighbouring Aberfan was carefully explained to us, we followed Sir Francis Chichester's progress around the world and marvelled at the world's first heart transplant, deeply saddened when Louis Washkansky died.

Just as I might have been turning the corner and starting to appreciate school, Dad was posted to Donnington. Another school; this time the Trench Secondary Modern School near Telford. Maths continued to be my nemesis. I couldn't understand binary arithmetic. My struggle seemed to infuriate the teacher, so I stopped asking for help. On one occasion, I was unable to recite Pythagoras' Theorem. After the subsequent punishment, I learned it by rote under threat of even more punishment and can still recite it word perfectly now, fifty-four years later. The problem was I could say it, but I didn't understand what it meant at that time. Looking back, I can see that fear was becoming a reason to do things; many different things, fighting, talking my way out of situations and taking calculated risks but it didn't make me more intelligent; it was a coping strategy.

I finished my schooling at St John's in Singapore on 28 June 1971 and we were to return to the UK for my dad to serve his final tour of duty in the Army. My dad was a heavy drinker, a compulsive gambler and a heavy smoker. On one occasion, at a social function in his Mess, I looked on aghast as he lost 6 weeks' advanced pay at an all-night poker school. The advance of pay was meant to see us through the journey back to the UK. My late mother was very good at coping with his weaknesses and protected us from his excesses largely by concealing them. On this occasion, I witnessed first-hand his gambling and total loss of control with this addiction which completely undermined my personal security. To this day, I get angry at the explosion of online gambling and the plethora of patronising TV adverts proclaiming how safe it is.

His last posting was at Central Ammunition Depot Kineton. He was in B Company and worked out of an office above the old guardroom next to the A41. He was the NCO in charge of stocktaking, and he had a most endearing and forgiving boss, Major Bill Baker, which was probably just as well. On arrival, I couldn't find a job; ammunition depots are not known for being located near populated areas and the bus service was non-existent. I left home and went north to find work.

I landed a job as a Van Boy at the Alfred Morris Fur Coat Factory at Shildon. It traded as 'Astraka of London'. This was somewhat pretentious; the factory was in Shildon, and Alfred Morris had a very small accommodation address in London. To be fair, Astraka had achieved a 'coals to Newcastle' business coup by selling a large consignment of furs to Russia. My new-found joy at finding employment started to disappear from the start. I would have to wash, wax and polish the boss's Jensen Interceptor which, during the winter, was painful. However, the over-arching reality was that fur coats tend not to sell in summer so, in the following spring, I was made redundant. I was now jobless and homeless. Despite the ringing endorsement of my loyalty and devotion to Queen and country expressed at my Long Service and Good Conduct Medal presentation in 1988, my motivation to join up was only to get a roof over my head and three meals a day, and maybe learn a trade. Whatever my motive though, it was the best choice I ever made in my life. In retrospect, I made some bad early life choices, but I have no regrets as even those bad choices helped shape my character and lay a solid foundation for future success.

In concluding this summary of my formative years, I have offered this background so that any readers who knew me during my Army Service might understand me better for who and what I was. Perhaps bizarrely for one who progressed into the world of explosives, guided missiles and bomb disposal, I believe one of my strongest motivators was the fear of the consequence of failure. In my teenage years and throughout my Army Service, I suffered from frequent migraine headaches, and I usually had a mouthful of painful ulcers at any one time. I initially put this down to stress and anxiety stemming from not wanting to fail. With very considerable hindsight, however, my headaches and ulcers ceased from about 1999 when I elected to avoid mercury-containing amalgam fillings at the dentist. My late wife's research into veterans started to lift the veil of ignorance from the opportunity cost of a no-madic childhood, where there were no long-term friendships or grass roots to call home. I left the Army in March 1999 after twenty-seven years, adopted the City of Dunblane as my new hometown and focused on providing my two young sons with a stable family life.

My Life's Journey and Stops Along the Way		
Where	*When*	*What*
Gateshead, England	1954	Born
Chilwell, England	1954 - 1956	Army life in the UK and abroad. Each posting to and from the UK entailed a brief stay at my grandmother's home in Southchurch, Bishop Auckland.
Minden, Germany	1956 - 1960	
Ma'ala, Aden (Yemen)	1960 - 1961	
Khormaksar, Aden	1961 - 1962	
Bracht, Germany	1962 - 1963	
Munster, Germany	1964 - 1965	
Bunde, Germany	1965 - 1966	
Pembroke, Wales	1966 - 1967	
Donnington, England	1967 - 1968	
Lorong M, Singapore	1968 - 1969	
Ban Guan Park, Singapore	1969	
Mt Sinai Plain, Singapore	1969 - 1970	
Tanglin, Singapore	1970 - 1971	
Kineton, England	1971	Left home & started work in Shildon
Bp Auckland, England	1971 - 1972	
Blackdown, England	1972	Basic military training
Bramley, England	1972 - 1973	Ammo Technician's Course
Kineton, England	1973 - 1974	Depot duties
Lisburn, NI	1974	EOD Tour as No 2
Kineton, England	1974 - 1975	Depot duties
Armagh, NI	1975	EOD Tour as No 2
Kineton, England	1975 - 1976	Depot duties & technical training
Paderborn, Germany	1976 - 1977	Lance GM Platoon
Kineton, England	1978 - 1979	Depot duties

Belfast, NI	1979	EOD Tour as No 1
Kineton, England	1979 - 1981	Depot duties
Stonecutters Island, HK	1981 - 1982	Depot AT at ASD Hong Kong
Edinburgh, Scotland	1983 - 1984	521 EOD Company
Oman	1984 - 1986	Loan Service
Rheindahlen, Germany	1986 - 1987	Ammo Operational Planning HQ BAOR
Bessbrook, NI	1987	EOD Tour as No 1 at ARB
Rheindahlen, Germany	1987	Ammo Operational Planning HQ BAOR
Herford, Germany	1987 - 1989	221 EOD Company – SAT 4 Armd Div
Falkland Islands	1989 - 1990	SAT in charge of depot & Inspectorate
Saudi Arabia	1990 - 1991	Gulf War
Herford, Germany	1991 - 1992	221 EOD Company – SAT 4 Armd Div
Shrivenham, England	1992 - 1994	SAT at RMCS
London, England	1994 - 1997	621 EOD Squadron
Longtown, England	1997 - 1999	Oi/c Accounts & retired from Army
Edinburgh, Scotland	2000 - 2002	SO2 Resources Logistic Support
Stirling, Scotland	2002 - 2014	3 SO2 staff posts in HQ 51 Brigade
Dunblane, Scotland	2014 - 2021	Estate Manager Queen Victoria School
Dunblane, Scotland	2021	Retired.

For abbreviations, please see the jargon-buster at the back of the book.

The remainder of this book will generally follow the journey outlined above, expanding into greater detail. Photographs can be found embedded within the relevant chapters. In the hope I may attract a wide readership, I will explain aspects of military life, abbreviations and procedures. A possibly confusing aspect to readers with little or no military experience is the amount of change that took place during my military career and the twenty-four years that have elapsed since then. The RAOC Bomb Disposal unit in Northern Ireland had name changes from 321 EOD Unit to 321 EOD Company and then became 321 EOD Squadron upon the formation of the Royal Logistic Corps. My childhood and service in Germany was during the Cold War when Germany was divided into East and West. All of the views and opinions expressed are my own, based on my direct experiences. I will avoid identifying individual people except where they are deceased or have consented to be named. However, I have often used first names and nicknames so those who served with me may spot mention of themselves. Looking back at it all, I have no regrets, although I could have done some things better; that said, some things could have turned out far worse than they did. I do have a quixotic tendency to try and put things right. This was often misunderstood by peers and superiors alike and once, after vigorously rebuking one of my young corporals for suggesting that I thrived on conflict, I wondered if he was right; however, I didn't share this with him at the time! So then, back to the fear of the consequence of failure and how it shaped my life.

CHAPTER 1

The Fuze is Lit

I was always attracted to fireworks and the opportunity to take on dares; a dangerous combination. As a child, as Bonfire Night approached each year, I would 'procure' what fireworks I could and experiment. Never satisfied with outcomes, I would mess about. I would attach bangers to rockets and launch them like improvised mortars. I would consolidate fillings from bangers I had opened in search of a yet bigger bang. Eyebrows were regularly sacrificed in this research. I was probably very lucky not to blind myself or end up residing somewhere at Her Majesty's pleasure. It was chance that led me to become an Ammunition Technician and it enabled my pursuit of a fascination with explosives to become a career which I enjoyed; well, most of the time anyway.

As a teenager in Singapore in 1968, the fireworks at Chinese New Year were awesome. Bangers were the staple of Chinese celebrations and the louder the better to scare the evil spirits away. The more extravagant displays at Chinese New Year consisted of huge chains of bangers with interlinked fuzes suspended up the sides of high-rise buildings. These garlands of bangers draped around buildings would be simultaneously ignited at pavement level with spectacular results as the advancing flame accelerated up the central fuze. Bangers would fall clear in their hundreds as the fuze ignited and would explode somewhere below. As the flame raced up the fuze, the deafening noise and blinding flashes roared to a crescendo as they approached the final sequence of even bigger bangers at the top. The bangers were made of stiff red paper, red being a lucky colour for the Chinese. At dawn the next morning, the streets would be carpeted ankle-deep in red confetti which usually concealed a lot of duds. We would collect these and mess with them. There was a favourite of mine which could be bought individually. It was labelled as a 'Thunder'. There was nothing to prevent us from buying these even though we were children. The Thunder banger was easily on a par with the British Army Thunderflash. One afternoon, as a group of us walked home along our street, we spotted a massive rat on the pavement which scampered into the monsoon drain as we approached. Stooping down to see where it had gone, we could see a nest had been dug into the earth underneath the paving slabs. We raced off to get ammunition and quickly returned. A lookout confirmed the rat was still in situ. We prepared a bundle of six Thunder bangers, configured in a way to ensure one single big blast. The bangers were taped to the end of my mum's yard broom shaft and we marked the length needed to reach the nest beneath our feet. The fuze of about 20 seconds was lit and the device was deployed (for those in the know, this was a bit like an improvised Bangalore Torpedo). We had blocked the far end of the drain to ensure the rat would not escape. We retired to hide behind a nearby large gatepost and waited.

Then, through the heat shimmer coming off the road, we saw the 'collateral damage' on its way down our street in the form of a policeman on his bike, now intent on investigating what we were up to. We promptly legged it and watched from afar, aghast as the policeman dismounted, erected the bike on its stand and approached the entrance to the drain. We could see whisps of blue smoke rising as the wretched man's face levelled with the kerb and he looked up the drain. He then shifted onto his knees to get a better look when, fortunately for him, the bangers exploded just when his face was out of harm's way. Two paving slabs were hurled vertically up into the air in a massive cloud of white smoke. The petrified policeman saw the genie! He flew backwards and fell over his bike. After three fumbling attempts, he eventually remounted the bike and then realised his cap was on the other side of the road. Pausing only to retrieve it, he pedalled and wobbled his 'rent-a-tank' bike furiously up the road as we emerged to inspect the damage. There was a crater two feet wide and about the same depth in the footpath. Tellingly, a severed rat's tail lay in the bottom of the crater but nothing else was left of him. We tried to replace the slabs before disappearing. Later on, I remember Mum was puzzled at how her broom was suddenly shorter. She knew it was something to do with me, but she didn't press the matter.

By the time we moved from the east coast to central Singapore, I had perfected methods of attacking the huge rats that lived nearby in the filthy drains and canals with concealed remote-controlled bangers and bangers that could be launched on rockets or projected out of scaffolding pipe using another banger as a propelling charge. In later years, when it came to investigating ammunition incidents caused by horseplay or tampering, I already had a head start on the guilty. I was literally the poacher turned gamekeeper. To be fair to Singapore, their president, Lee Kuan Yew, a most remarkable man, launched a campaign to clean up the city and the outcome was dramatic. The Siglap Canal by our house had been an open sewer. In my subsequent visits to Singapore, I was amazed to see that canal is now clean and populated with fish and the length of it is a pleasant connector park where parents walk their young families. A once crowded, polluted and dirty city-state of about two million people in 1968 had been converted into a Garden City where the population, now of about five and half million people, enjoy an incredible and modern environment. There are even otters roaming confidently about in large family groups around Marina Bay and the Kallang River.

One of the best dares I accepted was in early 1971 and it nearly caught me out. It was hatched one evening as a group of us were larking about in a field in GHQ Tanglin. It was dark, we were bored, and we wanted to partake in some mischief, but we did at least have a social conscience and so vandalism was out of the question. I lived in Harding Road and to one side of the front of our house was the garrison church of St George's. The field was large and contained two very high radio towers. From our vantage point in the dark, we could see the comings and goings at the guardroom about 100 metres away. The place was well-illuminated and that meant we couldn't be seen. At the entrance to the guardroom, through its large veranda and louvred doors which were usually propped open, there was a spoof wooden sign, depicting the guardroom as 'No 10' in black paint on a white background. As a pseudo-symbol of authority, this became the focal point of our attention and we discussed how we might somehow undermine this pretentious logo. After various suggestions, one of our group suggested we simply nick it and hide it. This would be an audacious act if it was pulled off. Perhaps we could ransom it or re-erect it on another building. The sign was located underneath a large and bright lamp. It was attached to one of the large louvred doors and was right in front of the guard commander's desk. We knew from experience that after the orderly officer's check visit, and especially after midnight, the guards would retire to a dormitory in a back room, a two-man patrol would walk the camp and the guard commander would usually doze off at the desk. We watched and waited as the hours passed. The orderly officer arrived and inspected the guard and then departed. Things settled down. We crept in closer to watch. The guard commander's head kept falling off his hand and he eventually settled his head on the desk. We drew in closer and could see the storm of insects and bats attracted by the light. I had borrowed my dad's Army-issue clasp knife. As a knife, the blade might just as well have been made of plasticine, but it had a really useful screwdriver blade at the base of the handle, ideal for unscrewing the big brass woodscrews securing the sign to the door. The odd passing car failed to rouse the sleeping guard commander and we knew the two-man patrol was now hundreds of yards away. I walked directly up to the door, ready to make a pretend report of some odd occurrence which would be a credible reason for being there. The sleeping man didn't stir. The ceiling fan inside was clanking as it spun, and I hoped this would mask any sounds I made. The sign was at head height. I reached up and loosened each screw in turn, pausing between each to ensure I had not been detected. After the last screw was out, I realised the sign was stuck to the door by layers of paint. With the knife blade, I scored the edges and then prised the sign away and it came free with a cracking noise which seemed as loud as a gunshot. Still no reaction. Noting the now-vacant shadow of different coloured paint where the sign had been, I tiptoed away to rejoin the gang only to find they had all gone home; bugger! I went home and upstairs into my bedroom. I hung the sign on the wall opposite the bedroom door and went to bed.

I was tired the next day but enjoyed regaling my friends on the bus to school with my exploits the night before and reproaching them for doing a runner and leaving me to it. We agreed to meet that night and consider what to do with the sign. In the early afternoon, I got home from school to a warning from Mum; "Something's happened at work and your dad was called to a Scale A parade and the RSM is raging. You'd best keep out of his way". Dad was settled in his favourite armchair, dressed only in his Y-fronts, cooling off with a bottle of Tiger Beer under the ceiling fan and muttering; it seemed he'd had a few. I slipped out the back, met up with the gang and we crossed over

Holland Road to the Botanical Gardens to lay low. Because our family was large, our house in Harding Road was actually a pair of semi-detached houses knocked into one. This meant we had two staircases. My parent's bedroom and my own were at the front of the house. My parents usually used the stairs on their side of the house but for some reason, Dad went upstairs for a nap using the stairs on my side of the house. As he reached the top of the stairs, the object of the RSM's Scale A parade was hanging in plain sight before him. I heard him shout for me all the way from the Botanic Gardens! Perhaps the only thing that saved me from a sticky end at his hands was his instinctive urge to get rid of the evidence and that I would survive if I 'disappeared' the sign. I hid the sign and rejoined the gang as night began to fall again. They all told the same tale. This was not just any sign, it was the RSM's pride and joy, and it had been taken from under the noses of his guards. His humiliation was complete. It seemed the only way to stop the ongoing manhunt would be to restore the sign to its hallowed place on the guardroom door. Perhaps, with hindsight, I should record that this was to be my first, real 'high-risk' manual approach. As I recce'd the guardroom in the small hours, I had watched the same routine unfolding except that the orderly officer was strutting about and pointing his cane at the vacant square of paint on the door. He left and then I noticed the guard commander was the same one who had been on the night before. He must have been placed on extra duties. I empathised with him, but the brutal reality was that he had fallen asleep on duty. My advantage for a safe replacement was that he was bound to be tired. At about 2 am, I snuck in as he slept. I replaced the sign but with only two screws, not wishing to spoil success for perfection, and then fled the scene. I kept a low profile for the next few weeks, but the furore died away. If the British withdrawal hadn't taken place just after this, I reckon the poor guard commander would still be on extra duties!

We flew back to the UK in an RAF VC10 at the end of June 1971. The fun was over, and the need to find employment occupied my mind. We landed at RAF Brize Norton and were taken first to the Sergeants' Mess, which was then located two miles away from Kineton, at RAF Gaydon. After a grand meal, we went to our new married quarter at 12 Byron Walk. It was a four-bedroomed house, and we were treated by our new neighbours to a 'get you in' pack of basic provisions. We were to live out of suitcases for about three months until our boxes (coming by sea) arrived from Singapore. Dad had packed hundreds of cigarettes in the boxes and was disappointed to find they had all gone mouldy in transit. My bedroom faced the ammunition depot, and I would stare at the distant explosive storehouses (ESH), wondering what was inside them. There was a storehouse outside the wire, not far from our house, which I gather had been requisitioned as a general store by the Quartermaster's Department. This was where our boxes were collected from.

Most of the camp was quite old, and the buildings were mainly Nissen Huts except for the six main barrack blocks. The Burton Dassett Beacon overlooked the camp and the weather that summer was quite warm and sunny. The main road which skirted the camp perimeter was the A41 which was a very busy trunk road and was very bendy and there was a lot of goods traffic thundering by; accidents were common. One day, a refrigerated lorry left the road and crashed through the perimeter fence, bursting open and scattering frozen lamb carcasses over the small grassy field which stood between the nearest house and the fence. It was to be the Kineton version of 'Whisky Galore' and Dad rushed out and managed to fill our new chest freezer. Eventually, that section of road was straightened out, but the trunk route is now served by the M40.

I left home and headed north. I got a job within days but the work was seasonal. After six months as a van boy, I was made redundant and that made me homeless. Hard choices had to be made. I clipped the coupons in the paper for all of the Armed Services. The Army came looking for me first. The recruiter who came to pick me up took me to the Army Careers Office and I was interviewed and tested. It turned out I could apply for any of the technical trades in the Army. Although I had been an Army child, my knowledge of the Army was quite limited. Dad was serving out the last 12 months of his service in the RAOC. I asked if there were any technical trades in the RAOC; the recruiters pulled their faces but reluctantly got out the trade brochures and looked. One of them found the trade of Ammunition Technician. I was put in a room on my own to watch a film about the RAOC. In this film, there was an officer in Service Dress standing on a sheet of wood in the middle of a muddy field. I remember being preoccupied with how he had managed to get onto the piece of wood in his shiny shoes without getting messed up. Then I was told to report to the Army Careers office in Coventry where I would be enlisted. It happened on 12 April 1972. Days later, I arrived at Brookwood railway station. I had travelled with some other recruits and we split up at the station to report to different units. I was taken to Blackdown Barracks and was accommodated in a holding platoon to await the arrival of the remaining recruits who were to form Malta Platoon.

The accommodation was brand new. I was put in a six-man room by a friendly, avuncular corporal who showed me around. It was explained that our formal training would start once the platoon had formed up. He noticed that the large brown trunk I had with me was of the kind bought in the Far East and guessed I was an Army child. I was instructed to write a letter home to my parents and there was some care taken to ensure I did this. I got a sense that my new environment was wholesome and caring with a lot of attention to detail. The food was good and plentiful. The next day, I was joined by another recruit who seemed to have come from a chaotic and disorganised lifestyle. He was in his late 20s, white and very smartly dressed in a green suit with coordinated accessories and had a shock of long black permed hair down to his collar. Dad had insisted I get a 'good haircut' before I reported for recruit training, and I was curious about this somewhat incongruous recruit. He explained that his grandmother had died some time ago and had bequeathed him a lot of money. During a lengthy discourse, he explained that he had blown it on cars, clothes and women and was now broke and homeless and the Army was one way to get back on his feet; a bit like my own story but without the inheritance! I wasn't sure about whether to envy or sympathise with him and, although we were being treated quite well, with none of the stereotypical callousness I had expected, the 'rough treatment' must be imminent, and I wondered how he would fare.

Over the next few days, our numbers increased, and we were taken to the quartermaster's clothing store for our initial issue of clothing and personal equipment. There was none of the expected 'Carry On, Sergeant' capers at the issues counter. A lot of care was taken to ensure the clothing, especially boots and berets, were a good fit. So far, so good. After we got back to our accommodation, we were shown how to put together our 1937 pattern webbing and how to wear our uniforms. There was an informal talk given to us about loyalty, integrity and duty. We were sternly warned that stealing from comrades was about one of the most heinous of crimes and the so-called 'tea leaf' could expect to have his fingers broken through barrack-room justice. Another heinous crime was absence without official leave (AWOL). If we did a runner, we could expect to be mercilessly hunted down. A training programme was placed on the noticeboard and next Monday morning, it was all to start. Before then, each of us was interviewed by a corporal in the training company office.

This was where the unpleasantness started. We hadn't met this corporal before, and he was aggressive, surly and foul-mouthed. The purpose of the interview seemed to be about our personal administration and then what Her Majesty would expect us to do every single day henceforth. Firstly, I was asked if I smoked. The answer "Yes, Corporal" resulted in my pack of 10 No 6 tipped cigarettes being scrounged off me. I was then told that I must bathe or shower and shave daily without fail. My next of kin details were checked and then I was ordered to fall out and I acknowledged mentally that the 'shock of capture' phase had begun. Our standards were henceforth to be measured against seemingly implausible levels of perfection attained by trained soldiers who had gone before us. The threat of being 'back-squadded' through failure was ever-present. Back-squadded recruits came in two sorts: Those who had picked up an injury and consequently enjoyed 'minor-celebrity' status amongst us as they already knew what was coming, and those who had failed mandatory training tests. Back-squadding entailed leaving your training platoon and joining the following, newer intake of recruits in order to repeat training and hopefully make good on past poor performance. The most common reason for failure that I perceived in them was perhaps aptitude-related. With very considerable hindsight in later life, I could see that dyspraxia was a probable major cause of this and the unfortunate 'misfit' would be hounded in the pursuit of perfection, but they were usually a lost cause. I went back to my room and was accosted by a now quite frantic and still long-haired fellow recruit from day two, who looked really odd in his baggy denims and lumpy jumper. I thought about warning him about the 'Mr Nasty' corporal but dismissed it as pointless. I didn't want to increase his anxiety as he was clearly now having second thoughts about his decision to join up. The overall impression I had of the Army at that point was that it was a curious mix of new and old. National Service had ended in the previous decade but much of the banter expressed by the permanent staff was rooted in that era. We were now meant to be serving in the professional and volunteer Army but, as the transition from 'new recruit' to 'trainee recruit' proceeded, it started to feel less of a vocational choice and more like a term of incarceration. On our last Saturday before formal training began, most of us walked into Frimley Green, carrying kit bags of dhobi, to use the launderette. We alternated between there and a nearby pub until, dhobi washed and dried, we tramped back to barracks.

CHAPTER 2

Enlistment and Training

I enlisted on 12 April 1972, aged a few days older than 17 years and 6 months. In the terms and conditions of service then prevailing, I became a 'Young Soldier'. I was too old to become an Army Apprentice but not quite an adult. A young soldier was treated as an adult with the exception that before coming of age, I could leave the Army if I chose. As you would expect, the initial training regime was quite tough. Once the recruiter's kid gloves were off, there was the initial 'shock of capture' period. After a few days forming up, training started for me in Malta Platoon which was a squad of about 30 recruits to be trained by several Non- Commissioned Officers (NCOs) and a somewhat daft Second Lieutenant who was completely entranced with the hit *Vincent* by Don Maclean; he would wander around singing it as the NCOs aped his tuneless cavorting behind his back. The erstwhile, avuncular corporal, who lived in a bunk next to my 6-man room, underwent a Jekyll and Hyde transformation which wrong-footed all of us.

We were taught basic hygiene, laundering and ironing, making our beds (bed boxes – a sort of Origami for blankets), polishing boots, cleaning and Blancoing our webbing, how to dress and the topic of 'Interior Economy'. This was a grossly misleading pseudonym for endlessly cleaning our accommodation. My father had already warned me of 'Blackdown Fever' (dust) and our trainers had the gift of finding it anywhere and at any time. The idea that we recruits were in it together was firmly implanted when the corporal took us into one of the communal bathrooms. There he ordered a tepid bath be drawn. When the desired depth was reached, we were all ordered to urinate into the bath, following his lead. We then took turns to wade up and down the bath wearing our new DMS (direct moulded sole) boots. It was explained this was the first stage in making the uppers more supple and therefore comfortable and quicker to break in. The next day, we were shown how to burn the pimples off the uppers using a candle flame to heat the back of a spoon. With some irony, we were sternly warned that damaging the boots would constitute a Court Martial offence as it was against the Queen's Regulations. It seemed everything was against the Queen's Regulations. A particularly heinous crime was to cheat by using seal liquid polish to achieve the required mirror finish to our toecaps. It seemed that even Her Majesty knew about this act of treason and, you guessed it, this was allegedly also proscribed in her Regulations. Pimples removed, the next task was to bull the boots to a high polish. To be honest, this was easy for me as I had been bulling my dad's boots and Blancoing his webbing for years. We also had to polish our belt brasses but we didn't have to polish our cap badges as these were stay-bright.

During the bed-making demonstration, our attention was drawn to the coloured stripes running centrally down the blankets. These were to guide us in achieving the most accurate folding to create a bed box. As we looked on, the NCO noticed a passing frown on the face of one of our number, Foxy. This was instantly deemed to be 'silent insubordination' and was immediately (and very loudly) challenged. "What stripes, Corporal?" asked the hapless trainee. "These effin' stripes," came the reply. There were a couple more exchanges about the disappearing stripes, accompanied by various threats of imprisonment and how bad it was going to get before it transpired that Foxy was actually colour blind. The NCO stormed out in a rage. The RAOC medical standards for recruits permitted colour blindness at the time but nobody told the training NCO.

One morning, we were to be subjected to our first room inspection. We were to be barracked in (confined to accommodation) the night before in order to clean kit and accommodation. All of us had been allocated additional cleaning duties in the shared facilities such as the ablutions, stairs, corridors, windows and outside areas. Our personal turn-out and bearing and our bedspaces and lockers had to be spotless and perfectly arranged. At 2200 Hrs the night before, a cursory glance by an NCO at our achievements elicited permission to go to the NAAFI bar for a pint. This was a trap! Most of us drank too much, nearly all of us smoked and, by now, we had become veterans and were bomb-proof; or so we thought. This self-delusion ended dramatically at 0600 Hrs when an NCO burst through the door and struck all of the steel personal lockers with a pick helve to wake us up. He then disappeared after we had all sat up and put our feet on the floor to his satisfaction.

Side Note: One of these NCOs later became a minor celebrity by appearing in character in the TV reality series 'Bad Lads Army', so there is no need for me to elaborate, assuming readers have seen at least one episode. I can vouch for his performance, but he wasn't acting - he was just being himself! In 2011, I was at the Shell Island camping site in North Wales when I saw someone familiar. Everything about him screamed 'WARNING'. I needed to walk in front of him in a TV room next to the camping site's Tavern Bar to reach the gent's toilet. He looked up as I excused myself and our eyes briefly met. It was those eyes! His hair was very long, and he was hunched up in a chair, which was confusing. Back at the bar, I told my brother what I'd just seen. Initially, I couldn't remember the name and then the penny dropped. My brother was amused and suggested I go and ask if it was him. Briefly, my reticence to tempt fate after nearly 40 years held me back but another Guinness firmed my resolve. I went back into the TV room and asked if it was him. It was. Forty years was stripped back in an instant. We reminisced and since then have met up several times. Physically, age has changed him, as it has me, but the spark is still in those eyes. Mind you, in the old days, you never looked an NCO in the eyes!

The trap I mentioned was that our brief liberty the night before had undone most of our earlier efforts. The afore-mentioned bath was still streaked with black boot marks, the contents of our bedside lockers were hurled out of the windows, bed boxes followed them and then we were personally inspected. Interior Economy failings were punished with further 'barrack-in' nights. If our uniforms were in bad order, we would be placed on Show Parade. This took place at 2200 Hrs each evening outside the company office in the dark! If you were lucky and the Company Orderly Sergeant was an old sweat, the inspection would happen in the dark and would be over quickly. One night, however, we were marched into the office one at a time for a closer inspection. That night, I had been cited to 'show belt and buckles'. The orderly sergeant was smoking a cigarette as he laid my belt down on the desk in front of him. He looked up at me to say he was going to look under the buckles for Brasso stains and I saw a flake of ash fall from his fag and land under the now-raised buckle. He saw the contamination and started to shout. I leaned forward and blew the flake away and it vanished before his very eyes. He had obviously had a few in the mess before taking the parade and this vanishing stain perplexed him. I was hastily dismissed with a 'don't do it again' admonition. If our turnout was really bad, the heart-breaking punishment of 'change parade' would be imposed. To explain: We had several uniform types including Service Dress, Working Dress, Combat Dress and PT kit. In a change parade, you would parade in front of your accommodation block. You would then be ordered to change into a different uniform and report back in an impossibly short time. After several changes, the platoon would be reduced to a sweaty exhausted heap; it was especially bad for those living on the top floor.

Our military training started with basic drill and weapon training. One morning, the NCOs greeted us enthusiastically. No shouting, no screaming; just plain pleasant. We suspected a trap. What happened next was outside their control, but it changed the lives of Malta Platoon immediately. In the Aldershot Garrison area, there was an abandoned military showground known as the Rushmore Arena. It had last been used almost 50 years earlier for a military tattoo before being locked shut and abandoned. The military authorities had decreed that the 68-acre arena should now be restored to its previous condition. This was going to take a lot of physical hard work as the arena was completely overgrown. In fact, when we first saw it, it looked like the jungle version of a burst mattress trying to explode out of the chain link fence it had outgrown years earlier. To achieve this end, the authorities ordered that every garrison unit, including ours, produce a work party. Therefore, our basic training was stopped and we became cheap labour. My progress through military training to my career choice required that I be a trained soldier in time to undergo pre-selection for the Ammunition Technician's (AT) 1972B training course. There was a shortage of ATs at the time, and eventually, someone realised that myself and another potential AT in Malta Platoon were languishing as landscape gardening labourers instead of being trained. After a few days, we were moved into Delhi Platoon and our basic training resumed.

Delhi Platoon was a little larger than Malta Platoon so an efficiency to expedite our drill training was introduced. The platoon was split in two and each half of the platoon would do drill training in different venues in Blackdown Barracks under separate instructors. For readers unfamiliar with Army drill, you would need to know that after a word of command is called out, the drill movement is usually broken down into choreographed parts. Thus, a right turn at the halt would be accomplished by a soldier swivelling his body around on his feet 90 degrees to the right and then pausing briefly before raising his left leg off the ground and then banging his foot down next to the right foot. The banging of the foot needs to be synchronised perfectly so that the platoon produces one satisfying crack and not multiple bangs. Multiple bangs would send the instructor into a fit of apoplexy which had to be avoided at all costs. At the early stages of training, to help with timing, recruits have to call out loud their timing, typically, they call out together "1, 2-3, 1". They move on the 1s and keep absolutely still on the pause of 2-3. We trained in this way for a couple of weeks to the point where we didn't have to call out the timing and then the platoon had to be brought back together to learn more advanced drill as well as rifle drill. My half of the platoon had the use of the main square at Blackdown as our instructor was a full corporal who was senior to the other training staff. After we had been marched to the agreed rendezvous place on the square, we were halted and awaited our colleagues. At a given signal, they marched on.

They and we had been producing most satisfactory and perfectly synchronised cracks of boots on tarmac so far. As the other half approached us, we were called up to attention. The other half converged on us and halted perfectly; the instructor purred like a cat. The new arrivals did a left turn to the front, so we were all facing the same direction, which was perfect (cue more loud encouragement from the instructor). We were then all ordered to 'move to the right in threes, right turn'. At this point, I must reiterate the importance of moving on the '1s' and keeping still on the '2-3'. The turn we carried out had two distinct sharp cracks instead of the obligatory one. The instructor screamed, "As you were!" at us and we repeated the previous manoeuvre, sadly, with the same result. Cue apoplexy; then the dawning realization of what had happened. The junior drill instructor spent most of his time on weapon training. His knowledge of drill was not as good as that of the full corporal. After the two halves of our platoon had separated, such as to be out of earshot of each other, it was obvious that the other half had been trained to stand still on the 1s and move on the 2-3s!! It was priceless!!

In the middle of this surreal experience, I caught the 'lurgy'. One night after 'lights-out', I felt an odd tickling sensation on my right inner thigh. Thinking it was maybe some creepy crawlie, I ran my hand over it and discovered a small, sharp bump on my skin. As soon as I touched it, fiery itching started. I put on the bedside light and peered under the covers. The skin at the top of my legs had turned a bright red colour and dozens of these prickly bumps had erupted. I soon learned not to scratch them and with considerable willpower, I managed to ignore them and go to sleep. At any other time and place, I might have got up to investigate the matter but there was no way I was going to disturb the NCO sleeping in his bunk just outside our room. Anyone who has seen the film Full Metal Jacket will know what I mean. In the morning, we had our usual 'courtesy call' to make sure we were up. As I sat up, the Mancunian lad in the next bedspace saw the rash and alerted the whole barrack room to this outbreak of plague. He strongly reminded me of Ken Goodwin, the comedian who starred in the 1970s ITV Show The Comedians. He empathised with me and claimed that he too had a rash and we should attend sick parade together. Closing in on me to preclude being seen by the other occupants, he pulled open the front of his pyjamas to reveal a tiny red spot in the middle of his chest. He was either a total hypochondriac or was completely deluded. The thought of attending sick parade with anything less than a traumatic amputation was terrifying, but by then, my rash had spread to everywhere on my body except for the palms of my hands, soles of my feet and my face. Plus, the itching was by now unrelenting. In fact, I think I would have preferred a traumatic amputation!

Another recruit sent for the NCO which obviously interrupted his ablutions and someone was going to have to pay. He came striding up to me in my bedspace and I stood to attention. Then he saw the rash and asked how much was there. I showed him; his eyes lit up like saucers. He immediately ordered everyone out of the room and I was left alone in some sort of quarantine. Then the Platoon Sergeant arrived and inspected me. He was on his last posting and, as a younger man, had a full head of bright auburn hair. Nature had been unkind and, in his late twenties, he had suffered male pattern baldness. On the Norwood scale of baldness, he was a definite seven! So, he had spent a fortune on a wig. I had never seen him without his peaked cap before and now he was looking down at me, head uncovered. I was looking at a bright red crown topper bordered by thinning and greying flanks. All I could think of was 'ginger skunk'! I tried to stifle an uncontrollable laugh but it escaped, sounding like a cough. He ordered me into my No 2 dress and I had to pack my small pack. Then the 'Ken Goodwin' character appeared and said he had the same thing. The two of us were marched post-haste to the medical centre. He went in to see the Medical Officer (MO) before me. The medical orderly sergeant looked like Uncle Fester chewing a wasp. As soon as the MO saw the diminutive pimple, the cry of "DEFAULTER" rang out. Ken Godwin reappeared and was subsequently double-marched under escort to the guard room to face some terrible fate. Uncle Fester then sized me up and asked if I had the same symptoms. I nodded. I was ordered into a shower cubicle and told to strip. The curtain was suddenly pulled back. My bright-red nakedness was exposed to the MO, Medical Orderly, two nurses and about six WRAC girls. When they saw the rash, the curtain was ripped shut and the waiting room was rapidly emptied as though I had Ebola virus. The MO came back and was now masked and gloved. He checked me over and prescribed Whitfield ointment for the rash which he diagnosed as 'Khaki Rash', an allergic reaction to the still-new uniform I was wearing. I was bedded down on my own and my fellow recruits brought me my meals. After two days of smearing the greasy, burning ointment all over, the rash vanished as quickly as it had appeared. I resumed training with the others. Ken Goodwin's pimple was never seen again.

There was a more unsavoury aspect to our drill training. One of the purposes of drill is to instil discipline. Of all the subjects we were trained in, drill was invariably the subject where most of the verbal abuse was directed at us. The matter of abuse directed at Army recruits has been a hot topic for many years. To a point, however, military training must be robust; the recruit is ultimately being trained for war. During my basic training, it was normal to be sworn at, occasionally shoved about and always instantly and roundly rebuked for errors. In our drill training, this was taken to another level by an instructor who is now deceased. I will not name him, but I will write of his methods to instil fear of the consequence of failure in us.

Between teaching the various drill movements, the instructor would occasionally speak of his own experiences of what went on during his own apprentice training. He told us he had served twelve years and his ambition was to achieve a transfer into the Small Arms School Corps (SASC). In the apprentice dormitory at night, they would allegedly have masturbating competitions where the winner was the first to ejaculate into a cup placed on a table and he extolled the personal qualities of the winners. I personally believe this was made up to intimidate us as to his lack of inhibitions about what he might do to us if we failed to come up to his standards. The nearest we came to an actual verbal threat concerned sloppy or lazy foot drill whilst standing to attention. In British Army foot drill, when a soldier is in the position of attention, his fists are clenched tightly with the arms held straight down at the sides. The thumbs are pressed down on the closed forefingers such that the soldier feels for and aligns his thumbs down the outer seam of his trousers. A common fault is for a soldier to relax and allow his closed fist to open. On one occasion, when the instructor was standing behind us, he shouted at a recruit in the rear rank accusing him of allowing his hand to open. The threat he issued was that he would place his penis within any such open hand and masturbate. I remember being shocked and revolted by this threat but quickly dismissed it as simply not being credible. Some days later, however, his temper peaked during a rifle drill period. He had borrowed a rifle with a bayonet already attached in order to demonstrate a rifle drill movement. He was standing about 20 metres in front of us and then ordered us to imitate what he had done in the conventional British Army technique of Explanation, Demonstration, Imitation (EDI). We tried but we messed up. He became furious and hurled the rifle he had been holding in our direction. The rifle was never going to hit anyone, but, as it tumbled end over end, the bayonet tip dug into the tarmac and the barrel snapped at the flash eliminator joint. Fear of the consequence of failure was definitely reinforced that day. On another occasion, during a temper tantrum, he threw his Number 1 Dress Hat towards us. I feel certain he didn't intend that it would hit anyone, but it sailed like a frisbee and as it rotated, the peak spun around before striking a recruit in the front rank across his Adam's Apple, causing him to collapse to the ground. The instructor was remorseful and apologised profusely. He was clearly someone determined to get his own way, including by intimidation if nothing else worked. Later, after qualifying as an AT and having been promoted to full corporal, I met him whilst on another training course. He seemed affronted by my casual ease with him and then noticed my badge of rank was the same as his own. He seemed ill at ease with my familiarity despite my being respectful. I thought it ironic but strangely curious that my quite rapid progression to the same rank was due in no small part to his determination to make us all succeed; almost at any cost.

On the 9ᵗʰ of June 1972, the newly built Blackdown Barracks were opened by Queen Elizabeth. Although the barracks were brand new, it seemed to me that everything along her route was painted and then re-painted. Trained soldiers were to parade on the main square and receive a royal inspection. As recruits, we were set up to do a weapon training demonstration with 9mm Sterling Sub-Machine Guns. We were outdoors near the gymnasium, sat on our ponchos. HM swept past at the appointed time, glaring down at us, but we were forbidden to look at her. She had just returned to the UK from a long trip to Kenya but I noted that her complexion was a pasty white. She looked bored with us all.

In the penultimate week of basic training, we were taken to the Thetford Training Area where we were to undertake a so-called 'Battle Camp'. We were accommodated in Nissen Huts with cast-iron, pot-bellied stoves for heating. After the first day, we were to deploy into field conditions and dig trenches and would occupy them for about 48 hours and be subjected to mock attacks by the instructors as we practised our all-round defence drills. We also conducted ambushes and two of us were selected to carry out reconnaissance on a simulated enemy position. As we were paraded in single file to conduct pre-exercise weapon safety drills, we were ordered to 'make safe' our weapons. One of our number, Harry, then made a bad mistake. Our weapons had been loaded with blank ammunition and Harry somehow messed up his 'make-safe'. This drill, which we were now expected to conduct without any prompting, involved unloading the weapon and then re-loading it with a fresh magazine. The unload was meant to conclude with the 'easing of springs' which meant checking the chamber first for the presence of a round and then closing the working parts, taking off the safety catch and squeezing the trigger which normally resulted in a click. It seems Harry missed out the all-important check for the presence of a round in the chamber. Although we only had blanks, the bang seemed to reverberate around all of East Anglia! Our Platoon Sergeant exploded into fury. We were meant to be tactical and quiet as the virtual enemy was deemed to be close by. Harry's faux pas had compromised our location. Another aspect was that the unintended firing of a weapon was labelled a 'negligent discharge' and somewhat publicly, Harry's sin was reviewed, and the question of punishment was considered.

The Platoon Sergeant decided to deal with this informally but in a way that Harry, as well as the rest of us, wouldn't forget. I might explain that Harry was of the body type built for comfort and not for speed. He was popular with us because, despite his size, he invariably tried hard to succeed, especially in the more physical aspects of training. We knew he had to work at his fitness far harder than the rest of us and his spirit and work ethic were admired by us all. Now he was going to suffer. The sergeant went away and then returned carrying a grey cylindrical object in his hand. He raised his hand up to Harry's face and pointed the object, which we could now see appeared to be a pressurised spray can of 'something', directly at him, at a distance of about six inches. The actuator was pressed and a jet of something hit Harry between the eyes. He immediately collapsed writhing to the ground, gasping and clutching at his face. The spray was CS and Harry's informal 'field punishment' had been summarily dispensed. As Harry struggled for breath, unable to see, the sergeant justified his actions by saying that it was an important 'lesson learned' and Harry would not be encumbered by a disciplinary entry on his Army record (a document known as the Conduct Sheet). This last point was moot; we had been receiving lessons about military law from the same sergeant and we knew that the Conduct Sheet was destroyed after a recruit passed out of basic training, under the principle of a 'fresh start'. This episode was damaging in our eyes. Harry had messed up, but his public punishment was brutal and upsetting to witness. The Platoon Sergeant went from 'inspiring' to 'arse-wipe' in an instant.

Battle camp was also great fun. In some nearby woodland was an assault course which ran along and through streams and ponds. It was three-dimensional with lots of challenging obstacles, long, high, deep and shallow, requiring teamwork or individual agility to negotiate. We were walked along the course first and briefed on how to tackle the obstacles. Then we arrived at the world's smelliest pond. The water was black and still. An instructor prodded the bottom with a long stick from the bank and that prompted a prolonged fart and bubbles rose from the now-disturbed and malevolent gunk living at the bottom. It seemed to be about waist-deep. Crossing this pond required that we sprint up a steep ramp and throw ourselves headlong over the water before catching a rope attached to a tree thrown by an instructor from a ramp at the other end. Catching the rope enabled the recruit to swing over to a ramp on the other side. An instructor worthy of performing as a trapeze artist demonstrated the technique and flew over with grace and aplomb, catching the thrown rope and alighting, dry as a bone, on the far ramp. As Buzz Lightyear would say three decades later, it was "Falling with style". I wanted to fly like that! As I ran the course a few minutes later, I came off a cargo-net obstacle and sprinted towards the take-off ramp. Terry, the tall cockney ex-butcher instructor, shouted encouragement from the far ramp and prepared to throw the knotted heavy rope for me to intercept midway. Then I noticed all the instructors were gathered around laughing and shouting, "Come on, Robbo, go for it". Well, I should have known a trap was at hand; why else the informality? I pounded up the wooden ramp and flung myself forwards into heavier-than-air flight. I saw Terry's arm swing forward and release the rope which sailed out to meet me. Then, Terry's hand jerked backwards. The knotted rope stopped dead and then swung back, and Terry caught it. My assignation with the rope now cancelled, I went head-first into the black water and the lights went out. The bottom of the pond was soft with a primordial slime and all of me passed from the surface water into this viscous, sucking porridge as I face-planted. I managed to get my head above water and sucked in a lungful of air before the revolting stench started me heaving. I struggled to the opposite bank where I noted that Terry had a ball of fishing line in his hand. This was the invisible means by which to snatch away the rope swing in mid-flight. All I can say is thank God this was well before the era of smartphones with their ubiquitous cameras because the footage would have reaped me infinite internet infamy. As the late, great Kenneth Williams said, "Infamy, infamy, they've all got it in for me"! I saw the funny side, however, and had no trouble in getting an uninterrupted shower afterwards.

Following the evening meal, we were awarded some downtime and I remember the TV was on in the dining room. The Six O'clock News came on and featured a soldier being hit by a house brick thrown during rioting in Belfast. Earlier that day, we had been conducting internal security training and the Platoon Sergeant got off his feet at the sight of the injured soldier and started shouting about how his injury was due to his lack of tactical alertness. The 'arse-wipe' was really gambling with what little credibility he had left. I think the nearest he had ever gotten to hostilities had been in a NAAFI queue at closing time.

As the day of our passing out parade approached, we noted a sea change in the attitudes of our instructors towards us. From about week five, the occasional word of praise was issued. That had a dramatic effect on us. In reality, having had our individuality hammered out of us, we had now been melded into a close-knit and credible platoon. In the final week, we were to have a dress rehearsal for the parade. Something incredible happened; the full RAOC Staff Band marched on and played as we drilled. I swear everyone grew six inches taller! But that was as good as it got. The Staff Band wasn't available for our passing out parade and a somewhat sub-calibre bunch of people with drums and whistles turned up. If they had issued us with kazoos it would have sounded better, something like the Pelaw Hussars Majorettes who featured in one of my favourite old Michael Caine movies, *Get Carter*. The other disappointment was that not all of the platoon had been issued with No 1 Dress peaked caps as the factory in Northern Ireland had been fire-bombed. We would instead march on wearing berets. Nevertheless, the great day came and went and some old fart smelling of mothballs took the salute and told our proud mums that each of us "Had a Field Martial's baton" in our backpacks. Ginge and Terry, our lance corporal instructors, actually seemed to be the proudest people there. Ginge was a 'Weegie', short but louder than anything in the known world. Terry was a tall cockney man who had been a butcher before joining up. Together, they had performed a miracle and converted us into trained soldiers. The saying 'what comes around goes around' was confirmed almost twenty years later when Ginge, Terry and myself were deployed to the Gulf War. We had very different roles to play but their investment in training me to be a soldier set me up for life and then us serving together in a war seemed somehow most fitting. I never got the chance to thank them properly, so, thank you, guys! I remember babysitting for Ginge's baby son after training when I was 17. Ginge later told me that tiny bundle had grown into a six-foot-tall Marine Engineer.

Having revealed a darker side to training methods in one individual, I must extol the virtues of most of my other instructors. Even the loudest, most aggressive and intimidating of them shared a common bond of dedication to their task. In a word, most of them were inspiring. I had already figured out that the initial harsh treatment meted out was designed to eradicate individuality and force us to act as a cohesive team, almost like turning us into a murmuration of starlings!

Having passed out from military training with Delhi Platoon, I moved on to the Trade Training Wing. There was no direct entry to the Ammunition Technician trade and each candidate had to have an existing trade qualification. I was loaded onto the Staff Clerk's B3 course which was to take six weeks. From the outset, clerical training felt like an experiment in brainwashing. Our theory instruction took the form of so-called Programme Learning. This entailed reading through pamphlets seemingly designed for 6-year-olds. At the end of each section, you had to answer questions on what you had just read through. On second thoughts, the age range was nearer that of 4-year-olds. The instructor was a Warrant Officer Class One Staff Clerk who seemed to know everything there was to know about filing cabinets and Tags India. Our classroom featured a huge, illuminated typewriter keyboard mounted high up on the wall at the front and, between Programme Learning sessions, we had to participate in touch-typing training. Suddenly, learning about railway warrants from childish pamphlets gained a new appeal. Touch-typing training was like Chinese water torture. Our typewriters did not have letters on the keys. Each keypad was blank and the home keys featured a tactile raised pimple by which you orientated your fingers. With a fresh sheet of paper on the platen, we would commence typing letters in strict accordance with which finger was deemed appropriate for that letter; hunting and pecking for the right key with one finger would instantly expose you to the instructor. We all had to type in step, bizarrely like some form of finger drill, with a loudspeaker monotonously calling the time: "A now, B now, C now....." As a letter was called, the demon screen at the front would light up and we had to stare at it. Looking down at the keyboard was strictly verboten. I found this extremely stressful. The object of the training was to establish muscle memory and cut out the conscious recognition of the actual letter you had to type. Worse was to come.

After two days, the demon keyboard started demanding letters at random instead of in alphabetical order. It was so unfair; arms, wrists and fingers ached. Muscles in your head spasmed as your ears swivelled, trying to sense where the instructor was so you might relax if you were not under his direct scrutiny from behind. We progressed to 'the quick brown fox jumped over the lazy dog'. Someway, somehow, the instructor could instantly detect a mistaken keypress by any one of us, despite there being thirty of us to monitor in what we imagined was like 'Resistance To Interrogation' training. In week 3, I escaped briefly to attend yet another career interview on the rocky path to becoming an AT. After being called out, I walked up the aisle away from the demon keyboard feeling like the character Papillon in an escape movie. As I turned to quietly close the door on exit, I glanced at the demon and, for the first time, I could see all of the scripts in the typewriters as the monotonous death march continued. Then the secret of the instructor's infallible scrutiny was revealed to me; from behind, the demon's ranting resulted in an amazingly symmetrical pattern on the scripts in the typewriters. Even a single wrong letter by only one victim would instantly expose him to censure. As I hurried away, I laughed at the psychology of it all.

After my interview, I returned all too soon to the demon's lair. As I knocked on the door, the omnipotent instructor called the class to a halt. He looked at me and asked what was so important that I could evade the demon. I told him I was a potential AT and it was a career interview. He pulled an enigmatic smile and muttered something like, "Ahh, so *you're* the potential plastic bag". Feeling somewhat puzzled, I regained my seat and the relentless marching of fingers resumed. A little while later, it was a pleasant relief to return to railway warrant stuff. When we went to lunch, I got confirmation of what muscle memory was. As I reached for my knife and fork, my fingers twitched, adopted the home key resting position and I automatically looked up to comply with the imagined demon's demands. I swear as we all ate our meal that our hands rose and fell in perfect unison and jaws masticated in harmony! The day before we were to sit our final theory test, I took the typing test. We had to achieve 30 words per minute with up to three errors allowed on the page. I managed 50 words with no errors, and I couldn't remember anything at all about the topic. The brainwashing had clearly worked. Twenty-seven years later, after leaving the Army, I registered with a commercial employment agency and when they found out I had been a B3 Staff Clerk, they insisted I do a typing test. Protesting aloud, I was ushered into a test booth as, from outside, Christine smirked the grin of schadenfreude at me. Oddly enough, I achieved 50 words per minute, no errors and, if you pull up a comfy chair, I'll tell you all about MoD Railway Warrants!

After the trauma of Staff Clerk training, I was summoned to the presence of the Training Company Sergeant Major. I had apparently been on the wrong course for a potential AT, and I was to start the next B3 Storeman's Course. Before then, I was to be given various administration tasks in the Holding Platoon. This was to become heady stuff as I was now in the world of trained soldiers. The weather at the time was warm and sunny and my favourite activity was delivering leaflets to the occupants of the married quarters. I got to talk to normal polite people as I did my rounds and, on one occasion, I even got to babysit for the baby son of one of my basic training instructors. I suddenly felt that I had been welcomed into the Army circle of trust; there was an amazing sense of belonging. However, the next week, it all changed again. The Holding Platoon was to deploy to Bisley for the Army's Annual Shooting Competition, and we were to live in a field in a marquee by night and perform General Duties by day. Day one was real National Service jankers stuff, peeling our way through a muddy potato mountain after the cookhouse potato rumbler had died. The next day, I was appointed as a batman to an officer called Lieutenant Colonel George Styles GC. He didn't know I was a potential AT, and I didn't know who he was except that he had recently been awarded the George Cross for Bomb Disposal. Perhaps the sergeant major was having a laugh? As his batman, I would bring him tea in the morning, clean his kit and make his bed in the Officers' Mess whilst he was at breakfast. In the mess, he would stride around in a huge cowboy hat, often whilst wearing distinctively striped cotton pyjamas. If his bed wasn't made to his satisfaction or I hadn't folded the pyjamas properly, the Chief Steward would intervene, but it was only for a few days which passed by without incident. Being batman to George Styles was just one of those odd coincidences, but I was largely unaware of who he was, and I still didn't know that ATs did bomb disposal, assuming it to be a lofty calling conducted by those on high. In 1972, as I prepared to join the trade, six EOD Operators were killed in action in Northern

Ireland, but their loss and role were never mentioned to me outside the AT fraternity; it was almost as though they weren't in the RAOC.

Another random event happened whilst I was in Holding Platoon, connecting me, in my youthful ignorance, with the trade. The sergeant major had gotten especially anal about the condition and fit of our No 2 Dress uniforms, which we normally only wore on formal parades. We were made to wear it and we were sent up the hill to the old Apprentice's College where we were drilled up and down on the square. On reflection, there was a haunting similarity with the Monty Python Meaning of Life 'Would you rather be elsewhere' comedy sketch featuring Michael Palin. But it wasn't funny. After settling on who was going to be selected for a forthcoming parade, we were squadded up and ordered into a slow march. This resulted in chaos. Although the 'slow march' was in the common military syllabus for recruits, we hadn't been trained on it. Cue more apoplexy but this rapidly settled into a determined effort to learn quickly when we were told what we were to do. We were to be the Marching Escort at a military funeral at St Barbara's Church, Blackdown. The deceased was a captain in the RAOC who had been killed in Northern Ireland. I was still blissfully ignorant of the trade's involvement in bomb disposal. The officer concerned was an Ammunition Technical Officer, Captain J H Young, who had been killed in action at Silverbridge on 15 July 1972.

The storeman's course was more interesting than the Staff Clerk's course and the instructor was amiable and knowledgeable. I scored very highly in some of the tests, and one day, after he lauded my 100% score in the ammunition examination, he asked me to remain behind for a chat. He tried to persuade me to go into the storeman's trade as a career and not to pursue a career as an ammunition technician. He felt I would go further as a storeman and there would be greater employment potential when I eventually left the Army for Civvy Street. I was somewhat taken aback by this intervention, and I tried to establish his motives. He mentioned that my parents would probably worry less about me if I was a storeman. I believe in retrospect that he knew my father quite well although I didn't know this at the time, and he didn't admit to it. He beat about the bush quite a lot about the pros of being a storeman versus the cons of being an AT. I was getting suspicious, but I was being thick. I pressed him on why he felt I was on the wrong path, so, he told me and I was left speechless! The 'plastic bag' nickname suddenly made brutal sense. I was still only 17 and I had already participated in one ATO's military funeral. There and then, I felt a sense of anger at my ignorance, but I was not in the least bit fazed by what he had explained. It had the opposite effect. I had watched TV news about events in Northern Ireland and already had some misgivings about the employment of the military in what I saw as a political and social crisis. Bomb Disposal, on the other hand, was a neutral, perhaps nobler undertaking where the focus was on the bomb itself with, I imagined, the luxury of impartiality in the violent struggle between the warring factions. My views at the time were grossly naïve and I was completely unprepared for the sectarian hatred I would later experience.

After the storeman's course, I was posted to the Army School of Ammunition, then at the Central Ammunition Depot Bramley, which was roughly halfway between Basingstoke and Reading. I had to travel in No 2 Dress, carrying all my kit, and this was hot and sweaty. At the guardroom, I met yet another sergeant major who inspected me. It was obvious from the start that he didn't like potential ATs. I was allocated a bed space in a spider hut (single-storey structure with ablutions in the centre, bracketed by two barrack rooms, each having six bed spaces). I spent the next week in a classroom, being taught about basic explosives, basic nuclear physics and sample lessons on different types of ammunition. There was a test to see what I had retained. I think there were about thirty of us. Our number was culled to twenty and then I had to go back to the Regimental Depot to do even more regimental training. My course colleagues included other potential ATs who had been on the same pre-selection. Three of them were potential transferees from the Intelligence Corps - Keith, 'Deadly Tedly' and Ski. It started with us being on a muster parade. In those days, working dress was boots, anklets, denim trousers, web belt, shirt sleeve order (rolled up or down) and beret. Our anklets and web belt had to be spotlessly clean and freshly Blancoed. I might also explain that we were issued with 1937-pattern webbing. Although this was superseded by 1958-pattern webbing, we had to persist with the 1937 version and, yes, I know, it was then 1972. The 1937-pattern webbing had to be scrubbed clean daily, after wear, and Blanco applied. Straight away, the drill pigs threw a track and had a right hissy fit when they saw the three Intelligence Corps soldiers parading next to us. I need to explain that the colour of the Blanco worn by the Intelligence Corps was a slightly green tint; different to that of the RAOC. It was the end of the world! Anyway, we survived this brush with square-bashing and were duly deemed to be qualified regimentally for promotion to full corporal, provided we actually passed the AT Course.

Back at Bramley, we started the 1972B AT Course and the peaceful classroom atmosphere on day one was disrupted mid-morning, when Deadly Tedly's baggage in the QM's store burst open, cascading shot-gun ammunition all over the floor. Ted was an endearing character with a huge interest in firearms and I'm going to suggest he was a bit like Eugene Tackleberry in the Police Academy film series; hence the nickname Deadly Tedly.

Our days followed a routine of classroom lessons where we chain-smoked and my habit went from about 10 cigarettes per week to almost 40 per day. On Wednesday afternoons, we were allocated a private study afternoon which meant skiving off to Basingstoke for most of us. On the course, we had twenty military students and an endearing civilian from BAD Longtown. This was Harry Cartner, a most genteel man in his fifties who required the theory phase as a qualification to manage ammunition processing work at his home depot. The attrition rate on the course was quite high. With hindsight, I would characterise the selection process we went through then as more of a collection process. I started quite strongly but got bored, lazy and discovered girls, and had to take two resits, finishing ninth out of the twelve graduates. Exam failures were the usual cause of leaving but one of our number was something of a Walter Mitty. It came to light that he was playing the money game with multiple bank accounts and he had been moving his limited funds between them to keep solvent whilst enjoying a lifestyle beyond his means. It all came crashing down around his ears when a string of bounced cheques resulted in him being exposed.

[To give any familiar readers a chance to recognise the origins of some of our mutual colleagues, I will try to list the class of 1972B by their first names (bit of a struggle after 50

years). There was Mick, Paul, two Colins, Deadly Tedly, Andy, Keith, Reidy, Clive, Bill and Phil and Harry Cartner. Sadly, Harry passed away some years ago.]

One of the distractions available to us was the other courses, especially the Commonwealth and Foreign Ammunition Technical Officers Course known as the CFATOs. Many were from third-world nations and some were from regions of strife, such as Israelis and Arabs. Some had acquired rather pompous British habits and one day, we were ticked off for not saluting one of them. Well, at the start, there were twenty of us and we outnumbered them. We would often pass by the CFATO course on the road as we walked to and from classes. We arranged to walk along in single file, several metres apart. The CFATOs coming the opposite way tended not to bunch up. After several days of having to return salutes twenty times, peace was declared!

In those days before personal computers and the internet, our trade knowledge base was contained in a series of publications known as Ammunition and Explosives Regulations. These contained storage regulations and were also a sort of Haynes Manual for the many hundreds of types of ammunition in service. There were also many other publications and so a type of examination we were required to pass was called the Reference Exam. These were introduced about two-thirds of the way through the course and, by then, I had already had to take two resits. I responded well to a warning and pulled my socks up and went into the Proof Reference Exam feeling quite confident and well-prepared. To pass the exam, you had to answer a question correctly for one mark and then you had to write down where the information was found in the publications for the second mark. It turned out the first question on the script was at the bottom of the page below the instructions on the first sheet. That question flummoxed me so I went on to the remaining questions and answered them all. I had about 15 minutes left in the exam so I turned to the first page and pondered the question. At that point, the invigilator walked up the aisle and paused behind me on my left side. He stood there for about a minute before returning to his station at the front. There, he wrote something on a piece of paper which he then screwed up. He came back up the aisle and as he passed my desk, he dropped the screwed-up paper ball on my script and walked on without saying anything. I unravelled the paper and discovered that written on it were both halves of the answer to the one question I had skipped. The exam concluded and we returned our completed scripts and left the classroom. He called me back. He said I could have all the answers for future written tests if I paid him

£5 per exam. I was quite shocked. I refused the offer and walked on. The topic was never raised again.

Eventually, we reached the Disposals Phase. We studied all manner of ways to dispose of ammunition available to us in the 1970s. These included dumping ammunition at sea, destroying it by explosive demolition, burning in a reinforced incinerator, burning in the open and burial. Burial could apply to chemical forms of ammunition and was deemed at the time to be a permanent method of disposal. Apparently, we had been burying chemical forms of ammunition for decades. That might sound completely irresponsible today, and it would be, but in the post-war era, there were vast quantities of surplus ammunition, nowhere to keep it and we needed to transition back to peacetime normality. It turned out that burial was not so permanent after all and this came back to haunt us when the Bramley depot was closed, sold on and contractors started excavation activities near where the old demolition ground had been located, however, that would be a topic for an even bigger book than this one! We went to the ranges on the coast at Lydd for our practical demolitions phase. The range was quite close to the sea and the ground we were working in was primarily shingle. A short distance away was the Dungeness nuclear power station and it seemed odd that we were conducting large-scale explosive demolitions so close to it. We got to go to a staff disco there and it was said we had cracked the power station's foundations with one of our bigger blasts.

In the middle of our time there, we had to pause to allow an explosive trial (experiment) to be conducted. Car bombs in Northern Ireland were wreaking havoc in urban areas and someone came up with an idea to contain or attenuate the blast from such a bomb. This was going to be interesting. A very basic rule with explosives is that low explosive, such as gun propellant, could be confined in gun breeches and made to do useful work in firing projectiles. In other words, low explosives could be said to be 'controllable'. High explosives, on the other hand, detonate, which is a totally different scenario from the 'fast burn' properties of low explosives. If you put high explosives in the breech of a gun and detonate them, the gun will be destroyed. You cannot practically confine a detonation. In this trial, that principle was going to be challenged big time! As we watched in awe from a safe distance, a caterpillar-tracked crane lumbered into view, heading towards the hulk of an old Army car sited on the shingle. Hanging from the jib was an enormous box. We got the chance to close in and look at it. The box had been made from foam concrete blocks held together in a matrix of steel rebars. It was amply dimensioned and was an easy fit over the top of the car. In the car was said to be about 50 kgs of military plastic explosive (PE4). We moved back and a countdown started. The explosion was epic. The box vanished and bits of foam concrete and rebar started to fall from the sky. The bang was ear-shattering. Well, the trial proved you couldn't control high explosives and the shingle was now mixed with jagged chunks of what vaguely resembled pumice. We were allowed to inspect ground zero (the seat of the explosion). Aside from small pieces of the car, the shingle under the car had been superheated and had then cooled into a solid chunk of a glass-like conglomerate. To be fair to the people who have these great ideas, we do need to 'cut them some slack'. Necessity is said to be the mother of invention, and during conflicts, the military often invents things with great spin-off value to society. However, looking back at what we had just witnessed, and considering the practicalities of it, the whole thing seemed implausible. If the trial had succeeded, how on earth would there be enough time to fetch a huge box on a crane and then risk the crane operator's life in placing it over the bomb? In the early 1970s, terrorist car bombs tended to detonate within a few minutes of being deployed. But it was fascinating to watch the trial and most entertaining to see how fast the MoD could get rid of concrete boxes. The pre-occupation with attempts to attenuate blasts from car bombs continued and, in 1974, the Foaming Pig arrived in Belfast. The concept that a water-based foam could attenuate rather than confine blast was probably quite sound but, as before, the issue of the lack of time before the bomb would explode made the concept impractical.

We graduated in June 1973. There was no ceremony. We packed our bags after sewing on our new trade and rank badges and several of us went to Kineton. Sadly, I never met Harry again. Years later, in 1997, I saw a commemorative photograph of him on the wall of the conference room at Longtown. It recorded that Harry had suddenly passed away, after retiring, whilst playing lawn bowls. Way to go, Harry!

CHAPTER 3

The Kineton Years 1973–1976

Including Northern Ireland tours in 1974 & 1975

I arrived at Kineton, this time as a soldier, in late June 1973. I was to be accommodated on the top floor of a barrack block next to the main square. The accommodation was a mixture of six-man rooms, each with an NCO's single bunk at the entrance to the corridor. I lugged all my kit to the door of the six-man room and opened it. Although it was about midday, everything was dark. The lights were off and the curtains were closed. In the gloom over to my left, I could see movement. Hushed voices stilled as we all contemplated my entry into this crepuscular, twilight zone. I introduced myself and walked towards a group of four men who were clustered around an object which seemed to be on a tripod. A part of this object appeared to be pointed at the window and the curtains were fastened around its business end. The room had been blacked out and the object was a telescope. Their attention returned to the telescope as one of them reported movement outside. Another one pointed at an empty bedspace in the far corner, apparently earmarked for me, and I moved my kit over and surveyed the scene. As time went by, I realised this was some sort of surveillance operation. It was distracting as I wanted to unpack my kit and sort out my bedspace. I watched the huddle as they took turns at the eyepiece. After a while, the lights came on and I become a temporary distraction for them as they lost interest in the erstwhile attraction at the telescope. I walked over and saw that the telescope was pointed at another barrack block on the other side of the square. One of them described the scene outside. I already knew the Nissen hut complex in the front left foreground was the NAAFI shop and a cinema. To the right was the cookhouse and beyond it was the boiler house. It turned out the object of their attention was the WRAC (female) block. Interest had waned as the inhabitants had returned to work after their lunchtime had expired. Outside the room in the access corridor was a drying room, strangely locked, toilets, baths and showers. The smell coming from the drying room turned out to be batches of home brew. The camp was a mixture of new(ish) and older buildings. It was scheduled to undergo a major refurbishment which would sweep away the dispersed Nissen huts and replace them with modern buildings, however, the older buildings were quaint and had a certain charm about them.

Over the next few days, I was shown around the administration area and then into the explosives area inside the wire. At the time, there was no apparent presence of enforced discipline. In my room, spare six-foot lockers had been pushed together to create some privacy around the occupied bedspaces. There seemed to be no routine of room inspections. There were no muster parades except that a daily works parade would take place in the ammunition process area (APA) where we would be detailed to attend our respective workplaces. The APA was an RSM-free zone! To get in, you would walk through a pedestrian access gate where your tally number would be called out. This caused the MoD Policeman inside to record your entry. It was a bit like the tally system used in coal mines. If disaster struck, they would know who was left in the rubble... provided this control point survived the explosion. Just outside the APA entrance were the stores, forklift parking bays and the A Company headquarters. Inside was an improvised canteen. At break time, the elderly canteen ladies would brew copious quantities of tea. The brewing was done in two-gallon galvanised buckets and your order would be passed through a small wall hatch.

Dozens of us would be crowded around a gallery of melamine tables in an impossibly small space for so many. The whole setup had a primitive, improvised ambience which was warm and welcoming. The roaring waterfall of chatter inside was like a bingo hall between houses being called.

Inside the APA were about twelve ammunition process buildings (APBs) known colloquially as 'labs'. The first two were quite small and were used for specialist inspections, such as initial acceptance, where the volume of ammunition looked at was small. The others were larger and were used for major repair tasks. The smaller labs were preferred by most. Typically, there would be a handful of staff and the pace of life was leisurely, the atmosphere informal and you were closest to the canteen! The larger labs were more strictly controlled with larger work parties in them, sometimes up to thirty people. A typical work party would comprise ammunition technicians, storemen and store-women, Royal Pioneer Corps soldiers employed on manual handling and civilian industrial staff. There would be output quotas to work to and it was a classic industrial setting. We had a workplace mantra - 'SQAP' - which stood for Safety, Quality, Accounting and, finally, Production. The era I describe is pre-Health and Safety at Work Act, but we had an ostensibly strict set of regulations based on law and also our own Ammunition and Explosives Regulations. Each process task had to have an Inspection and Repair Instruction (IRI) approved by the Senior Ammunition Technical Officer (SATO). Despite these measures to preserve safety, we would have incidents. Once ammunition has been unpackaged, it is susceptible to all manner of misfortune. On one occasion, a fused shell was picked up whilst the handler's hands were still coated in barrier cream. The shell slipped and struck the APB floor nose-first. The top detonator in the fuze exploded but the fuze's internal safety design features prevented disaster. On another occasion, a friend of mine felt the need to answer the phone in the Initial Acceptance lab. Unfortunately, at that precise moment, he had a red smoke grenade pinned in a special clamp so that the inside of the fuze could be inspected. He became distracted and hadn't noticed that the locking pins to hold back the grenade's striker weren't secured. The striker pounced, the grenade emitted dense clouds of red smoke as everyone bailed out and the once-white walls were turned pink! That sort of thing was hilarious; provided it didn't happen to you. Safety and quality don't need explanation but perhaps the accounting principle merits a mention. If you were conducting a major component replacement task, you were supposed to reconcile all of the components before and after each process session. When employed on the tedious task of removing, inserting or replacing hundreds of components each day, it was easy to miss one; or two. It often happened that as the last pallet of a large repair job was sealed, someone would find an unused fuze which would trigger apoplexy in the ammunition technician in charge (AT i/c). Becoming an AT i/c attracted a certain amount of kudos but most of my peers avoided it. There was no pay differential between an AT on his first day at work and another corporal AT in charge of the lab. Another source of anxiety was the visit regime of the Line Foreman and the Senior Ammunition Technician (SAT). They would sweep into the lab, sometimes annoyingly with a pet springer spaniel that would piss all over the place, and then they would set about trying to catch people out. One Line Foreman had a fetish for the Nucleonic Test Set which used a radioactive isotope to detect the position of the arming lever in a Barmine fuze. He would almost invariably pounce on the operator and ask him to identify the radioactive isotope. Fifty years later, I still recall that it was Americium 241. I also recall that next to it was an open bath of trichloroethylene used to clean the threads on fixing bolts. The hazards of this solvent are now very well-known but, in those days, in what we would nowadays call 'lost in the hierarchy of risk', it was a good way to get gunk off your fingers!

In the early 1970s, binge drinking and drink-driving were not socially unacceptable. I was fully immersed in this culture although, at the time, I could not drive and didn't own a car. One day, on the demolition ground, I found a private car inside a large ISO container. Knowing glances were exchanged between my bosses when I reported it to them. One of them was the owner and he was banned from driving at the time, having been convicted of drink-driving. It was apparently 'bad luck' if you were caught. At the time, the sergeants' mess had an honorary member who was a local policeman, and it was said that if he caught you, he would take you home and the crime would not be reported. The RSM would allegedly deal with it instead. It appeared that being caught drink-driving was indeed a case of bad luck. I have referred to 'attrition by alcohol' in several places in this book and I would like to clarify my position on it. I was then indifferent to the consequences of binge drinking and didn't really care about drink-driving. It seemed to me that it was condoned; however, things were going to change.

One day, a group of soldiers went to Banbury on Market Day in a battered old car. Almost every aspect of conformity with licensing and roadworthiness was breached and ignored. The pubs were open all afternoon and the party imbibed. On the way back from Banbury, the driver lost control on steep and winding bends and struck a group of parked cars on a layby near the infamous Warmington Hill. The collision resulted in the deaths of four people. All of a sudden, our flippant attitude to drink-driving was brought into sharp focus. At the time, I blamed the driver who was a colleague but, with hindsight, I have come to appreciate that the incident was caused by him but enabled by the indifference of the Army and wider society to drink-driving. The consequences of 'attrition by alcohol' were going to get even closer to home in the near future.

The largest labs, furthest away from prying eyes, were often the venue for mischief and fun. Horseplay was supposedly strictly forbidden but it thrived in the nether regions of the APA. At the tame end of it, we would play cricket in the very large indoor inspection rooms. This would consist of an improvised ball made up of multiple windings of adhesive black tape which we knew as 'jungle tape'. For bat and wickets, we would fashion these from bits of dunnage. As things progressed towards the reckless end of the spectrum, it could turn unpleasant. A new person was usually put through some sort of initiation process. At break time, you could be grabbed and held down whilst you were taped to lengths of wood. You would then be lifted up onto the open double doors of the transits and 'crucified' by spending your break dangling there as your peers disappeared off to the canteen, leaving the fading shouts and screams behind them as they went. As we had to change into specialist clothing before starting work, you could be held down whilst your boots and socks were shellacked to your feet. In the returned ammunition group lab, where ammunition was inspected to see if it was fit to go back into the stockpile, there was an especially cruel trick. If CS spray canisters came in and if we had a newbie, and if the newbie was suspected of being in the slightest bit gullible, there were going to be tears. Depending on gender, the hapless newbie would be shown a spray and would be told it was 'combat deodorant' or 'combat hairspray'. The victim would be left at the inspection bench, on the pretext of tidying up, with one of these sprays left deliberately on prominent display.

The workers would lie in wait in the changing rooms. Within seconds, the mischief would elicit a subtle 'hiss' from the inspection bench immediately followed by howling!

Our working lives were none too demanding. Responsibility levels were low. I recall we had over thirty corporal ATs in A Company and it was easy and tempting to be the 'grey man' and get lost in the crowd. At the time, there was a promotion ban in force so that you could not get promoted to sergeant until you had accumulated five years' service as a corporal. Five years is a long, long time when you're only 19. We seemed to be insulated from real responsibilities.

An interesting task arose in a special building called the Major Proof Centre. This was a highly specialised facility where you could dismantle stuff like fuzes and was cushy. The staff sergeant supervisor was about the most laid-back man in the world. This building had a lot of windows and parts of it were like a greenhouse; indeed, the staff sergeant actually grew tomatoes on the windowsills. Three of us were detailed to dismantle artillery fuzes. These particular fuzes had a nasty habit of becoming dangerous with age as the explosive azide compositions in their detonators reacted with the copper in the lining of the detonator cup holders. This would result in the formation of a far more sensitive azide composition; too sensitive, in fact, to withstand the shock of being fired from a gun and this was suspected of causing fatal bore prematures. The purpose of our task was to dismantle the fuzes and then extract the detonators which would then be tested for the dangerous version of azide. Getting inside the fuze was easy but the detonator cup holders were externally screw-threaded. Once assembled correctly into the fuze, the manufacturer would then employ a process of 'punch-stabbing' to distort the thread in three places to prevent it from becoming undone. The punch-stabbing was applied around the periphery of the detonator. In the middle, just millimetres away, sat the bullseye-like most sensitive part of the detonator. Striking the bullseye would be bad form! Initially, we were quite wary of the obvious hazards. To remove the punch-stabbing, which was quite deep, we had to use a drill. The drill bit had to be carefully aligned with each of the three punch-stabbings in turn and then drilled deep enough to allow the detonator cup to be unscrewed. To spell it out, the drill bit alignment had to be perfect and an act of carelessness could easily result in the drill bit hitting the detonator.

The other less obvious issues were dwell time and depth. If the spinning drill bit was left in contact for too long, frictional heating could set the detonator off, and drilling too deep could result in the drill bit entering the side of the detonator. There were some basic precautions. The three of us were in 'one-man risk' bays. The jig holding the fuze was mounted on a stout bench and there was an armoured glass screen between the operator and the detonator. You had to be conscious of where your fingers were at all times and ensure they were well away from the detonator at critical times.

Bet you're probably getting a bit bored with all of this pre-amble! We were too, as we had hundreds of these bloody fuzes to dismantle and our initial wariness wore off as the whole thing became a drudge. Muscle memory replaced the conscious act of aiming the drill bit carefully at the punch-stabbing and our production rate increased. Did I mention our lunchtime drinking habit? Each lunchtime, we would get a snack and a beer in the NAAFI. Typically, we would have three or four pints, depending on the group size around the table as nobody wanted to be labelled as tight. Now we all know peer pressure can get you in trouble. We were joined by a newbie who entered into the process activity enthusiastically.

After a particularly heavy lunchtime session in the NAAFI, we got back to the Proof Centre, ready to resume. Our staff sergeant had spent lunchtime in his mess having a liquid lunch too. We weren't allowed to start work unless he was present so we waited for him. He rolled in and promptly put his feet up on his desk and went to sleep. We returned to our workstations and we were soon drilling for Britain. Suddenly, a loud bang reverberated around the Proof Centre. The staff sergeant woke immediately and shouted the question, "What the hell was that?" Quick as a flash, one of our number shouted back, "Sorry, staff; I left the door open and the wind blew it shut". Satisfied with this explanation, he returned to his nap. We investigated and found the Newbie transfixed behind his armoured glass screen, speechless. We counted; he still had ten fingers! He couldn't hear what we were saying to him but there was no blood. We walked him into the changing room and sat him down. As we looked anxiously at him, he suddenly laughed out loud. We checked his workstation; the drill bit was gone. Bits of metal gleamed on the black shiny conducting floor and there was an acrid smell. We suddenly decided it was time for maintenance so we cleaned his bay and got rid of the incriminating evidence. We think he had struck the detonator with the drill bit. It didn't happen again.

One day, the generally lackadaisical air changed abruptly. Employment policy was that corporal ATs were not sent to N Ireland on EOD Duties. By 1973, it was clear that N Ireland was becoming a permanent state of affairs. It was decided to send corporals there as Number 2s where they would pick up valuable experience and could offer more technical assistance to the Number 1. The announcement about this was made in the canteen one day after the technicians were ordered to remain behind. I remember the announcement well and it seemed to pierce the easy comfort zone we worked in. I was up for it on a technical level but I was also very concerned about the political and social failures that seemed to both cause and prolong the need for troops to occupy and enforce public order in a part of the UK. I got hold of a number of books on Irish history and learned for the first time of the potato famine, absentee landlords and the discrimination practised in the north against the minority Catholic population. The sectarian violence was horrifying; as a soldier, I felt reluctant to be deployed to quell the violence but then my role was not face-to-face against protestors. In bomb disposal, the bomb would be my opponent, regardless of who made it. This appeased my reluctance to deploy. The horrific scenes after bombings were televised and it produced in me a sense of moral impartiality. The people who used the bombs were repugnant and worthy of condemnation and the full force of the law. The innocent victims seemed caught up in a persistent horror and no outrage seemed bad enough to quell the bloodlust of the terrorists; it was almost as though they were trying to outdo each other. Bomb disposal seemed to me to be a bit like being a paramedic or fireman. The injury or the fire was the immediate focus and not what had caused the issue. In hindsight, this was an easy way out for me and was perhaps simplistic.

I got my marching orders for my first tour in early 1974. A couple of my friends at Kineton had volunteered right at the beginning but had not thrived and both were sent back. I had apparently performed well at an exercise near Thetford and an ATO captain had given me a pat on the back which was upgraded to a shove into operations. I was OK with that but first was the 'small matter' of pre-operational training and the newly introduced Psychometric Test. I was nominated for a course and was also ordered to attend a pilot Psychometric Test at the then School of Ordnance at Blackdown. At the time, I was single but was dating Rose who was a medical orderly in the Kineton Medical Centre. As the course and future operations would involve the use of ionising radiation, I was required to become a classified radiation worker. This entailed registration and, as the late, great Tony Hancock would say it, giving a 'whole armful of blood' for the blood count! I reported to the Med Centre and was put in a cubicle. From inside, I heard an approaching and familiar giggle; it was Rose, come to take my blood. By then, I was a regular blood donor so what could possibly go wrong? Well, it seems I was one of Rose's first victims. Stage fright intervened and my arms started to resemble those of a mainlining junkie. The medic sergeant intervened and the armful was harvested. Next up was to be a pep-talk from the Commandant, Colonel K D Bangham. The RSM marched me in and I promptly trampled the pet dog which tried to protect its master from the incoming stamping boots. From a script written by somebody else about somebody else, the hapless commandant gave me a huge heart-given earful of praise for doing so well on my course and said he was proud and confident I was going to represent Kineton in Northern Ireland and not let him down (no pressure there, then). I glanced at the RSM at the obvious error and the withering, reproachful return glance was worthy of Windsor Davies in the sitcom 'It Ain't Half Hot, Mum'. Thus browbeaten into accepting the misplaced praise, I was asked if I wanted to participate in a BBC Panorama documentary about Bomb Disposal men. I declined; the dog started whining and it was time to march out.

The Psychometric Test was odd. I travelled down to Blackdown in the company of fellow corporals Nobby and Terry. On the staircase outside the venue, I met Captain Nigel Wylde who, seeing I was a mere corporal, then exploded with indignity when he found out I was not just merely a corporal, I was a mere class 2 corporal. Inside the classroom were a lot of people in the trade who, if not already preceded by their reputations, would go on to greatness in future years. Some for acts of derring-do, others because they were great characters and some for both! All of this was recorded for posterity by the Panorama production crew, headed up by Jenny Barraclough. She was sat at the front with an Army psychiatrist. She appeared to be heavily pregnant, and I had a passing thought it might be a reaction test, such was the atmosphere of paranoia. (Remember, this was almost fifty years ago when it was rare to see pregnant ladies in the place of work.) The 'shrink' spoke unconvincingly about the origins of the test and that it was to protect those of us lacking the emotional stability to conduct EOD operations in the high-threat environment of Northern Ireland. It was less than reassuring to hear the test was developed from one used to test would-be submariners. We did the test on day one and the Panorama filming was done on day two. I had elected not to be filmed but maybe that was a mistake; every now and again, I review the documentary, which is still available online, if only to remember absent friends. In excluding myself from the filming, I was influenced by what was being said and done about our personal security. If you were warned for duty in Northern Ireland, you were excused haircuts and we were told at one point that terrorist organisations were collating our personal information. Some of the candidates were quite feisty. The room went very quiet when it was asked if the test could disclose homosexuality. One candidate asked if the failure of the test would see him leave the trade. The answer that it would, if only to protect him from himself, was rebutted by the swift riposte that he had already done a tour and had been decorated for gallantry. I felt then, as I do now, that I had an 'Emperor's Clothes Moment'. The whole episode seemed patronising and condescending.

[Whilst on the topic of the Panorama documentary, I will signpost readers to another documentary made by the BBC in 2012 called Bomb Squad Men: The Long Walk. It features three old friends, one now sadly deceased, and retraces their experiences thirty years earlier.]

My performance on this test was sufficient (I think) to allow me to proceed. At least until I became 25 years old when I was obliged to resit it in case my brain had changed, which was a widespread belief; so much so, car insurance premiums dropped after that age. I then attended a pre-operational training course of four weeks. My instructors were worthy men of seeming irreproachable character. There was an exception, however. There was one instructor who was unbelievably pompous and totally full of himself. He would bounce up everywhere like Zebedee, pouncing on and reproaching anyone for the slightest real or suspected deviation from the taught line. I would listen attentively to the wisdom of the late Tom Galloway. He was an erudite graduate of the University of Life and I hoped to be like him one day but feared I would never be good enough. He would set practical tests with hook and line and stand by while we totally messed up but would then painstakingly illustrate best practice with an ease and patience worthy of Job. On the last Friday of the course, I was told I had passed. The next morning, I was getting off the ferry in Belfast. I was completely unprepared for what I saw. Unlike most soldiers, we did not undergo the typical Northern Ireland training package; our training was focused solely on bomb disposal. I was largely ignorant of the overall security situation. I had spent a sleepless night surrounded by drunken passengers vomiting in the toilets; pools of vomit on the deck flowed from port to starboard and back as the ferry rolled during the crossing. I was travelling alone, in civilian dress; everyone else could have been a terrorist. I had to share a berth with strangers. After docking, I looked down from the foot-passenger ramp and could see two men with my name on a placard. I was ushered into a Sherpa van. We climbed in through the sliding front doors. In the back, it was dark. There were no windows. The van was evidently used for cargo as there were no rear seats. Instead, there was a free-standing battered old armchair; the kind that would steal the coins from your pockets. As I watched the driver and escort, they removed their Service 9mm Browning pistols and placed them under the floormats. We drove out of the docks and I remember seeing the rows of terraced blocks, made bleak by the houses within that were burned out, blitz-fashion. The van suddenly slowed down and stopped. The front seat passenger opened the window and was challenged for identity. As he showed his Service ID, I caught a glimpse of the man who had stopped us. He was wearing obsolete British Army green combat clothing and a balaclava. We had been stopped by a terrorist manning an illegal vehicle checkpoint (VCP). It was the first day of the Ulster Worker's Council (UWC) strike. When I got to Lisburn, I was greeted and shown the ropes. When not on task, I was to work from a desk situated in the clerk's office in HQ 321 EOD. I sat at my desk and noted a large black scorch mark on the portacabin ceiling. It was directly above a burned-out metal litter bin on the floor next to the desk. The others watched on as my gaze went around the office looking for other signs of damage. It turned out my predecessor had made up some incendiary composition to be used in EOD lectures but had left a lot of the stuff in the bin and a discarded cigarette did the rest. Burning sugar chlorate is very exciting stuff in the confined space of a crowded office!

On task, I could find myself acting as No 2 for one of three operators, an ATO captain, The SAT or the Statistics Sergeant (Statscat). The ATO was wedded to higher things and never missed an opportunity to lecture me on stuff that would 'come in handy' as I progressed through my career. The SAT was inspiring and quite mellow; the kind of warrant officer who didn't need to shout although I probably merited the occasional earache from him. Statscat could be hilarious. We once attended a disruption day when the Belfast Section was overwhelmed with real and very large car bombs. The first one we attacked with what we called a Torpex Candle. There was a wooden box on the back seat of a Cortina, and I had got through a side window with the Wheelbarrow (EOD Remote Handling Equipment) and dropped the candle next to the box. It blew out the windows but then the car caught fire. On the radio, we heard that we were needed urgently around the corner in Bedford Street. Five large car bombs were now being worked on in the city centre. Thousands of people were milling around outside the cordon, unsure of where to go to get away safely and yet drawn moth-like to the flame of curiosity in front of them. Somewhere near the Europa Hotel, an 84mm Carl Gustav gun team opened fire on a suspect car. The inert practice round was capable of damaging car bomb mechanisms and, in extremis, could save the day, but the reality was that it was a weapon that produced window-breaking backblast and very few firers had the requisite calm disposition to aim steadily to ensure a hit. Our burning car bomb looked to be all but burned out. We ran down towards it, Statscat intending to clear it and I was to recover the Wheelbarrow. Halfway down, several hundred pounds of ANFO (Ammonium Nitrate Fuel Oil) in the boot detonated and we tried to hide from the falling car debris and slashing shards of glass now scything through the air. Incredibly, bar a few scratches, nobody was injured.

We packed up quickly and set about the car bomb outside Bedford House in Bedford Street. I managed to get an explosively projected heavy steel plate perfectly aligned with the bomb inside the car (probably more by luck than judgement). On the cusp of firing, we were ordered to stop. The foaming pig was brought in, and we had to wait about 20 minutes whilst vast volumes of foam were pumped into the entire street. The theory was that the foam would attenuate blast and reduce damage. Hypothesis then hit the wall of common sense with a massive bang as the bomb detonated before the foaming was completed. Statscat was beside himself. At the end of that day, six large car bombs had been put into the city centre. Five detonated and only one was rendered safe. Miraculously, I believe the only real injury was an old lady with a gashed leg, but the damage was awesome. It 'snowed' in Bedford Street after our second bomb detonated. Bedford House was a government building where row upon row of filing cabinets could be seen through the glass-walled frontage. All the windows were sucked out by the immense blast and the filing cabinet contents fell like confetti onto the chaos below.

On one occasion in June 1974, I assisted at the scene of a car bomb explosion. The bomb had detonated without warning, killing a 13-year-old girl. The would-be bomber had abandoned the device in the car park of a greyhound racing circuit near Hannahstown. This was the first fatality I saw on operations. I had seen dead people at the scene of road traffic accidents before then, but the memory of this incident stayed with me. I often reflect on this child being robbed of life and the chance to become a mother and grandmother. Who has the right to steal an innocent's life like that?

During this time, I was recruited as a crew mate for a sailing dinghy race by Chippie, who was a lance corporal in HQ 321 EOD Unit. We were to race as novices in a big Army sailing regatta around Strangford Lough. In the first round, we set off and the first leg seemed fine. I already knew about the sailing technique of tacking from reading about Sir Francis Chichester's exploits on his epic solo tour around the world in Gypsy Moth in 1966. But I didn't know that 'Ready About' was another expression to mean 'Duck'. After several whacks around the head from the boom, I got the message and by some counter-intuitive miracle, we managed to come first in our class. Sadly, this meant we had to race again. In the next race, the wind got up. It was too strong for us to navigate, and we lost the sail. A rescue launch eventually took us in tow, and we got back, soaking wet and freezing cold, hours after the other participants had left. I was never to try sailing a dinghy again!

The Wheelbarrow we had in 1974 was quite basic. It had one black and white CCTV camera and could carry a 5-shot semi-automatic Browning shotgun on its boom. Twin disruptors could be mounted in scaffolding clamps at the front of the boom and, despite the Wheelbarrow's development being supported by an MoD agency in the UK, it turned out the best sights for the disruptors were nothing more than a loop of black tape stuck on the disruptor's muzzle. You would reverse a small piece to expose the pale-coloured adhesive side for contrast and the sight indicated you were on target when you saw the loop of tape distorted in the CCTV picture as it touched the target. The development of Wheelbarrow over the years was dramatic but the equipment could be temperamental. It didn't like heavy rain; it was powered by two lead-acid Land Rover batteries with a limited useful charge but it was simple. What you never did was stand in front of it once the weapons were loaded. The method of initiating the explosive charges or weapons also meant a departure from conventional demolition practices. Weapons had to be cocked and the safety catch set to fire before the Wheelbarrow set off towards its target. If it was carrying an explosive charge, the detonator had to be inserted and connected to the firing cable. The disruptors, which were electrically initiated, were very powerful and could easily kill. These would be connected to the Wheelbarrow's electrical circuit to enable firing through the control box. We used to laugh at our own black humour, saying that if the EOD incident was dangerous, it got even more dangerous once the EOD Team arrived. If we became a little too fond of blowing things up we would be accused of doing the terrorists' job for them; it was said the IRA would provide the coded bomb warning and we would provide the explosion!! Although we had quite strict precautions relating to weapon and explosive safety, EOD Teams were constantly pushing the boundaries, trying to cut corners to save precious time. Disaster was always waiting in the wings.

On one occasion, to save time, an EOD Team decided to fire an explosive charge using the Wheelbarrow's integral circuitry rather than the safer off-board firing cable. As they assembled the charge in the control point, they connected one terminal, thinking they would only need to touch the other terminal with a cable to complete the circuit. What they didn't appreciate was that the 18-way main controller cable was actually being used as a 19-way cable as the earth return through the armoured sheath was being utilised for the CCTV circuit. As they connected only one half of the circuit to the detonator, the charge exploded. It was counter-intuitive and baffling when it happened. The Team were blown off their feet but injuries were only slight. On another occasion, I had a nightmarish incident when my No 1, who was very tall and tended to stand with his legs astride, hands on hips, stood in front of my loaded Wheelbarrow. The shotgun had the standard long barrel which was uncommon as most of them had been sawn off to increase the spread of shot. His life was narrowly spared when the Wheelbarrow suddenly discharged all five shotgun rounds between his legs, inches from his groin. The control box was connected but nobody was holding it. It turned out that the main controller cable used an 18-groove hub to allow the drum to rotate as the Wheelbarrow advanced without twisting the cable. A loom of sprung contacts transferred control signals as the drum rotated. In this case, the nut securing the spindle had loosened and fallen off. The drum jumped off its spindle and created a massive short circuit. The gun was loaded with the Army version of buckshot which was nine 7mm balls. Forty-five of these balls passed just under his balls and tore up the tarmac behind him! If the barrel had been a sawn-off or he had been shorter, he would have been disembowelled. EOD equipment can be extremely dangerous when it plays up.

As I was based at Lisburn, I would occasionally assist in weapon trials. One of these involved a remote firing stand for the 84mm Infantry anti-tank gun known as the Carl Gustav. It had been used against short-delay car bombs where the infantry could fire it against a suspect car if the nearest EOD Team couldn't get to the scene quickly enough to attempt a 'render safe'. I have watched the Carl Gustaf in action in Belfast City Centre. In use, the firing team were relatively exposed as it is a back-blast weapon which cannot be fired from inside cover. The engagement range was usually about 100 metres, often much less. It was common for even an experienced gun team to miss. In one incident, I looked on as a team fired at the broad side of a bus and missed it. The boffins proposed that it be positioned and fired from a bespoke stand which, on paper at least, seemed to reduce the danger to the firing team and the stand didn't suffer from the shakes.

We trialled the prototype stand on the ranges at Ballykinler. We mounted the gun, carried out bore-sighting and aligned it with the hulk of a car. There were two methods of firing. One was electrical, using a battery, a lengthy firing cable and an electrical solenoid to pull the trigger. The other method used a length of Terry Cable and a large D-shaped handle, and the firer could pull the gun trigger mechanically from behind cover. Both methods worked fine, and we fired about five rounds of TPTP (practice) ammunition without incident and with consistent accuracy, using each method. Eventually, only the Terry Cable method of firing was introduced to service as it was simple and reliable. There was, however, an inherent danger. A freak accident occurred at the ranges when a unit was practising with it. An attempt was made to fire a gun and the trigger appeared to be stuck fast. The firer placed the pull mechanism on the ground and went forward to investigate. It turned out he was on the wrong side of the gun so he elected to go around the muzzle, stooping low to pass under the gun to stay out of harm's way. As he did so, it is believed his foot struck the Terry Cable which had become coiled and kinked. The firing cable within was under tension and the kick released the tension. Sadly, the firer had not stooped low enough under the muzzle and he was killed as the gun fired. EOD is dangerous, even in training.

My tour ended and I returned to Kineton in early September 1974. It was very difficult to adjust to the unreal environment in the depot. Some of my peers continued having issues with what those on high identified as 'leadership failures'. Then one of our superiors had a 'bright idea in the bath'. The solution would be a four-week leadership course at the Regimental Depot to be taken prior to a tour of duty in Northern Ireland. As the date for the inaugural course neared, the company sergeant major called for me. I was asked if I had a serviceable No 2 Dress Uniform. I said that I did. He then gave me joining instructions for the new leadership course. My protests that I had already completed a successful operational tour in the Province came to naught. I was sent on the training course which could have been the inspiration for 'Bad Lads Army'. Although we were all full corporals, it seemed to us that the instructors had been ordered to toughen us up and it was like being a recruit all over again. There was an ex-Parachute Regiment sergeant who had suffered an injury to his wrist in Northern Ireland. He needed to wear a brace and was downgraded medically and was obliged to transfer to the RAOC if he wanted to stay in the Army. I would readily admit that is some fall from grace; Parachute Regiment to RAOC? But it wasn't our fault. We were beasted at dark o'clock each morning, respirators on, running towards Camberley with logs. There were, however, three things I appreciated about that course. The Skill At Arms Wing hosted us and it was led by RSM JJ Thomson.

I thought the man was an absolute legend. The next thing was that we were trained up as Unit Shooting Coaches and the third thing was Brad. We would drown our sorrows each evening in the NAAFI, and this made the early- morning road-run beastings even worse. Up until then, I hadn't taken to Brad. He was an absolute clown. He had a heart of gold but was, in my view, completely off the wall. He had that knack of putting me on edge if he was anywhere near me. He probably had the sharpest repertoire of wit in Christendom, scant regard for authority and would mercilessly deride anyone who appeared to be an 'establishment man'. As a somewhat 'anal geek', I was the golden target of opportunity. Now we were on this course from hell; what could possibly go wrong? Brad turned out to be pivotal in the maintenance of our group morale. I can only speak for myself, but I felt a powerful sense of resentment at being put on the course. My performance qualities were more than sufficient as a corporal, I had completed a tour in Northern Ireland and my leadership abilities on exercise were praised by my officers; in fact, my performance on exercise was the very reason I had been selected to go to Northern Ireland in the first place. As for nearly all the others on this 'leadership course', there was nothing in their respective characters that I could see that merited additional leadership training, especially with the apparent onus on ridiculing us and denigrating us as over-promoted geeks. However, as time went by, I suspect the training staff started to see our worth.

It was small things at first. The RSM was lecturing us one day about small arms and spoke of the mix of tracer and ball and the usefulness of tracer as an indication of fall of shot and target indication. We countered this, quoting the modest ballistic differences between ball and tracer ammunition and that the 7.62mm tracer burned out at about 1100 metres. His initial scepticism was replaced with some apparent respect for us when we produced various bits of official publications that corroborated what we had said. The emphasis on bawling _at_ us was replaced by talking _with_ us as we were mentored through the Unit Shooting Coach phase, which I enjoyed. By that stage, I had already experienced a lot more regimental and leadership training than the average RAOC corporal. To get onto the ammunition technician course, I had to attend rigorous regimental training as a pre-cursor. After graduating as an AT, I had already passed my regimental proficiency training for promotion to sergeant. I had real experience of firing support weapons on trials whereas the instructors had not gotten beyond limited training in this area; for example, our Carl Gustaf instructor had only fired the weapon on an indoor sub-calibre training device.

Towards the end of this absurd leadership experiment, we were to conduct a night navigation march with only very limited navigation aids. In my syndicate, we had the late Harry Bazen. Harry was tall, quiet and unassuming. One of the challenges in night navigation was in measuring distance. Younger readers may need to be reminded that GPS devices had not even been thought of at the time. We had been told that our appointed navigator had to keep track of paces covered by counting them in his head and then, by using small stones in a pocket, he should keep a tally of the paces. To maintain a steady heading in rough featureless country in darkness, we would have to put a man out in front and march in stages using compass bearings and back bearings constantly to ensure we did not deviate. The leg we were marching on was about three miles long and we were to find a man concealed in a bush somewhere out in this wilderness. We were not allowed to call out to him, and he wasn't allowed to call us in if we were nearby. This navigation test required determined concentration by the navigator and flawless teamwork. As we trudged on, feeling ever more pessimistic that we would fail, Harry remained cheerful and confident, encouraging us on and all the while keeping track of our progress while talking to us. We eventually reached a small clearing and there was a bush in front of us. Just as Harry said the rendezvous point "Should be here", our contact stepped forward out of the bush to give us the instructions for the next leg. We had gone three miles over broken ground, in the dark, and our navigation had been inch-perfect. Our group was being supervised by a lieutenant colonel. This officer was obviously overawed by our achievement and offered huge praise (I actually think he was lost but then you may know what soldiers think of officers with maps). When I say, 'our achievement', I really mean Harry. This quiet, thoughtful man had led us in the darkness without fuss and had demonstrated leadership and integrity in spades. It was a fine example of being a leader without all the unseemly shouting and screaming that seemed to characterise the regimental model.

Now I'll come back to the topic of Brad in a paragraph I would entitle 'Spirit in the Sky'. Brad was a total extrovert and the way he responded to our mistreatment showed moral courage and his hilarious antics buoyed us up, especially when we had been paraded together to await a beasting. One morning, we were in three ranks outside an accommodation block. By tradition, we were five minutes early and perhaps our next tormentor was a little late. Our spirits were low, not broken, just fed up and suffering from the 'same shit, different day' syndrome. Brad suddenly broke ranks and stepped out in front of us to recite some sort of doomsday prophecy about how we were to imminently face our maker at the hands of the next screaming drill pig. Anxiously scanning for any approaching killjoy, we started to laugh. Brad pointed up into the sky calling out that he saw the spirits of the dead on high (or some such daftness). The merriment was infectious and even I creased up at his antics. Just then, a young soldier opened a window on the first floor of the accommodation block, looking quite distressed. From the window, he announced that he had just found a dead body in that room. This was really bizarre. It turned out that the occupant of the room had died in his sleep overnight and had just been found. It was a tragedy with a twist and the irony was not lost on us.

The four-week course ended on Friday 20th December 1974. During the last week, one of our group celebrated his 18th birthday; or tried to. We had to complete some night-time tactical exercises and the weather was freezing. The birthday boy was of Greek heritage, Nick Nicholaides, who was known to us as Nick the Greek. On his birthday night, we had been put into an ambush position somewhere out in the woods. We were there for hours. After midnight, the RSM appeared. He checked our positions and handed a bottle of rum to Nick for his birthday. The course had started acrimoniously but ended on a better note. And the rum hit the mark as we waited for the enemy who was to stand us up!

We returned to Kineton, took our respective leaves of absence for Christmas and I went home to Birmingham. Leave over, I returned to Kineton and pondered over what was going to happen next as we started 1975. The spring passed with me being moved aimlessly around the labs. The preoccupation amongst corporal ATs with leadership capabilities, or the lack of them, continued. The next bright idea was the establishment of 'competence' levels. To manage a small APB or part of a process task in a large APB now required the corporal to have a certificate of competence at Level 1. To manage a larger APB required the corporal to have a certificate of competence at Level 2. The day the new policy edict from the technical directorate at Didcot arrived (known then as the Chief Inspector Land Service Ammunition (CILSA)), I was summoned to the Line Foreman's office and told I was to put my APB into maintenance as I was now deemed 'incompetent'. That afternoon, I was called back and handed a newly typed Level 1 certificate of competence. The next morning,

I received my Level 2 certificate. Business resumed as I had become competent overnight.

The new policy of certifying competence required that we be regularly rotated around the different process buildings. One morning after muster parade, the company sergeant major ordered three of us with Northern Ireland experience to report to him in his office. I suspected a trap; the last such assignation had resulted in four weeks of purgatory in the hands of drill pigs at Blackdown. A common saying in the Army is 'never volunteer'. It turned out that a corporal AT had been short-toured in Northern Ireland and an urgent volunteer replacement was needed. Now I was desperate to escape Kineton, apparently more so than my two peers, as I executed a rapid 'One Pace, Step Forward, March' and beat them to it. Away I went, now familiar with the route to Belfast, I boarded the train for Liverpool at Leamington Spa. The train didn't get far. After waiting for ages at an unscheduled halt, we were informed that a man had thrown himself in front of a train ahead. As a result, I missed the boat train. I had to stay overnight in transit accommodation in a barracks in Liverpool. The journey resumed the next day and I arrived at HQ 321 EOD Unit the following morning. The SATO briefly interviewed me on arrival. He didn't seem terribly convinced about my excuse for lateness but perhaps the size of the lie, had it been a whopper, convinced him otherwise. I was then collected by the Armagh EOD Team which was based in the old Gough Barracks in the city. We were in a Ford Transit and the No 1, Colin, then a staff sergeant, hammered the Transit along the road and at one point, we nearly reached a ton. We entered Gough Barracks and turned right. The resident unit was the 9/12 Lancers. We were accommodated in a small block with an EOD garage off to one side. The Team was a mixed bunch of characters. The driver was a short, portly and accident-prone RAOC lance corporal. I noted he was armed with a Webley Revolver which was inside a massive holster, sited on the front of his belt where it sagged down between his legs. I think this was a compromise as a conventional side position was awkward in the cramped Transit cab which was required to seat three of us. We had an escort provided by the resident unit who lived with us. My room was the Team office, and I didn't have a bed. Instead, I would retrieve a grubby mattress each evening from a cupboard and place it on the desk. It wasn't too uncomfortable. Opposite our little block was the REME LAD; for those not in the know, this was a sort of garage for maintaining Army vehicles.

The Ford Transit carried the Wheelbarrow and a change from my first tour was that the Ford Transit had an integral battery charger for the Wheelbarrow. You could plug the Wheelbarrow into the onboard charger and then you plugged the Transit into an electrical socket on the wall inside the garage. There was an obvious 'accident-waiting-to-happen' if the Transit drove away before being unplugged; mitigation was provided in the form of a big cardboard warning placard which would be positioned over the steering wheel whenever the Transit was plugged in; provided, that is, the driver remembered. Not long after I arrived, we were called out late one night into Armagh City. Rubbing the sleep out of our eyes, we tumbled into the Transit's cab, the engine was fired up and the blues and twos were switched on. We charged forward and then there was a brilliant blue flash followed by a pop in the back. Yes, the plug had been forgotten. By the time the over-stimulated driver was brought to a stop, we had almost reached the guardroom and we had succeeded in tearing out the steel conduit tubing from all of the garages. The hapless driver had also had a very near miss. He had been crouching behind a wall when his Webley suddenly fired. It turned out he had loaded all of the chambers, which meant the hammer was resting on a round and he had somehow clouted the hammer as he dived for cover. It was symptomatic of the somewhat chaotic conditions we endured in Gough Barracks.

One day, my No 1 handed me a new piece of electronic equipment. It had to be mounted on the skid of a Sioux helicopter which was on the helipad on the main square. It was a bright sunny day and I walked around and found the chopper. I opened the box and read the instructions. They said I had to scrape the paint off at the mounting point to ensure a good earth connection. As I attacked the paintwork with a knife, the shadow of one extremely angry 'Driver Airframe' suddenly passed over me and I was chased.

Because of our operational standing, we had no trouble getting supplies. Other than food. The cookhouse in Gough Barracks was a magnet for vermin and the food was disgusting. A prized possession from the supply depot was a very large tin of Swarfega; it went missing one day as we took a tea break. From my improvised bed in the office, I could see into the REME LAD opposite, and I noticed that one of their vehicle mechanics liked to roam around our vehicles like an urban fox whenever our backs were turned. Suspicions aroused, we procured another tin of Swarfega and pondered how to keep it safe. Believing in the value of deterrence over detection, I resolved to punish the suspected thief and deter all others from messing with our kit. I cleaned out the new Swarfega tin, putting the gel into other containers. I fitted the tin with a microswitch in the base and set it up as an anti-lift booby trap. In those days, we didn't have sound units. There was an Igniter No 84 which was well-loud indoors, but this scavenger merited something more upmarket. The alternative was Fuze Instantaneous; not the modern stuff - we had stock of the obsolete Fuze Instantaneous. Six inches of that could make your ears ring for a week. Ten feet of it fitted nicely in the tin. I secured the lid tightly after setting a delay-to-arm timer and placed the tin on the bonnet of a Land

Rover in front of our building. With bated breath, booby trap primed and waiting and the Swarfega label to broadcast temptation to anyone with greasy hands, we watched from behind closed Venetian blinds. After a while, the scavenger appeared, scurrying between the parked vehicles. With furtive glances, he crouched down and crept around the parked vehicles, ending up within grab range of the Swarfega. We saw his hands reach up for the tin. He lifted it and a brilliant flash, followed by a cloud of grey smoke enveloped the front of the Land Rover. The bang was something else. The tin lid took off like a frisbee and he fled back to the LAD. The tin lid landed near the guard room. People started running around thinking we had just been attacked but the guard commander found us all doing the 'dying fly', creased up with laughter and realised it was ATO home-grown humour. The REME guy never bothered us again.

Shortly after I arrived, the No 1 had to leave us on compassionate grounds and he was replaced by a man known in the trade as 'Gentleman Jim'. At this time, we had already suffered casualties in rural areas. We hadn't yet developed an effective EOD doctrine and, in hindsight, some of the ways we operated were extremely dangerous. If we had suspect devices in rural areas, our approach was often similar to the way suspect devices would be dealt with in urban areas; we would simply drive up to within about 100 metres, or sometimes closer. If we were lucky, there might be an RUC Constable or member of the UDR who would have some understanding of why we had been called out. Very often, we didn't even have an effective cordon, perhaps only protected by our four-man escort team. We attended the scene of an alleged gunshot next to a five-bar gate which had been fired as a farmer member of the UDR went through the gate to attend to his cattle. We drove up to the end of the lane and the whole team walked up to greet an RUC Constable standing at the open gate. We looked around and noticed a small patch of disturbed turf next to where you would be standing whilst unlatching the gate. On the bottom rail of the gate was some fishing line, betraying its presence by glinting in the sun as it fluttered in the wind. On the end was an improvised wedge; this betrayed the presence of a booby trap so we legged it, sharpish. I then expected at least some form of discussion and a more circumspect follow-up. Instead, Jim asked me to get him a spade out of the Transit. I offered to carry out an electronic sweep with the very basic equipment we had in those days but he declined the offer. With the spade and no other equipment, he then walked back to the gate. As I looked on in horror, he dug up the disturbed ground directly, as if he was chasing earthworms for fishing bait. Then he put the spade down and bent over, tugging at a heavy object in the hole he had made. By now, I was watching through a Swift scope. We were only 60 metres away and I could see the hairs in his moustache, such was the power of the scope. The object he pulled out of the ground was large, wrapped in clear plastic and pink in colour. Then Jim straightened up and beckoned to us to approach. I was initially reluctant. Whilst watching him, I had been rehearsing my statement for the Board of Inquiry as I genuinely expected him to be blown up. When I got to him, he was pleased as punch. He had pulled 30 pounds of Frangex out of the hole. On the top of this charge was the splash-like witness mark of where the detonator in this vicious booby trap had functioned. The charge 'failed to propagate' as we say in the trade. I won't explain precisely why; suffice it to say that this escape from certain death was as lucky as it could get. The initial report of a gunshot arose because a detonator can sound something like that if it explodes alone. The would-be victim's surname was Fluke! Would you credit it? He was identified in the local press at the time and was quite self-assured. He didn't seem to appreciate how lucky he had been and was quite fatalistic, if not to say sanguine about the incident. When we detonated the main charge to dispose of it later, the blood drained out of his face and he almost passed out when he saw how big the explosion was.

Perhaps the more fatalistic character was Gentleman Jim himself. A man of almost invariably cheerful disposition who seemed quite indifferent to danger, he had almost a complete disregard for his own safety. From my perspective, I found this to be quite frightening. Jim had a side-line in commercial explosive demolition work and, at this time, he demolished a chimney. I don't recall the exact circumstances, but it was authorised as military assistance to the local community, a sort of hearts and minds job. I think there was even an article about it published in the Army's Visor Magazine.

I was to discover in another job the limits to his self-professed commercial knowledge of quarrying and demolitions. We were called to a disused quarry well out in the countryside. A rockfall near the bottom of the quarry had exposed a shot hole and there was an unexploded Quarrex charge in a helical cardboard tube visible. The rockfall had only exposed part of the charge and you couldn't see above or below the charge. There was no link to crime or terrorism. It would simply be a matter of recovering the charge and disposing of it. However, we couldn't excavate it as it was in solid rock. Cutting into it would be a foolhardy proposition so destruction in situ was the preferred solution. A reasonable assumption as to how this situation came about was that a prepared shot hole had been filled with explosive charges and perhaps an air gap had prevented all of the charge from detonating. Jim placed a small demolition charge against it and sent me back to the Transit to radio the Brigade Operations Room with a warning of an imminent controlled explosion. Having ignited his fuze, Jim returned to the Transit and checked to see how much burning time was left. "Anytime now," he said. Then there was a thunderous roar and a massive column of rock fragments shot up into the air. The ground heaved under our feet. To our good fortune, the blast was directed away from us by the rock face and the debris fell back into the quarry. The charge we had just destroyed was not alone; the entire column had contained a full charge and I estimated it to be about 200 pounds based on the size of the charge and how many could have been in the shot hole. Jim looked on bemused as I called the Brigade Operations Room to explain that the controlled explosion at our location wasn't!

The last significant jobs I did with Jim were on the Ballygawley Road. We were sent to the scene of an explosion. When we got there, we were confronted with chaos and devastation. A large stone cottage at the end of a terrace had been completely destroyed. Only about two feet of the base of the original thick walls remained. Some of the rubble had fallen onto cars parked in front. We walked straight into the exposed foundations of the destroyed building. Body parts littered the scene. The victims were adult siblings from one family, two brothers and their married sister. They had been working to set the house up as a marital home for the sister who was heavily pregnant. We were able to locate the seat of the blast which had been inside a hot press cupboard on the ground floor. From the disposition of the body parts and the traumatic amputation of one of the forearms, we could discern that this was probably a booby trap, triggered when one of them opened the cupboard. It looked as though the main commercial explosive filling had been concealed inside the hot water cylinder. The scene of horror we were confronted with is beyond description. Death would have been instant and I would say no more about it out of respect to the families. The UFF allegedly claimed responsibility but the creatures who perpetrated this callous act can never, ever justify what they did to fellow human beings, including the unborn child. And they have the gall to call themselves loyalists. All terrorist murderers stand beyond the bounds of the accepted norms of society and should never, in my view, merit compassion of any kind. I would prefer they were executed upon conviction or at least jailed for life with no hope of parole.

A few days later, we were back in the area. In a tit-for-tat bombing, a family home was blown up without warning. Fortunately, there were no fatalities but that was a matter of good fortune; there was a clear intent to murder.

The last operator I assisted in that tour was a well-known and like-able man who had recently been an instructor at the Army Apprentices College, Chepstow. He was a careful and thoughtful man and I had no need to worry about him. I left shortly after he arrived and returned to Kineton. It was late spring, I was contemplating marriage and getting curious about where I might be posted to next. Another point was that I would likely be loaded onto a three-month Class One upgrading course and this would shape my activities in the short term. Shortly after returning to work at Kineton, I had a phone call from one of my peers on my basic ammunition technician course. He had learned that he, myself and the afore-mentioned Gentleman Jim were to be posted to a new unit and that we would be promoted to sergeant. Between that eventuality was marriage, the Lance SSGW course and upgrading course.

I got married in July and then attended the upgrading course. Because my basic course had been the original longer course, there was much duplication. The really challenging part of the course was the EOD phase of which there were two parts: Dealing with stray conventional ammunition and then terrorist bomb disposal which was technically known as Improvised Explosive Device Disposal (IEDD). The real hurdle was getting through the IEDD practical tests. Typically, each student would undergo up to four two-hour sessions covering simulated terrorist incidents in a variety of scenarios. I distinctly remember that one of my jobs involved dealing with a man murdered by terrorists; a so-called body job. These were never straightforward. Great emphasis was placed by the directing staff on respecting the dead. I recall being reproached by one examiner who was unhappy that I was showing insufficient sensitivity to the deceased and family and he then suggested the widow was watching me from the cordon. I passed the job but I was left with the impression that we seemed to go through phases or trends in Northern Ireland where, in one year, you would respond, blow up a car and then get back to base as quickly as possible, and, in another year, you might be expected to deal with a suspect car in a slower, deliberate fashion with damage being limited. Another factor was the recovery of forensic evidence but, except for jobs where there was an imminent threat to human life, the operator's own safety was deemed paramount. There seemed to be an ambivalence, perhaps personality-driven by whoever was in charge; or was I being cynical?

By this time, I had received a posting order to the newly formed Lance Guided Missile Platoon of 43 Replenishment Park Company, 1st British Corps Combat Supplies Battalion, otherwise known by the sobriquet 1 Complete Surprise Battalion! We were told we had been specially selected. We encountered two officers and three warrant officers who had attended a Lance training course in the US. They had come back to the UK to design a UK-based training package and create the new platoon. The trainers produced an effective course which was interesting. The pilot course also included personnel who were, or would be, based at the RA Ranges Benbecula in the Hebrides. This was the only place in the UK where the missiles could be fired. The Lance missile had a range of up to 75 miles and, on Benbecula, it was to be fired out to sea and tracked by radar. The version of the operational missile we had procured was nuclear with a warhead designed to detonate as an air burst, high above advancing Warsaw Pact armoured formations. The fast neutrons it generated were to penetrate enemy armour and irradiate enemy tank crews with a lethal dose of radiation. The missile itself was a beautifully sleek descendant of Hitler's V2 rocket. On the ranges, it could be fitted with a practice warhead. It was stored in a robust, two-piece shipping container. It contained pre-loaded fuel and oxidiser. These were known as 'hypergolic' as they would spontaneously ignite when mixed. Being so reactive, these chemicals (fuel: Unsymmetrical Dimethyl Hydrazine (UDMH) and oxidiser: Inhibited Red Fuming Nitric Acid (IRFNA)) were extremely dangerous. To mitigate the danger of a reaction in storage or transit, we were equipped with Draeger air samplers (a bit like breathalysers) and we constantly used these to monitor for leaks. If a leak was detected, we were to suit up in heavy-duty chemical suits and would use oxygen re-breather sets. Breathing in any fumes would likely have a rapid and fatal outcome. To deal with a leak, we were equipped with Propellant Disposal Kits (PDKs). These were palletised propellant draining kits which included a variety of tools to either seal a small leak with a circumferential band or to enable the complete drain-down of a damaged main missile assemblage. We carried out intensive response training where we would practise our techniques to make a leak safe. As I completed this training, where I was to be a PDK Team Commander, I contemplated how a real leak scenario might proceed.

The most likely cause of a leak would be when the missiles were being moved; in other words, some sort of transportation accident. As we had to regularly remove the missiles from storage for periodic inspection, the next, and probably more likely scenario, was if we accidentally dropped a missile as it was hoisted out of the shipping container and placed on an inspection trolley in the bespoke process building.

I must admit to being hugely sceptical of the potential efficacy of any leak-sealing or draining task except perhaps in the most trivial of leak circumstances. The whole shooting match had too many working parts, was too ponderous and needed several men in their protective suits with working oxygen re-breathing kits to work. However, that was what we were trained to do. Touch or inhale any of the propellants and you would be up shit creek in a wire mesh canoe.

CHAPTER 4

Lance Guided Missile Platoon 1976–1977

In January 1976, I flew to Germany and joined the embryonic Lance GM Platoon. Straight away, budget uncertainty and changed MoD planning poisoned the well. We were accommodated in Barker Barracks in Paderborn. Married officers and soldiers were based around that town, living in the community. The single soldiers lived in Barker Barracks despite there being a domestic site located near the Pombsen ammunition depot at Neheim. This depot was sited 25 miles away on top of an impossibly steep hill. The domestic site included single soldier accommodation and married quarters were meant to be procured to enable Pombsen to function independently with personnel located nearby. This plan was halted. We now had a 25-mile commute to work and the same to get home. As the Lance Platoon, we provided direct support to the Royal Artillery's 50th Missile Regiment, which was based at Menden, near Dortmund, another lengthy commute. All of this detracted from the whole point of the Lance Missile. It was supposed to be a fast-response weapon system to counter the massive and real threat of a Warsaw Pact invasion. In the event of an alert, which we practised periodically, we would all have to be rounded up from wherever we were accommodated in and around Paderborn. In the era before mobile phones and radio pagers, and with most of us not on the telephone at home, this would take hours.

Initially, I had been allocated temporary married accommodation (a hiring) with a German family in what you might call a 'granny flat', in Dom Weg, near the impressive Paderborn cathedral. Our landlords were nice people. We stayed with them for several months until we got a married quarter on the other side of town. To get to my work, we would start at Barker Barracks and then commute to Pombsen. If it was winter, we would often not be able to drive up the hill to the depot. At some point, we might need to outload the stock of Lance main missile assemblages. The operational warheads were kept somewhere else by the Americans. The mobilisation procedure was complex and the only way that mobilisation was even remotely possible was if we used our private cars to supplement the inadequate road transport. It gets worse. The Lance missile main assemblages required a specialist forklift truck known as a Sideloader. We had two of these lumbering ancient and unreliable beasts at Pombsen. In use, they would have to negotiate a steep and bendy incline to get between the storehouses and the process building. This so-called high-readiness plan had more Achilles' heels in it than a Greek tragedy. But we soldiered on. The missiles were transported into the depot. To get them, most of the platoon deployed by rail to a port as the missiles were coming in by sea. We arrived ahead of the docking and had a couple of days to kill while we waited. The boss took the platoon to an upmarket brothel to drink the expensive beer and not touch the exhibits. Me and Harry took off elsewhere and we found a delightful little bar near the seafront where the beer was cheap, and we could get fast food such as Frikadellen and pommes frites (faggot and chips) for 50 pfennigs a portion which was outstanding value. I think we spent about 36 hours there, drinking the

German way which was to sip your beer slowly instead of gulping it down. After a night's sleep, we were good to go and boarded the train which took us to a railhead near Pombsen. We were relieved to get the missiles into storage and away from the hazards of transportation. After that, we started to get visits and, on one occasion, I was to admit a high-ranking officer into the storehouses to view the Lance Missile 'Holy Grail'. At a temperature of minus 10 degrees C, with locks frozen, I was unable to open the doors!

The Russians knew all about us. Under the terms and conditions of arms control agreements, they were allowed to drive around Germany in specially marked cars, so-called Soxmis missions. NATO forces were afforded a similar facility over the border. It was stipulated that these Soxmis vehicles were not permitted in sensitive locations and Pombsen was one of these. There was a rough but passable track that skirted the perimeter fence of Pombsen ammunition depot. It was accessed by driving up the steep and winding main access road and turning off about 150 metres before the entrance, onto a forestry vehicle access road. Being conscientiously British, when the Lance process building was constructed, we erected all the liquid rocket propellant warning signs around it, spelling out the hazards and that 'Here is Lance'. These signs were easily visible from the track and one day, a Soxmis vehicle was seen on the track, observing our Lance process building. The OC of 43 RP Company was something of a Colonel Blimp character. When he heard of the Soxmis car's presence, he ordered us to search for it in our private cars to shouts of 'Tally Ho' and 'On, On'! It was embarrassing. It was like our own home-grown version of Dad's Army.

I mentioned Harry briefly and I think he merits a little more. He was from Lancashire and was the son of a miner. He was an endearing character and, even then in his late thirties, he was very fit and had been a

Combined Services rugby player and at one time, held the Army 200 metres sprint record. He had a huge sense of humour, a wicked wit and a powerful sense of social justice. For a variety of reasons, none of them sinister, Harry failed to achieve promotion as an ammunition technician beyond the rank of staff sergeant. He had been decorated for gallantry following his 1974 EOD tour in South Armagh. He was eventually told he would not achieve warrant rank whilst he was an AT. He was affronted by this and decided to act incisively to correct it. He relinquished his trade as an AT and became a Storeman. Some years later, I met him at Bicester when we were both attending the same training presentation. He had achieved his promotion after all. His time in the Army was drawing to a close and his ambition was to become a taxi driver. I wasn't to see Harry again until 1998 when I was sent to carry out a Board of Officers audit on an Engineer Field Park in Ripon. I had been commissioned by then, which fulfilled Harry's earlier 'piss-taking' prophecy of my career prospects when I first arrived at Pombsen. The Board members arrived the night before the audit and stayed in a small hotel in Ripon Marketplace. As we waited at the hotel lobby for our transport the next morning, my attention was drawn to a taxi rank about 30 metres away. Specifically, I noticed a man standing with his back to me and he was talking to the other taxi drivers in an animated fashion and, even after all those years, and from behind him, I instantly recognised the idiosyncratic gait and his mannerisms. As I approached him, the other drivers stepped away thinking I was a prospective fare. He turned and looked at me, a little uncertain at first, but I spoke his name and the grin confirmed it was Harry. Then he noticed I had indeed been commissioned and he laughed out loud. That evening, Harry collected me from the hotel and took me to his home where he lived with his wife Gill. I hadn't seen her for over 20 years. It was a special evening. Harry and Gill had bought themselves a thatched ancient cottage which had originally been a saw pit. The odd thing was that Harry was from Wigan, Lancashire and yet he had settled in Ripon, Yorkshire. I was delighted to see he was comfortable and settled, in good health and his sense of humour was as good as ever.

In June of 1976, we had an athletics competition in the stadium at Sennelager Training Centre. For some odd reason, and with no prior experience at all, I was nominated to compete in the pole vault. I was handed a heavy, thick pole which was more like a tree trunk than the sleek poles you would see on TV. In fact, it was a bamboo pole. To be fair, I did reasonably well, although I suspected I could have jumped higher without the pole! I ended up in a jump-off with a colleague. On my last vault, I tried too hard and lost momentum as I tried to clear the bar. I ended up having a bad fall and my lower back struck one of the concrete blocks holding up the jump frame. The pain was incredible. Eventually, I was taken to the Sennelager Medical Reception Station (MRS) where I was admitted for observation. A large swelling had appeared over the point where the corner of the block had dug in and I couldn't straighten out. After several days, I was discharged but I needed crutches to walk for the next two weeks. I was given an appointment to see a medical officer but the only transport I could get from Dom Weg to Barker Barracks was a push bike. I eventually arrived but couldn't get off the bike. There was a ramp with railings at the medical centre and I used these as a climbing frame to get off before struggling through the door like Quasimodo. The Army receptionist in the empty waiting room declared I was late and refused to let me see the doctor until I had gone over to my Battalion headquarters for a different form. I was bent over and could only walk with great difficulty. In the Orderly Room, the well-grumpy Chief Clerk, who out-ranked me, gave me a bollocking before issuing the all-important F Med 4, made out in red ink because I had been late and would now be attending a 'special sick parade'. The return to the medical centre was as slow and painful as the previous walk and I went back into the empty waiting room and was ushered in to see the medical officer. I was given light duties and a bottle of painkillers. I look back on that period of indifference to my suffering and how hard the administrators made my life at the time and I wish a plague on all their houses!

I didn't thrive in the Lance Platoon and I rarely enjoyed my time there. I was easy meat for the older senior NCOs who appeared to resent my youth. Some of them lost no time in declaring they had joined up before I was even born. My own SAT made his scornful attitude towards me quite plain. He liked to project an air of supe-riority and had a graph on his office wall upon which he plotted the various statistics relating to our work activity. After the first month, it became unreadable as it was on a sheet of A4 paper and he was plotting too many variables. He was very highly organised and sched-uled his working week meticulously, including half an hour to update the impossible graph. One day, I overheard him briefing the Platoon Commander on how bad I was. This breakdown in trust was a barrier to the all-important mentoring function an SAT should maintain with his younger sergeants. One evening, while we were on some sort of response exercise, we were at the Neheim domestic site about two miles from Pombsen. A report was telephoned through that a box containing a tank shell had fallen off a pallet in the depot. I was despatched to reseal the box and ensure it was returned to its rightful place. When I got there, however, the real story unfolded. A forklift truck operator had tried to lift the top pallet off a stack three pallets high and the pallet had accidentally swiped the wall, displacing the box which fell to the concrete floor where it burst open, ejecting the shell. The operator had carried the shell and box outside and reported the matter to his Line NCO. When I learned the truth, I opened the damaged box and lifted the shell out to inspect it. As I did so, I felt certain that I heard a short high-pitched whirring sound. I put the shell back in its box and then checked the technical manuals in the office relating to this ammunition. It was a 120mm High Explosive Squash Head (HESH) shell with an integral Fuze Base Medium L56. Mechanical fuzes typically contained an escapement mechanism, and my concern was that however unlikely, the fall might have damaged the fuze. The fuze's inbuilt safety mechanisms would prevent disaster, but it would be a bad idea to leave the shell with serviceable stock. The operator's story of how the box came to be damaged didn't score highly on my credibility scale and I felt loath to simply return the shell to stock in case it was indeed damaged internally. In the trade, there is an expectation that we refer up when in doubt. If I categorised the shell as damaged, it would cause a fuss and there would have to be accounting action taken, not to mention an accident investigation. I called my SAT to seek his advice. He received my call with obvious disdain. When I explained what I had found, he told me I was a qualified sergeant AT and I should just get on with it. He refused point blank to have any further involvement. I segregated the shell and reported the matter. The next day, to cut to the chase, a huge fuss erupted. An EOD Team from the Ammunition Inspectorate was called out. I explained what had happened. I was roundly scorned and criticised for what was presumably seen as an overreaction. It was decided to destroy the shell in the woods behind the storehouse which is quite extraordinary but that was not my choice; I saw the shell as potentially unserviceable, not dangerous. This happened in 1976 and the tale of me and my 'buzz click' episode in Pombsen, much embellished, was still being talked about 23 years later in the year I retired. But there was an epilogue. In 1994, I was commissioned and had to undergo a formal medical examination. When I had my hearing test, it revealed chronic mild tinnitus and hypersensitive high-tone hearing. High-tone hearing usually degrades with age but mine went the opposite way. Did this lie behind the 'buzz click' experience? I'll never know. But what I do know for sure is that in the ammunition technician trade, any mess-up, real or invented, would follow you forever!

The platoon had a distinctly different role from the rest of 43 RP Company, but I felt our bosses took this one stage further and we weren't encouraged to mix. There was no overt policy on this but there was a strong Lance Platoon identity which seemed to distance us from our colleagues in the rest of the company. The Pombsen ammunition depot had been sited on a very steep hill and the explosives area buildings were aligned with the contours so, from a distance, the drab grey concrete storehouses seemed to be strung like a multi-strand necklace upon the headless neck of a forested hill. The views from the top were outstanding and on a clear day, you could see the Hermannsdenkmal monument in Detmold. For technical facilities, we had a process building, a propellant draining area and two explosive storehouses. There was an ongoing surveillance programme for the missiles which meant we had to move them from storage to the process building where the transit container would be opened and the missile hoisted out onto an inspection trolley. The trolley would be rolled into the main inspection area where the missile's protective boat tail cover would be removed, and we take off the end plate which sealed the forebody at the place where a warhead would be mounted. We would then disconnect the internal cables before attaching the guidance and control system to the guided missile system test set (GMSTS). The GMSTS would then be run on a programme of diagnostic tests to ensure the missile was in good health.

The inspection area was cavernous. The ceiling was high up and festooned with an impressive array of sprinklers designed to flood the inspection area in the event of fire. The floor had a slight fall in it to encourage water to run off into a covered drain which exited the building and led to a large underground tank where effluent could be stored. At the far end was another large room, designated as an engine inspection area. The original design had envisaged that we would do some work on the rocket engine which would necessitate controlled environmental conditions, but this didn't materialise. The conducting floor, unlike most explosive process buildings floors I was familiar with, was light grey in colour instead of black. Clean conditions were meant to be maintained but our black boots would leave scuff marks all over the place and this required regular scrubbing to keep the floor looking pristine. During slack periods, we would often play ball games in the inspection hall when there were no missiles present. Inevitably, this meant even more black scuff marks but then a brainwave was had. The most tedious aspect of scrubbing the black marks away was rinsing the floor which entailed the use of dozens of buckets of water drawn from a tap in the toilets. It was discovered that very careful taps on the main emergency drench valve lever would elicit a very slow dribble of water from the overhead sprinklers, almost like soft rainfall. It meant we could rinse the floor rapidly. This went on for several weeks until one Monday, we came into work to find the floor was badly marked and we had an important visit coming up. We scrubbed the floor and one of us started to gently tap the drench valve lever. I might add the pipe this was mounted on was thicker than my thigh, in fact much thicker. The requisite amount of indoor rain dispersed the dirty water, and the valve was shut, and we prepared to go to break. Then all hell broke loose. A large fire engine screeched to a halt in front of the process building and German firemen carrying fire-fighting equipment ran in. There was a tense stand-off as each side struggled to understand what had happened. It turned out that, unbeknown to us, the drench valve was fitted with an electronic monitor and if any water flow was detected, it would automatically trigger a major alert at the regional level due to the perceived hazard that a missile fire would present. We laughed about it later on; much later on, that is.

The visit we were expecting came to pass and it included some pretty important people and a major from the technical directorate in the UK. The posh visitors left but the major remained behind. He was involved in the technical management of these missiles but I think he had never actually seen one before. He asked for a demonstration of a GMSTS diagnostic test, and I moved to prepare the missile by disconnecting the internal components and plugging the guidance and control system into the GMSTS. However, being eclipsed by the junior sergeant was more than the pride of my more senior colleagues could cope with. I was assigned to some more mediocre tasks as they hurried to impress the visitor. Normally, I did the test preparation and was well-versed in the procedure. The colleague with the technical superiority complex peered into the guidance and control section and stared at the connections. He unplugged one of them and plugged in the GMSTS. He went over to the GMSTS control panel and started the test. I now need to explain the technical bit so please bear with me. The Lance missile is steered in flight when streams of pressurised propellant are injected into the rocket motor efflux. This is done through four thrust vector control valves, and these are opened and closed by really strong solenoids. Just to make it more complicated, the Lance missile spins slowly in flight so the thrust valves have to 'chatter' constantly or the rocket motor efflux will end up pointing the wrong way as the missile spins. Actually, when I say 'chatter', what I really mean is the valves go off like multiple machine guns. Sadly, the overlooked disconnection stage meant that the four valves were still connected to the test set and were about to be cycled multiple times. To add a little more spice to what happened next, the visiting major wrapped his arms around the boat tail, hugging it and feigning a kiss of affection. The lights on the control panel flashed their way through the various test sequences and then reached the bit where the four thrust vector control valves would be cycled. Normally we didn't leave them connected in order to reduce wear so none of us had ever experienced what was going to happen next. With the visiting major still wrapped around the boat tail, the four 'machine gun' sound effects started up, and the banging echoed around the whole building. To say the major shat his pants would be an understatement. We all legged it for the exit but as we reached the door, the fact we were still alive loaned the situation a measure of common sense and logic. With the look of 'knew it was going to happen' on his face, the AT in charge of the building switched off the test set. People slowly and sheepishly returned to the process area. The visiting major departed and thought better of telling our boss what had just happened.

The Lance missile had a liquid propellant engine which used two nasty components for propulsion. The fuel was unsymmetrical Di-Methyl Hydrazine (UDMH) and the oxidiser was Inhibited Red Fuming Nitric Acid (IRFNA). When mixed together, these would spontaneously ignite (hypergolic). As a part of our training, we had visited the Rocket Propulsion Establishment where a nutty-professor-type lectured us about how bad it would be if we encountered either liquid. We noticed that his brown leather shoes and the turn-ups on his trousers had pockmarks in them. Standing on a concrete apron, with a beaker of liquid in each hand, he tipped a few drops of each to the ground between his legs where they angrily spattered and fizzed as they mixed; nuff said. That's what hypergolic means and it's not good for your clothing and footwear or for anything else. What this meant was that a Lance missile represented a significant potential hazard in storage, and especially in transit. If a missile was seriously damaged in something like a road or rail collision, the likely outcome would be a massive fire and the only steps needed would be big ones in an upwind direction. An incident which resulted in a so-called leaker was the kind where you would really earn your pay. In short, you would get dressed in special suits with oxygen re-breather kits. You would then approach and try to contain the leak by strapping heavy-duty patches to the missile. There were various scenarios where you would be required to pump out a propellant tank into a palletised draining kit. Dry nitrogen was used to provide an inert means of pressure, so, what was already a potentially dangerous incident got worse as we had to manage high-pressure gases. One day, we were sent to Menden to conduct a Weapon System Integration Test (WSIT). This is American jargon meaning put it together and see if it works. We were standing around a palletised propellant draining kit (PDK), watching one of our bosses as he twiddled various valves and connected pressure release stubs to venting pipes. An important safety precaution before opening the large cap on top of the propellant receiver tank was to vent any possible gas before flipping the toggle clamps to open it. He connected a venting stub to the vent pipe and then flipped the toggle clamps. The bang was well impressive. The large cap, which was about half the size of a dustbin lid but heavier, launched upwards, forcibly enough to snap its retaining chain. It flew up and struck the roof before falling to the concrete floor where it bounced and rattled loudly as if to attract the attention of as many would-be critics in continental Europe as possible. The person concerned was quite tall but, fortunately, not tall enough for his face to be in the way. He had neglected to open the valve after connecting the venting stub. The pressure within was not great, perhaps just a few PSI, but when that is applied to a lot of square inches, it's a lot of energy! We stifled the urge to laugh out loud as we were browbeaten by the near-victim.

One evening, as Christmas 1976 approached, I was the Battalion Orderly Sergeant which was a duty performed at Barker Barracks. After handing over my report the next morning, I went to the sergeants' mess for a late breakfast. This was usually a pleasant perk. The dining room would be empty, Uncle Bill (Bill Mitchell) of BFBS fame would be narrating a children's story from his 'Tales of Big Wood' series on the big gramophone radio in the dining room and the German mess steward would fuss over you and deliver a huge breakfast. This particular morning, the kitchen was quite busy, and I peered in through the door to see what was happening. The staff were working on the buffet for the forthcoming Christmas Ball. There was a tradition of providing the Christmas Ball with a magnificent spread of food and the chefs of the Army Catering Corps (ACC) would almost invariably deliver brilliantly on these occasions. My breakfast and a pot of tea arrived and I got stuck in, but as I ate, I heard a loud squealing. The Mess Chef, Ernie, was a sergeant in the ACC and he suddenly appeared at the dining room door, white-coated and struggling to restrain a wriggling piglet under his arm. He apologised and brushed past into the kitchen. Every now and then, the piglet would burst into wild squealing and peals of laughter would erupt from the staff. When my breakfast was complete, the mess steward appeared to clean up and I asked her what was going on. She scornfully related that Ernie had procured a live piglet for the Christmas Ball buffet in order to save butchering costs and they were to roast it today. In her best broken English, she tried to explain that

Ernie had yet to decide how the piglet would transition from lively squealer to roast suckling pig. I was amused and intrigued. I finished my tea. The kitchen had gone very quiet and the only sound was Uncle Bill on the radio talking about animal adventures in Big Wood. I looked through the door into the kitchen and couldn't see or hear anyone. I went through into a back room and saw about six people standing around a tiled table. I drew closer to them and heard Ernie whispering instructions. His team was mostly female and four of them were each holding a limb of the hapless piglet as it lay on the tiled table. A tea cloth had been placed over the piglet's head and it was quiet, so quiet that I thought the deed had already been done. Then Ernie raised his right arm and I saw he was holding a claw hammer. He brought his arm slowly down and rehearsed the anticipated swing, aiming to strike the piglet a fatal blow upon its head. The arm went up for the last time and just before it could deliver the coup de grace, the female stewards screamed and let go. The piglet's head jerked up, displacing the improvised blindfold and it realised the end was nigh; or was it? As the hammer descended, the piglet took off. The hammer hit the tiles, smashing them and eliciting a curse from Ernie. The whole team then chased after the piglet. There was no obvious escape, but the piglet sprinted around the kitchen, pursued by the howling team. Then it came towards me as I stood at the now-ajar door into the dining room. It shot through my legs and I held the door open so as not to impede the pursuit. I decided a tactical withdrawal on my part was prudent. I drove up to Pombsen, chuckling all the way. On the Friday night, we attended the Christmas Ball. As was customary before eating, we would tour the buffet which had been laid out like a king's banquet on the carefully covered snooker table, the table lights making the whole mountain of food look spectacular. Between the honey-roasted hams, whole salmon and trout and game birds lay the roast suckling pig on a silver salver. It had been roasted to perfection, filleted and put back together. There was an apple in its mouth and then I noticed the dent on its head, between the ears; I went for the salmon!

CHAPTER 5

Kineton 1977–1981

In November 1977, I returned to the UK and back to Kineton. I went back into the ammunition process area. As a sergeant, I was usually in charge of a process building and I was involved in the processing of 25-pounder and 105mm shells, Barmines and the refurbishment of stocks of an anti-lift booby trap dating from the Second War. In-service booby trap mechanisms were designated euphemistically as 'demolition switches'. This one was specifically the Demolition Switch No 12. Its role was that once refurbished, the 'switch' could be used to complement the way anti-tank Barmines were deployed. Random Barmines would be laid alongside others in a minefield with a switch concealed underneath them to deter de-mining operations. I remember the first rusty box coming into the lab and inside it, I found a yellowed instruction booklet on how to deploy the 'switch'. The booklet was marked in bold red ink, top and bottom, 'SECRET'. It was the kind of thing you might see on the popular TV series The Antiques Roadshow; er, the booklet, not the booby trap! In early 1978, my marital woes worsened, and we separated, and I moved into the sergeants' mess. I'm not sure if the powers that be wanted me out of the way, but I was then sent on an unusual assignment. I went to a training area near Stafford called Swynnerton to perform administrative duties in support of the Kineton annual summer camp. The point of the summer camp was to get personnel away from the depot and put them through all of their mandatory annual regimental training and annual tests in eight weekly residential phases.

The person in charge of the camp was a lieutenant. I was next in line, and we had two corporal instructors, none other than the two who had trained me as a recruit at Blackdown, Ginge and Terry. They were then full corporals and I was a sergeant, but it definitely wasn't a case of turning the tables on them. There was, however, an element of robust rivalry and mischief. They kept me on my toes, mainly through humour and incessant practical joking. One day, they appeared in my office, hurled a fizzing object at me and shouted "grenade!" before locking me in. The object was a Thunderflash which is an industrial-strength banger capable of causing serious injuries in confined spaces. This one was now fizzing away in my lap; time to react! I flicked it away and dived behind the desk to put something substantial between us. There was a bank of single-glazed windows behind me, and I expected a lot of glass damage. The fizzing subsided; it's a blind, I thought. I waited a little while before looking at it through the smoke from the fuze. Then I realised they had removed the main filling; I didn't know whether to laugh or cry. I wasn't their only victim.

The Officer Commanding the camp was not one of the more effective officers I have worked for (that's a poor attempt to be diplomatic). Although we were the camp's permanent staff, we were still required to complete the same military training and training tests as everyone else. The syllabus included physical training, fitness tests, NBC training and a gas chamber confidence test, weapon training, fieldcraft and battle tactics. The permanent staff did the gas chamber test together. The training NCOs ignited CS Gas pellets and we circled around the smoke-filled room. As we did so, the pellets, which were only supposed to smoulder to generate a cloud of smoke containing CS in the form of micro-particles, flared up producing flames. These flames reduce the efficacy of the CS and a common tactic to put the flame out was to blow it out, but you had to make sure your action sequence was perfect. Aside from that, the gas chamber was improvised. There was only one door and it opened inwards. One NCO started his unmasking drill. When ready, he inhaled deeply, removed his mask and with his eyes tightly closed he blew hard on the small fire which immediately went out. He replaced his mask, blew out hard with his remaining breath to expel any gas particles inside the mask and resumed the confidence test as if nothing had happened. Even from inside my mask, with diminished senses, I could tell the young officer was in absolute awe of what he had just witnessed. We finished the test, and the young officer approached the NCOs and asked if he could conduct the next test. I sensed he was deliberately going to use too many pellets in a tight pile which was guaranteed to cause a similar fire because he wanted to emulate what he had just seen but with a bigger audience. I also noted an exchange of knowing glances between the NCOs. The following week came around and the gas chamber was readied for action. Sure enough, a large pile of pellets was stacked on the makeshift hearth. With a nod of approval from one NCO, the young officer ignited the pellets. The other NCO was outside with about a dozen test candidates, readying them for their practical test. After a cloud of smoke had developed, the test candidates were ushered in and started walking around the hearth and moving about to ensure the gas-tight fit of mask and equipment. Suddenly, the dim room glowed with the flames erupting from the now-burning pellets. The young officer started his unmasking drill, ripped his mask off, put his face immediately above the pellets and inhaled deeply. Instantly realizing his grave error, he opened his eyes. This compounded the first mistake; CS gas particles have an affinity for mucous glands, the eyes and sweaty skin. A strange gasping noise erupted as the panic-stricken wretch bolted for the door. We bundled the helpless young dilettante outside where his face was bathed with water between spasms of vomiting. After a few minutes, he was able to stand up and he staggered off to his accommodation. After that, he didn't show his face again at any of the training.

Some readers may harbour sympathy for this young officer. He was certainly an odd character. He had retained a CS gas spray after some earlier NBC training, unbeknown to me, and he had it in his room. He didn't like the cold and I found his room was unbearably hot. I went to see him one day and as I entered his room, my eyes started to sting. I noticed he had put his combat jacket over a radiator and assumed the stinging was caused by trace remains of CS on his jacket from earlier training. That night, we went to the local pub; the place was in full swing and was tightly packed. The young officer was seated near me on a bench seat. Suddenly, a commotion erupted at the bar and several people were rubbing their eyes and sneezing and coughing. Several of them ran outside. I looked around for clues as to what was happening. Then I noticed a cylindrical bulge in the trouser pocket of this young man. At one end of this bulge, I saw a small circular stain which appeared to expand and then contract. It was a CS gas spray, and the actuator was being pressed in his tight trousers every time he moved. I bawled him out and sent him back to camp in disgust. Fortunately, the small amount of CS released cleared rapidly and the locals soon forgot and resumed their drinking.

I took the opportunity during the camp to improve my physical fitness. I participated in every weekly basic Fitness Test and, as the weeks went by, my time improved. During the last test, I tried especially hard to achieve my personal best. I found myself out in front in the last few hundred metres, but I could hear the steps of someone coming up behind me. I pushed harder but the gap between us shortened. Harder still, but to no avail. With the last hundred metres, my pursuer effortlessly cruised past me, so I tried to match him, stride for stride. It didn't work and I had no stamina left. The winner was a warrant officer (Dave) who I thought I knew but clearly, I didn't know him well enough. It turned out that he was a worthy long-distance runner of considerable repute. I did improve my own time though!

There were several incidents during that summer camp which caused me very considerable worry and could have ended my career. Each evening, I would tally the cash takings from the camp bar, seal the cash in an envelope and hand it to the OC for it to be locked in his safe. Shortly after the camp concluded and we returned to Kineton, I was introduced to a brewery representative in the Sergeants' Mess. He asked if I had been running the bar at camp and I said I had. He then asked where the takings were as the brewery hadn't yet been paid. I explained my part and told him who to approach for payment. A few days later, I was called into my Company office to be told that a quantity of live ammunition had been discovered in the training camp's ammunition store after we had left, and the Camp Commandant there had complained to my commanding officer. I was then called to a meeting in the Regimental Headquarters concerning the overdue payment to the brewery. In the Orderly Room, I met the young officer who was kissing an envelope and thanking his father out loud for sending the cheque to him to pay the brewery. There was no sign of contrition, and no explanation was forthcoming. The meeting was cancelled, and I heard no more about it. On return to the company office, I was informed that formal disciplinary action was to be taken against me in the matter of the ammunition found at Swynnerton. I was subsequently charged and remanded for Commanding Officer's Orders. Prior to appearing before the CO, the RSM spoke to me about how I should conduct myself and I was warned the CO was very angry and had a mind to remand me for court martial unless I accepted his punishment. At the time, I was in a marital crisis and the last thing I wanted was this axe hanging over my head. I subsequently pleaded guilty, agreed to accept his award and was awarded a Severe Reprimand.

Relieved to have survived this threat, I put it all behind me and soldiered on. A consequence of a Severe Reprimand is it disqualifies a soldier from being awarded the Long Service and Good Conduct Medal (LS&GC). Later in my service, whilst on an EOD Tour in South Armagh, I got an unexpected letter from the Army Medal Office. The letter explained that I was now time-qualified to receive the LS&GC but the severe reprimand was a barrier to the award. However, I was invited to write a plea of mitigation. I hadn't reflected on the injustice of that episode since then, but I knew all along I hadn't left ammunition in that armoury. Now, with vastly more experience in unit ammunition procedures and with the benefit of hindsight, I thought through what had happened to me. I recalled that there had been several units lodging ammunition in that magazine, all with unsupervised access and that the individual bays could not be locked. Occasionally whilst at camp, I would find wet dishevelled sandbags full of small arms ammunition burst open with the ammunition scattered on the floor. This matched the description given in the original complaint by the Camp Commandant to my CO. The day we left the magazine it was empty, and it appeared this ammunition had been 'fly-tipped' in there after we left. Aside from that, the RSM's advice that I plead guilty, however well meant, was profoundly wrong. I submitted a plea of mitigation and a short while later I received a notification that my plea had been accepted.

Another reconciliation with my first wife took place. This lasted, on and off, until we left Kineton for Hong Kong in 1981. By the time we left, we had two children, which seemed to settle things, but it was not to last. At Kineton, we would be required to perform periodic security and overnight administrative duties. The security duty entailed being the last to leave the ammunition process area at the end of the working day. We had to walk around all of the process buildings and check they were properly secured and locked up. This duty was a right pain; the simple truth was that a process building could not be effectively secured. The sliding transit doors were secured with bolts on the inside which were never padlocked. There was often a gap between the wall and the door, and it was a simple matter to reach in and lift the bolt up. The window catches were the same specification as domestic window catches. They were frequently found to be broken and were commonly a sloppy fit in the frame. Our security check was perfunctory at best and was an 'arse-covering' exercise as the MoD Police would come around on patrol overnight and would repeat the checks. If they found an insecure building, the buck stopped with the Security NCO. An incident report would be raised and the SAT would deal with the hapless Security NCO the next day. Typically, the informal punishment was an extension of the security duty period for an additional week (extras). At that time, on Friday afternoons, the Security NCO would typically be the last one into 'Happy Hour' at the Sergeants' Mess. You would dread the ring of the phone on the bar in case it was the MoD Police to report an insecure building. I had a friend who had been caught out so often that he had carried out six weeks' worth of consecutive extra duties. On that last Friday, we were waiting for him to join us at the bar to celebrate the completion of his 'turnkey marathon'. As the welcome pint slid down his throat, the phone rang. It was the MoD Police! I swear he'd still be there today, trapped in a never-ending cycle of extra duties if he hadn't been posted away.

The other duty was Orderly Sergeant. This entailed reporting for duty to the RSM which usually entailed a verbal 'wire-brushing' from him as, other than the weekly parade, it was one of the few times he'd see you. One of his pet hates was if any of the junior officers addressed him as 'Sergeant Major' as they wished him a good morning. He would spontaneously ignite into a tirade of abuse at the hapless subaltern and march him around to the Headquarters Company Sergeant Major's office. He would point inside and angrily declare, "That's a Sergeant Major, Sir! I am <u>THE REGIMENTAL</u> Sergeant Major".

Part of this duty was to shut the NAAFI bar at closing time. You would get the occasional drunk, but it was usually a routine affair. On one evening, the NAAFI Manageress phoned me to say there were rival factions of Paratroopers in and a riot was about to kick off as closing time approached. I pondered what to do to avoid getting 'filled in' and body-swerve the massive paperwork effort that would follow. At home, I had a rough-haired German Shepherd. She was huge and soft as muck, but she was very defensive. A mate of mine was the Dog Section Commander. He had given me a baksheesh Army-issue collar and lead. When Shandy, as she was called, was wearing this kit, she was indistinguishable from a Dog Section War Dog. Now for a word about War Dogs. They are not police dogs, and they are not your friend. They are 'land sharks' who regularly ate bits of their handlers. The NAAFI Manageress called time. Glasses started to fly and drunken tempers erupted. As the opposing sides squared off, I opened the door with Shandy at my side. I ordered her to 'speak' which was her cue to get angry and bark. The melee paused and looked at us.

Shandy's hackles went up and her top lip seemed to go right over the top of her head revealing the white, gleaming tools of her trade.

Grown men, once intent on beating the pulp out of each other and destroying the NAAFI, started to scream. The bar was on the first floor. The windows were opened, and the main protagonists climbed out into the dark, preferring the vagaries of gravity over the certainty of Shandy's wrath. The remainder surrendered and quietly filed past me to safety as Shandy growled like a chainsaw. The Manageress was speechless at the near miss. I locked up and said good night. I took Shandy home and returned to spend the night in the duty bunk. The next morning, as I de-briefed the RSM, he looked me in the eye and asked me if there was any bother in the NAAFI. "No sir," I replied, to which I was awarded extra duties for having a pet dog in the NAAFI. Some people are never satisfied.

Some weeks later, I was called in to speak to a warrant officer. He said I was to report to the Orderly Room at a given time that day but wouldn't explain why. At the appointed time, I was there and was ushered into a small office which was empty other than there being a table and three chairs. Two men in dark suits were seated behind the table and gestured for me to sit on the third chair. They didn't speak for about a minute and then introduced themselves as being from the Special Investigation Branch of the Royal Military Police. This was well before the Police and Criminal Evidence Act (PACE 1984) and so the interview was actually an interrogation. They never actually said what it was they were investigating. It was simply "Were you, at the said time and place, the Orderly Sergeant?" Like most people, I don't have a Filofax in my head. I replied that I didn't know but it was in my work diary in the office and was also detailed on Part One Orders. This seemed to them to be an admission of guilt on my part. The next questions assumed I was at an apparent scene of crime, and I was asked if I had entered the orderly room alone after hours. I had indeed, as part of the duty was to check the windows and ensure nothing untoward was happening. This reply raised the ante and they became more intense. Had I opened any cupboards? Nope. Had I issued any railway warrants? Nope. "You can go for now but don't discuss this with anyone else." Mystified, I returned to work and immediately quizzed all of my mates about it. Nobody seemed to know anything. A few days later, the Orderly Room corporal vanished. We later learned he had been selling railway warrants to his mates. Railway warrants, at the time, were a bit like cheques. They came in books and were serial-numbered. A record of an issued warrant was kept on a stub in the book. The corporal had used the old ruse of tearing warrants out of the back of the book and the crime was spotted during a standard audit.

Mystery over but I can only assume the RMP must have been having a quiet period then.

One of the funniest episodes happened whilst I was the AT in charge of a large process task right at the far end of the APA. I think we were processing artillery shells; bloody thousands of them. It went on for months. As we were so far away from the precious warmth of the canteen, we were allocated a walking time. One morning, we were returning from tea break. The weather had turned really bad, and it was overcast and raining. Although it was mid-morning, it was very dark and the security lights at the labs had all come on. We all prayed for lightning as this would force a cessation of work. As our lab came into view, the four WRAC girls walking out in front suddenly stopped and gathered around an object on the road. They were quite upset at the discovery of a small rabbit suffering with well-advanced myxomatosis. This was an appalling and deliberately introduced way to kill rabbits and we would get periodic outbreaks of it as the rabbit population waxed and waned under its influence. As we caught up with them, they pleaded for someone to put the wretched thing out of its misery. As I looked down at the pathetic sight of the rabbit, mutilated by the disease, a swishing sound made me flinch. Ginge, the Lab Storeman, lunged at the rabbit with an excessively sized piece of dunnage which had been lying at the side of the road. The blow was worthy of a home run.

Bits of the rabbit flew into neighbouring postcodes. The girls were furious and mobbed Ginge all the way back to the lab. As lunchtime approached, I noticed Ginge had been in and out most of the time but that was normal for the Lab Storeman, who would be moving tools and equipment to and from the stores as a regular part of his job. I called lunchtime and everyone moved into the shift lobby to change. Outside, the wind howled and the rain bounced off the windows; it was still dark. I was the last out and I locked the doors behind me. Then I noticed everyone was clustered together looking up at Ginge who was high up on the traverse singing (badly) a number that was popular at the time. The song was Art Garfunkel's Bright Eyes and as Ginge crooned on, he gestured to the security light above our heads. Something was on it. Ginge had recovered the rabbit and had skinned it. He had then placed this improvised rabbit cloak over the lamp and secured it with sealing wire. The apparition was made all the more sinister because beams of light were now shining through the wretched animal's empty eye sockets. The girls screamed with bloodlust and lunged for Ginge, who had a head start being high up on the traverse. He sprinted off into the gloom, pursued by the girls intent on revenge. They didn't catch him and the rabbit was given a decent burial. Every time I see or hear of Art Garfunkel, all I can think of is that gloomy morning in 1978; and Bright Eyes!

Each Wednesday morning, we would have to attend RSM's parade on the main square. One Tuesday night, I had spent a pleasant evening playing snooker with a friend, John Grant, a fellow sergeant.

We messed up badly when we got suckered by a senior warrant officer into a session of 'double or quits'. It turned out he was something of a hustler. We drowned our sorrows at the bar; too much. The next morning, I slept in. I tore out of the house, getting dressed along the way and ran towards the A Company Barrack Block as I could see the Company was forming up and preparing to march off to the square. I approached the company from the rear as they marched along the road. The company sergeant major hadn't clocked me (or so I thought) and I was able to run along the rear rank before inserting myself covertly into a blank file. Feeling somewhat smug and emboldened after the erstwhile panic, I picked up the step and we marched onto the square. The parade was its customary shouting and screaming match. When it was over, we marched off to the process area. When we arrived there, we fell out and started to file through the pedestrian gate but my collar got felt. I was pulled into the sergeant major's office. An explanation for my tardy arrival on parade was demanded. I told the truth, but the sergeant major got a strop on. "You're going in the book," he said. He reached into his drawer and took out an orange, alphabetically indexed book. With a flourish, he thumbed the tab to select 'R'. He then made a note of my misdemeanour before replacing the book on his desk and dismissing me from his presence. I thought this was all a bit 'over the top'. For the next few days, I felt he was stalking me, waiting for the opportunity to pounce and record the next offence in his little orange book. I found myself on security NCO duty the following week and part of this duty involved checking that the A Company office block was secured. It wasn't. Inside, all the internal offices were open and files and paperwork were scattered all over the place. I knew someone had just been promoted so I surmised they had gone to the mess to celebrate. The sergeant major's door was ajar and there was the little orange book on his desk. I leafed through the copious entries to find all

126

manner of notes and observations. My newfound knowledge seemed to gift me with valuable insight, but along with my crime, there were entries relating to some of my friends. All I can say is the little orange book vanished. There was no inquest and no mention of the missing 'tome of crimes'. However, there are people out there who owe me and they know who they are. Honour and integrity would be redeemed with a modest donation to the Felix Fund.

During this period, I had to transition from poacher to gamekeeper. I was promoted to staff sergeant during my third tour of duty in Northern Ireland (this tour is described in the next chapter) and I was appointed a Line Foreman when I got back. There were two Line Foremen in the conventional ammunition part of the process area and a third in guided weapons. One day, we were called to meet with the conventional ammunition warrant officer, Frank. He actually lived a few doors away from me. His wife was a lovely person and they kept an enormous cat which she would often have to retrieve from a tree in my garden. He stated matter-of-factly that "His wife would die in six weeks" and we were to share his duties between us whilst he was on compassionate leave. He would return after her death, expecting a seamless handover from us. We were both profoundly shocked. I didn't know anything about the poor woman's illness which I heard informally was uterine cancer. I couldn't understand how anyone could be so blunt about something so awful. The six weeks passed and he didn't return. His wife had apparently exceeded the prognosis. Out of respect for them both, I won't detail what was actually going on, but I was conscious that this terrible period was seemingly corrosive and, if most people in the know were like me, we were walking on eggshells. She eventually passed away and I was left puzzled and totally confused by what I had witnessed. It was nothing like Ali MacGraw's depiction of terminal decline in the 1970 film Love Story; this was even more tragic; more messy. I only include mention of this deeply saddening episode because it happened to me when my wife was diagnosed with terminal cancer in 2015. In many ways, I was to reflect on this episode as I struggled to cope with my own issues. My own, later experience seemed to lift a veil from my eyes. I knew that my mental health was going downhill fast as I tried to remain functional and support my wife. I knew then what Frank had gone through; I knew then what empathy really meant.

I was then put on the advanced guided missile course. This four-week course was fairly intense. At the time, we had surface-to-surface missiles, air-to-surface missiles and anti-aircraft missiles. Some of these missiles were made by the same manufacturer and this meant that they often had common design features. When you are monitoring missiles during firings, you need to have a crystal-clear recall of the launch sequence and how and when the arming sequence takes place. Earlier courses before mine had set an examination at the end of each week. Course critique feedback from these courses indicated a desire by students to reduce the number of examinations and have them all at the end of the course. By the end of the first week, I started to realise that the downside of this new arrangement was that it was easy to get hopelessly mixed up with the various and confusingly similar launch and safe-to-arm sequences. An additional distraction was that a colleague claimed to have come by the course syllabus, and this included the bank of examination questions, so would I like a copy? I said no. I foresaw trouble coping with the end-of-course examination so I was at pains to swot intensively at every opportunity. The last day arrived and we sat the exam. Out of about 24 students, only two of us passed and I was one of them. The other student to pass was a bright young corporal called Larry who was to gain a middle-entry commission a couple of years later and he transferred into the Royal Army Education

Corps. I returned to the depot and was moved into the guided weapons department. I initially worked on Blowpipe anti-aircraft missiles, including the refurbishment of fired practice darts.

The next nightmare was Swingfire anti-tank missile warhead changes. The process for this entailed the use of the world's most complicated multimeter. It was fiddly work and you had to remain focused on what you were doing lest you really screwed up. I'll now relate a tale of woe concerning these missiles which is funny but deadly serious at the same time.

The Swingfire missile came into service in the 1960s and was so successful, accurate and lethal, not to mention being ahead of its time, that it was still in service in the 1990s and was deployed in the 1991 Gulf War. It had a range of 4,000 metres, a large warhead containing a shaped charge of almost 3 kgs of a French explosive called EDC1A and was wire-guided. It had been fired from a variety of vehicles and ended up installed on the Alvis Striker armoured fighting vehicle which was one of the Combat Vehicle Reconnaissance (Tracked) range of fast and lightly armoured vehicles. By then, Swingfire had been upgraded to become a semi-automatic, command line of sight (SACLOS) missile which is awful jargon meaning the firer only had to keep the sight trained on the target; the missile's guidance system did the rest. The missile was ground-breaking in many ways when it first came into service. It was boxed inside a launcher container which could be mounted directly on or in the launch vehicle. Inside the box, the missile's fins, folded and spring-loaded, were located in grooves. The forebody was supported within a bespoke plastic cruciform whose outer edges ran in the same grooves in the box. The box was sealed at both ends with a vapour-proof barrier made of Mylar. Electrically, the missile was connected to the box via a connector we called a 'carrot'. On the outside, the launcher container would be plugged into the firing vehicle's electrics with a so-called Smart and Brown Connector. The missile was steered by a 'jetevator'. A similar device is often used in jet skis. The jetevator is a throat-like collar which surrounds the rear of the rocket motor blast pipe. When the missile launches, the rocket motor efflux passes through this collar which is mounted on gimbals. Shortly after launch, guidance demands result in the gimbals moving the jetevator somewhat like a rudder behind a boat. This deflects the rocket motor efflux and enables the missile to be guided in flight. For safety reasons, the missile does not arm or become controllable until a failsafe known as the 80-metre loop is severed as the control wire deploys off the wire drum in the rear of the missile. Non-technical readers may be flagging somewhat at this stage, but the picture I am painting is of a brilliant design concept which suffered from the MoD's addiction to eking out the life of weapon systems with mid-life enhancements whilst trying to save money at the same time.

Whilst this missile gave the firer more bang for his buck, technically, it was a pig to manage. Firstly, the explosive limits at the factory where it was made were too small to allow the fully assembled missile to be completed there. It went elsewhere to have the warhead fitted. In transit, the lack of a warhead could cause balance problems and damage, so it was transported with a dummy warhead, painted pink to differentiate it from a live warhead and filled with concrete ballast. The next issue was that the warhead's shelf life was shorter than the rest of the missile. This meant the missile had to have its warhead changed for either a new one or the practice variant if it was to be transferred from war stock to training stock. This happened in the GW lab at Kineton. The job was not constantly running and, with most lab staff being military with a high turnover, maintaining the skills base was very difficult. The lengthy in-service life of Swingfire of over 30 years caused a problem. 20/20 hindsight permits crystal-clear clarity in the rear-view mirror of life but we should have known better (that's the 'royal we', by the way). Whenever a missile was to be head-changed, it would be brought into the process building and the box would be opened. This entailed aligning the box with a jig before removing the vapour-proof barriers. These had to be removed by unscrewing a large number of nuts which were mounted on threaded studs. The vapour-proof barriers would be replaced. Someone would have to spend the best part of an hour scraping the sealing cement away from the mating surfaces and this usually entailed that 'someone' losing a lot of skin from his knuckles as he inevitably caught them on the vicious studs. The missile would then be electrically separated from the box by the carrot being disconnected. A special hook used to sever a snatch loop component in the safety-arming mechanism would have to be unscrewed and then parked out of the way. After this, the plastic furniture would be removed as the missile slid forward on the grooves in the box. As the rear end emerged, the jig would keep the spring-loaded fins in their folded positions. At this point, the now-naked missile could be operated on and tested with the aforementioned complicated multimeter. The outer casing would be unscrewed, collars would be removed, and you could then see the guts. The usual head change was to replace the shelf-life-expired live warhead with a practice warhead. In compliance with standard ammunition markings, the practice warhead was painted blue. The live warhead was olive green with a yellow band signifying high explosive content. The transit warhead was painted pink to ensure it was never fitted to a missile that might be fired.

If you are still following me, take a break, drink some caffeine and clear your head because there's more to come.

At the rear of the warhead was the safety and arming mechanism. In the live setting, the explosive charge in the S&A Mech was positioned forward to detonate the warhead. When a practice warhead was fitted, the S&A Mech would be fitted back to front so that the explosive charge rested against the front of the rocket motor housing. Thus, it could be used as a self-destruct device. This expedient was very prudent. Typically, the missile launched at an angle of about 35 degrees elevation. Under control, the range was up to 4,000 metres, but if the missile failed to arm properly, it would fail to gather (that means to come under effective control) and would fly a ballistic trajectory which would dramatically increase the range to the point where it could stray outside the range boundary. The head-changing of missiles to become practice missiles was generally done just in time to provide stock for firing on ranges. After the head change was completed, electrical testing would take place before the missile was replaced back inside its launch container. A critical issue was that every single step in the unpackaging of the missile had to be faithfully reversed. If not, things could go drastically wrong on the ranges. The whole head-change operation was complicated and slow. There were no shortcuts; distractions and interruptions had to be avoided at all costs. Errors could not be detected after the missile had been sealed back inside its box.

Other things were going on in the life of Swingfire. The manufacturer went metric, and this meant that replacement stocks of the Mylar membrane for the vapour-proof barrier became marginally thicker to conform with the nearest metric equivalent. This tiny margin had a major effect. When a Swingfire missile launches, the thrust as it takes off is only just sufficient to get it off the ground. It was said (if you were daft enough) that you could stop a missile from being launched by holding it down in the launch box with one hand. There was a shortage of practice warheads. As an expedient, direction was issued permitting the use of the pink-coloured transit warheads. This configuration led in one case to a missile going ballistic and flying outside the range boundary before striking an isolated dwelling house. The nickname for missiles fitted with the pink transit warhead became Pink Panthers! At manufacture, the missile's jetevator would be centrally positioned so if a missile failed to gather, it would follow a ballistic trajectory. To avoid a recurrence, an instruction was issued to technical staff on ranges that they should break the rear vapour-proof barrier and re-position the jetevator in the hard down position. If such an adjusted missile failed to gather, this would cause it to dive down and strike the ground some distance in front of the launch vehicle, which was preferable to it flying uncontrollably outside the range boundary.

We had a significant range day approaching and the user unit needed 50 practice missiles. Government ministers and VIPs would be guests at the high-profile firing and so colleagues of mine were instructed to prepare the Swingfire line for a head-change task. Thankfully, I was employed on a different task. At the same time, we had a mobilisation exercise coming. For this exercise, we were instructed to dress in full nuclear, biological and chemical warfare (NBC) suits, including respirators and remain dressed in this manner for a full weekend. As an exercise aim was to process ammunition against an urgent user requirement involving round-the-clock, triple-shift work, some bright spark decided that the Swingfire head-change task would be an ideal use of this time. That weekend was the weekend from hell. In a respirator, your breathing and vision become diminished. Normal conversation is near impossible. Even in a temperate climate, hyperthermia is a distinct possibility. Nevertheless, the Swingfire line was ordered into continuous round-the-clock production.

A short time later, the unit attempted to fire 50 missiles in front of the great and good. A large proportion of missiles failed to function as expected. The range AT, who was known to be mild-mannered and reserved, issued a scathing report. It detailed almost every mode of failure, every single one attributable to incompetence or negligence during the head-change task. There were misfires where he discovered the carrot connection had not been restored. In some cases, the S&A Mech loop cutter had not been restored to its correct position. Some missiles tried to launch but became hung up in their launch boxes. The cause appeared to be badly fitted packing pieces which jammed in the box grooves which would otherwise ensure a smooth launch. Another potential cause was the breaking of the rear vapour-proof barrier to reset the jetevator position prior to firing. This allowed the rocket motor efflux to escape at the precise moment that the rocket motor ignited, preventing a build-up of pressure that might help to develop forward momentum, not helped by the marginally thicker Mylar membrane. In the Striker vehicles, the rocket motor efflux coming out of the rear of the missile for much longer than designed allowed smoke and flame to penetrate the vehicle obliging the crew to evacuate. The choice of egress was grim; should they go forward in front of a missile that was desperately trying to become airborne or out the back door where the smoke and flames were worst? Some missiles got away and went ballistic, while others crashed into the ground, precariously close to the firing point. The whole range-firing deteriorated into chaos and mayhem. AFV crewmen's lives had been endangered and the Director of the Royal Armoured Corps wanted scalps.

At Kineton, a witch hunt started. On the face of it, the Swingfire Process building staff were culpable. The man in charge of the Lab was a conscientious sergeant known to be reliable and effective. If he had indeed been negligent, it was wholly out of character for him. At the time, we had a warrant officer in A Company who had the understanding, integrity and moral courage to intervene on behalf of the process-building staff. He had already been selected for a commission. This was Mick Watkins. Although we weren't party to any of the choicer interviews he may have had with higher authorities, the word went out that he had defended the would-be scapegoats and had even threatened to resign. Eventually, the matter was resolved but I think there was a limited sanction applied to the sergeant in charge. I cannot be sure of how it concluded as another drama was developing not long after.

A popular warrant officer was killed in action in Northern Ireland, and I was to be a member of his bearer party at the funeral. I was also preparing for a posting to Hong Kong, and I had a newborn son. Mick Watkins had already left but he returned to offer us encouragement as we rehearsed for the funeral with gymnasium benches in the drill shed. It was typical of the man and the care he exercised on those around him. That period of time was a very disruptive and mind-blowing period and guess what? As far as I know, the buffoons in authority who had allowed the Swingfire debacle to happen on their watch weren't held to account. It confirmed the soldiers' self-fulfilling prophecy that 'shit trickles downwards'.

The military funeral we rehearsed for took place as planned and we expected the experience to be challenging. We had been sized, which means we had been sorted by height, and this dictated where we were sited on either side of the coffin. I was at the foot of the coffin on the left-hand side. We met the undertaker and hearse at a school close to the church. This meant seeing the coffin containing our friend for the first time which triggered an intense reaction, but we remained sternly resolute, keeping everything inside and our emotions in check. The undertaker explained that the casket was sealed, and the orphaned children had been unable to have any tributes to their father enclosed within. The coffin was draped with the Union Flag and a stuffed toy had been safety-pinned to the Union Flag by its ears to secure it whilst we marched to the church and then the graveside. The undertaker then briefed me that my task at the graveside would be to unpin the toy and drop it into the grave on behalf of the children. The dam burst and hot, unstoppable tears scalded my face.

Towards the end of June 1981, we departed for Hong Kong. If I thought things were going to get better, I was being woefully over-optimistic.

CHAPTER 6

Belfast 1979

1979 proved to be another hectic year. In February, I had deployed in support of 42 Royal Marine Commando in the far north of Norway on their annual exercise programme where they trained enthusiastically in their NATO northern flank protection role. Specifically, I was there to monitor the performance of the newly procured Milan Anti-Tank Guided Missile system during firings in extreme cold weather. The following month, on return from Norway, I started pre-operational training for a tour in Northern Ireland. This would be my first tour as a No 1 in the high-threat situation in the province. I hadn't been allocated a location or tour dates which was fairly normal as your course performance would often dictate where you should go. The high failure rate on the course also made it almost pointless trying to solve the enduring puzzle of who should go where, and when. In the summer, my first child was born. Immediately after this, an EOD Operator in Belfast was short-toured, and I was nominated to replace him. I was to join No 1 Section of 321 EOD Unit in Belfast, based in the Parcel Post building next to the Grand Central Hotel (GCH). It seems there was a herd of cats in 1 Section then, comprising four teams named Bob Cat, Bear Cat, Wild Cat and Tiger Cat. I was to join Tiger Cat. By 1979, it had become normal for troops to travel to the province by air, which was something of a relief. As an individual reinforcement, I flew from Birmingham Airport on a commercial flight. On arrival, I was housed in transit accommodation in Lisburn, at Thiepval Barracks. The next two days were spent doing induction training and arrival administration before I was moved to Belfast. On arrival, new EOD Operators would go out with experienced operators and shadow them for a day or two, depending on how many and what kind of tasks were encountered. Then, roles would reverse, and the newbie would take over and the erstwhile mentor would take a back seat. If this takeover period was deemed satisfactory, the newbie would be fully assimilated into his designated team.

The picture shows me and the Tigercat Team No 1 Driver (Chalkie) posing on the bonnet of our No 1 Pig. I had to black out Chalkie's face as I haven't been able to secure his permission to publish. Behind me, to my left is the 40mm grenade launcher within a protective cover and the eagle-eyed may be able to pick out the mounting clamps for the semi-automatic Browning shotgun behind and above the spotlight. The photo was taken in the parcel post building next to GCH.

The accommodation we had was basic but comfortable. The EOD Operators, Infantry Escort Sergeant and RCT Sergeant occupied a space known as The Kremlin. This was an open-plan lounge and our bedrooms opened into it. The lounge was carpeted and well-furnished thanks to a recent car bomb job where Jim, the SAT, had saved the day for a well-known furniture retailer and they kindly donated the furniture as a gesture of gratitude. We had a TV and a small kitchen and there was a speaker on the wall with which radio transmissions to and from deployed EOD Teams could be monitored. Well before my arrival, a fiendish arrangement to promote best behaviour when out on task was installed. Pinned to the wall in the Kremlin was a cloth bag. It was absolutely full to the brim with 50-pence pieces and even looked like it might pull the wall down! Whenever any of us was out on task, the others would listen to the radio conversations. Any error in your voice procedure, or other misdemeanour, would be noted and you would be fined 50p on return for each transgression. This was the infamous Duncairn Gardens Fund. Its origins had been lost in the past but I think it was related to a busy period when a lot of IEDs were encountered in that street. The street had been something of a hotspot for trouble, but during my tour, it was relatively quiet. There was a highly contrived way for an Operator to win the proceeds of the fund. You had to render safe a viable IED in Duncairn Gardens and bring the bits back. Just when it seemed the swollen bag might cause a structural collapse, the prize was claimed, and the circumstances naturally led to many protests. Ian Rimmel had been tasked to a shop in Duncairn Gardens, to a suspected IED. Sure enough, when he got there, he found a blast incendiary and rendered it safe, and brought the bits back. We were beside ourselves to find a technicality which would void his claim! When I explain the circumstances, you will see why. Some time previously, the shop had been undergoing a refit, including a complete new set of enclosed staging in the shop window. During the work, there was a bomb attack and several blast incendiaries had been placed in the shop. It turned out they were rendered safe; but not quite. The terrorist had concealed one of the bombs within the partially constructed staging. The bomb was overlooked, the refit was completed and the bomb, which had failed to explode, remained there. Its subsequent discovery occurred when a joiner was doing another refit. Ian turned up to do the necessary and it was a case of 'Bob's yer mother's brother'. But there was a steward's enquiry. Was the bomb viable? The battery was completely flat and the homemade explosive in it had degraded to the point that the fuel oil had dried out and it had gone hard as rock. Eventually, Ian's win was deemed morally justifiable, and the prize was awarded. I think that most if not all of it was actually donated to a nearby orphanage.

The manner in which we were tasked to an incident was quite dramatic. We had a small operations room where the various radio nets were monitored. 39 Brigade operations room was the tasking authority. Typically, you might pick up an escalating incident as the infantry discovered something or responded to a warning. The sequence of operations in a bomb incident had to be correct. The unit on the ground would carry out the 4Cs: This mnemonic stood for Confirm, Clear, Cordon, Control. Another C was added later. At the appropriate point when the Incident Commander was ready, a tasking request would go to the Brigade and they would then transmit a standard tasking message on the Brigade Radio Net. The message would start with the callsigns of the units to be involved followed by "Felix Request, Over". All hell would then break loose. Our ever-overly enthusiastic watchkeepers would hit the 'panic button' which would set off an enormous bell which had been recovered some years earlier from a burned-out building. I think the gong on it was about a metre in diameter. Our vehicles were kept in a state of high readiness in a loading area surrounded by ramps. The team being called out would burst forth from their accommodation, grabbing weapons, flak jackets and helmets. They would mount up, rev up and move the vehicles in convoy order to the main ramp. The usual convoy consisted of four armoured vehicles: The No 1 Pig, the No2 Saracen, the Lilliput in a Pig and finally, the medics in a Saracen Ambulance. The Alpha Operator would go to the operations room and collect the tasking message. This was a model of brevity as it simply listed: A. Brief description of suspect device. B. Location and grid reference of suspect device. C. Location and grid reference of rendezvous point. D. Any other information. Armed with this slip of paper, the operator would go out onto the ramps, pass the information to the team over the cacophony of two-tone horns being tested and revving engines and then Wacky Races would begin. Segment gates would be hurriedly opened, and we would roar away on a terrifying race to get to the scene. The journey to the scene was usually the really dangerous bit, if I base my judgement on how hair-raising the trip usually was. The journey back was usually slightly more sedate and dealing with the bomb between the two frantic journeys was like a brief respite on R&R! The duty roster in No 1 Section was based on a four-team, four-day cycle: Day one was Alpha where you were on immediate standby and would be the first team to respond to a bomb alert. Day two was Charlie where you would be on a reduced notice to move. This enabled essential team administration, training and some relaxation. Day three was Bravo where you were on immediate standby but would deploy only after the Alpha team had already gone out. Day four was the blessed Delta Day where I think the notice to move was 12 hours. You could go out into safe areas, relax in civilian clothes and have a long lie in the morning. There was a delightful twist to this routine. Whoever

141

was on a Delta day on a Saturday had to go out and buy cream cakes for the entire Section from a nearby baker. This was the worst-kept secret in EOD. It was unbelievable how many people from outwith No 1 Section would find an excuse to visit us on a Saturday morning!

Another aspect related to the four teams was the degree of modifications made to the lead No 1 Pig. Each Team's lead Pig was different. The Section Commander's Pig had a hinged drawbridge affair welded on the front. When ready for deployment, the Team's Wheelbarrow equipment would ride on the drawbridge. This was meant to enable a very rapid Wheelbarrow deployment to a bomb as, on halting, actuators would extend this 'drawbridge/ rampy thing' forward and downwards. The Wheelbarrow could then drive off the end into immediate action. Well, that was the theory anyway. I recall with horror the experience of crewing this Pig whilst the Section Commander was on R&R leave. We responded to a suspect car call and burst out of the Parcel Post building at speed before turning out onto Royal Avenue where this drawbridge thing out front would scythe over the footpaths threatening to cut down pedestrians. It also badly affected the handling and the Pig would literally go down on its knees to negotiate bends. I found the prospect of emergency driving to a task in this vehicle, in the uninhibited hands of the RCT driver who seemed fearless, to be more daunting than the prospect of dealing with an unexploded bomb!

The Tiger Cat Pig's modifications were benign in road safety terms by comparison to the boss's Pig which I visualised as something like Brighton Pier welded to the front of a lunging, leery green monster. On the roof above my front passenger seat was a 5-shot semi-automatic 40mm grenade launcher and we had specially made disruptor grenades for it; now we're talking! If that firepower was not enough, on the nearside wheel arch was another mounting for a 5-shot Browning semi-automatic 12-bore shotgun. These additional weapons had been installed to counter the threat from multiple blast incendiaries. Another feature, which was obsolete and the REME refused point-blank to resurrect it, was a legacy item from the 1950s when these Pigs had been deployed during the Malaya Emergency. This was a device designed to prevent hostile crowds from swarming all over the Pig in a riot and worked by switching tens of thousands of volts into the vehicle's hull. Having been caught up in a few riots in my time, the thought that I might fry any hostile interlopers at the flick of a switch was overwhelmingly tempting but, on reflection, the presence of electrically fired weapons and detonators inside a vehicle with 50,000 volts in the hull was probably even more of a danger to life than the boss's Pig!

The terrorists had started to use improvised detonators, especially in their blast incendiaries. These were made up in lengths of copper plumbing pipe and contained quite large fillings of home-made mercury fulminate. A modified flash bulb provided the ignition source and these detonators were potentially very hazardous; we certainly couldn't submit them for forensic examination. We would store recovered detonators in evidence bags with records to maintain evidential continuity and, every few weeks or so, we would destroy the arisings of these improvised detonators in a basement room of the parcel post building. To do this, we would radiograph a detonator and would then place it in a large steel, sand-filled box, connected to a Shrike Exploder. We would then initiate the detonator and record the results, the aims being two-fold: The safe destruction of the detonator and the maintenance of an evidential record that would attest to the viability of this device. The first time I did this was with a more experienced colleague. When we went down into the basement room, I noted it was mostly in darkness as the lights didn't work, there was meant to be a working extractor fan to remove the fumes, but this was inoperative, and the floor was pocked with small puddles. My colleague demonstrated the procedure and I think we destroyed about six detonators. With hindsight, perhaps the darkness obscured the clouds of fumes. After each explosion, the box full of sand would be raked through for fragments and these would be bagged and labelled. When I sifted through one box, a sharp pain went through my right forefinger, and I saw that a sharp shard of copper pipe had pierced through my glove and had gone right through the fleshy part of the finger. A few days after this, I was assaulted by a drunk person by being headbutted on the left side of my face. This resulted in some small cuts on the inside of my cheek where it was pinched between the cusps of my teeth and the forehead of my assailant. About a week after this, I was obliged to report to the medical officer. I felt quite unwell and the inside of my mouth had become inflamed; also, the cuts were ulcerated. The medical officer seemed perplexed and then he noticed my AT badge and asked if I had been in recent contact with any explosive chemicals. I related my experience in the basement room with the improvised detonator disposal and that they contained mercury fulminate and that we were working in a confined space with a lot of fumes present. Next thing I knew I was on the way to Musgrave Park Hospital (MPH). This then really played on my mind. I was on a guilt trip that I had been negligent and was worried that I would be sent back home under a cloud. I should have been more focused on the health implications. I was checked at MPH and prescribed diuretic medication in the hope this would flush through any mercurial compounds I had ingested. I remained in Belfast to complete my tour and was reviewed at the Queen Elizabeth Military Hospital at Woolwich afterwards. Nothing untoward was reported back to me.

I recall I probably did about 60 tasks during my 1979 tour with the majority being false alarms. These could be funny, but the joke would often fall on me. One rainy horrible evening, I was called to the scene of a suspected time bomb placed in the worker's entrance around the back of a small factory. After the usual pre-cursory drills, I was dressed in the bomb suit, tooled up with so-called lightweight weapons and equipment (not), and made my way to the pitch-black entrance. My torch was pointless. In the dark, I saw an object answering the description of the suspicious item silhouetted by the light from a distant lamp post. I positioned a disruptor next to it and returned to the vehicles. The disruptor was fired, and I went back to assess what had happened. I couldn't see a thing at first but, after lifting my visor and as my night-vision improved, I could make out a smashed clock face. Cue the standing up of hairs on the back of the neck. The occasional tick came out of the now-dead object. I rummaged carefully through the bits until I was certain the thing was harmless. I arranged little piles of debris based on what I thought they were; clock bits here, container there, wet slippery fabric tape over there and then decided to collect the bits for later investigation. I had lifted the steamed-up helmet visor from my face right at the start and was constantly wiping rain off my face. The helmet and its visor were a mixed blessing. It kept your ears warm, and the ballistic visor was capable of stopping all sorts of incoming. On the downside, it would steam up as soon as you put it on, leaving the operator lurching about like a drunken 'Mr Blobby'.

I returned to the team. "What was it, Boss?" "I think it was false or maybe a hoax," and then I saw the whole team staring incredulously at my face. In the dark, I had disrupted the factory worker's clocking-in clock which contained a wet ink fabric ribbon to stamp their in/out times on their cards; it was obviously dark purple in colour as that was now the same colour as the rest of my face!

On another occasion, I was working on a car which had been abandoned near the Europa Hotel. There was a system of control zones in force where any vehicle parked would elicit an immediate EOD Team callout if the owner could not be found. The usual Wheelbarrow remote approach had enabled access and the main load-carrying areas were seen to be empty; it was time for a manual approach. Just before my No 2 completed the standard helmet and visor sensory deprivation exercise, a somewhat jaundiced RUC Constable ambled over and whispered into my ear. I followed his outstretched pointing finger and saw that someone was watching us from a disco on the top floor of the Europa. Was it someone with a finger hovering over a radio control bomb transmitter, I thought? "No, sir, it's the driver. He's blootered and he ran away before we could breathalyse him and now he won't come down to face the music. But he left the car in a control zone and rules is rules." There was no point remonstrating; we'd be there all night. I approached the car and, as I walked down the middle of the road, I could see the cordons blocking access at each end. Suddenly I saw headlights coming towards me at speed accompanied by the sound of squealing tyres.

Shouts went up and I could hear rifles being cocked as they were readied to open fire. The car kept accelerating and was driving straight towards me. I tried to do a runner but the EOD suit, helmet and all that lightweight kit wouldn't let me. I hid behind the suspect car, but the rogue car was heading straight for it. Behind me was a typical townhouse, the front door access being via a concrete staircase. At pavement level was a brick wall; ideal! I made for it and hit it square on. My momentum and the weight of all that kit carried me over the wall to the other side. Sadly, the other side was a 10-foot drop into the basement flat entrance of the house. I sailed over and performed a neat half somersault and landed flat on my back. Winded and stunned, I looked up and could only see a streetlight and the lights in the house above. I was too winded to call out. On the road above, the rogue car had gone silent, and I could hear my team and the cordon troops calling for me. Nobody had witnessed my fall and they were mystified by my apparent disappearance. However, I had left a trail and the team followed the firing cables to the scene of my demise. It turned out the rogue car was another drunk driver who missed me and the suspect car but crashed further on. He was gently assisted into a pair of handcuffs and very carefully 'placed' in the back of an RUC Hotspur Land Rover. The original suspect car was a write-off by the time I got through with it.

Most of the real devices I dealt with, or tried to deal with, were blast incendiaries. Typically, each one was a small homemade explosive charge attached to a container of petrol. These were usually deployed against commercial properties or buses. Upon the expiry of a short delay, designed to allow the evacuation of bystanders but timed to function before a bomb disposal team could stop them, the device would detonate, blowing out windows and doors and both igniting and projecting a wall of burning petrol into the premises. An instant major conflagration would result. If used against vehicles like buses, the bus would be toast. In more traditional buildings of lath and plaster, the fire would be uncontainable, and the complete destruction of a building would usually result. After shopkeepers and others concerned with the preservation of properties started to carry these devices away, the IRA placed the explosives inside metal casings, often short lengths of pipe or scaffolding which we designated as Cased Metal Charges

(CMC). The idea was that the resultant shrapnel would deter people from going anywhere near them. This still did not prevent people from carrying them away and so the IRA incorporated anti-lift booby traps in a very small proportion of these devices.

Out of the incendiary campaign against buses emerged an amazing individual. His exploits became so well-known that we were taught about him during our pre-operational training and the 321 EOD Unit even had a specific Standard Operating Procedure (SOP) on how to handle him if he appeared whilst we were dealing with bombs placed on Ulsterbus buses. The man was called Werner Heubeck. During WW2, Werner had been a member of the Hitler Youth before being conscripted into the Luftwaffe in the Hermann Göring Division. For him, that war was over after a transport ship he was on was bombed and sank in the Mediterranean. He swam almost 5 miles to Cape Bon off the coast of Tunisia, rescuing several colleagues along the way. Werner was obviously the kind of man you wanted on your side. Since his tenure at the helm of Ulsterbus, he had steered the company to profitability largely through delivering innovation and efficiencies. The mounting loss of buses was threatening the viability of Ulsterbus and so Werner would often appear at the scene of a bus bombing and would carry the blast incendiaries off his precious bus before driving it away to safety. The man was a legend in his own time, but we couldn't make our minds up on whether he was a hero or just mad. He was certainly single-minded and dismissive of the threat presented by possible booby traps. I heard it said that one blast incendiary he had removed actually contained a booby trap which failed to function, but I cannot verify that. Werner was awarded an OBE in 1977 and this was upgraded to CBE on his retirement in 1988. He eventually moved to Shetland where he passed away aged 85; a true character.

My first experience with blast incendiaries presented as a potential gift which morphed into disaster. I was on Alpha duty when a call came in to say we were about to be tasked to a suspect incident. What followed would be too farcical for even a comedy film script. The IRA had decided to place four blast incendiaries on the fourth floor of a carpet warehouse. The bombs were in plastic carrier bags and up the side of the building was the highest and 'bendiest' wooden ladder I have ever seen. Unbelievably, the terrorist intended to climb this ladder encumbered with the four bombs which he intended to deliver through a window.

Each bomb had a time and power unit, cased metal charge and about a gallon of petrol in a plastic container. The all-up weight was easily over 20 kilogrammes. Understandably, he got off to a slow start. When he was challenged by the RUC on about the second rung of his climb, he jumped off the ladder and had the presence of mind to start the timers on each of the four bombs, this being the only rational act he carried out before abandoning them on the pavement and running off. When the tasking message arrived in the form of a 'Short Felix Request', I was given an excellent description of the devices and I had already decided the fastest and safest 'render safe' would be achieved by using the world's sexiest piece of EOD equipment; the Special Water Dispenser (SWD). To orientate the younger readers, I need to spell out the technical stuff I just wrote about. Firstly, a "Short Felix Request" was an abbreviated tasking message designed to get the EOD Team to the scene of a multiple-blast incendiary bombing in the shortest possible time. Secondly, the Special Water Dispenser was truly special. This equipment was a Saracen Armoured Car with a Saladin gun turret mounted on top. On each side of the vehicle, clamped to the over-wheel running board was a pair of very large cylinders of compressed nitrogen gas. Internally, the Saracen had a water tank and fitted in the gun turret, was a specially adapted anti-riot water cannon. This was not just any ordinary water cannon - it was not even a Marks & Spencer cannon - this beauty had been upgraded so it could fire a massive slug of water at very high speed at blast incendiaries. In action, you would drive right up to the suspect bomb, looking at it through a heavy glass vision screen. You would then aim the gun at the bomb and squeeze the trigger. On Delta days, we would go to Moscow camp and practice endlessly with the SWD. We would long feverishly for the opportunity to take on multiple blast incendiaries with it. As I prepared to leave base, anticipating glory in battle and the accompanied bragging rights, I was called back to the operations room. There was a phone call for me. It was the Chief Ammunition Technical Officer (CATO). He had heard the Short Felix Request over the radio. He asked what my plan was. I said SWD. He said no. He wanted me to use the 40mm grenade launcher on my Pig. I pleaded 'Operator Discretion'. He countered by threatening to have me on an evening flight out of the province if I didn't comply. He pointed out that development of the 40mm was lagging behind schedule due to the lack of data from operational use. Crestfallen, I swapped vehicles and we raced to the carpet warehouse in my No 1 Pig. In the ICP (Incident Control Point), I loaded the grenade launcher and fitted a semi-automatic 12-bore shotgun to the clamp over the wheel arch. Fully closed down, we advanced until I was at a distance of about 12 metres from the four bombs which were on the left side of the vehicle. Through the CCTV system, I was looking down into the tops of the open shopping bags. I could see the time and power units, the detonators in the cased metal charges and the petrol containers. The bags were clustered together. There was a laser sighting system which enabled me to align the grenade launcher. Declaring on the radio the intent to fire, I fired the first grenade. There were two thuds barely discernible from each other; the one above me from the launcher was muffled and the second was louder. The grenade was a newly developed munition designed to be effective against blast incendiaries and specifically designed not to ignite petrol (allegedly). As the CCTV picture settled down, I could see the devices were now engulfed in an intense fire. My immediate consideration was to try and separate the various explosive components from the burning petrol before they could burn to detonation. I fired the remaining four grenades in what resembled cannon shots on a billiards table. Try as I might, I couldn't get the explosive components out of the pool of burning petrol. I turned to the shotgun and tried the same tactic. There was limited success, but defeat was snatched from the jaws of victory when the first of four cased metal charges detonated. A large fragment struck the door of the Pig. Inside, I was safe, but the CCTV Monitor was between my legs, and my left knee was pressed firmly against the door. The shock of the impacting fragment passed into my knee. It was briefly quite painful, if harmless, but I pressed on trying to move the remaining charges. However, I was out of ammunition. The remaining charges detonated one after the other, almost mocking me. I was devastated. Just a few minutes earlier, if I'd had my own discretion, I would have had four IEDs in the bag. Now I had four explosions which was pants by comparison. After a safe waiting period, the bits were collected, and we returned to base. The failure of the 40mm system in what should have been a very simple test of its design capabilities proved worthy of a detailed investigation. I was quizzed endlessly about how I had used it; had I had sufficient practice? My report was sent back to the boffins and a few days later, a serving officer visited and interviewed me. The pet theory as to the cause of the failure was an error on my part as I was accused of being so close to the four bombs that the grenade fuzes hadn't armed. The nominal arming distance was 10 metres. I was angered by this baseless accusation and with good reason. I had already practised a lot with the system, and I was well aware of its physical limitations. I took the doubting Thomas officer out onto the ramps and demonstrated that with the grenade launcher fully depressed, you couldn't engage a target to the left at less than 12 metres. The pet theory was clearly wrong. The officer returned to the research establishment and back to the drawing board. Another few weeks later, an official report arrived. The incredible conclusion as to the cause of the failure left me thinking someone was having a laugh. It seems the trial firings in the UK had targeted containers of Army-issue 2-star petrol. It was said that the real bombs in Belfast had contained 4-star petrol. What can I say?

The most dramatic incident I attended with blast incendiaries concerned the East Bridge Street gas building. This task started with a 'Short Felix Request' and I responded accordingly in the Saracen-mounted SWD. An RMP POINTER Team guided us in and the bombs were said to have been armed but abandoned in a cardboard box which had been left just inside the main entrance which was a solid revolving door. I assessed we had two options open to us given that we couldn't actually see the bombs, but we knew exactly where they were. One option was to do nothing and allow the bombs to explode. The second option was to engage the bombs with SWD through the front door in the hope that the door would yield and expose the bombs and that we might then at least limit the incendiary effect with the SWD. It wasn't much of a choice, but I loathed the idea of doing nothing. We advanced to the front door, and I trained the gun on the door and fired. The door splintered and was holed. Inside it was dark and we couldn't see anything. More water seemed like a good idea, and I prepared to fire again. At that point, the bombs detonated, and a huge fireball engulfed the reception area. I kept firing the gun hoping more water was good and not knowing if any bombs were yet to explode. Over several minutes, the fire turned into an inferno, aided by the lath and plaster interior finish. I don't recall how long it took but the building suddenly underwent a full-scale collapse, the facade falling onto the Saracen. Inside the closed- down vehicle, we were safe, but it was very noisy. The debris, which had covered the vehicle completely, meant we couldn't see what was happening. The Pye Westminster radio burst into life with colleagues asking if we were OK. I told the driver to extract us from the ruins and he rocked the vehicle back and forth, causing the rubble to fall clear of the vision block and gun sight. Now able to see, we were able to withdraw to the ICP where we were shocked at the sight of the complete loss of the building. It was not just the SWD that was special. The driver of the SWD was a specially trained RCT driver; in other words a private soldier. He was a young man, keen and conscientious. I believe I can speak for all of my colleagues by saying that we thought his courage, faith and trust in the design of the SWD and the safe judgement of us operators more than warranted formal recognition; I hoped he would be awarded the Queen's Gallantry Medal. However, there was a seri-ous incident towards the end of his tour, for which he was blameless, but it put official recognition of his achievements beyond reach. This was deeply saddening but I regret I am not at liberty to disclose what happened. I hope he reads this book and this bit where I record my admiration and gratitude for his exploits. For those in the know, the clue is that his surname could refer to an astronomical body '-).

My next outing against blast incendiaries left me saddened due to the effect on the victims. I was called out to a suspected bombing of a hotel. When I arrived at the scene, I saw many elderly people on the cordon wearing night clothes. The RUC explained to me that several devices had been carried into the building which presumably had been targeted by the terrorists in the belief that the hotel was a commercial target. The hotel had, in fact, become an old folk's home in recent years and these old folks were now standing outside in the cold, bewildered and distressed. The blast incendiaries started to explode. I was surprised at the power of the explosions which seemed to dwarf the blast incendiaries I had encountered to date. Some elderly ladies became extremely distressed; they had just lost everything except the clothes they were standing in. I believed the explosive charges were bigger or more powerful than the blast incendiary charges I had encountered before. In my report, I increased my estimate of content to up to 1 kilogramme per device. When my peers learned of this, some of them accused me of over-egging things. I stuck to my guns and left the new estimate in the report.

About ten days later, I was called to the scene of a find in a hide in the roof of a house. An intelligence-led operation resulted in several arrests and the discovery of what was thought to be bombs in a transit hide in the attic. I went up to the roof and entered the attic. The suspected devices were said to be underneath an old-fashioned, riveted steel water tank of about 100-gallon capacity. When I looked underneath, I could see the bases of cased metal charges. These were of a new type, of box-section steel construction and it turned out the explosive fillings were homemade ammonium nitrate and aluminium. This was a new trend which needed to be investigated. Getting at the bombs safely was not going to be easy. The concealment was partially obscured by the stout joists as the bombs had been hidden between the joists and the base of the water tank. Other than a short briefing left by the special forces personnel who executed the search and arrest operation, there was no other reliable information to be had. Time for some lateral thinking.

The tank was full of water and appeared to be functional. I couldn't see how I might easily drain it, so I decided to tape the ballcock valve shut. I then cut the flow pipe with a hacksaw and the water gushed out. Now I needed to move the tank which was certainly going to be heavy. I got the car tow rope attached to the tank by passing it through a nearby skylight, and Stubbsy, my Saracen driver, was delighted to be asked to pull the tank clear with his Saracen which he did with his usual enthusiasm. When I returned, there were four brand new and complete blast incendiaries on show in the now-wrecked attic and they were completely exposed. I still needed to ensure there were no concealments. I noted that these new cased metal charges were finished to a high quality for homemade devices. The explosive filler had been sealed in at the top by what looked like a layer of Isopon body filler, so I used standard EOD techniques to clear these. I felt vindicated that these new charges had a much higher explosive content than the previous types and believe that similar charges were used to bomb the old folk's home.

My last outing against multiple blast incendiaries was at the Cliftonville Golf Club. Terrorists had placed four devices, contained in large black bin bags, on the floor of the bar in the clubhouse on the eve of a pro/celebrity match. I had a lucid witness account of where the bombs were. All of them were on the floor, close together and could be seen from outside with the aid of binoculars. There were opened veranda doors at the rear and a very handy bunker at a safe distance from where I could contemplate my next move. My No 2 was a Vehicle Specialist, Tony Blount, and we discussed the remote options. It was very unlikely that the Wheelbarrow would be of any use. The situation was time-critical, and I was reluctant to stand by and do nothing until the bombs exploded. So, I went for a compromise course of action. I hoped at best that I might separate the components by firing 12-bore solid shot into the four bombs from a safe distance. I knew from the witness, who had looked into the bin bags, that the explosives were in cased metal charges fabricated from scaffolding pipe and the improvised detonators were inside the protective sheath of stout steel tubing. If this worked and they didn't explode, it would be the best I could hope for. The most likely outcome was that I could burst the petrol containers, which were five-litre polyethylene jerricans. The petrol would drain away and significantly reduce the devastating fireball effect. The fire brigade was present and there was a reasonable chance that any resultant fire would be contained by them provided I could verify their safety. I knew from experience that even one detonating blast incendiary would destroy the building. The memory of losing the old folk's home was fresh in my mind so I wasn't going to wait.

In the dark, we hurriedly set up a firing point. I had sent Tony back to the vehicles to fetch the shotgun, solid shot ammunition and the swift scope, and to brief the cordon commander that we were about to open fire. I was well-practised with solid shot and was confident I could hit each bomb. Tony was to observe with the swift scope and confirm hits as I fired. I took aim and fired and saw the first bag jump as it was struck. All around me, I heard the characteristic sound of SLRs being cocked and a shout of "CONTACT" went up. Tony had forgotten to brief the cordon commander! I shouted back in the dark that it was us and we were forgiven but only after a salvo of expletives came back. I fired at all of the bombs several times and Tony confirmed the hits. Tony had loaded the shotgun for me and reloaded it whilst I reviewed the scene with the swift scope.

Eventually, I was ready for a manual approach. In addition to my 'light-weight EOD equipment' and my EOD suit, I carried a fire extinguisher under each arm, just in case. As I entered the bar, there was a stench of petrol. I took this as evidence that the jerricans had been burst.

As I got near the first bomb, I noticed the white skirting board behind it had lots of little grey indentations in it. This was odd; solid shot would have gone through the bag and wall like a train. Then I noticed small pellets on the carpet. I had unwittingly been firing No 6 Shot (birdshot) and at that range, the effect on the bombs would be negligible. I looked inside the bag. The improvised detonator had already exploded but the case metal charge was intact. The other three bombs were the same. I suspect the bombs had 'tried' to explode before we even arrived at the scene. I bagged the components and brought in the fire brigade to deal with the now petrol-soaked carpet. The Club Captain was well happy. The match the following day would go ahead, and they would ventilate the bar until the petrol had all evaporated. We were happy too; we hadn't stopped the bombs from trying to explode but neither had we made things worse. And we didn't get shot by our own cordon troops!

In the somewhat chaotic pace of life, it was essential to try and maintain a military routine with regular inspections of soldiers and their accommodation and our equipment. Another aspect was welfare and periods of inactivity would often lead to boredom. Keeping a balance was tricky and humour played no small part in this. We regularly hosted visits from the headquarters, and this meant inspections and checks. One day, as I paraded my team on the ramps, we were joined by a well-known member of the headquarters who was the nemesis of the lazy but inspirational to the willing. He set high standards and few people were able to match them. As he progressed along the line of Tiger Cat Team members, he would pause and ask a question or would check specific things for conformity. On this day, he stopped in front of Stubbsy, my Saracen driver. Stubbsy was a larger-than-life person, sharp-witted, funny and big-hearted. He was one of those characters who would inevitably find an object of fun in even the most austere set of circumstances. I was in dread of what was going to happen next. The visiting officer asked to see his identity card. Stubbsy correctly executed a check pace and then opened his tunic's upper left pocket. The card was then flourished to the inspecting officer. I swear I saw the faintest gleam of mutual amusement in their exchanged glances. "Very Good, Stubbs, put it away". Stubbsy returned the card to his pocket and resumed his position of attention in the line. The visiting officer then wanted to conduct a stock check of the ammunition and equipment on the vehicles. Cue the focus on my No 2. He was of a nervous disposition at times, and this was one of them. As he escorted our visitor into the rear of the parked vehicles, I grabbed Stubbsy and demanded to see his ID Card. In those days, our identity cards were laminated in layers and the photograph of the holder could come out if the plastic had cracked. That had indeed happened and Stubbsy had replaced his own picture with one he had clipped from the Beano. It was of Dennis the Menace with Gnasher the dog; I just didn't know where to put my face and hurriedly rejoined the stock check. The officer asked to see the Clam. This was a manufactured explosive device with an explosive filling in a plastic casing and featured magnets to attach the Clam to ferrous objects. This Clam was a veteran passenger of the Pig; it was old and battered, the casing was cracked, and the magnets were loose in their housing. The officer attempted to attach the Clam to the back door of the Pig. The clam couldn't hang on as the weakened magnets struggled to grip. The Clam slid down the door until it reached the bottom and then fell onto the ground with an embarrassing clatter. Cold, unsympathetic eyes now focused to transfix the No 2 in a glare of blinding scrutiny. "When did you last charge these magnets, Corporal?" The No 2 struggled but he couldn't get the words out. "Go and fetch the charger," demanded the officer and the hapless No 2 turned and ran into his accommodation. (Portable chargers for small items of equipment were usually kept under beds in the Team's room.) Almost immediately, the No 2 re-appeared, red-faced and empty-handed, to be appraised of his folly by the now-grinning officer. The poor man was so anxious that he failed to detect the obvious spoof question about recharging the Clam's magnets.

During one of the lulls in activity, we agreed to let our teams re-paint their accommodation to their own choice of décor. Tiger Cat leapt into action behind closed doors and, several days later, I was invited to inspect their efforts. Flanked by my grinning team, I was escorted through the door into their room. It was pitch black; I was puzzled. Maybe they wanted to switch the lights on after I had entered for dramatic effect. I asked for the lights to be switched on only to be told they were already on. As my eyes adjusted to the gloom, I could see the ghostly blue of ultraviolet strip lights, like those often found in discos. Then all I could see was dandruff and fluff. They had painted every surface, ceiling, floor and walls in their room matt black. Cue instant claustrophobia and my immediate exit.

Stubbsy was the arch comedian and, on Delta days, we were allowed to attend a local bar inside the segments provided we consumed only moderate amounts of alcohol (yeah, right!) and that one of us was carrying a radio pager. These had been recently issued and were viewed with mixed blessings by the Team. Stubbsy didn't like them. One evening, we were sitting around a table and a round had just been bought. My radio pager was on the table, and it suddenly burst into life, buzzing and vibrating and started to crab across the table. Quick as a flash, Stubbsy grabbed it and dropped it in my beer. The pint started to foam immediately, and the beer overflowed onto the table. We returned to base with me dreading how I was going to explain the pager's demise.

A few days later, karma restored the balance of fortunes. Stubbsy and the other RCT drivers took huge pride in the upkeep and appearance of their armoured vehicles. His Saracen was an outstanding piece of hot-rod art. He regularly painted all six roadwheels with shiny black tyre-wall paint. He would then painstakingly pick out all of each tyre's moulded markings in gloss white paint. This was indeed showroom stuff but the piece du resistance was the tiger's jaws and teeth he had lovingly painted onto the front of the Saracen. There was some kind of heavy gauge rubber waterproofing cover right at the front which was tough but flexible and this bore the most impressive paintwork. We were called out to a really urgent job at Musgrave Park Hospital. As we prepared to leave, the Section SAT told me to get a move on as patients' lives could be in danger. We managed to get the No 1 Pig and Stubbsy's Saracen up to just over 50 miles per hour on a downhill section as we approached the hospital but when Chalky, the No 1 Driver, tried to slow down for the rapidly approaching bend, we all realised that the brakes weren't man enough. We took the bend on two wheels and got round. Right behind us, the Saracen was over on three wheels and then it ran into the back of us. The resultant Saracen 'face plant' totally destroyed Stubbsy's art; he was heartbroken. Oh! And the hospital job turned out to be a false alarm.

The EOD world is over-endowed with characters, and it is often the case that the best of them making the greatest contribution are the quietest and least well-recognised. One such man was a civilian engineer who worked for the MoD in a vehicle research department. The great man was Lofty Pattinson. He was a kindly, hands-on man with the patience of Job. His entire focus, to which he was totally dedicated, was the development of engineering innovations where remote machinery could be used to reduce the need for EOD Operators to make manual approaches to bombs. He would make visits to Northern Ireland to nurse experimental equipment through the rigours of operational duty. Although a civilian, he would accompany us onto the streets and actively work on the kit with the No 2s during EOD tasks. He was usually dressed in combats with no rank markings. He would stay out with us in all weathers. When we got back to base, he would not stop to rest until he had repaired or serviced the equipment he was developing and, often, equipment that was not under development where he saw a No 2 needed help. He was a tall man and can be seen in many EOD Group photographs, standing at the side in anonymity. In tribute to his commitment to his work with us, he was awarded a so-called Felix tie. These were usually only presented to EOD Operators who had actually neutralised an IED. Sadly, he passed away some years ago and I heard that his wish to be buried wearing his Felix tie was respected.

During my tour of duty, I was to trial a new piece of remote handling equipment. This was the upgraded Mk 7 series Wheelbarrow which was radio-controlled. It was radically different to its predecessor and, having already been stung by being forced to use the 40mm grenade launcher, against my better judgement, I was initially doubtful. Lofty put me at ease. His enthusiasm was infectious, and his dedication was total. The trial was, however, complex.

Having been equipped with the experimental equipment, we had to carry a second set of existing equipment in case the new kit failed on task. I have previously described a typical EOD convoy in Belfast as comprising four armoured vehicles. However, I didn't mention the remote-controlled Eager Beaver. This was a rough terrain forklift truck which could be used to move vehicles at a safe distance and even lift the Wheelbarrow up to the first floor of buildings. The original Eager Beaver sported a Makrolon armoured cab to protect the driver on the journey to and from tasks. On arrival, the driver would dismount, switch the equipment over to remote control and the Eager Beaver would move forward on its own. Since I now had to be accompanied by twice as much kit, the EOD convoy responding to a suspect car bomb got huge. On one occasion, we deployed with 17 vehicles, including all sorts of ancillaries and an RMP POINTER Team. This coincided with the RCT Drivers leaving us en masse, having completed their tours, and the new drivers didn't know their way around Belfast; what could possibly go wrong? It did and the whole shooting match once got lost on the way to a job near the Falls Road. As we desperately tried to turn the convoy, fearful of getting bricked or even worse, we were puzzled at the complete absence of protests. Then the penny dropped; there were so many of us that the locals must have thought a re-run of Operation MOTORMAN was in progress.

I must now add a word of praise about the RMP POINTER teams. The acronym POINTER stood for Photography, Operational assistance, Investigation, Notification, Tracing, Examination and Recovery. These small teams comprised RMP NCOs who were on two-year tours of duty in the province. Thus, they could provide continuity (we only did four-month tours and barely got the time to learn our patches). If a POINTER Team deployed to a suspect bomb, they would toot their two-tones as they departed to alert us. We could then listen in to their radio-net and get a sense of what was up. By the time we got to the scene, they would have assessed the situation, collated all relevant evidence and would have checked the ICP location history in case it had been used previously and might therefore be a potential 'come-on'. With Short Felix Requests, they would often drive ahead of the SWD to clear traffic in front of us and then guide us to within metres of the actual devices. They were very experienced, calm and did 'everything it said on the tin'. Typically, when we returned to base, the POINTER

Team would deliver still-wet, just-developed prints of photographs taken at the scene along with detailed contemporaneous notes. It was an outstanding example of cooperation.

When I arrived, the Section SAT in Belfast was an unflappable WO1, Jim. I think he was on at least his second EOD tour and possibly had a somewhat jaundiced view of things and would almost certainly have experienced the loss of close friends. The rest of us were younger, on our first tour of duty as No 1s, and all we wanted to do was defuse bombs. I have already described what would happen when a 'Felix Request' was received over the radio with the massive bell ringing loudly and the duty team sprinting into action. Jim was a far more measured man. One day, that massive bell started jangling its call to arms. I was next out, so I ran into my room, grabbed my gear and ran to the operations room to get the tasking slip. Veterans of the days when we wore the old flak jackets might have experienced getting an arm-hole of the jacket caught in a door handle; one second you're running through a door, and the next you're flat on your back, looking well stupid! As I left the operations room and ran out onto the ramps, I was swinging the flak jacket over my shoulder to get it on when, without warning, I was stopped dead in my tracks. I was nowhere near a door, but something had caught me, and I was held fast. Then, the voice of calm and reason was in my ear. "John, lad, slow down and calm down or, one of these days, you'll get out of here so fast, you'll arrive before the bomb explodes and then you'll have to defuse it". At that, I was released. Somewhat appalled at this apparent heresy, I proceeded to the scene of the incident and returned about three hours later. I mulled over what had been said to me, puzzled at the apparent contradiction but the puzzle eventually matured into sound reason, especially when I deployed years later to Bessbrook Mill where you certainly learned to be more deliberate than rapid in your approach to bomb disposal.

A few days later, on a quiet day in Belfast, we were watching the TV in the afternoon. It was 27 August 1979. A newsflash suddenly appeared, and it was announced that a bomb had exploded at Narrow Water near Warrenpoint and there were significant casualties. A few minutes later, another newsflash announced that Lord Mountbatten's boat had been involved in an explosion at Mullaghmore, south of the border. I remember speculating that it was probably an accidental ignition of accumulated gas in the bilges as a terrorist bomb was just too unthinkable. Sometime later, a third newsflash announced a second bomb had exploded at Warrenpoint with heavy casualties. The rest, as they say, is history. I remember feeling quite stunned at the enormity of what had just happened. I resolved to heed the sound advice I had been given days earlier; after all, it seemed nobody was safe. The next day, I delivered some bagged exhibits from a scene clearance to the Northern Ireland Forensic Science Laboratory (NIFSL). I recall seeing a large vehicle already there and being unloaded. My colleague Arthur was handing in exhibits he had recovered from Warrenpoint; dozens of bags which summed up the graphic loss of human life for me in but one glance. As the Bessbrook EOD Operator, he and his team worked alone. I felt lucky to be in Belfast, living with my peers amongst four large EOD Teams and having their support and incisive humour to fall back on. Bessbrook looked to be a lonely and bleak place. That view would come back to haunt me in 1987.

At the end of my tour, my replacement had arrived, and my flight home was booked. Then, an odd helicopter escort task came in. The Army in Northern Ireland wanted to trial the use of photoflash cartridges in South Armagh to illuminate rural areas at night to enhance imagery. The ammunition involved was already in service and was normally used with the AN USD 501 (Drone). It turned out that the ammunition's hazard classification (it contained metallic powders) meant that there were strict conditions attached to its movement by air. A Wessex helicopter was going to fly from Moscow Camp to Kineton to collect the ammunition. We were involved as a technical escort was required. The chance to fly to a helipad 300 metres from my door was too much to pass up on. I volunteered. With hindsight, I probably shouldn't have. The Section Commander would fly with us to provide a technical escort for the ammunition on the return leg. On the day, the weather was awful. It was cold, very wet and intermittent gales were blowing through. We got to Moscow Camp and boarded the helicopter. It took off and headed out to sea and the weather worsened as the aircraft laboured against the gusting wind. The plan was to fly to RAF Valley on Anglesey to refuel and then continue south to Kineton. The weather was worst somewhere near the Isle of Man. The aircraft was badly affected by severe turbulence and on several occasions, it rolled over on its side. I recall two of the three-man crew suffering airsickness, their brown paper sick bags being placed at their feet as they were filled; you could see their feet from the passenger cabin. We eventually arrived at RAF Valley. The pilot elected to land the helicopter like a fixed-wing aircraft, touching down on the wheels without stopping to hover. We taxied to the refuelling point. After being refuelled, the loadmaster measured the wind speed with a venturi speed meter. It was said that the gusts of wind were just below the maximum allowed for take-off but I wasn't convinced. We took off and headed inland but as we tried to cross the Menai Strait, the wind increased causing the aircraft to buck and rear alarmingly.

The pilot flew back towards the coast and reduced height as he neared the north Wales coast and then threaded his way through a natural gap in the hills below which seemed to be deflecting the wind upwards at us. We flew on and the turbulence reduced. We eventually met up with the main road network leading to Kineton and we flew along it. We landed at Kineton and five minutes later, I was sat at home. A rapid if unsettling transition from high readiness in Belfast to domestic normality.

I returned home from my tour which I would describe as unremarkable in the bigger scheme of things. That is the way of EOD; I had dealt with a small number of viable terrorist bombs but nothing that I would describe as outstanding. Some months after my tour, however, I was recalled to Northern Ireland to give evidence against three alleged terrorists who had been arrested and charged following their attempt to attack a Bookie's shop in Belfast with a hand grenade. The procedure was that Army personnel would be hosted by the Court Witness Section of the RMP. You would be accommodated in Lisburn and shown a video of how to give evidence, and what not to do, when in court. The video showed an enactment of a military witness being torn to shreds by a defence advocate because he failed to remain objective under cross-examination and lost his temper. After the video, my RMP 'minder' said I shouldn't worry about being interrogated as "This never happens". The case was being heard at the Crumlin Road Crown Court under the Diplock rules (no jury). As no jury was required, the case was actually heard in the coroner's court. As I arrived at the courthouse, I was met by an RUC officer who said he didn't expect me to be called as the accused were expected to plead guilty. I was taken into the court and sat in the public gallery. It turned out I was surrounded by supporters and families of the accused. It was intimidating, to say the least. The plea was not guilty. The first witness called was an official surveyor who produced charts and maps and his evidence was basically to establish that the premises existed at the time of the alleged crime. I was absorbed by interest in the way all of this came together and not expecting to be called, however, I was rudely jolted out of my thoughts as I heard my name called as the next witness. I entered the witness box and took the oath. The prosecuting advocate took me through the events at the scene and it all seemed quite reasonable, and I found myself agreeing with the points he was making. Then it was the turn of the defending advocate. As you might expect, he was quite inquisitorial. I expected that and avoided talking to him directly, looking instead directly at the Justice, on whose behalf the advocates test the evidence. The advocate had a copy of my EOD report which had presumably been supplied to him through official sources. He started asking me questions on it. The technical bits explaining my actions were encoded for security reasons and had also been redacted. This was a bone of contention with him, and I repeatedly found myself explaining that the report was a technical document submitted for technical reasons and that it was my personal statement that was of greater relevance. The report had been two pages long, but the second page was apparently missing. At the bottom of the page, clearly written, were my comments that the grenade "was found in the rear of the footwell..." The bit that was missing, from page 2 said, "in the front passenger seat". He was trying to exploit an apparent discrepancy and was suggesting that I reported finding the grenade in the rear footwell which would have been at odds with my personal statement. There were none of the courtroom calls of 'objection' which I thought might stop this obvious attempt at obfuscation. We moved on and it got worse. The advocate made a number of allegations against me which, in essence, suggested that I had fabricated the evidence, my motive being to seek approbation for my actions at the expense of his clients. This elicited some anger from the accused's supporters. I calmly refuted the suggestion, which, in my opinion, was a breathtakingly arrogant attempt to show that the guilt was mine for being an incompetent or a glory hunter. I was then asked to describe the grenade and how it worked. It was a British

Army No 36M grenade. The now-empty grenade was passed to me. I removed the base plug and checked for the presence of a fuze. There was none. I then unscrewed the loose filling plug on the grenade's shoulder and looked inside. The explosive filling had been removed. I reassembled the grenade and, whilst holding it up, I described it in detail. To demonstrate its functioning, I placed the grenade on the bench in front of me, holding the body in my right hand and pressing the base firmly against the large condenser microphone positioned in front of me. I pulled the pin out and then let go of the fly-off lever. The loudspeakers enhanced the whack of the striker hitting the base plug in a most satisfying way and the crack echoed off the walls. The fly-off lever flew towards the advocate and clattered noisily off the furniture and then onto the floor. Everyone in the room flinched; there were gasps and many squirmed uncomfortably in their seats. The inert demonstration did the trick and any lingering doubt that the grenade was an effective lethal weapon was dispelled. There were no further questions and I was dismissed. I had intended to await the verdict but now I just felt dirty and affronted. The accused were entitled to a fair trial, and their advocate had the freedom in court to raise any explanation to assuage the guilt of his clients, but, however untrue, my integrity had been maligned in open court. His clients nearly succeeded in murdering several people. I didn't know who they were, I didn't see them at the crime scene and my evidence related solely to the hand grenade. They will be free men now, presumably, no doubt proud of their contribution to their cause. My view is different; anyone intending a gun and grenade attack against unarmed, anonymous and innocent people in a crowded bookie's shop is a potential murderer; no excuses; plain and simple.

CHAPTER 7

Stonecutter's Island Hong Kong 1981–1982

In June 1981, we arrived in Hong Kong where I had been posted to the Ammunition Sub Depot on Stonecutter's Island. This was a sub-unit of the Composite Ordnance Depot, which was located in Kowloon, near Kai Tak Airport. Amid the frenetic 24-hour pace of life in Hong Kong, Stonecutters was an oasis of calm. With the exception of the Royal Navy Chief Petty Officer, who ran the locally enlisted naval ratings training school, the only other inhabitants were the staff and families of the ammunition department and the Fire Officer. There were two other units: 415 Maritime Troop RCT, which operated RPL launches, and Naval Party 1009, which operated two hovercrafts from a ramp next to East Pier. Most of their staff were only on the island during working hours. Shortly after we arrived, my young son, aged three months, seemed to be suffering from a heavy cold. One morning, he started screaming in his cot and seemed inconsolable but strangely distant. I phoned Sister Stella Ma who was the nurse based in the small medical centre on the island. She hurried over and, after one look at the child, declared that he was very ill and she made arrangements for him to be transported promptly to the British Military Hospital, Hong Kong. He was quickly diagnosed with bacterial meningitis and declared to be very seriously ill. Antibiotics were infused directly into his head through a cap made of Plaster of Paris. After a couple of days, he recovered, and didn't appear to suffer any longer-term complications. His illness led to an odd clerical error. In those days, the families of service personnel overseas were referred to with a reference to the head of family's regimental number preceded by an abbreviation indicating the relationship. In this case, my son was referred to in official correspondence as S/O (son of) 24285109 S/Sgt Robinson RAOC. Official correspondence concerning my son's serious illness had been sent to the RAOC Manning and Records Office in the UK (HR department, for those not in the know). The RAOC Corps Gazette, a monthly magazine, had an office there and they gleaned much of what they published in the magazine directly from this HR department. In the summer, I received a very posh-looking letter. The address was handwritten with an expensive pen, the stationery heavy gauge and textured. I was either in deep shit or was on the cusp of glory. I opened the letter after repeatedly reading the address to make sure it was definitely for me. It was from the editor of the RAOC Corps Gazette. In those days, the drafted magazine would take about three months to get published and distributed. The letter was an apology in advance of the apparently unstoppable publication of my obituary. This was to be published in the forthcoming September edition and an explanation for how this came about was offered. A clerk (don't they always get the blame?) had allegedly found a note that S/O 24285109 S/Sgt Robinson was very seriously ill in BMH Hong Kong. Now this clerk was 'said to know' the gazette did not publish details of illnesses, only deaths. Also, the clerk was supposedly unaware of the significance of the prefix 'S/O', so this clerk assumed the note was about me and that I had subsequently passed away. The clerk then drafted an obituary notice in my name. I would love to hear this clerk's version of the truth! My demise was to be announced to the unsuspecting world on Page 371 of the September 1981 edition of the RAOC Gazette and it was too late to prevent it. I phoned my OC to let him know. He laughed his head off which annoyed me. Quotes attributed to Mark Twain started to fly and I had to tell him my father did a full career in the RAOC and would likely see the obituary. He relented at this and took it more seriously. A signal was sent back to the UK to notify people of the error. It wasn't entirely successful, and I recall bumping into an old friend at Kineton many years later who looked at me in disbelief; he thought I was dead. Your present reading of this author's book is evidence that rumours of my death are exaggerated... for now!

Stonecutter's Island was a place where bizarre things could happen. There was a drinking culture, and I became a part of it. It all seemed quite benign, but a shocking event took place which revealed the extent to which excessive drinking was costing lives in the Services. The Chief Petty Officer, who ran the locally enlisted Naval training facility on the island, was a gregarious man, generous and great fun to be around. He had spent most of his career afloat and this current draft was perhaps the only time he had been shore-based. He was a single man and lived in a room above the bar in the sergeants' mess. He would be in the bar almost every evening. As far as I can recall, we never saw him in an obviously drunken condition. He was a great raconteur and even had an EOD anecdote. In the earliest days of the troubles in Northern Ireland, he was on board a naval vessel which was docked in or around Londonderry. His appointment on board ship was that of Buffer, which appears to have been an important role on board, involving a wide variety of activities. From what he told me, I think it was a post respected by all on board and he could perhaps be labelled a 'jack of all trades'. This, he claimed, involved EOD. By then, EOD in the Royal Navy was a role for Clear-

171

ance Divers but prior to them being given the IEDD role, where that was appropriate, Charlie claimed that it was a Buffer's responsibility and, during his time, he had been ordered to deal with a suspect device which had been discovered ashore, not far from where his ship was berthed. The suspect device was within a dustbin and Charlie had evaluated it using improvised hook-and-line techniques. It turned out to be either a hoax or false alarm and by the way Charlie described the incident, what he said was both lucid and believable.

Although he was a single man, the wives in the mess were all fond of him and he was invariably at the centre of functions in the mess and very much a part of our community. One evening, very late at night, there was an incident. Charlie had gotten up, perhaps to use the loo. His foot had apparently become tangled in a TV coaxial lead and he had pulled the aerial down off the top of a tall locker and had suffered a minor but bloody head injury. His condition was puzzling to the people attending to him. He was eventually evacuated to BMH Hong Kong, and we later heard he was very ill. All of us were stunned by the rapid switch from 'life and soul of the party' to very seriously ill. Charlie was stabilised and evacuated to a UK hospital, and it was heartbreaking to hear the news some days later that he had died. Charlie's demise led to an investigation which revealed a side to him that we were unaware of. Bar sales records appeared to show that he was consuming a large quantity of vodka in his room after the bar closed. By day, he was always well turned out and he displayed none of the usual warning signs of his condition. Royal Naval personnel recovered his personal effects from the mess, and we were left with nothing but memories of a lovely man with a terrible hidden addiction that killed him. His replacement was another lively character and, pointedly, he was a married man with a young son. There had been some consideration that drafting in another single man might lead to a repeat situation. There was some thought from above that loneliness had contributed to Charlie's condition and that the loss of his shipmate's company caused his condition. I felt this was wrong, but it felt disrespectful to speculate. The new CPO, Pete, was great fun and his son eventually became an ammunition technician; what a small world!

On a more jovial note, we entered a period known as the Bicycle War. The island was quite small, and bicycles were the main form of transport. After the monthly mess meeting, members would adjourn to the bar and get a skinful. After time was called, members would leave and go home, hopefully on their bikes. When they got outside, however, the slower leavers would find their bikes had already been taken! This meant they would be late getting home and would be inconvenienced in the morning, having to leave home earlier to walk to work. Something needed to be done. The depot staff broke up into factions and bicycles started to be taken and hidden away on an industrial scale. The bicycle war escalated to a peak when we came into work one morning and saw a bike propped up on its stand, atop one of the highest watch towers in the depot. Height was relative. Much of the depot was underground in a very rugged system of ravines, caves and sharp hills. This bike over- topped everything in sight and how it got there was a mystery. For all I know, the People's Liberation Army may well have inherited it when the island was handed over to them in 1997!

A persistent urban myth during my time on Stonecutter's Island was that the Japanese military established a snake farm there in 1943 and this was abandoned after their surrender. There may be truth in this as there are online Wikipedia references to it and we did have a large population of venomous snakes. As I had access to an EOD shotgun,

I became the appointed vermin controller on the island and was often called upon to deal with snakes and potentially rabid dogs. Not only was the snake population large, but most of the snakes I encountered were very large; in fact, close to their known maximum sizes. What puzzled me was what was maintaining this unsustainably large population? The human footprint on the island was quite modest and we had very few road vehicles. The most common large snakes seemed to be Banded Kraits and several species of cobra. These snakes are known for co-existing with humans and the reason behind this is usually the presence of rats and mice. I couldn't find any obvious magnets for rats and the very large numbers of large snakes defied the logic that they were predating on mere rats. Whilst I was there, a very large rifle range was constructed, and this resulted in a significant loss of potential habitat for all sorts of animals. Most of the island was covered in dense vegetation, probably much of it capable of being categorised as secondary jungle as it was so dense. The cutting back of the vegetation for the new range certainly displaced the resident beasties and sightings and encounters increased at the time. Two memorable encounters are worthy of writing about. In late 1981, I lived in No 1 Wuthering Heights. Opposite my house lived John Knight, who was the SAT. One Sunday afternoon, our wives had entrusted us with our kids, and we took them with us to watch a matinee film in the mess; something called The Life of Brian. We had a whale of a time and probably indulged a little too much in the 'bad decision juice'. Afterwards, as we strolled back up the road towards Wuthering Heights, we walked around the back of the houses along the road as the children's buggies made using the concrete steps up the hill too difficult. We laughingly recounted the funniest parts of the film and then stopped dead in our tracks directly behind my house. To the left was a small chain link fence, a two-foot verge and then the edge of the single-track asphalt road. To the right was the wood store attached to the back of the house. The door of the wood store was closed. The distance from the wood store to the road's edge was about three feet. The object of our attention was a thick blue-ish-grey snake with dirty-white bands around its body. The thinnest end was still out of sight under the fence on the left. The business end had already entered the wood store through a large gap at the bottom corner of the door. In the middle, the snake was thicker than my arm; that's not especially thick but it is thick enough. Thankfully, the snake hadn't noticed us and continued to traverse the gap and disappear into the shed as we looked on with eyes on stalks! The tail eventually passed under the door at which point we fled, pushing the buggies urgently to our respective front doors. We pondered what to do. We didn't actually use the wood stores, which did have small piles of chopped wood in them, but the kids would play in them. The scene was now set for an intervention where ambition clearly eclipsed capability.

With Heineken-infused bravado, we returned to the wood store to evict the beast. Along the way, I found an old mop on a shaft. The mop head was mostly gone. All that was left was a metal triangular piece to which the mop itself would be attached. Using the mop, I pulled the door open to John's encouragement, albeit from behind me... well behind me. The shadow cast by the door over the small pile of cut logs retreated as the sun shone inside. The pile of wood was quite small. We couldn't see any sign of the 'Loch Ness Monster' hiding within. Emboldened by this and the thought the beast had already fled, we drew closer, our shadows then fell over the wood. At this point, the angriest creature I had ever seen erupted out of the logs. Whatever species this was, it did not slither on its belly. Its head bounded up into the air level with my face. I spun around and ran straight into John. He staggered away to the right, and I bounced off to the left.

175

As I looked over my shoulder, I saw the snake bounding after me, seemingly intent on catching me. The reality was we had cornered it and it was reacting typically but, at that time, I was in the flight mode of the 'fight or flight' paradigm, and this bloody monster was inches away from the back of my neck. I ran into the small courtyard where the Amah would dry the washing on the clotheslines, hoping the snake would choose to go back into the jungle, but it followed me and this time, I was the cornered one. I turned and faced it; the head reared towards my face, and I lunged at it with a roundhouse swing of the headless mop. I felt the blow as the snake was struck and as the mop shaft followed through, it got very heavy and slowed down. At the end of the swing, my elbows bent, and the mop came back towards me complete with snake. Instincts to prevent the snake from getting wrapped around my neck kicked in and I let go of the mop which then flew away due to centrifugal force, just like a field athlete throwing the hammer. As the mop/snake combo flew towards the wall, I ran back to where I had last seen John; he was gone. Checking I wasn't being followed, I went to his front door; he refused to come out! I tip-toed back to the scene of my desperate defence. The snake was now tightly coiled around the metal mop head but wasn't moving. Above it on the wall was a blood spatter. Not convinced of the snake's injured state as I'd heard some of them could play possum, I grabbed a long clothes prop from next door's washing. I prodded the snake and then pushed it. The head was upside down, the pale belly was up, the mouth was open and its tongue protruded. It was completely still. As my gaze followed its coils, I saw that the sharp end of the triangular mop head holder had impaled it, about two feet behind its head. I ran back to John's front door and pleaded with him to come out, but he wouldn't. He'd actually locked the door. After a few minutes, he relented and followed me back to where the snake lay. Using the clothes prop, I straightened out the coils and then placed the prop along the body to gauge its length. The snake was longer than the prop which was about nine feet long. We pondered what to do with it. Then John had an idea. He phoned the locally enlisted Chinese members of 415 Maritime Troop RCT who were in their hut by East Pier. They came trotting up the hill and chopped off the head before disappearing back to their hut with the snake's remains in a plastic bag. We learned the following day that the head, complete with venom glands, had been sent to the mainland so the venom could be harvested. The rest of the snake was the main course for their evening meal. The moral of the story? Heineken does indeed 'refresh' the parts of the body that other beers fail to reach, including that vital bit of the brain that would normally inhibit foolish risk-taking!

Another snake adventure happened by accident. We had an RAOC Vehicle Specialist on the island employed as a driver who had the secondary role of being the crane operator for the depot's 3-ton Iron Fairy crane. By happy coincidence, this was Tony Blount who had spent some time with me as my No 2 in Belfast in 1979. We had already had one or two adventures together and trouble seemed to have a knack of following us about. He had two lively young sons, and they were a constant source of entertainment. One day, Tony was driving us along a single-track road past a landmark on the island called the Geisha House. This was a deserted building completely surrounded by dense vegetation and rumour had it that Japanese troops had kept kidnapped women there in the war and they used the venue and the wretched women as a 'comfort house'. Most of the time, vehicular traffic was almost non-existent. We typically had about three Land Rovers on the island at any one time and the commonest mode of transport was push bikes. Tony would like to drive along this deserted road at speed and we shot along, taking the many bends on two wheels.

As we passed the Geisha House, we saw something like a pipe lying across the full width of the road, but we couldn't stop. We ran over it. He screeched to a halt, and we walked back to it. We had struck a King Cobra. The wretched snake had been almost chopped into three parts. Bits of it were writhing but the business end was still. We were in a long-wheelbase Land Rover and the snake was about one and a half times its length. This monster had apparently been basking in the sun on the warm road. We left it and drove back to the depot to get a sack to recover it and bring it back. We were back a few minutes later to find it was gone. All that was left was bloodstains covered in ants indicating where our wheels had cut it up.

I had a theory about how these large and numerous snakes were able to survive and grow so big despite the obvious lack of prey. Hong Kong was home to one of the biggest concentrations of Black Kites in the world. These magnificent birds were almost as common as seagulls around a municipal dump; indeed, squaddies labelled them as 'shite hawks'. Their diet was mainly carrion, sometimes roadkill, but more usually, as islanders, we would see them retrieving dead fish from the sea. These birds would then squabble for their scraps of food on the wing, and it was quite common to find dead fish on the ground where they had been dropped. I had noticed that we had a large population of feral cats on the island although they were very shy and active at night, but you could still hear them. Unlike the rest of Hong Kong, the loudest thing at night on Stonecutters was the sound of waves lapping on the beaches. In some bizarre animal kingdom pecking order, I fancied that fish fed cats via the fighting kites and big snakes ate cats having graduated on rodents whilst young. I didn't see many small snakes at all and many of the larger snake species, like Kraits and the King Cobras, preferred to eat smaller snakes. The large snake population was too big for our small island to conceal and so it was inevitable that confrontations were common. One of my favourites was the time a cobra emerged from a toilet when the lady of the house was in the shower! I saw neither of them by the time I got to the ground floor flat, and neither was injured by their experience, but it certainly makes you want to look twice before you sit down to do your business!

On the island, we had a lively social life for the whole family, and we had a fancy dress party for the kids. Tony's two sons were to come as Incredible Hulks. His wife Annetta, ever the attentive and fussy mother, did a brilliant job with their outfits; she even dyed their skin green with food dye. I believe they were so good they won prizes. The next morning, as they awaited the ferry to take them over to Kowloon, peals of laughter erupted, and Annetta was frantic. The dye wouldn't come off; it was priceless.

Dogs were another potential hazard on Stonecutter's Island. Rabies was endemic in the region and dogs were kept by most Chinese families, including those who lived aboard the ubiquitous Chinese junks which frequently sailed around our shores. The sea currents around the region tended to cause floating objects to be washed ashore on the tide and this included human remains too. These would be the remains of illegal immigrants who had tried to swim across Mirs Bay, often tethered to makeshift buoyancy aids like balloons. Mirs Bay was shark-infested and some of them perished. In my time, several bodies were washed up and the Hong Kong Urban Services Department staff would come over, wrap the bodies in some sort of bamboo matting and take them away. It was all very sad and was like watching a human form of roadkill being swept away. The most exciting dog operation happened when a British member of 415 Maritime Troop was carving graffiti onto a prominent rock which the ferries would go past as they commuted to and fro. His big idea was to record his details and tour dates for posterity along with some artwork. Halfway through his endeavours, he scrambled down off the rock to admire his handiwork, and there to greet him was a large savage dog. Realising the danger he was in, he scrambled back up the rock, leaving most of his bloodied fingernails behind in his urgent desire to gain purchase on the slippery rock. After the dog disappeared, he got to the nearest telephone and called for help. The boss phoned me in the office and asked if I would deal with the animal and he authorised the use of the EOD shotgun and SG Shot with which to destroy it. As there were married quarters nearby, I asked if the clerks would telephone warnings for everyone to get inside until the job was done. The information I had was that the dog was a big one with bloodshot eyes, foamy saliva around its jaws and it was very aggressive. That could have been rabies or the symptoms of a badly dehydrated dog that had been swimming in the open sea for hours. I was accompanied by one of the three corporal ATs. I can't remember who it was for sure. It could have been Geordie, Owen or another Tony. I recall we swept along the beach trying to find it. There were a lot of bushes and rocky outcrops; I could easily end up face to face with the wretched animal and my defence was the long-barrelled shotgun which would be unwieldy in confined spaces. The shot loaded was SG Shot which was similar to buckshot; each cartridge contained nine 7mm balls. If struck, any animals would be torn apart but my main concern was this ammunition had a much longer range than bird shot, and I constantly nagged my assistant to stay clear of my possible arc of fire; the look on his face reassured me that he didn't need to be told.

As we passed by the area of the last known dog-sighting, a diesel-powered boat chugged past about 50 metres offshore. These were what we called bum boats and they would sail along with a characteristic diesel-engined growl. I stopped in the shade of a large bush which was between me and the sea. As my eyes peered into a large hollow space in the bush, the glare off the water meant I couldn't see inside. It was then that I realised the bum boat had gone out of sight, but the engine note was louder. I brought the gun into the shoulder and made ready to fire as I realised this growl was not a diesel engine. My assistant was behind me to my right, out of harm's way. I still couldn't see the dog. I slowly shifted position as I tried to find a way of seeing past the blinding reflected glare. Bending my head and neck over to the right, I found a welcome piece of shade and waited a few seconds for my eyes to adjust. Then I saw Batman! It was a silhouette of a large dog about two metres in front of me. The dog was erect, sitting on a large boulder and his sharply defined ears gave his presence away. At first, I couldn't tell if he was facing towards or away from me. Also, I couldn't now see if the area beyond the dog was safe to fire into. At this range, the shot would pass right through. I had to move. Fortunately, I was standing in soft sand which deadened the sound of movement.

Then I saw the dog was facing away from me. As his head traversed left and right, I could see large bubbles of saliva ballooning out of his mouth before bursting as he panted and growled. I inched backwards up the rising ground behind me to where I could see the area beyond the bush; it was thankfully clear. I now aimed at the dog and moved back in. I was again about two metres away and I put my forefinger inside the trigger guard and, recalling my shooting coach training from RSM JJ Thomson in 1974, I brought my breathing under control and applied pressure. My finger started to hurt. I squeezed harder, it hurt more.

Buggar, the safety catch was still applied! Imagining the dog would sense my incompetence, I moved my finger to the safety catch and pushed it in. It was the loudest click in the world, but the dog didn't react. I re-applied trigger pressure and the gun fired. At that range, the group size of the SG shot would be minimal. The dog fell forward and disappeared from view. Was it a hit or a miss? I waited a minute and then went forward. All that was left of the dog's head were its ears. Its death was humane and certain, and I felt relieved by that. I phoned the graffiti artist to tell him the coast was clear, but I gathered from his response that he had completely lost interest in his rock art.

The final doggie story again ended badly for the dog concerned but the collateral damage extended to my reputation. I was walking past the small NAAFI shop on the island which was next to a beach and there was a concrete boat ramp nearby. There was a rubbish incinerator on the ramp which was burning whenever I went past it. I think the NAAFI staff burned cardboard packaging in it. A mother and her two sons were walking nearby and were fussing over something she was holding. It was an adorable, heart-melting puppy. I asked about it and was dismayed to learn she had just found it on the beach, and she thought it had come ashore there. I warned her of the rabies risk and the danger to her and her family. Her eyes filled and the boys stared angrily at me as though I was the Grinch that just stole their Christmas. I was asked what could be done; they wanted to adopt the dog. Putting on my best snake-oil salesman face, I suggested she commit the puppy to my custody. I would arrange for the puppy to be tested for rabies on the mainland. If the result was negative, she would be able to request permission to keep it. If it was positive, the animal would be euthanised. The families' hopes soared, and I was instantly transformed from Grinch to saint. Trouble was that the only effective way to test for rabies in a dog at the time was at its post-mortem. The reassuring white lies poured forth and I reconciled my dishonesty with the importance of the common good. What they didn't know wouldn't harm them. We parted company, me with the puppy and them with renewed hope and an excited debate on what to name the dog!

I took the dog with me to retrieve the shotgun. I returned half an hour later, intending to do the business and dispose of the dog's remains in the incinerator. It seemed a well-rounded plan; what could possibly go wrong? I had placed the dog in a hessian sack and carried it close to my chest. It was relaxed and it suited my motives not to stress the animal. After all, I was to euthanise the animal, not torment it. I took it down to the foreshore, placed the sack on the ground and patted the head through the sack to both comfort the dog and set up my target for a clean kill. I fired the shot and the outcome was clean and instant. Nearby, the incinerator was well alight. I put the sack inside and then felt I was being watched. As I turned in response to the instinct, I saw my audience was the would-be adoptive family standing aghast about 30 metres away. No words were said but the glances were like bullets. A strategic withdrawal was prudent and I could only hope that time would be a healer; some hope!

We had a fairly busy EOD workload. It was mostly false alarms. I had already cleared a suspect bomb in the car park at HMS Tamar. It seemed to be attached to a car, but it turned out to be a harmless radiosonde device from a weather balloon that had randomly fallen there from a great height. When deploying from the island, we almost invariably flew by helicopter, usually an RAF Wessex and sometimes an Army Scout. Our only EOD Wheelbarrow was notoriously unreliable, and it would take hours to move it by ferry and road so we would deploy with lightweight portable scales of equipment. We would exercise regularly with the Royal Hong Kong Police and the Gurkha Field force. The war role of the military in Hong Kong was confined to Counter Insurgency and Internal Security but training for this role had been badly disrupted by the illegal immigrant emergency. Each night, at the peak of the emergency, hundreds of illegal immigrants from mainland

China would attempt to cross the land and sea borders. Their awful journeys, usually on foot and sometimes over thousands of miles, were tempted by the so-called 'Touch Base' policy. This policy allowed for eventual Hong Kong citizenship if the immigrants were able to cross the border and reach the RHKP police station on Boundary Street in Kowloon. Just after my arrival, this policy was rescinded and the flow of immigrants reduced to a trickle, allowing the military to return to their war-role training. On two occasions, we were to carry out exercises in newly built satellite towns in the New Territories. This was very useful as we were able to exercise in built-up areas with intact infrastructures before the new residents and factory owners were allowed in. Our boss at the time was deeply into all aspects of EOD. He had a personal project of trying to construct a piece of miniature radio-controlled remote handling equipment out of a radio-controlled model racing car. Tony built the thing, and we were going to test it in a new high-rise building to see if the radio control was degraded by the high metal content in this type of structure. It nearly ended in disaster. We were given permission to train on a high-rise vertical factory, namely the new YKK Zipper factory in Tuen Mun new town. This was high; It was over 20 storeys. We were to deploy onto the roof of the building by fast-roping down from a Wessex. It was late at night when we went in, and it was well-windy. We hovered over the building, reassuringly close to the flat roof. The Loadmaster indicated that I should descend. I had a fairly heavy bergen of kit on my back and I unstrapped from my seat and moved to the door, taking hold of the rope as practised many times before. I exited and looked down. My field of view was full of the solid 'terra firma' of the roof. I've never had a fear of heights and enjoyed activities like abseiling. I started to descend. People might think the downwash of a helicopter is like trying to stand up in a wind tunnel but when you first exit a helicopter, there is very little down-

184

wash because you are close to the centre of the main rotor where the airflow is minimal. As I accelerated downwards, I was trying to judge when to start braking. The rope-end was coiled below me on the roof which was a handy reference for judging distance. Then a strong gust of wind blew the helicopter sideways, off-station.

The rope end disappeared over the side of the building. I was now approaching the end of the rope at speed and instead of being about 20 to 30 feet above my landing point, I was now well over 200 feet from the pavement far below. I could see the glow of lights in the deserted streets below me. I managed to lock my grip on the rope and stopped with a yo-yo-like jerk. I was outboard of the roof and just below it. The rope was now swinging back towards the building. I looked up to see what the helicopter was doing, and I could see the Loadmaster looking at me. The helicopter climbed a few feet, and I avoided hitting the wall. I swung over the railings and got my feet onto the flat roof. I ran towards the middle of the roof, let go of the rope and crouched down as the next man started to descend. Abseiling can be great fun; human conkers? Not for me.

My next adventure with a helicopter was with an Army Scout. I was providing technical cover for an International Mortar Competition at Castle Peak ranges. I think there were five nations competing and the winners by far were New Zealand. Their team consisted of huge Māori soldiers. The competition was conducted in the dismounted role where the mortar men would distribute the load of baseplate, bipod and ammunition among themselves. They had to race to a firing point, come into action, come out of action, redeploy to a location several hundred metres away up and down steep and rocky terrain and repeat. They were awesome and deadly accurate. The ammunition for the teams was delivered by helicopter-underslung loads in nets. As the unfired ammunition was recovered, I noted that the steel boxes were missing, and the ammunition had been hurriedly shoved back in its 'greenies'. These were paired green plastic inner containers that each held two complete bombs. I could see that that ammunition had been poorly packaged and was unsafe to be moved until properly repackaged. I gestured urgently to a Loadmaster as his aircraft lifted away. The top had come off a greenie and the bomb had slid out and was caught by its fins in the cargo net, dangling precariously above us. The load was promptly ground-dumped, and I noted some exchanged glances of reproval from the ground-handling crews towards me. The helicopter departed without load, and I berated the bemused handlers for their carelessness. Among them were members of the air liaison team and my displeasure was conveyed back to the aircrews by radio as they plied their trade above me. My intervention was going to slow everything down for them, but I was firm and insisted that all bombs had to be correctly packaged before flight. The air liaison team were concerned about the delay affecting their schedules. To the question, "How long will this fuss take?" I replied, "As long as it takes". It was clear that I would be the last to be extracted. There was no access where we were for vehicles, and I would need a helicopter. I was also carrying a lot of explosives in a demolition kit, and I would need to be flown directly to Stonecutter's. I checked the remaining bombs, got them properly packaged and placed them in cargo nets. As the last lift departed, they promised someone would come back for me; I swear I noted a knowing glance exchanged between them, or was I just being paranoid?

About half an hour later, I heard the sound of an approaching helicopter. It was an Army Scout. As it came into land, I noted that the doors and back seats had been removed. The Scout didn't shut down and I got a thumbs-up to approach. I went to climb into the back but the P2 had got out and gestured for me to stand on the skid with my back to the aircraft and sit on the edge of the cabin floor. Puzzled, I did as I was told. He then produced a long canvas strop which he connected to attachment points on either side of me. The implication became clear, I was going home on the outside! I'd never done this before; I'd never even trained for it. No spoken words of instruction were uttered but I wouldn't have heard them over the engine noise in any case. With a cheerful wave, the P2 resumed his seat and strapped in. The strop meant to secure me was long and loose; in fact, it was drooping level with my knees. I then thought I could enhance my precarious perch by ensuring the heels of my boots were shoved hard into the skid which thankfully had a non-slip, textured paint finish. The small of my back seemed to find itself a nice tight fit against the airframe. I felt a little more secure; only a little. The engine note increased, and the aircraft started to lift off. As it did so, I was dismayed to feel the skid moving away from my perch. Even though it was a skid, it had some sort of suspension. The strop drooped even lower, and I could no longer wedge myself between skid and airframe. The pilot headed into a gorge and used the plunging ground as an opportunity to pick up speed. As I tried to gain a worthwhile grip on the flaccid strop, my left hand felt the D shackle the strop was attached to. I managed to squeeze the tip of my little finger inside the D shackle and my right hand tried to pull the strop tighter but, as the aircraft manoeuvred in flight, I found I seemed to be floating like some pendulum in an absurd experiment. I dreaded the thought the pilot might pull a high-G turn to starboard. Thankfully, he didn't. We headed back over the water a few hundred feet up and flying straight and level at what I estimated as about 100 knots. Then we passed under a low rain cloud. Droplets started hitting my face like bullets, and I had to close my eyes which made the whole nightmare even worse. A few minutes later, the rain stopped, and I could see Stonecutters in front of us. The Scout swooped in with a final turn to port which pressed me reassuringly into the airframe. As we landed, the skid's positioned changed and pushed me back upwards. The P2 jumped out, unfastened the entirely pointless strop, handed me my demolition box and, with a grin, gestured that I should leave the aircraft. I stooped down under the rotor and staggered away towards the headquarters building. It was the nearest I had ever come to shitting my pants!

Sometime later, I was tasked to attend the discovery of a shell in a trench at Lye Mun on Hong Kong Island. We had a fast patrol launch on the island which was named 'Joseph Hughes GC'. A plaque commemorated his heroism in fighting an ammunition fire on the back of his heavily laden truck. This was in 1946 when there were vast quantities of Japanese and Allied ammunition dumped all over the place. Hughes died two days after his truck exploded. The plaque didn't mention that the subsequent conflagration ignited a massive fire in an underground magazine at Lye Mun which led to a huge explosion. Thousands of shells were scattered several hundreds of metres in all directions. Fortunately, a massive rock outcrop above the magazine had fallen in on top of it, bringing about an expeditious, if not entirely safe, covering up of the disaster. As long as nobody started digging holes there, it would be OK. As I said, the rockfall was expeditious. However, Hong Kong's brilliant Mass Transit Railway (MTR) system was scheduled for expansion and soon the excavators were cutting trenches in Lye Mun where there was to be a new station. Tony drove us over to this job and we joked about the likelihood of a controlled explosion revealing yet more shells from the Lye Mun disaster. We were only joking but our black humour had tempted providence and now fate would intervene and take her just revenge. We found the shell which was still partially concealed at the bottom of a trench. In the hot, humid conditions, we took turns with the shovel to expose it. As I dug, Tony remarked, "Wouldn't it be funny if the shovel gave off a clang of metal on metal?" We laughed. At the next stroke of the shovel into the soft sandy soil came the sound of a shovel scraping a metal object. We were in a nest of shells. We exposed what we could and destroyed them in situ. When I approached to check the trench was safely cleared, I just knew I would find another shell... and I did. This went on all day until we thankfully ran out of shells. It was clear that a major battle area clearance task by the Royal Engineers was merited.

In November 1981, I 'inherited' responsibility for the island's Bonfire Night celebration which was to feature a bonfire and outdoor drinks, followed by a return to the mess and a party. I was promised some ammunition items to help get the fire going. The fire had already been built some time previously. Heavy rain had completely soaked the fire but at the time of intended ignition, the weather was dry. The families circulated around the fire, impatient to see it lit. The ammunition I was promised turned out to be a solitary destructor incendiary. Although this device was quite small, I was hopeful that its very high-temperature burning properties would do the trick. It was already positioned at the heart of the fire and was connected to an exploder. As darkness descended, the kids counted down to ignition. At the shout of "ZERO", the world's most pathetic anti-climax took place before us. The silhouette of the dark fire's conical structure was picked out by the many lights of ships moored out in Victoria Harbour. The flickering glow of the igniter as it burned and ignited some of the diesel could be seen. The wet timbers resisted ignition and the fire spent the next hour struggling to stay awake. The Island's Fire Officer was standing next to me, his attendance completely pointless. We eventually traipsed back to the mess to drown our sorrows. I was furious; I had been bequeathed a damp squib and everyone was crestfallen. Next year would be different.

On the island, we had a commercial explosives factory. Hong Kong's previous brush with terrorism had resulted in very strict controls over explosives. There was high demand for blasting explosives and the island presented a natural solution to meet the needs of safety and security demanded by the highly populated colony. As the explosives were manufactured, there was a requirement to conduct test firings of samples for quality control.

I had a good working relationship with the owner and as time went by, I learned more of how the plant operated. I had taken a strong interest in the commercial explosives industry and had joined the Institute of Explosives Engineers. I planned ahead for the next bonfire night. I acquired barrels of heavy oil from the Maritime Troop. Pete in the LSP school helped with various bits of the fire's construction. At its heart was a central core of post pallets. These were steel pallets which would support the fire and provide a chimney effect. The built-up fire was approaching the size of a house. From the explosives factory, I received a donation of two full sets of half-second delay detonators. I had seeded the fire with unserviceable propellants and diesel. The plan was to have a memorable and spectacular ignition. I had hinted at my intent but very few people knew what was to happen. We had a Guy Fawkes competition, and the winning Guy was hoisted atop the massive pyre. The young boy whose guy was best was selected to ignite the fire by plunging down on an imitation exploder. The small crowd gathered as the light started to fade into nighttime. The Island's Fire Officer was standing next to me. We had issued warnings to the statutory harbour and airport authorities, and I could hear chatter on the radio he held in his hand. The time for ignition arrived. I had planned the fire as if it was a standard demolition, with safety distances and procedures in place. The countdown started; behind my back, I had prepared a Shrike military exploder which would actually start the firing sequence. The prize-winning guy maker had his hands on the plunger. As the crowd counted down and shouted "ZERO", the plunger went down, and I pressed the fire buttons.

There was a brief pause, just sufficient to make people think something might have gone wrong. In the darkness in front of them was an avenue of small blast incendiaries, each one primed with a delay detonator. The outermost pair of incendiaries would go first and then five more pairs would detonate in sequences half a second apart, racing towards the dark form of the fire. Half a second after the last pair detonated, the fire would ignite. The initial short delay was planned and was the delay built into the detonators. Then, the world of explosives special effects lit up the night sky as the blast incendiaries boomed out and fireballs hung in the air just long enough for the next pair of blast incendiaries to be passed what resembled the fiery baton in a pyrotechnic relay race. The audience gasped and stepped back involuntarily. Impatient, muttering children were stunned into silence. The last pair of incendiaries had exploded and then the fire itself instantly transitioned from being dark and inert into an instant blaze. The shouts went up and the jungle fringe behind us was lit up as night became day. In the low clouds above us about two miles distant, a wide-bodied jet emerged as it approached Kai Tak airport. The island was the runway outer marker and aircraft were constantly overhead, lining up to fly directly at Lion Rock before pulling a steep right-hand turn into their final approach. The landing lights came on and seemed to swivel like startled eyes; I imagine the pilots would have had a grandstand view. Despite our warnings to the statutory authorities, someone on the Fire Officer's radio reported that an oil tanker may have caught fire and exploded in Victoria Harbour. Whilst the Fire Officer attempted to placate the anxious callers, we saw a Fire Boat charging towards the island, training its spotlight on us and made spookier by the fire's light now reflecting off its upper decks and windows. The huge fire raged on and we could feel the heat on our faces. It burned for a little over half an hour before fading into a glowing pile of ashes. Honour was restored from the previous year's debacle. My tour in Hong Kong was rapidly coming to an end. On reflection, if I had stayed for another year, I guessed I wouldn't have been invited to light another bonfire. The late, great Dr Fred Dibnah MBE, yet to emerge as a celebrity figure on television, would have asked "Jer like that?" It had been a spectacular swansong.

Early one morning, I was walking along the perimeter fence which, at that part of the depot, was just above the high-water mark. The beach was below me and was a mixture of sand and pebbles. My eye was drawn to what looked like a large diameter metal pipe but one end of it was rounded and it wasn't that long. It was rusty and I noticed that it had two holes through the upper surface and there was a lug halfway along the top. Curiosity kicked in so I walked around to the gate and then walked back up along the beach. With a stick, I scraped away the sand obscuring its ends; I realised I was looking at what appeared to be the empty casing of a large aircraft bomb. The holes in the casing looked like practice trepanning holes and the fuze pockets were empty. I took some rough measurements and went back to my office to ponder this discovery. I was tempted to recover the object, tart it up and put it on a pedestal outside the Depot Ammunition Technician's office. I grabbed Tony and showed him the find and asked if the Iron Fairy crane was capable of hoisting it up and over the perimeter fence. He said it was, so planning commenced. To refurbish the empty bomb would require a replacement tail and fin unit, a good clean up and painting with the appropriate colours and role bands. I needed some authoritative references, and I knew the SAT's technical library had some books on WW2 air-dropped US ordnance. By then, John Knight had been posted back to the UK and replaced by Dave. I knocked on his office door and asked if I could borrow some books from his library and he nodded approvingly in the direction of the shelf unit. As I was reading off the book covers, Dave asked for the reason for my newfound interest in US air-dropped ordnance. My somewhat coy response elicited tangible suspicion that I was up to something and my denials of an ulterior motive, other than that of wanting to improve my technical awareness, just made the hole I was now in, even deeper. I 'fessed up' that I had found an aircraft bomb. I was then frog-marched to the scene, and we were accompanied by the OC and Admin Officer. As they stared disbelievingly through the chain-link fence, one of them started to talk about flash signals to the UK base for a team from 33 Engineer Regiment (EOD) to be scrambled. Another voice opined it was a Royal Navy task as it was below the high-water mark. I couldn't suppress the laughter any longer and was pounced on as they realised it was a jape. The empty bomb was hoisted over the fence, tarted up and became a monument to folly; quite whose I wouldn't confirm.

In early November 1982, my wife and children flew back to the UK. I was now living in the sergeant's mess pending my own return to the UK. Very early one morning on the 17th of November, the Admin Officer, the late Major Stan Woods, for whom I had huge respect, woke me up with the terrible news that my brother-in-law, RUC Constable Ronald Irwin, had been murdered by terrorists the day before as he manned a security barrier in Markethill. His colleague was also murdered in a brutal attack where four gunmen cornered them and fired dozens of bullets into them at close range. Ronnie was a charismatic man, the father of two young boys and I was enormously fond of him. It added to the growing enormity of obstacles in my way to getting my life back into some semblance of order. I have written elsewhere of what had happened to me but there was a sense that nothing I could do would improve things.

CHAPTER 8

Edinburgh Detachment 521 EOD Company 1983–1984

After disembarkation leave spent in Birmingham, I went north on a train to report for duty at Catterick Garrison where the HQ of 521 EOD was based. This was the base of the northernmost EOD company in mainland UK and had troops in Nottingham, Catterick and Edinburgh. I was picked up from the train station and taken directly in to see the officer commanding. He spoke to me with empathy about my recent experiences and said he was sending me even further up north, to the Edinburgh Troop, to 'keep me out of the way'. My recollection of that interview was that the OC (Major Alan) was kindly, firm and encouraging; so much so that I felt greatly relieved and uplifted for the first time in many months. I was taken straight back to the train station and eventually arrived at Edinburgh Waverley. From there, I was taken to Craigiehall which was then Headquarters Army Scotland. The Edinburgh Detachment was based in a listed building called the Stable Block. I was to live in a relatively modern sergeants' mess in a tiny bunk and in front of the mess was the actual headquarters building, which was a 1960's flat-roofed, glass-walled building. The only business I had in there was occasional visits to Supply Branch to resolve supply problems with ammunition. I was keen to avoid that building. Just inside the main door on the right was one of the Camp RSM's two offices. The RSM himself was an utter disgrace to his battalion. More so than any other RSM I had ever met before or since, he was, in my opinion, a tyrannical despot. My arrival interview with him was an interrogation. In contrast, my arrival interview with the Camp Commandant was convivial and he expressed much concern for my welfare. I was to discover later on that Major Hamish Grace was a grandson of W D Grace. He was a kind-hearted and courteous man, perhaps eccentric, bordering on being as mad as a box of crabs! Seriously, Major Grace was a soldier's officer and was invariably a genteel soul. Coming on top of the kindly welcome by my new OC in Catterick, I felt I could now see the light at the end of a very long tunnel.

In judging the Camp RSM's character, I was minded to consider the maxim that power corrupts and absolute power corrupts absolutely. He was abrasive and appeared to resent the fact that, as EOD Operators, we did not carry out the Camp duties he controlled such as the Assistant Duty Officer (ADO) duty. During weekday mornings, we could hear him bawling out the wretched ADO from the previous evening and then bawling at the incoming ADO. Aside from the occasional rude outburst in the mess, my first real 'crash and burn' session with him arose out of me asking if I could have an electric kettle in my room. He went 'pear-shaped' on me. We were not allowed in the kitchen under any circumstances and my EOD duties, being somewhat like 'out-of-hours' tourism, meant I could spend days on end driving around Scotland, dealing with routine EOD incidents where I might collect items from police stations which had been handed in by the public. I often missed the evening meal due to arriving late back at camp. As I was often alone, driving a vehicle containing both serviceable explosives in a demolition box and large quantities of unexploded objects, I could hardly stop anywhere and leave the vehicle unattended. If I was in one of the marked bomb disposal vans, I couldn't stop anywhere at all and would have to refuel the vehicle and replenish any ammunition used before I could park it in our secure garage and then stand down. His observations on my allegedly bad personal administration being the cause of missing meals and that I could submit travel and subsistence claims for missed meals were completely illogical. Some weeks after arriving at Craigiehall, I was joined by another EOD Operator who lived in, making two of us in this situation. The new guy was Ron, who I knew already from Germany and Kineton. Ron had the kind of sense of humour that autocrats didn't like. We found ourselves being regularly reported to the RSM by his 'nark' for alleged misdemeanours.

One day, as the two of us visited Supply Branch in the HQ Building, we heard a newly promoted sergeant getting the 'Foghorn Leghorn' treatment. The guy had only been a sergeant for a few days and was getting a real '110-decibel wire-brushing'. As Ron and I came back down the stairs, the opportunity for mischief presented itself. The RSM's office door was adorned with an antlered stag trophy. Underneath it was a shield bearing his rank, name and regiment mounted atop his regimental tartan. Next door to his office was the gent's toilet. The sign on the door of the toilet seemed to have similarly spaced mounting screws and we were carrying multitools. Confident that the noise within would mask any sounds we made, we hurriedly swapped the signs over before legging it back to our sanctuary in the stable block. Having escaped detection, our laughs attracted the attention of the civilian Chief Clerk, Margaret. "What have you two buggers been up to?" We laughed so much we could hardly speak. Then Margaret started tickling Ron and the whole thing turned into a Laurel and Hardy sketch. We blurted out what we had done, and Margaret disappeared back to her office with a mock 'tut-tutting' mingled with the giggles. Margaret's best workmate was the Chief Clerk at Catterick. Margaret phoned her and told her what we'd done. The Catterick Chief Clerk laughed so much, the SAT asked what was going on. He was not amused. He came straight up the road in the Company Command Car in record time to berate us. If I'd had the nerve, I might have reminded him of when he was involved in painting the bear statue at Hounslow dayglow pink many years before. But I didn't. And he got caught!

The 1983 Edinburgh Military Tattoo was awesome. Ever since the 1971 bombing there, the Tattoo's security plan included having a bomb disposal team pre-positioned under the seating. We took turns to conduct this duty at what I think were the best seats in the house. While the Tattoo was in progress, we were joined in the mess by two temporary members. One was a pay warrant officer to pay the cast and the other was a catering warrant officer. After the final performance, the catering warrant officer let it be known that he had a rather large surplus of perishable foodstuffs and he offered to let us have it in the mess. We emptied out one of our vans and collected the surplus. It was a big load, predominantly game such as salmon, trout and pheasant. We had food hidden everywhere but our glee was short-lived when the well-known RSM's nark got wind of it and grassed us up to the RSM. Ron had just started dating Anna, the mess chef, and she told us the RSM was going to come over later to check all the ration cupboards and fridge-freezers. We got a couple of vans emptied out and put all the surplus in them. As the RSM approached the mess, Gus, our civilian driver, followed him at a safe distance and radioed his progress in real time as the vans stayed one step ahead. He didn't find our stash and living-in members fed like royalty for the next month.

Late one evening, I got a phone call from the Operations Centre to task me to the discovery of a mysterious substance that had put two teachers into hospital. The location was in a north-west facing bay near

Lochinver in northwest Scotland. I telephoned the local police contact. As we spoke, I could hear the occasional spitting sound in the background. He described to me that he had a piece of a pale brown substance in an ashtray, and it would hiss loudly when he prodded it with a stick, emitting dense, sweet-smelling white smoke. I realised he had somehow gotten hold of white phosphorous and didn't realise that he was quite literally playing with fire. I told him to put the substance into water and then secure it in a safe place. He explained the two teachers had found an even bigger piece of the substance which was lodged in a crack in rocks at the high-water mark in the bay. I left immediately to respond; it was going to be a long drive. I got to the location in the early hours, retrieved the lump of WP from the police office and then went to the scene of the discovery. The tide was on the way in and access from the beach was already cut off. The WP was inside a man overboard marker which had been washed ashore. If the tide came in all the way, it would likely float away and come ashore somewhere else. I decided to destroy it in situ with a large charge of plastic explosive to ensure all of the WP was consumed. The bay was close to the officer's home, which had the police office in a lean-to on one gable end, so he knew the area well. Normally, we didn't conduct controlled explosions in darkness for safety reasons, but time was limited; two people were in hospital and waiting for daylight was out of the question. I put him through a standard range of questions aimed at establishing if there were any people, livestock, hazards or other considerations that might be affected by an explosion. There weren't any. The rock formation was like a mini cul-de-sac facing out to sea and this would help direct blast and fragments seawards. I set up the demolition and we sought cover. As the charge detonated, a brilliant white flash illuminated the bay for a split second, lighting up thousands of white objects. As the darkness came back, the thousands of sea gulls who had been sleeping on the water took off in a panic, some of them obviously into the path of rock fragments that went out to sea, almost as though I had fired a punt gun at them. Then bloodied feathers started to fall like autumn leaves around us; it was time to leave!

About then, we were joined by a new Detachment Commander. Before his arrival, the SAT had deployed to Australia for about three months on an exchange programme called Exercise Long Look. From the outset, the new Detachment Commander was something of a control freak. He had a personal organiser which he took everywhere with him and he wanted to record everyone's personal details in this book, which he kept in his pocket. We were not too happy about this but he insisted we comply. He accompanied me on a unit inspection as an observer and made a huge fuss when he noticed one empty cartridge case under a pallet in the unit ammunition store. On one unit inspection in Glasgow, I found a unit store in very bad order. I phoned him to say I was considering awarding an 'unsatisfactory grading'. His reply was emphatic and without merit. I was "Not to award an unsatisfactory grading on his patch". On one occasion, after I had dealt with an unexploded artillery shell on a remote hillside in Dumfries and Galloway, he was critical that I had used safety fuze to initiate the charge. My electrical firing cable was only 100 metres long and, at that distance, I was exposed to a significant shrapnel hazard, the ground being swampy peat and there was nowhere to shelter. He seemed well capable of rattling off the theory from his course but incapable of understanding the hierarchy of risk that can present itself in the real world. This was a personality conflict in the making and this one would last until I retired in 1999.

In Chapter 18, I have written about Christine who I was yet to meet. Ron and Anna invited me to go on a blind date where I would meet her and we eventually married. In late October 1983, we decided to marry and we went looking for rings in the various jewellers in Edinburgh. The Detachment Commander had apparently seen us and, on the next weekly meeting, he rebuked me in front of the whole Detachment for not having requested his permission to marry first. He did have his good points and there was a conscientious and caring side to him but that didn't mitigate the growing and mutual dislike we had for each other.

In October 1983, I went to Kenya to conduct the annual ammunition inspection of the British Arm Training and Liaison Staff Kenya (BATLSK). Two weeks prior to going, I suffered a scaphoid fracture of my left wrist after falling whilst playing volleyball. Word of my injury flashed around the Battalion, and I had many phone calls asking if I would still be able to go to Kenya; I never knew I had so many friends! When I arrived at Brize Norton, my injury was noticed as my lower arm was in a plaster cast. This caused my mostly empty aircraft, an RAF Tristar, to be classed as a medical evacuation (MEDEVAC) flight. I was seated alone in the centre five seats and was able to lift the arm rests and put my feet up. When I got to BATLSK, I was based in Kahawa, in pleasant surrounds and comfortable barracks. The soldiers there had even made a DIY swimming pool by lining a hole with plastic sheeting.

One of my first inspections was of a small ammunition store near the Voice of Kenya Radio Station in Nairobi. The entrance to the store area was guarded by Kenyan soldiers. As our Land Rover approached, they cocked their rifles and aimed them at us nervously. When we produced our identity cards and they realised we were bona fide British soldiers, they seemed very relieved. I learned later that the Voice of Kenya Radio Station had been captured by only two mutinous Kenyan soldiers in the abortive 1982 coup d'état and these soldiers feared instant retribution if they failed to preserve security. In the following days, my escort, a British Army lance corporal, guided me to the Gilgil ammunition depot. He was unable to drive so I drove and over the week I was there, the plaster cast on my left arm was all but destroyed with gear changes. Getting there was quite special. We had to drive up out of the Rift Valley and the Land Rover engine would struggle as we got near the top. I had a most pleasant meeting with two Kenyan Army Ammunition Technicians who had trained as Commonwealth and Foreign Ammunition Technicians (CFATs) at Kineton. Whist there, I had a nasty encounter with a Gaboon Viper. As I approached an ammunition store in the depot, I encountered the snake in front of the door as I turned a corner around a bush. It was about five feet long and I was struck by how thick it was as I jumped backwards; I had almost trodden on it. I've always had a fascination with snakes and have handled many in my time, but the Gaboon Viper has a reputation for having huge fangs, copious amounts of lethal venom and the fastest strike speed of any snake. It had a bit of a hissy fit, so I moved away until it disappeared.

On Friday nights, the single soldiers in BATLSK would get a liberty transport lift into Nairobi city and back. I was invited but declined to go when I heard the explanation of what they did there. They would do the rounds of bars and then go looking for 'bim-bam', which apparently meant women of ill repute. The big deal at the time was of the emerging global HIV/AIDS epidemic and sub-Saharan Africa was said to be a hot spot. Unprotected sex by the BATLSK singlies was quite common and my escort quite frankly explained that the following Monday after an exposure, they would see the medical officer for a course of antibiotics.

Meanwhile, back in the Inverness area of Scotland, a GP gave a very public warning to females about the soldiers in Fort George who had recently returned from an exercise in Kenya and that they posed a threat to public health from HIV/AIDS. I never encountered my escort or his colleagues again during my service and I often reflect on their promiscuous and perilous behaviour and how it all turned out for them.

When I flew back from Kenya, our refuelling stop-over was at Cyprus. We were to be joined by a darts team of military wives who were travelling back to the UK to participate in a female darts tournament. In those days, military personnel and dependants could get concessional travel on RAF flights, if there was available seats, in an arrangement known as 'Indulgence'. These ladies were 'indulgence passengers' but they had been delayed which delayed our flight. We took off, hours late, and I suddenly realised how much I now loved Christine when it dawned on me there was insufficient time to make my connecting flight to Edinburgh; too late to meet her as we had planned. As we approached Brize Norton, an announcement warned us of severe weather with strong crosswinds blowing over the airfield. On final approach, I cursed my luck as it was already too late for me to get from Brize to Heathrow for my connecting shuttle to Edinburgh. Through the window, I looked down and saw the lit perimeter fence as we flew over it, buffeted by the wind. Then I heard the sound of the engines spooling up as the pilot aborted the landing to execute a 'go-around'. We went up into a holding pattern where the pilot announced that Brize was too risky, and he was re-routing to Heathrow. My heart soared higher than the Tristar at that news and I started calculating the odds of me catching the last shuttle. Christine would be waiting for me at Edinburgh Airport, and I had no way to warn her that I might be late or not arrive at all. We landed safely at Heathrow and, as an unscheduled arrival, we were herded into a makeshift lounge. There my heart dropped as I saw the dreaded Movement Controllers. We were going to be corralled like cattle and bussed to a nearby transit barracks only to return in the morning to fly to Brize so that I would then have to make my way back to Heathrow. It was absurd. I spoke to the Movements Controller who eyed me like the jaundiced DHSS character Martina used to look at the Boswell Family dole claimants in the 1980's sitcom Bread. I was his 'bitch' and would do as I was told. Suddenly, a side door opened and a Heathrow Airport Ground Stewardess appeared. She spoke briefly to the Movements Controller about organising our onward travel arrangements and I seized my chance. I can only describe what happened next as analogous to an 'interception try' in rugby! I told her I was booked onto the Edinburgh Shuttle, and could I catch it? The Movements Controller now looked more menacing than that Gaboon Viper I just wrote about. He claimed jurisdiction but the smiling stewardess wagged her finger and said, "My passenger, I think". She escorted me through the side door and then whizzed me around to Terminal 1 on an electric buggy for the Shuttle. The gate was about to close but she called ahead on a walkie-talkie. I boarded the Shuttle, hardly daring to believe I was en-route. For me, it was all meant to be; Karma if you like, but I was now absolutely sure, despite the massive loss of confidence I experienced after the acrimonious separation from my first wife, that Christine would become my soul mate and wife.

In late November 1983, I was tasked to provide EOD support to Police Scotland (then Strathclyde Police). There had been a theft of a large quantity of Special Gelatine 80 explosives from a mining location near Shotts. Intelligence had subsequently been gleaned by Special Branch which had identified who did it and who they were linked to. It was believed that both the Scottish Nationalist Liberation Army (SNLA) and the Irish National Liberation Army (INLA) were involved. Police surveillance had tracked INLA members coming over from Northern Ireland on a ferry, possibly using the cover of an Old Firm football match in Glasgow as cover.

The explosives had been divided up into two caches. One cache was in the boot of a car from where it was expected to be passed to the INLA. The second cache was in a tenement flat in Great Western Road. I had already discussed the optimum way to minimise disruption at the point of arrest and recommended to Special Branch that the arrest teams handcuff the suspects at scene and hold them there until I had recovered the explosives so that the scene would be categorised as an occupied find. The EOD protocol in those days for an occupied find meant the operator could deal with the scene expeditiously and without causing mayhem in the city. I was accommodated in the VIP Suite of the Pitt Street Police Office as the various suspects were being observed and followed. As the time of interception and arrest drew near, I was brought into the Special Branch operations room where surveillance radio traffic was being played on a tannoy. That date became infamous for another reason. It was the 17th of December 1983, and as we waited for the transfer to take place, we got word of the Harrods Bombing where three civilians and three police officers were killed. Over the tannoy, we heard the command issued for the arrest operation to start. The suspects offered no resistance and were quickly subdued and cuffed. We moved to the scene where the explosives, still in their original packaging, were recovered. On another occasion, the suspects in Great Western Road were arrested and held at the scene until I arrived. The explosives had been concealed in a bag in a fireplace. The case against the six accused came to court in early April 1984. I had asked for and received a witness anonymity arrangement whereby my identity, address and other personal details would not be stated in open court; written notes about me would instead be shown to the jury and both advocates. Despite this, the defence advocate argued that my anonymity would prejudice the case against his clients by giving the circumstances a sinister appearance. The day after my court witness appearance, the press published all of my details in their coverage of the case.

Christine and me then started planning for our future. We decided to marry just before I was due to go to Oman unaccompanied. I was entitled to request married accommodation for her in Edinburgh, in a surplus married quarter. We both wanted to marry in church; not for religious reasons, however. As a divorced man, I expected some push-back from the minister, but our wish was to celebrate our marriage in a communal and solemn way as distinct from the banal Registry Office experience I had in my first marriage. Fortunately, the minister didn't mind a bit and he agreed to marry us in church. The venue was really special. It was to be the thousand-year-old St Margaret's Chapel in Edinburgh Castle, on the Easter weekend, 21st April 1984. We hired the limousines of the two Scottish Brigade Commanders and Christine was brought in style from her family home in The Cornton, Stirling. At the Castle, the Guard turned out and did a Present Arms as the limousines crossed the drawbridge over the dry moat. There were thousands of tourists milling about, many of them Japanese with their new camcorders. The crowd parted to allow the limousines to drive up to the Half Moon Battery where Christine, on her dad's arm, alighted. The tourists thought it was an act to entertain them and many applauded. Me and my best man, Ron, watched from above at the door of the chapel, before scuttling inside to await the bride. She was piped in by Pipers from the Royal Scots and piped out after the ceremony to Mairi's Wedding, a traditional Scottish folk tune. We then moved to Cragiehall for our reception where Anna, Christine's cousin and chef, had done us proud with a magnificent buffet. By then, the RSM had moved on and had been replaced by a man of charm, dignity and empathy. He was also a Royal Scot and had become the President of the Mess as his battalion had celebrated the 350th anniversary of their founding. He gifted us a bottle of champagne at our reception.

CHAPTER 9

Loan Service in the Sultanate of Oman 1984–1986

I flew to Oman on the 7th of May 1984. My job was primarily a desk job in Force Ordnance Services where I would keep tabs on the ammunition stocks in the depots of the north and south, carry out EOD Duties, and conduct quarterly procurement reviews. I also carried out inspectorate duties in the north consisting of unit inspections and the investigation of ammunition performance failures, defects and accidents. Additionally, I would periodically fly down to southern Oman, to the Dhofar province, to stand in for the AT based in Salalah. This was Nick Nicholaides, who I mentioned earlier in chapter 3. My living accommodation was in Muaskar Al Murtafar (MAM) which was where the Omani MoD and Headquarters of their Armed Forces were co-located. I worked for an ex-RAOC retired lieutenant colonel who was on contract service as a major. In turn, he reported to a British contract officer who was serving as lieutenant colonel. He in turn reported to another retired British officer who was serving as the Head of FOS in the rank of full colonel. Over the next few months, this preponderance of retired British officers would reduce as the Omanis implemented a process called 'Omanisation' as more of their own gained sufficient qualifications and experience. At the time, the British Prime Minister was actively promoting a large arms sale agreement with Oman. Oman had a mixed inventory of arms and ammunition, procured from all over the world. This included Soviet and Chinese communist weapons and ammunition. We regularly hosted Arms Sales Teams as the Omanis upgraded their defence capabilities. However, whilst I was there, an economic crisis and fall in the price of oil hit the value of the US dollar to which the Omani Rial was linked.

When I arrived, the Daily Mail was running a series of investigative articles on corruption in Oman, perpetrated by British ex-patriates. There was a lot of it going on. Corruption, it seemed, was an embedded sub-culture in my opinion. There was also a big difference in propriety standards between Britain and Oman which meant that some trans-actions could be viewed as corrupt in Britain but compliant in Oman. I had no doubts whatsoever on that score and always measured my conduct by the values and standards expected of a British soldier. My own status was that I was still a member of the British Armed Forces and was seconded, or loaned, to the Sultan of Oman's Armed Forces (SOAF). In addition to the technical line management chain of com-mand over me, there was a Loan Service Office in the headquarters where a Regular British Army lieutenant colonel was my commanding officer. I lived in the No 4 Mess in MAM and the office was a ten-minute walk away. Life was pleasant and I found the work fascinating. I had never had a technical staff job before and I learned a great deal under the mentoring of Tom Galloway, who was now a contracted warrant officer in FOS, and Bob, who was still serving and was now a WO1. I was teetotal at the time and was struck early on by the incredible amount of binge-drinking, especially among the contracted warrant officers, Tom Galloway excepted. With Oman being a quite moderate Islamic country, we were permitted to drink alcohol within the mess, and our diet included those items usually proscribed in Islamic culture. The majority of mess members were contractors. Typically, they would have served a career in the British Army and then come to Oman as ex-patriate contractors. They were not subject to British Military law, and they usually had fixed working hours and limits on their personal liability in terms of what they could be ordered to do. Most were quite amiable. Some were a downright liability. There was a contract warrant officer stereotype. They weren't a majority by any means, but they had easily observable traits. They were approaching middle age, they were now earning a relatively high salary, the children had grown up and left home and their wives, now alone at home, had established themselves in new careers; some were conducting extra-marital affairs. We knew this because the men concerned would binge-drink to extreme and then pour out their sorrows in the bar. Some would be homesick and would spend a fortune on phone calls home. This led to them running up horrendous bills. They would then be caught in a trap; they couldn't afford to resign and return home. The worst ones would have their passports confiscated so they couldn't do a runner back to Blighty and leave unpaid bills behind them. Perhaps for some of them, this made the taking of bribes more palatable, but the things I witnessed in Oman reinforced my own views that the most well-off were often the greediest. On my regular forays down south, the main effort was battle area clearance (BAC). This is normally a Royal Engineer task but there were no established RE assets then to do this. The Salalah Plain was absolutely carpeted with unexploded ordnance from the Dhofar War. The War had seen prodigious amounts of ammunition fired at the adoo (enemy). At the time, Oman was a very backward country, and the Sultan was quite isolationist. His son and heir, Qaboos, was a more worldly man and had been trained at the Royal Military Academy Sandhurst before serving with the British Army with The Cameronians

(Scottish Rifles). It was rumoured that Qaboos was placed with them as his short stature would not stand out as they too were allegedly of short stature. On his return to Oman, his father kept him isolated in a palace in Dhofar. In 1970, with the help of British Special Forces, Qaboos mounted a coup d'état and succeeded to the throne. He implemented modernisation, put down a communist rebellion in the south and ended Oman's isolation.

The situation with the vast amounts of unexploded ordnance was quite serious. Nick Nicholaides dealt with many thousands of unexploded objects in his twenty months and, when he eventually left, he was awarded the Sultan's Distinguished Service Medal (WKhM). My own tally was in the mere hundreds, but the work was fascinating, sometimes funny and sometimes quite dangerous. There was a high casualty rate amongst civilians who were handling blinds (failed to explode) and so Oman implemented a bounty scheme whereby Omanis discovering ordnance would be rewarded substantially. This triggered something of a job opportunity scheme and some Omanis would actively seek out unexploded ordnance. It got to extremes when some of the more avid collectors started to cache their burgeoning collections in case they were stolen. This could mean you might respond to the discovery of a mortar bomb only to find that you would be directed to a cave where there could be hundreds of blinds, some in a very dangerous condition. We did a study on the blind rate and our finding indicated that up to 30% of all shells and mortars fired failed to explode. The causes were usually the poor storage environment and fuze mechanisms which failed to detonate in the very harsh terrain where they were fired. There was another quite bizarre phenomenon. Sometimes you were taken to the base of what looked like a termite mound on the Salalah Plain where there would be an exposed shell or mortar bomb. On investigation, you could find dozens of projectiles clustered tightly together at or just under ground level. These were not termite mounds, however. They were symmetrical, cone-shaped mounds varying from a metre to 5 metres in height. I formed a theory about what was going on.

In southern Oman, there is an annual monsoon called the Khareef where the monsoon blows dense clouds and fog in from the Indian Ocean. This would inundate the dry, hard-packed clay of the plain with heavy rainfall for about three months. The temperature would plummet and in days, the arid, apparently sterile ground would erupt into dense vegetation. After three months, the clouds would vanish and the hot arid conditions would return. It seemed to me that the deep clay on the plain was being subjected to a slow, swirling seasonal movement, somewhat similar to a convection current. Shells and mortars being extremely heavy for their size were being graded and collated as they moved, something like the grading of rocks in glacial till. Whatever! I learned very quickly to carefully excavate around these conical mounds whenever faced with a shell or bomb in case it was just one of many; the veritable tip of an iceberg in the desert. How's that for mixing my metaphors?

This was one of the smaller mounds where several blinds had been amassed.

An Omani family poses with a policeman next to a blind shell. The policeman had to countersign the claim form for the family to receive the bounty which, for this item, would have been about £30 in Sterling.

In 1984, action was taken to proactively deal with the large numbers of blinds still visible on the surface, on the Salalah Plain. All available EOD personnel were assembled at Um Al Gwariff and we were joined by an Omani infantry battalion. This was to be Operation Al Hadh, a large-scale clearance operation where the infantry would sweep across the Plain in organised segments and each soldier was to mark anything suspicious with a small pennant mounted on a stick. We followed along behind, investigating all discoveries and destroying them in situ if required, once the advancing infantry were sufficiently far ahead to be out of harm's way. We made excellent progress until two armed Jebali men robustly stopped the entire battalion. In our terms, we would say there was a certain lawlessness there at the time. Culturally, Oman was still in transition from the Dhofar War, tribalism was evident and, although every Omani I met was almost invariably friendly, they were no pushover when it came to confrontation. The Jebalis of the hills were especially resilient and distinct from the lowland population in language and customs. Once the two Jebali men had been treated with the respect they demanded, and were reassured that the operation was only to clear the menace of unexploded ammunition, honour was restored. An impromptu meal was had, the two men were introduced to us, and all was smiles. The operation resumed and was successful, albeit this was temporary due to the aforementioned way that blinds would erupt back up onto the surface the following year.

Uncompromising confrontation Jebali style

One of my various duties was to stand in for my boss whenever he was out of the country. We shared a two-man office with our desks joined in the middle. Behind him was a steel cabinet which he kept locked as it contained sensitive information relating to ammunition. While he was away on leave, I needed to open the locker to file the latest ammunition stock states in the two main depots. He had left me the key for that very purpose. When I opened the locker, my eye was drawn to a small pile of completed EOD Reports. That concerned me as one of my jobs was to check and file them on receipt. Someone had extracted a lot of reports. I could see they were originals and not copies and then I noticed that white error correction fluid had been applied to each report over the box where the operator would list the explosives used to complete the task. Under the pile of reports was a transmission copy of a telex. The transmission journal in the header indicated it had been sent from a travel agency just outside the base to the potential supplier of PE N1509. I read the telex which said that in-country experience with PE N1509 explosives in the EOD role had been most favourable and copies of the (amended) EOD reports would be forwarded to the Omani Procurement staff to show that instead of PE4 and C4, PE N1509 had been used which was far cheaper and just as good. Some of the reports were actually my own and I knew for certain that I had never tried to use PE N1509 in the EOD role. There was a good reason. PE N1509 explosive lacks the shattering power (sometimes called brisance) to detonate thick-walled unexploded projectiles. PE4 and the US equivalent C4 were always the explosive of first choice. As I also carried out provision reviews, I knew there was a huge price differential between PE4/C4 and PE N1509. I had discovered clear evidence of corruption and the issue was compounded because sub-calibre explosives could increase the risk of avoidable harm on EOD tasks.

My boss came back from his leave and I pondered whether I should mention the adulterated reports. I decided against it, preferring to consult my more senior colleagues first but he then started asking me about my leave plans and whether I was going to purchase an additional flight to enable an extra visit home. Loan Service personnel were entitled to three flights home in their 20-month tour plus one family visit, all at no cost. It was common practice to purchase an additional flight and reduce the three leave periods by a week each to create an additional leave period. He said he had a friend in a nearby travel agency who could fix me up with a free flight. It was the same travel agency as the one that telexed the false report to the PE N1509 supplier. That telex terminal was safely beyond the scrutiny of the Omani MoD officials. I knew this was a slippery slope and the conversation confirmed his corruption to me. I declined the offer.

I took the evidence of this corruption to my Loan Service Commanding Officer and requested an urgent interview. I briefed him on what I had discovered and what it meant. He then asked me to wait outside while he discussed the matter with his Adjutant. After a few minutes, I was called back in. I was given two options: Firstly, I could persist with my allegation which would impugn my boss and the Omani owner of the travel agency who was also a senior official in the Omani MoD. It would result in my immediate deportation from the country. Or, secondly, I could keep quiet about the matter and there would be no further action. I was gobsmacked. I took the easy way out and kept my mouth shut.

I mentioned that I conducted provisioning reviews. These happened every three months and three of us would work overtime on them for about ten days. Every single type of ammunition in Oman was listed on its own bespoke, templated paper spreadsheet. The spreadsheet was on A3-sized sheets of paper, two sheets per item, with all four sides to be filled in. It was laborious, number-crunching work. At the time, my primary leisure activity was computer programming on the back of the rapidly expanding personal computer revolution. In the office, we had networked Wang computers and the software included the Microsoft Multiplan spreadsheeting programme. There was an empty office next door to ours and there was a spare computer terminal and printer in it. I was confident in principle that I could create a Multiplan calculator to do the provision reviews automatically. The capability was there, I just needed to learn the application and then create a calculator. I started small and modelled the simpler natures of ammunition. I won't bore you with the detail; suffice it to say that four sides of A3 paper is a lot of detail. I slowly built the Multiplan calculator and eventually managed to include every single item on the inventory. For each nature, the variable data such as consumption rates, war reserve minimum holdings, pipeline times, costs, entitlements and depot stock holdings were listed. To conduct a provisioning review, the main effort henceforth was to input the latest depot stock return and then hit Shift F1 which started the recalculation. In those days of 8-bit computers, they worked slowly, and you could actually watch the numbers on the screen changing as they were being crunched. I sent for the boss and demonstrated the new automated provisioning review. He sent for his boss who sent for his boss, and it was back-slaps all round. If they had known I had grassed them up for corruption, I was instantly forgiven. I had just automated one of the most laborious and boring tasks known to man.

One day, I was given the task of dealing with an unexploded 60lb rocket which had been found near the top of a sheer mountain in the Jebel Akhdar (the green mountains). I was to take two Omani AT staff sergeants and mentor them in what would be their first experience of EOD outside of training. We were to fly there by helicopter which pleased me. The Jebel Akhdar is almost 10,000 feet high in places and is extremely rugged. The 60 lb rocket was a leftover from the 1957 rebellion when RAF Jet Provosts attacked the rebels.

We boarded a SOAF Bell UH1D in MAM and flew over the flat desert towards the sheer escarpment that marked the climb up into the mountains. There were five of us onboard: Pilot up front in the right-hand seat, Loadmaster in the back cabin on the forward seat, sat with his back to the pilot, an Omani AT sat on the forward seat, left-hand side, me on the rear seat sat to the left side and the remaining Omani AT sat on the right rear of the cabin. We were many thousands of feet up and we continued to climb in a corkscrew pattern, occasionally buffeted by turbulence which I thought was unremarkable given the proximity of the mountains. The buffeting worsened, however, and then the Loadmaster did something quite inexplicable. He gestured to my Omani colleague sat in front of me to pass him a smoke grenade from the ready-use rack on our side of the cabin. These smoke grenades were not a type I was familiar with. They were small cans with screw tops on them and as he received one, he unscrewed it, revealing a small lanyard which I assumed would ignite the grenade if it was pulled. He placed the prepared grenade on the seat next to him and gestured for another. I think he had eventually gotten four of these smoke grenades prepared for igniting before he stopped and sat still. My colleagues looked at me with apparent alarm. We couldn't talk to the Loadmaster as he was wearing a helmet and we weren't, so we were not on the intercom system. The Loadmaster then appeared to shut down. He made no effort to communicate with us which contributed to an increasing uneasiness. The turbulence worsened. This aircraft type allowed rear passengers to see into the cockpit and I looked to see what the pilot was doing. He was making somewhat rapid and exaggerated movements of the cyclic column. In front of him, I could see that two warning lights were illuminated. One was for the rotor RPM and the other was a Master Caution. The aircraft movements became twitchy. The smoke grenade thing simply made no sense. Helicopter crews sometimes drop smoke at low altitude so the pilot can judge wind conditions in a prospective landing area. They can also be used as a signal to search teams, but we were far too high. Apart from that, there was now a possibility that a grenade could be accidentally ignited inside the aircraft. This would blind the pilot and could cause asphyxiation. The engine compartment was behind me, and I could see the main rotor above me through the green plexiglass roof. The engine note started to run down and the flickering shadow of the rotor as it spun above me seemed to slow down. I watched the pilot closely for a clue as to what was happening. He was completely preoccupied with the controls, and I saw him lower his collective pitch lever. The aircraft was now plummeting downwards, and the pilot pointed the nose down and we accelerated. I could hear the airframe rattling and vibrating now as the engine note had died away. I could see the desert far below us through the windscreen and to my left I could see the horizon. The initial sense in the pit of my stomach of going down passed. I started thinking through my options in the few seconds remaining before we either crashed or the pilot managed an auto-rotation landing. Trouble was, the main rotor was visibly too slow and the rotor RPM warning light was still glowing. To my left, I saw a yellow-striped pull cable which was an emergency door jettison. In my lap, I had a demolition box containing explosives. Aside from a lethal heavy impact, I knew that fire in a downed aircraft was another major cause of death or injury. I weighed up my chances of judging the time perfectly to jettison the door so I could throw the demolition box clear before we crashed. I had a passing thought that Christine would be mad at me if this ended in disaster. But, oddly enough, I didn't feel scared; I was quite calm and constantly alert. I gestured to my colleagues to tighten their straps. We were by now much closer to the desert. The nose of the aircraft started to come up very gradually and the pilot had started to raise his collective pitch lever. The rotor blades started slapping as they bit into the air. We transitioned into fast-forward flight, close to the desert floor. More collective pitch was applied, and we shuddered as the aircraft started to slow. I could see the desert floor clearly now and it had a consistency to it of soft yellowy-brown talcum powder with no sign of boulders or other hazards that could spell disaster. The aircraft went into a flare and we touched down, skids on sand, unexpectedly quite smoothly. We slid along before gently coming to a stop with a slight twitch to the left. Then everything was quiet except for a loud whining noise coming from the cockpit dashboard which I assumed was a gyroscope running down. Behind me, the engine was silent except for the ticking noise of a still-hot engine that was cooling down. We got out and the pilot said he had called for help which was now on the way. Sometime later, a SOAF Hawker Hunter jet, flying low and fast, flew over us. A little while later, another Bell UH1 appeared and landed beside us. We were given the option of waiting to see if the first aircraft could be repaired or would we prefer to continue to the mountain top in the second aircraft? I voted with my feet, followed by two bemused Omani ATs. To be fair, we continued up the mountain, located the blind rocket warhead and destroyed it in situ. To get us in, the second pilot put the left-hand skid on a large boulder, and we exited on that side; to our right was a sheer drop. My colleagues were calm throughout and took everything in their stride. I found a renewed respect for them.

The Huey just after landing safely

The blind 60 lb rocket warhead

I took home leave after the Christmas break in January 1985. We had each been sent what passed for an 'Islamic Christmas card'; this was a card from the senior Omani Commander which offered us congratulations and blessings on the birthday of the prophet Jesus and that we could have that day off unless we were committed to unavoidable duties. In the mess, Tom and Bob were hoping to arrange a Burns Supper, due a few days after my return from leave. I offered to bring back some haggis for the supper. I bought several before the journey back and froze them, storing them in an insulated bag in my suitcase. On arrival, I went to the customs desk and was asked to open my case. When the Omani customs officer saw the still-frozen haggis, he asked what they were. I explained what haggis was and why I was bringing it back with me. He fixed me with a suspicious eye and asked, "Is this the meat of the pig?" I replied that it wasn't. He checked the ingredients label. I had already done this, and the haggis was pure. His suspicions couldn't be assuaged. More officials were summoned and a gaggle of them debated what to do next. Eventually, a decision was reached. "We will keep this haggis here and have it tested." There was no point protesting. I was picked up by a colleague and taken to MAM. About six weeks later, I got a call from the airport. I was told the haggis was only of sheep meat, not pork, and then asked if I would collect it straight away as it smelled awful. I declined the invitation and wrote the experience off to a clash of cultures.

All of a sudden, it was time for my annual confidential report. I was summoned to the Loan Service Office, and I marched into the CO's office and saluted. My report was slid towards me and I was asked to sign it. I picked it up first to read it and noticed a flash of irritation across the CO's face. I read it and was disappointed. At that time, I had been a staff sergeant for five years and this report was medio-cre. I felt I deserved better. This officer had only seen me once and wouldn't have a clue about me. The narrative in the report contained several inaccuracies. I asked if I might discuss the report content and the flash of irritation went from ephemeral to persistent. He was well unhappy. Inwardly, I thought I'd blown it, but he gruffly agreed to listen to my critique. He listened as I reported the inaccuracies. I was on safe ground with these as they were factual and not subjective; I didn't want to gift this guy any slack. I was asked to leave and come back later. When I did, the report was slid forward with the comment, "I suppose you'd like to check it?" I did; version two was considerably better. I signed the report, saluted and marched out. The adjutant was waiting for me outside, and I was reproached for requesting last-minute changes. I was going to go with a swift riposte about the lack of consultation and warning but decided to quit while I was ahead and let it go; the worm had turned.

Loan Service personnel were entitled to a family visit. Oman was then a closed state and all visitors had to have a sound reason for coming in. As my wife, Christine ticked all the boxes. She had saved up all of her annual leave and she was going to spend a month with me. Our reunion in-country was amazing. She arrived at the start of the holy month of Ramadan in May 1985. The weather was extremely hot, even for north Oman and the mercury topped 50 degrees C several times. I worked during her visit, and she was obliged to languish poolside, in the mess, waiting for me to finish. The shade and waiter service was most welcome but the pool was too hot to get into! I took her on several visits including to Izki, where local Arab men competed for her attention in an amusing and almost childish manner. One of them captured a dozen small black scorpions from a nest at the base of a wall, deftly snipping off their poisonous stings before dropping them into Christine's hands. I thought she would panic but she took it all in her stride. She loved Omani sunsets on the shores of the Indian Ocean, the souks (markets) and touring the many ancient settlements. Her visit came to an end all too soon and our separation continued. By now, I had seven months left of my tour with one more home leave left for the autumn.

Beads, anyone?

Beautiful bolts of cloth in the souk

Sunset over Christine & the Indian Ocean

Respite from the sun in an oasis

In our office in MAM, we were looked after by a Pakistani contract military clerk called Mohammed Abbasi. Mohammed was a devout Muslim with an uncompromising devotion to his religion. He had a kindly and caring nature, was invariably polite and was always willing to go the extra mile to please us. When activity levels allowed, he would ask after our families and speak with great pride and humility about his own. There was also a sadness about his circumstances. Mohammed had been in the Pakistani Army. He had been captured somehow by Indian troops and was ultimately released. Repatriated prisoners could face great opprobrium over their perceived disgraceful conduct in allowing themselves to be captured alive. This made employment at home very difficult and there was no prospect for him to remain in the Army. Like many of his colleagues, he entered into contract service in the Omani MoD. There was a mixed bunch of both Pakistani and Indian ex-military clerks in our headquarters, and they got on cordially at work. Their pay was better than they could get in their home countries but, for clerks below the rank of sergeant, they could only go on home leave once a year. Mohammed was only a corporal. He was a committed family man. Back home, he had inherited a small holding, which was farmed by his family, consisting of a wife and six daughters. He was especially proud of his water buffalo. With great pride, he would speak of his nephew whom he was sponsoring at college. When I arrived in Oman, Mohammed went to great pains to make me welcome and was fascinated to learn that I had recently married. He asked me if my wife was 'with child'; it wasn't impertinence. He needed to know that God's will was being enacted. When I said Christine wasn't expecting, he asked if I had yet 'known' her, and I replied that I had. He said he would go to the mosque and pray for us. After several months, my first leave drew near. Mohammed was greatly excited and wished for Christine to be with child by the time I returned; in fact, he would make it certain with extra visits to the mosque. When I returned, he was waiting for me. With the sparkling eyes of anticipation of a child at Christmas, he asked, "And is your good lady with child?" I replied that she wasn't. He was crestfallen and asked for permission to fall out and visit the mosque to pray for me. When he returned, he asked if I had "known her" to which I replied that I had. He was clearly quite distressed, and I felt moved to explain that we weren't quite ready to start a family. I spoke of family planning. "What is this?" he pleaded. I explained the contraceptive pill to him. He rushed off to the mosque at this apparent heresy. When he came back, I noticed that he was much at ease and there was mischief in his eyes. Making sure he could not be overheard, he approached me closely and whispered coyly in my ear if I could get some of these pills for him before his next visit home!

At the end of October 1984, I noticed a sudden change in the clerical staff; they had become sullen and subdued. I sought out Mohammed in his office to find out what was up. In the background, an Urdu language radio programme was on, and I heard a voice speaking. The only words I recognised were 'Indira Gandhi'. Mohammed was tearful and very distressed. "Please, Sir, Prime Minister Gandhi has been assassinated." The news was shocking, but I didn't understand why a Pakistani man would be so upset. It turned out Mohammed was a hugely empathetic man, and his distress was caused by seeing the distress of his Indian counterparts. Such was the man; the sweetest and humblest man I ever met. In 1985, we unanimously considered that Mohammed was worthy of promotion to sergeant. My warrant officer colleagues, and the boss, lobbied on his behalf and Mohammed was overjoyed to be made up to sergeant. He would now be entitled to two leave periods per year, but thankfully, he didn't come asking for contraceptive pills again!

The consequences of corruption struck again when an Omani infantry soldier experienced an apparent negligent discharge on the rifle ranges when he was participating in a trial of rifle grenades. This trial was to evaluate a new rifle grenade of the type known as 'Bullet Trap Universal' (BTU). The first generation of rifle grenades required that a soldier unload his conventional rifle ammunition and reload with bespoke ballistite cartridges which were designed to propel the grenade when the rifle was fired in the usual way. This meant the firer's weapon could not be used conventionally until the normal ammunition had been reloaded. The BTU grenades were designed to fit over the muzzle of the rifle and were designed to withstand a normal ball round being fired into their base and this kinetic energy would propel them towards the target. There was no mucking about with unconventional cartridges and the rifle could be fired normally as soon as the grenade launched. The incident on the range was quite alarming. An Omani soldier fired a BTU grenade, but, as the grenade cleared the muzzle, his rifle fired again and the second round struck the now-airborne grenade, passing through it and causing it to tumble onto the ground in front of the firer. Smoke from the holed grenade was emitted for a few seconds which must have been quite concerning. Initially, an 'error of drill' was suspected. The way the Steyr AUG rifle fired was a feature of its 'progressive trigger'. The first pressure on the trigger gave semi-automatic fire, and pulling the trigger completely back gave automatic fire. The Omani soldier who fired the grenade was seen to be struggling somewhat to maintain an appropriate posture and it was thought he had accidentally pulled the trigger fully rearwards as he tried to keep the weapon aligned correctly. This was proved wrong, and suspicions turned towards either the rifle or the ball ammunition when accidental discharges were encountered when the rifle was being fired conventionally. The rifle was seen to fire spontaneously when being cocked, which is a very dangerous defect.

The investigation into this defect was complex and the mechanism of failure was not understood. This was a worrying matter as the Steyr AUG in 5.56mm calibre was now the primary personal weapon for all of the Sultan of Oman's Armed Forces. We knew the floating firing pin would contact the percussion cap when the rifle was cocked, but this was common to most, if not all, floating firing pin mechanisms in guns that fired from a closed breech. The primary suspicion then fell on the ammunition. The Omani MoD had procured tens of millions of rounds of 5.56mm ball ammunition from an overseas manufacturer. The procurement had been strongly influenced by a British ex-patriate retired Army officer who had been hosted on a visit to the manufacturer's country and he allegedly approved the purchase order personally, despite not having any ammunition technical qualifications or experience in this area. A sample of this ammunition was forwarded to a world-renowned testing laboratory; their report was shocking. It turned out that the metal forming the percussion cap was only half the thickness of the standard specification for this type of ammunition. When this was appreciated, the weapon specifications were examined and tested. The firing pin was found to be comparatively heavy. This combination of ammunition and weapons would never be safe unless all of the weapons in-country were modified. A modification was made whereby the firing pins were swapped out for a lighter version and the firing pin retaining spring was strengthened. This solved the problem but left the whiff of suspicion that, at best, the procurement process was badly flawed, or, at worst, the procuring officer was corrupt.

My Loan Service tour ended in the early New Year of 1986. I was overjoyed to be going home. We had saved very hard and had accumulated enough money to put a deposit on our first home. I was also saddened to leave Oman. I had an eventful tour behind me, and I had learned a lot. I had been promoted to warrant officer class two and was posted to the British Army headquarters at Rheindahlen, Germany. But that could wait; I now had three months of post-tour leave to enjoy. I looked forward to watching the launch of the Challenger Shuttle at the end of the month. The shuttles seemed to have made safe space flight a routine reality; but how wrong I was!

CHAPTER 10

HQ British Army of the Rhine 1986–1987

Ⅰarrived here in the spring of 1986. I travelled ahead of Christine and took over our married quarter, 41 Appleby Walk, which was on the base. I knew from my former landlords in Paderborn that German folk referred to Rheindahlen as 'Little England' and just about the only thing on camp to remind you of Germany was the side of the road you drove on. This change in environment suited Christine well. She had given up her job as a shoe-shop manageress. She found the whole retail experience to be stressful, from the everlasting pursuit of sales targets to the periodic stock checks. I didn't know until then that she suffered from obsessive-compulsive disorder (OCD). In fact, I didn't know what that was. I had noticed that she would repeatedly check door locks at her shop and would often insist on returning home if we had gone out so she could check her curling tongs hadn't been left on. Ever being a pragmatist and not understanding how OCD was caused, I contrived coping strategies to address the symptoms. I had her curling tongs connected to the mains via a timer so if she forgot to turn them off, they would be switched off automatically and I provided a heatproof base to sit them on. With door-locking, I would sit her in the car and do the security check myself. She would appear in the house halfway through my checks to reassure herself that the house was secure, and I would get angry because I didn't understand. I wanted to because I could see this was a big issue for her. However, as we settled in Rheindahlen, she made friends, started night-school, got a job on camp under the Army Dependant employment scheme and started to relax into her new life. Years later, as her terminal illness progressed, she said that Rheindahlen and Herford had been the happiest times in her life. Our married quarter in Appleby Walk was an end-terraced house with a garden. Between the gardens were belts of trees, mostly silver birch. Of very special delight to us, and especially her, we had a regular visitor; a red squirrel we named Rocky. He was quite tame and would come into our lounge from the garden through the French window doors. He was a fiery red colour with a beautifully contrasting white bib on his chest. During our separation whilst I was in Oman, we had saved hard, and we now had enough to put a deposit down on a house. Her childhood dream was to own a home in Dunblane. She had grown up in The Cornton in Stirling, and on warm summer days, the family would visit Dunblane and play in the Laigh Hills Park and swim in the Allan Water. The Cornton was acknowledged to be a deprived area with significant alcohol, drug and crime issues. But it also housed some tight-knit communities of good folk with great integrity on modest incomes who looked out for each other. The dream home in Dunblane materialised and was in Strathmore Avenue. It was a semi-detached house in a picturesque setting, but we were obliged to let it out as we were overseas in Germany. No matter; we had our own home, and it was in Dunblane.

On the job front, I was employed in Supply Branch in the main headquarters. This was an expansive, sprawling building which was a maze of corridors. At each intersection of corridors, there was a ceiling-mounted clock, and these provided navigational cues to help the unfamiliar find their way around. My own office was located inside a secluded secure zone which opened out into the so-called F Corridor, and resembled a barred, single cell you might associate with solitary confinement. The original windows had been removed and replaced with semi-opaque glass blocks. These allowed natural light in, but you couldn't see outside. Inside, there was just enough room for a desk and a cupboard. On the desk was a computer. My job title involved ammo operations and plans but there was a long overdue project which I was assigned to and, as soon as I heard what it was, I could understand why it was overdue. Some years earlier, there had been some ground-breaking work on how much ammunition an army might need to fight an intensive war. For the first time, this study identified specifically that, during war fighting, men and equipment would be lost to attrition which begged the question of why we should provide 100% of the ammunition required for all of the men for all of the forthcoming battles against an assumption that there would be no combat losses. This study was known as the Battle Attrition Study (BAS). There was also a study to identify how much ammunition each soldier and weapon platform would need in order to fight an intensive war over a set period of 'battle days', which was an attempt to produce a scaling which would hold true and suit a variety of war scenarios. This study resulted in a document known as the Revised Ammunition Rates and Scales (RARS). My project was to bring these two pieces of work together and produce a new plan for general warfare in Europe known as the 'BAOR Mobilisation Instruction No 1'. At the time, this work was very sensitive but that was almost 40 years ago and was in the Cold War era. What it meant was that I worked in isolation, but I needed to collaborate closely with other staff branches. My first attempts to do this were farcical and, yet again, alcohol was at the root of the trouble. Branches would frequently hold drinking sessions in the workplace during the working week, and because many of them were housed in secure enclaves, prying eyes could be kept away. I found it quite difficult to pin down sufficient responsible officers with whom to collaborate. I was a subject matter expert, confident in my own field, but I needed input from the other branches to underpin my planning assumptions. I seemed to be struggling against a view that everything would be alright on the day, and I was being a pedant. This was long before the time when the British Army developed and then espoused their so-called Values and Standards. There was no recent experience of general land warfare to act as a reference point and the Falklands War, four years earlier, was probably seen as largely irrelevant to battle planning in Europe as this was an expeditionary war conducted thousands of miles away. There was also a general sense that the Warsaw Pact was in decline and the Russians were bogged down in Afghanistan. This was hardly a fertile environment in which to promote highly detailed war planning with the other branches in the headquarters, but my project had been handed to me with a deadline, which, although it felt somewhat ambitious, I would try to meet despite the disruptive 'speakeasy' climate which seemed endemic in the headquarters.

Just around the corner from my 'cell' was a coffee vending machine; no frills, just coffee so viscous you could stand your spoon up in it. The nature of my project called for long periods of concentration. I needed caffeine and I ended up drinking several cups a day. Then I noticed I was getting massive, banging headaches on the weekends but within a few minutes of starting work the next Monday, I would be fine. The penny dropped; I was now a caffeine addict! I weaned myself off the stuff and haven't taken coffee regularly since. Whilst my job was primarily in an office working on this project, I was also on the duty roster for EOD duties. Under host-nation agreements, we had primacy in the

UK bases. Early one morning, the Royal Military Police (RMP) Duty Room staff phoned to say a suspected IED had been found in an Army staff car in the Motor Transport (MT) pool in Rheindahlen. A military driver had been doing his first parade checks before driving away and had found an object in the boot. I responded in the usual way. On arrival, I found that the boot lid had been left wide open (you wouldn't believe how many people lock suspected bombs away) and so it was a simple matter to use the Wheelbarrow and take a look. The device I saw on the monitor was one of the best-looking IEDs I had ever seen. I was convinced it was real so immediately put a call through to my boss to advise him of what I was dealing with. I then used a disrupter to neutralise the IED and, in the aftermath, I could see the results were excellent. The components were beautifully separated, and I was content to conduct a final clearance. As my eyes became accustomed to the gloom inside the boot, I noticed a white label on the outer casing of the container. It was an RAF Police and Security Service identification label which identified the object as a tactical evaluation (TACEVAL) device, to be used in testing unit drills. There was a contact telephone number on the label, so, in an atmosphere of farce, I called the number and reported the find, including the disruption and damage to the staff car caused by their negligence. (Over 30 years later, I was having a security-related conversation with a senior RAF Officer who told me of his IED experiences in Rheindahlen in the 1980s. He said enough to establish that he was the one who had misplaced the device. Did I spare his blushes? Not a bit of it!)

I got pinged at Rheindahlen for what was to be my second involvement at a court martial. The first one was at Paderborn when I was a sergeant, and I was nominated to act as the Court Orderly. The case descended into pure farce. The accused was nick-named Peanuts. All he wanted was to leave the Army. He had a girlfriend in the UK and missed her badly. He became difficult to manage so, in an example of bizarre military logic, this young man who was broke and had debts, was made the barman in the sergeant's mess. He was accommodated in a small bunk in the attic above the bar. He would sleep by day and work behind the bar at night. There was none of the supervision you might reasonably expect was appropriate for his circumstances. He went absent; it was alleged he had absconded with the bar takings, and he was apprehended. While waiting to be disciplined for these offences, he went downtown and got drunk. On his way back to barracks, something caught his attention in a closed newspaper kiosk. He claimed he tried to illuminate the object of his curiosity with his lighter. This resulted in some paper igniting and a small fire broke out. He then tried to urinate on the fire to extinguish it and, as he did so, the Polizei pounced. As he spun round to confront whoever had accosted him, he urinated on the hapless policeman. As the Court Orderly, it was difficult to keep a straight face as he was charged in court for a litany of pathetic and oh, so predictable acts of daftness. His case had not been managed competently and he had been illegally detained in the unit guardroom, pending trial. He was dismissed from the service and his sentence of detention was deemed spent by his time already spent in jail.

The second case was quite different. This time it was a warrant officer who had been accused of shoplifting. I was to be his court escort. He was a very tight-lipped man and hardly spoke during our time together. The court martial took place during a spell of very hot weather and the court was adjourned as we sweltered, and a request was made for all present to remove jackets. At this point, I shat my pants because under my No 2 Dress jacket, my shirt had no sleeves! (Don't ask - it's a long story). The President declined, much to my sweaty relief and we persevered. There was a public gallery which was occupied by about 20 German civilians. The accused was almost at the end of his service and was quite portly. The point I am trying to make here is that if he was to be judged on his appearance, he was going down. He had a lot to lose. He had been detained by a German store detective and the matter was referred to the Royal Military Police via the German police. It seemed to be an open-and-shut case of theft. There was no discretion available, and the matter had to go to a court martial. The prosecution case was brutally simple and brief. The defence case was, however, brilliant by comparison. The German store detective had already given in evidence that she was alerted to the accused's potential for shoplifting because he had a certain glazed look about him of a person preoccupied by some sort of psychological illness, so she followed him because she had seen that many times before. He had allegedly taken an item of clothing and went to leave the store. At that point, he was detained, and the German police called. She went on to explain that a German civilian in these circumstances would likely not be prosecuted and would instead be referred for counselling or treatment for depression. She said she was shocked to see that he was now facing a court martial. The German public in the gallery were clearly sympathetic towards the accused and, as the case proceeded, many of them tutted their disapproval of his treatment. It came out in evidence that his family were in the UK as his daughter was disabled and could not be taken abroad. He had a fine record of service and prior sporting prowess. It seemed that his posting to Germany with the consequential separation from his family had precipitated a bout of depressive illness. By now, the public gallery was fuming. I felt awful for him. It seemed to me inevitable that he would be found guilty, and his life would be trashed. The court adjourned as the panel considered the verdict. It didn't take long, and we marched back in. The verdict was not guilty, and he was told he was free to leave without a blemish on his record. When we got back into the holding room, he was desperate to use the phone. As I sat there, he called his wife, who, up until that point, had no idea of what had happened. He completely broke down as they talked. After a few minutes, he calmed down and regained a measure of composure. I took his hand and shook it firmly, congratulating him on the outcome and commiserating with his misfortunes. The verdict was bang on, and I thought he had been treated terribly. It reiterated to me, as had the first court martial, the importance of 'hiring silk' if you were going to be court-martialled because there was no way I would ever leave that to a military defending officer.

There was a meeting one day for Supply Branch staff in the main registry. After the usual updates, one of the senior officers held up a computer print-out which was a list of defaulters, and his mission was to expose them. I will explain. In the RAOC, we had a Corps Gazette which was a monthly magazine, bedevilled by financial woes. In an effort to preserve a sustainable future for the gazette, the RAOC had come up with a solution whereby soldiers would 'volunteer' to contribute one day's pay per annum and, in return, they would receive a gazette and would be included in an insurance scheme which would provide additional benefits cover where the MoD's liability arrangements were not applicable. Technically, subscribers were supposed to volunteer but there was a lot of 'arm-twisting' and unit commanders were expected to maximise the uptake of the scheme in their units. I was not a member of the scheme. The print was held aloft for all to see, and the officer read out entries in the 'list of shame'. After talking about several well-known RAOC units in Germany, he noticed that there was a defaulter in our very own Supply Branch. "Q Robinson is on this list;

there must be a mistake!" he exclaimed. Everyone looked at me. I declared it was no mistake and I did not subscribe. Cue gasps all round at this heresy. An explanation was demanded. I told the audience that the RAOC Gazette had published my obituary in 1981, and I was not prepared to subscribe to such a publication. This reply was met with considerable scepticism. I knew where the Supply Branch archive of gazettes was kept so I excused myself and retrieved the September 1981 copy and turned to Page 371 and read out the death notice which I then brandished with some defiance. It was 'no contest'. Not even the Superintending Clerk had the neck to press the matter. I returned to my solitary confinement and the BAS/RARS project.

In the autumn, I had a call from our technical directorate in the UK. The call was from our very own 'Grim Reaper' and I have written about this in the next chapter, Chapter 11, which covers my EOD tour in Bessbrook Mill. I was completely immersed in my scaling project at the time and had progressed beyond designing my approach and methodology. I was now researching the hundreds of individual units and producing scaling documents for each of them. This work was highly detailed and very intense. I had reached a critical stage and was making excellent progress but now I was going to have to interrupt the work and deploy to pre-operational training and the tour itself. I was left with mixed feelings. I was keen to finish the project but knew that I would have to focus all of my energy on the forthcoming tour.

Then I learned that I had been selected for promotion to Warrant Officer Class One. Immediately after this, I got word of my first short-listing for a commission in the RAOC. Life was suddenly getting hectic. My promotion would take effect in the summer of the following year and would trigger a posting after I returned from Bessbrook. A posting order then arrived, and I was to move up-country and join the Ammunition Inspectorate BAOR. It was a lot to take in and I had also just heard my father had been diagnosed with cancer. It sounded treatable, so I pushed that to the back of my mind.

When I returned from Bessbrook, I got on with the project, but on day one, I discovered that my office had been used as a store whilst I was away, and it was full of boxes. This irritated me considerably and I sent for the person responsible. Harsh words were issued, and the boxes were removed promptly but I was left with the impression that people didn't matter in this organisation. This was reinforced by the lack of messing facilities for warrant officers and sergeants. There were several officers' messes in Rheindahlen but only one sergeant's mess. There were several hundred members, and the mess was too small for all of us. If you wanted to attend either the summer ball or the Christmas draw with your partner, you had to draw lots for the seats. In the late summer of 1987, I completed the BAS/RARS project and handed it over, both pleased at its content and presentation, which met my twin aims of simplicity and detail, and delighted that I had gotten this 'monkey off my back'.

CHAPTER 11

EOD Tour in Bessbrook Mill South Armagh 1987

In the late autumn of 1986, I was completely immersed in a complex ammunition supply and logistics project at the Army HQ in Germany. The aim of this project was to draft an entirely new Mobilisation Instruction to be designated the BAOR Operational Order No 1. It entailed calculating the ammunition scaling for every single unit which could be mobilised in the event that members of the Warsaw Pact invaded. The project was long overdue, and I was working alone on it. I wasn't expecting Northern Ireland to come calling. I had a phone call from our technical HQ at Didcot, England. The caller was the staff officer responsible for nominating personnel to fill vacancies on bomb disposal tours in Northern Ireland. Holders of this appointment were usually Late Entry officers (commissioned from the ranks) and his appointment had the sobriquet of 'The Grim Reaper'. I was told that I was to deploy to Bessbrook Mill, South Armagh, in the spring of the following year. My mind was a million miles away from bomb disposal in Northern Ireland, although, at the time, I was on a duty roster to conduct bomb disposal operations on British Army bases in Germany. During the call, the matter of my pre-operational training was discussed. There had been controversy for years over the fitness for purpose of what I would loosely call advanced bomb disposal training. At the time, to qualify for promotion to Warrant Officer, an Ammunition Technician had to pass this training. I had friends who had their promotions shelved for the lack of this qualification, so it was a very touchy subject. I had obtained a pass on this course in 1979 prior to my Belfast deployment. As I was already a substantive warrant officer, the link to promotion was irrelevant to me.

The month-long pre-operational course, therefore, had two purposes; to prepare an operator for high-risk bomb disposal employment and to qualify him for promotion. Prior to each deployment to Northern Ireland, each operator had to complete this course. It turned out that there was a lot of content duplication, and it was also recognised that the course did not always meet the needs of operators. The course also tended to have a very high failure rate, occasionally as high as 100%! Rationalisation of the training requirement had taken place and I was informed that I didn't need to re-take this course. Instead, I would be loaded onto a newly created course entitled the Special To Theatre (STT) course which had a duration of several days. I was immediately dismayed. It had been years since my last formal high-risk training had taken place. In the intervening time, the sophistication of radio-controlled bombs had massively increased. South Armagh was one of the highest risk areas in the province; I foresaw the need to get as much EOD training under my belt as I could, grandfather rights to the advanced qualification or not!

I persisted with my reluctance to deploy with only a few days' training, and eventually, the Grim Reaper relented. I was loaded on an advanced course in the early new year, and this was to be followed by attendance on one of the new STT courses. In the event, I didn't perform very well on the advanced course, but I passed it and this reinforced my view that it was right to re-take it. I had less trouble on the STT course. To be fair to the Grim Reaper and staff responsible for developing the training, they were working flat-out to improve things and perhaps they saw my reluctant approach to be a challenge. During this training, I was probably the only student who already knew where and when in Northern Ireland he was to deploy. The others were mostly first-tour operators who would usually be allocated to post after the course and once the training staff had reviewed their suitability and aptitudes. There was only one opportunity in the final assessments for one operator to be tested on a simulated mortar attack scenario and I was the odds-on favourite for this: I almost sensed the staff were selling ring-side tickets! Joking aside, the anticipated mortar attack test did play on my mind somewhat. The night before, my sleep was troubled, and, as morning approached, I had an outrageous nightmare. In this dream, I was out in open countryside and multiple Mk 10 Mortar Bombs were dropping towards me from a great height, like aliens in a Space Invaders game. But these weren't ordinary bombs; they appeared to be capable of being guided and no matter which way I ran, they would pursue me. I awoke with a start, sitting bolt upright. I had obviously been shouting in my sleep and my roommates surrounded me, asking if I was OK. We laughed about it. Fear of the consequence of failure had apparently struck again! Later that day, I did get the mortar bomb task; I didn't perform perfectly but I got by. At the end-of-course celebration, I was presented with an adjustable spanner by my piss-taking pals. This versatile tool was particularly useful for dismantling large mortar bombs.

Prior to deploying, I learned that I had been shortlisted for a commission in the RAOC. I had also been selected for promotion to Warrant Officer Class One. My boss in HQ BAOR was very supportive and, if I was lucky enough to have a successful tour in Northern Ireland, it would do my commissioning prospects no harm at all. I deployed to Northern Ireland on 2 March 1987; or at least I tried to. On the journey by road to the departure airfield in Germany, a band of freezing rain swept over the country. We got to RAF Gütersloh and boarded a C130. The aircraft was readied for take-off and was hosed down with de-icer fluid which promptly froze! The flight was postponed until the following day, and I stayed with a friend who lived nearby who was on the same deployment (Pete H), although he was destined for Belfast.

The next day, we resumed the journey and got to Lisburn where we started induction training. Blood and fingerprints were taken. "For exclusion purposes if we submit contaminated evidence?" asked one of our number. "And to help identify your remains if the worst happens," replied our host. That quietened the slightly nervous banter. In an administration briefing, we were then subjected to a particularly intense diatribe about the abuse of Q Cars. These were the civilianised cars driven by military personnel in civilian dress. I sensed there had been a recent serious disciplinary incident which had perhaps irritated senior management. I noted what was said, especially about the perils of drink-driving, driving without prior authorisation, driving only on authorised routes and not running out of fuel. I was puzzled at the body language of the officer giving the briefing; it felt as though I had done something wrong and was being singled out! I was driven to Bessbrook via the Section HQ at Drumadd Barracks in Armagh. It was early evening when I got there but I had to crack on with my takeover of classified documents, weapons, ammunition and equipment. The

246

officer I was relieving (Rob) introduced me to the Team in their rest room. As we exchanged details, I noticed they seemed somewhat distracted. I followed the fixed gaze of one of them to a large trunk near the door, labelled as the 'Toy Box'. On it was a CCTV 'Jack-In-The-Box' monitor. In the picture was a standard army bed, made down, and the orientation suggested the camera was positioned in the ceiling above it. The roof above the accommodation in this part of the mill was of the industrial saw-tooth profile with almost half of it being glazed. The ceilings and internal walls were of some sort of plasterboard. Above the board ceiling was chicken wire which served to keep the roosting pigeons out of the rooms below. I looked back at the team and jokingly suggested I thought they were spying on the female accommodation, before leaving to continue the takeover. Later, before retiring, I went to the Team Room for a cup of tea. The monitor was still on and being watched, which was concerning, and I was getting distracted by this when I needed to focus 100% on my takeover. I remember saying to the Team words to the effect of "If that's what I think it is, you'd better recover it or there could be trouble". A few minutes later, in my room, I heard a crash followed by screaming. The female accommodation was close by and the two WRAC girls in it had run into the Operations Room, panic-stricken. My suspicions were confirmed when I was told the camera recovery operation failed when the man lost his balance and fell through the ceiling into the room below. In the resultant melee, the evidence of wrongdoing was spirited away and there it might have ended, but for the twisted squaddie logic of milking every opportunity for what it was worth. Members of the team decided to treat the same two girls to their beer allowance the following night in the canteen. Despite the two-can rule, the beer loosened the team's tongues, and the boys regaled the girls with exaggerated tales of covertly filmed lesbian episodes which they were then told had been broadcast on the Mill's internal TV network. This was completely untrue, but the girls fled and were flown back to their permanent accommodation at Aldergrove in a state of considerable distress. I was briefed the next day; it was an inauspicious start to a tour where the risk was meant to come from terrorists. Some days later, a knock at the door signalled the arrival of a female RMP Sergeant Major come to investigate, and she was not best pleased about things. I briefed my HQ staff and then wondered how long I was going to last as the boss of a team of voyeurs!

The days rolled by and activity was initially light. Activity of note was the ongoing killings and attacks by and between the various terrorist organisations. In one case, I deployed to the scene where an alleged terrorist, Thomas Maguire, had been executed by shooting. His body had been moved but I was able to search for the bullet heads that had passed through him into the ground where he lay as he was finished off. On 14 March, Fergus Conlon was murdered, and his body was dumped very close to the Irish border at the edge of a road. This recovery job was fairly straight forward but the close proximity of the border meant that the Search Team and cordon positioning was awkward. I was told that the Irish Army and Garda Siochana would provide assistance to us which was welcomed but I was somewhat concerned at the lax disposition of some of their people who I could see from my control point. We performed a number of tasks which turned out to be false alarms, including one which concluded in hilarious fashion. We were tasked to something suspicious in a hedgerow and the ground was incredibly muddy. We were surrounded by large fields separated by ancient hedgerows. As we worked, contractors several hundred yards away were grubbing up hedgerows and levelling the ground with an excavator and grader, presumably to increase the size of the field to favour modern farming techniques. We heard shouting and laughter and looked up to see four soldiers sprinting away from the excavator. They had apparently been in a concealed observation post in the hedge, which had nothing to do with our job, but they had to abandon their hide in haste as the excavator blade neared them.

The rest of the month was fairly quiet, so I put the team through regular training drills and got up to speed with the Operations and Intelligence officers on what was happening in our patch. Bessbrook Mill Army Base was on the outskirts of Newry. Originally, the mill was an early Quaker settlement built around the linen industry in the mid-19th century. As a functioning mill, it closed in 1971. Next door to the main mill, and inside our secure zone, was a carpet factory which was still open when I arrived in early March 1987. It had a large worker's canteen, originally part of the linen mill, and the gable end inside had an amazing frieze painted on the wall showing the Mill's world-wide linen export customer locations. As a classic Quaker industrial settlement, everything the mill community of the time could need, from housing to what we would now call infrastructure support services, was present. The main buildings were very substantial and made mostly of granite. There was a very high chimney roughly in the middle of the base area which featured CCTV cameras on top, affording nearly all-round vision. It had much to offer as a fortified base and was the hub of military operations in South Armagh. It was also regarded as Europe's busiest heliport as nearly all conventional military movement in South Armagh had to be conducted by air; the number of daily air movements was typically in the hundreds. The noise of helicopters and smell of aviation fuel was constant. The Army unit in the mill when I arrived was the 1st Battalion, The Royal Hampshire Regiment. I quickly came to respect the sheer professionalism of everyone in that unit, and I regarded it then, as now, as one of the best I have served with. The

Commanding Officer (CO) could be described as tough and strict but fair. His leadership and presence amongst the men was exemplary. I knew from direct personal contact with him that he was very concerned for the safety of soldiers of all units in South Armagh. We knew from briefings we had received that terrorists had recently been resupplied with arms and ammunition from Libya. Also, more sophisticated improvised weaponry had been developed, some of which was known to be capable of defeating or evading our various counter measures. It was quite a tense time; the terrorist in these circumstances invariably enjoyed the tactical prerogative and to disrupt this, the CO had an unrelenting patrols programme which aimed to project the maximum dominance of all ground in the Area Of Responsibility (AOR) and deny freedom of movement to the terrorists. I believe this was effective and that terrorists tried to counter the heavy patrols presence by exploiting every opportunity to distract us through pre-emptive activity.

I used to attend the daily CO's operations briefings. As I was the ATO at Bessbrook, I was in the one place in Northern Ireland where the ATO worked directly for the CO of the local Infantry Battalion, albeit with technical oversight from HQ 321 EOD in Lisburn. This relationship enabled greater cohesion, fostered trust and gave me direct access to the important players in the unit which was ideal when doing operational planning. We started to get warnings that a mortar attack was possible, if only because the 10th anniversary of the last such attack was imminent and Bessbrook Mill was a high prestige target. We took certain precautions, however, at a later briefing, we were informed that a mortar attack was now deemed unlikely due to the almost incessant overhead presence of helicopters. As soon as I heard that from the Intelligence Staff, I glanced sideways at the Operations Officer to find he was already looking at me and a spontaneous but tacit aura of misgiving occupied the space between us. On leaving the briefing, we agreed that it would be prudent to review the response if we were indeed mortared. We went into the operations room and started talking through our options. It should be said that there were already generic standard operating procedures in place throughout Northern Ireland to deal with mortars, but we needed something more in tune with what we both considered was a plausible threat. We both readily agreed that a post-mortar attack scenario would be chaotic, communications would likely be cut, and we would need to work together seamlessly to restore the base to full operations. I seem to recall that we discussed a rudimentary signalling technique where I could make arm signals which he might be able to see on CCTV, and that he could respond using the tannoy system. Usually, an ATO deals with a mortar attack in a highly structured and cautious manner and only after such an attack. The ATO would not be in the target area, casualties would have already been evacuated and the conventional clearance operation would be deliberate and start with ariel reconnaissance imagery, Royal Engineer search assistance and then a sequence of clearance dictated by the location of the baseplate, the flight path of the bombs and then the impact area in that order. If our base was mortared, this clearance doctrine would need modification and we discussed some scenarios, concluding that we would need a novel approach to clearance, very much as a reaction to how events might unfold.

The background as to why the threat was serious was not just that the mill was a high prestige target. We had a very busy heliport including exposed and vulnerable aviation fuel bladder tanks, we were supporting all of South Armagh and we were preparing for a forthcoming major planned operation which would see the troop numbers in the mill double for a short period. Finally, we received warnings that a mortar baseplate (launcher) was believed to be circulating in our vicinity, being moved gradually into a position from where an attack could be mounted. Coming back to the afore-mentioned carpet factory, the plot it occupied was vacated in the days immediately before the attack. If my recollections are correct, we were either unaware of this or we did not effectively review our perimeter security. With buckets of hindsight, the many buildings around the carpet factory created substantial dead ground, ideal to conceal a mortar attack, and I understand there could have been a CCTV blind spot. Hitherto, this was negated as a concern as we had a manned sanger (temporary fortified position) covering it until the carpet factory closed. From that point, however, traffic control was handed over to civilian contractors. It is believed they were no match for the gunmen escorting the baseplate when it was brought in, although I believe they were unharmed. The various and often contradictory intelligence warnings we received were immensely frustrating. There are many metaphors that can be applied but intelligence is neither evidential nor factual. We knew the terrorists wanted to disrupt the patrols programme to give them freedom of manoeuvrability, but we didn't know exactly why or how they would do this.

On 12 April 1987, the IRA abducted, tortured and murdered an alleged informer, Charles McIlmurray. They dumped his body in a car behind a fuel station at Killeen on the A1, very close to the border with Eire. It was believed the garage was owned by people sympathetic to the republican cause and the location was easily observed from a permanent hilltop observation post (OP) nearby. These circumstances, from our perspective, were highly suspicious and this would be my third 'body job'. Was my modus operandi being observed to try and catch me out the next time? By dumping the body there, they had disrupted the garage's business and had risked being seen from the OP. My first thought was that this was part of what is known as a 'come-on' where security forces are lured into an area to facilitate an attack and there was a recent history of such activity in this area. The other consideration was that a human body had been dumped next to a main road and it would dictate a fairly rapid response from us, whereas the two previous bodies had been dumped in remote areas. I had previously consulted the Battalion's Medical Officer over the matter of infection risk from human remains, specifically things like HIV/AIDS, Hepatitis and anything else and if there was any protective clothing. He replied that I could consider wearing an NBC suit and my service respirator. (That'll be a no, then, I thought to myself). Late that night, I did a helicopter-borne reconnaissance using forward-looking infra-red (FLIR). A priest had been seen administering the Last Rites, knowledge of which was helpful in the way the task could be planned. Early the next morning, we went in on a very hastily planned operation. We inserted by air and, after all of the standard physical and electronic search processes had concluded, a Wheelbarrow remote vehicle was used to approach the car. The car was a three-door hatchback. The body was in the rear and the tailgate was closed. This was opened remotely, enabling the next stage of safely extracting the victim to take place. After that, it was time for a manual approach. Dealing with a dead body in these circumstances is a highly intense experience. I had already been involved in the recovery of human remains on a previous tour and an RUC Scenes of Crime Officer (SOCO) had once gifted me some valuable advice; treat the victims with respect and talk to them as though they were still alive. Experience has taught me that this can actually help. As I approached the car, I would have to walk in front of the Wheelbarrow, so I made its weapons safe and then trained its cameras on the car and victim. This meant my team could see me and they must have been baffled at why I appeared to be talking to someone. The SATO (Mark) decided he needed to investigate, and he approached the scene. I was fully engrossed with the business (I've always hated working manually on vehicles) and didn't hear him coming as the EOD bomb suit isolates you from the outside world. All of a sudden, I heard a voice talking to me. I'll leave you readers to use your own imaginations to guess who I initially thought was talking to me and what I said next! It gave me a start, but the job concluded with no further drama. Overall, the impression left on me was of the brutal and inhumane treatment meted out by the victim's judge, jury and executioner. Whilst I remained objective, I did feel empathy for the victim and his family.

The EOD phase of this clearance operation was rapid, but it was only one small part of the bigger planned operation which involved a large number of troops, the RUC, helicopters and other specialist agencies, taking the whole day. We were puzzled that there was no secondary device or attack, but the patrols programme had been severely disrupted. What we didn't know was that a large goods vehicle covered by a blue tarpaulin was edging its way unseen, behind our backs, along country roads towards Bessbrook Mill. The lethal payload was 16 Mark 10 PIRA Mortar bombs. These bombs were big. Each one had a maximum capacity of about 22 kgs of explosive, normally homemade, and usually a mixture of ammonium nitrate and nitrobenzene (ANNIE). The bomb body was made of tubular steel, about 150mm diameter and 1.2 metres long. All up, each bomb weighed about 60 kgs. The propelling charge was black powder contained in the tail unit, to be ignited electrically by a modified flash bulb. The bomb would be inserted into a launch tube made of a heavy gauge gas cylinder and these would be welded into a steel frame. The range and azimuth of each bomb could be varied by the size of the black powder charge and the angle at which the launch vehicle was parked. The terrorists positioning the baseplate were usually motivated and committed people and they would align the vehicle with an aiming point, usually because there wasn't direct line of sight to the target. When the Mark 10 was fired, it was aerodynamically unstable and would topple slowly, end over end, with a whooshing noise. It didn't need to land nose-first to achieve its effect. In transit, this type of baseplate would be concealed by a full tarpaulin; thus, the load would appear innocuous to the casual observer. The IRA developed several versions of this bomb since it was first used in March 1979. The most lethal attack with the Mark 10 Mortar occurred in Newry in 1985 when nine RUC Officers were killed by one bomb, of a total of nine launched at the station, which struck their canteen as they prepared their evening meal. It was the single biggest loss of life the RUC suffered and a further 37 people were injured, 25 of them police support workers.

To set the scene on the day of the mortar attack: 16 April 1987. We started the day normally in Bessbrook. I was to host a planning conference with subject matter expert colleagues in preparation for a major operation which was due to start imminently. Troop numbers in the mill were almost double the norm due to this operation. An EOD Team from Armagh City arrived, as did our in-house expert on radio-controlled bombs who had flown into theatre from mainland UK. He was an endearing man with a lifetime of ammunition technical experience behind him. He had taught me my basic explosive demolition techniques during my Ammunition Technician course in 1972. He was affectionately known in our close community as the GOC (grumpy old chap) although I have changed the last word to 'chap' to spare his blushes! In the Mill, my accommodation and office were near the operations room. This part of the mill was not within the hardened granite structure.

It was a separate brick and blockwork, single-storey structure with a classic industrial building 'saw-tooth' wooden and glazed roof. This old and decrepit structure was reasonably weather-tight, but pigeons could get in. Within the roof, wire mesh served to keep the pigeons out of our accommodation. Internal walls and ceilings were nothing more than plasterboard; indeed, it was like living in cardboard boxes. The passageways had solid block blast walls intermittently sited to stop incoming horizontal gunfire or shrapnel from passing through the entire building, but there was no overhead protection against an incoming mortar bomb on a plunging flight path. The lighting was primarily fluorescent tubing which tended to be dim in places and was very flickery. Ventilation was poor; body odour mixed with the stale smell of beer from the canteen and blended with cigarette smoke and the ever-present smell of aviation fuel which served to assault the senses; but only for a day or two, then you didn't notice. The building had all the ambience of a cramped and smelly submarine! As my guests arrived, they came into the Team's communal room, renewed their acquaintances with old friends and those who were to attend the conference ordered refreshments and then followed me to my office. The door was closed, and the conference started but was interrupted by Taff, my lead Electronic Counter Measures Operator (Bleep), when he knocked the door and entered with the brews and biscuits. He left, the door closed, and we resumed work. What follows next is a somewhat lengthy and detailed description of what happened. An interesting feature of what happens in an over-stimulated mind in the presence of impending danger is that time slows down, and the brain enters a quick response mode and senses become heightened. As we started discussions, my senses reacted slowly at first to an odd sharp noise and a rumble in the far background. I must add that the internal environment at Bessbrook was noisy and there was a pipe range just outside my building where weapons could be test-fired. I could not identify the cause of the noise, but it wasn't alarming at first. Then there was a very loud bang and the plasterboard ceiling seemed to move, the lights went out and years' worth of pigeon droppings started to fall through the ceiling. Mortar attacks are usually chaotic and often very difficult to discern from a conventional attack. However, the mortar alarm started up but ceased almost immediately and so I shouted "Mortars!" and tried to get under my desk. Well, the afore-mentioned GOC might have been older than me, but he wasn't slow, and he was already under my desk! Having donned helmet and flak jacket, I told my sheltering colleagues to remain in place, follow instructions given by the tannoy system and then told them of the 2 ways to get out of the building if they needed to evacuate. I then entered the operations room through a small side hatch and told the Operations Officer I would do a rapid assessment and report back to him.

As I exited the Operations Room, I saw extensive but light structural damage along the corridor, mainly detritus that had fallen from the ceiling. In the gloom, I could see the prostrate form of a soldier lying still at the base of a blast wall, his silhouette enhanced by the daylight streaming through the main entrance door which was open and the bright flames of an intense fire in the car park. Not far from him was an unexploded PIRA Mk 10 Mortar bomb lying on the floor where it had landed after coming through the roof. There were bright orange sparks vigorously fizzing out from its bottom end which was the unburnt residue of the black powder propelling charge. I could smell the classic stench of burned black powder along with the sickly odour of nitrobenzene and I noted the bomb's cylindrical outer wall glistening in the reflected light. Black powder typically leaves about 56% of its mass in a greasy residue when it burns, and this is awful to clean up and is extremely slippery. I will return to the slippery handling feature shortly. As I reached the soldier, who I feared might have been seriously injured, I stooped to check him. He was very young. He was physically unharmed and asked me what was happening. I explained it was a mortar attack and told him to stay put and await instructions unless the fire forced him to move. The reason for this 'stay-put' instruction is that mortars often get fired in salvoes. Soldiers exposing themselves after the first salvo could be hit in subsequent salvoes. That said, it takes a lot of self-discipline to resist the urge to run. I noted he was alert, correctly dressed and although obviously anxious, he was responsive and capable; I was hugely impressed to see this resolve and self-discipline in such a young person. I ran back to the Ops Room and confirmed it was a mortar attack, then briefed them of the location of the first unexploded bomb and of the fire in the car park.

As I went up the reception staircase towards the car park, I could see absolute mayhem outside. There was a casualty on the ground receiving attention from another soldier. To my immediate left was a burning Ford Transit van; it was the Electronic Counter Measures vehicle from the Armagh City Team. There was a long dent in its roof, overhead electrical cables had been severed and there were clear signs of a hefty explosion. I surmised the incoming mortar bomb had belly-flopped onto the roof of the van and had then bounced upwards to deliver an air burst. The fuzes of these bombs were time fuzes, not impact fuzes. The blast overpressure had ruptured the van's fuel tank and it was well ablaze. Shrapnel littered the car park. For readers curious about what I was doing and why, I would explain that I was in something of a limbo between being a random 'intended victim' in a mortar attack and yet I was the ATO. We had very well-established procedures for responding to a mortar attack but none of them envisaged the ATO actually being in the target. One of the blind bombs had landed on the roof very close to the EOD Team accommodation. If this bomb had detonated, both the whole Bessbrook team and visiting Armagh Teams would have been taken out. The main toilet block was near-by to the right and the windows were blown out. Later on, after we had completed the recovery operation, a very important member of the Battalion, who I wouldn't dare to identify, told me he had been sitting on the toilet when the bomb exploded outside, and shrapnel flew around the inside of the toilets ricocheting off the walls. He hast-ily completed his mission but failed to notice a piece of hot shrapnel had dropped into his Y fronts. He hoisted his Y fronts up and the hot shrapnel started to toast his nether regions. He survived the ordeal, and I decided I did not need to recover that piece of shrapnel! Any-way, there was plenty outside. Readers might be puzzled about the mix in my narrative of deadly serious details and then the funny bits. Well, if you didn't laugh, you'd cry. Inside the fiercely burning van was an electronic main frame, two jerricans of fuel (40 litres), a reserve Wheelbarrow and a large military explosive device used to disrupt car bombs (Paw-Paw). I noted that my Number 2 EOD Assistant Opera-tor, Smudge, was already fighting the fire. I joined him and could see that the normal fire extinguishers were having no effect. The injured casualty was nearby and I had no idea how many casualties had been inflicted but I feared the worst and this area was a designated casualty clearing station. This fire had to be controlled quickly or there could well be another explosion; the situation was dire. I shouted for other soldiers to fetch one of the large, wheeled foam fire extinguishers from the helipad. This appeared rapidly and as we used it in the open back doors of the transit, it pushed back the dense grey smoke coming off the burning mainframe. I could then see the jerricans and, grabbing them one at a time, hurled them as hard as I could away from the

259

fire and the casualty. At that point, we were joined by an officer who asked what he could do to help. As we were shouting at each other over the noise of the fire, a series of bangs came from the van. The fire had reached the cab and the escort's clothing, draped over the seats, was on fire. The bangs were ball rounds in rifle magazines in the jacket pockets cooking off. The officer promptly departed! We got the fire under control and the casualty was stretchered away. The explosive EOD device, which was housed in a wooden cassette, had been scorched at one end but was safely retrieved. I needed to get an overview of what was happening as I transitioned from would-be victim to ATO. I ran over to the helipad from where the Buzzard was watching events. The Buzzard was the officer responsible for helicopter operations, a sort of air traffic controller. Several helicopters were airborne, and I asked if he could call one down for me so I could assess the situation from on high. This he did and a Lynx picked me up. We did a quick orbit of the base and, after a short while, we located the baseplate. It was a big one. From the air, I transmitted a follow-up contact message to the HQ Northern Ireland Operations Room, added a Situation Report (SITREP) and requested technical support. An important point was I could see the baseplate, mounted on a lorry. The flatbed load area was stripped bare following an explosion on board and was surrounded by craters. There was severe structural damage in nearby buildings, and I assessed the baseplate as destroyed. It posed no further threat to the mill. I decided to modify the standard mortar clearance and not start with the base plate. The multiple blinds in the target area needed to be assessed and dealt with first to restore the mill's operational function. I had recommended the mill be evacuated but this was immediately rejected on operational grounds. The baseplate could wait as it was not located where it could cause harm. I was greatly saddened later to find that the wonderful and historic frieze in the canteen, depicting the world famous and worldwide exports of Bessbrook Mill linen, had been destroyed.

On landing, I advised the Buzzard to establish a separate improvised helipad outside the base perimeter and not to allow any base overflights at low level as it was clear this was a very large-scale attack and there were many unexploded mortar bombs lying undiscovered. I briefed the Operations Officer and the Armagh City EOD Section Commander, Captain Tim. We then conducted a rapid survey trying to find unexploded bombs and identify their operating characteristics. This entailed climbing up onto the saw-tooth roof and we found five bombs which had bellyflopped on landing and were blind. The bellyflop spread the energy of the impact over the length of the bomb body which explains why they had not gone through the roof. If they had landed nose-first, they would probably have punched right through. One bomb had landed on the roof and then rolled along and had fallen inside a broken window. It was dangling precariously from the chicken wire, nose down, with a drop below it of several metres. I already knew from the first bomb that the bomb body had an anti-rotation lug welded to it. This would normally indicate that the type of fuze fitted contained a percussion mechanism. If it fell and struck a hard surface, the fuze could ignite and detonate the bomb. The way I dealt with this particular bomb merits its own detailed description but, as I was later to discover, the terrorists had modified these bombs so that the time fuze would be ignited electrically at launch, but I wasn't to know this at the time. This meant that each bomb was originally wired to two pairs of twinflex cable, running from the launch tubes, along the flatbed and then through the bulkhead to a large wooden firing pack. I was to discover later that the baseplate had contained 16 Mk 10 mortar bombs and I also believed a secondary device had been positioned under the flatbed near the left side rear wheel to disable the vehicle in the event that anyone tried to move it. As a Mk 10 bomb could contain up to 22 kgs of explosive, the approximate all-up explosive weight was about 350 kgs.

At this point, I was alerted to the presence of a bomb which had over-shot the mill completely and had fallen onto the pitched roof of a house outside the base before rolling off and then dropping into the road. This increased the area we needed to cordon, and the local civilian population was visibly distressed. With an escort, I ran to the scene and assessed the object, which was indeed an unexploded bomb. I elected to remove this immediately and ran back with it over my shoulder to the mill to a secure working area where I could dismantle the bombs and collate the bits. (Mortar attacks of this type usually result in huge piles of junk, explosives and evidence.) I then advised the Operations Officer to reduce the cordon perimeter. There were sheets of corrugated steel roofing nearby which I placed the bombs on as they would prevent the bombs from rolling away as I dismantled them.

So far, I thought we were coping well. The baseplate was no longer a threat, I had heard that casualties were light but sadly, the most seri-ously injured soldier, who was well known to my Team, was in a bad way. I feared he had suffered life-changing injuries. I was formulating an evolving plan and had recognised the primary hazards within a complex hierarchy of risk, to me as being working at heights as most of the unexploded bombs were up on the roof and then there was the prospect of something lurking for me at or near the baseplate. I had al-ready retrieved several pieces of partially exploded bombs. The home-made explosives contained a hazardous chemical which was a known carcinogen. As I was working at heights on most of the unexploded bombs, and, at times, in confined spaces, I inhaled significant volumes of noxious fumes and was heavily contaminated with nitrobenzene which had soaked its way through my uniform and gloves. I hadn't noticed the pungent smell after I started the clearance, perhaps because my sense of smell had become saturated. I could not wear any personal protective equipment for obvious reasons. I had tried rubber gloves, but they tore immediately I handled anything heavy. I settled for wearing my urban patrol gloves which were porous to nitrobenzene but enabled a good grip. A few minutes in, I developed a raging, pounding headache with dizzy spells and breathlessness. I sought out the Battalion's Medical Officer and asked if he had anything for my headache. As soon as he saw me, he administered oxygen and gave me strong painkillers. After a few minutes, I recovered well enough to resume work.

The Chief Ammunition Technical Officer (CATO) had arrived by road. I gave him a verbal situation report and outlined my proposed 'render safe' procedure which was unconventional but took account of the unique local circumstances then prevailing. But he wanted to go straight to the baseplate. He insisted I accompany him and, without the opportunity to brief anyone and take any of the well-established standard precautions, we approached the baseplate directly. I paused on the way to assess a Southern Irish-registered car which was parked near the baseplate. He barked at me to forget that and focus on the baseplate. I learned a long time ago not to turn your back on potential hazards, so I checked the car rapidly and then joined him at the baseplate. We stared through the open door of the cab at the large firing pack. He had already pulled the door open. There was a balaclava helmet, boiler suit and a split pin on a ring lying neatly in the driver's footwell. This clothing had obviously been taken off by a calm and methodical terrorist and deliberately left in the cab so it would not be found later in incriminating circumstances. The split pin on the ring was the way the firing pack had been initiated by pulling it out of a pre-drilled hole in a Perspex cover plate, where it restrained a pre-set mechanical timer. Again, the modus operandi was to leave components at the scene but the lack of an incendiary device to destroy clues by fire was perhaps an oversight. I was now inclined to be even more cautious, but he was like a kid in a candy shop. He then insisted it had been an 8-tube attack, but he had clearly overlooked the way the terminal block connectors were wired up. In simple terms, there were 20 available terminal block connections. These were numbered and 13 had wires attached to them. The last 3 terminals had been double-wired with white twinflex cable giving a potential capacity of 16 tubes. The actual tubes had been blown apart and thrown off the flatbed so, at the time, we could only go by the clues shown by the firing pack and the fact that I had already discovered seven blind bombs, one had exploded at Reception and the flatbed was surrounded in well-defined craters in the sold concrete road surface. By then, I was starting to get very angry with him. There were, in my opinion, developing suggestions of a major intelligence gaffe. I already knew the Operations Room staff had received a somewhat frantic call warning of an impending attack and this call was cut off as the first bomb detonated. The comments he was making were strongly suggestive to me, if not quite accurate, that he and others had some prior knowledge of the existence of this baseplate and perhaps expected the attack to be foiled by interception. His conjecture and various assumptions simply did not tally with him coming absolutely fresh to a completely unexpected attack. It was as if he was trying to fit what had happened to a previously anticipated scenario. For my part, I was keeping an open mind. At that point, I looked in to assess the firing pack. A large explosion on the flatbed had pushed the cab body forward. In the confined space behind the passenger seat, the firing pack had been partially crushed and the top had burst open. It was of plywood construction and through the displaced lid, I had a clear view inside of all of the circuitry and many batteries. The pack had apparently been designed to fire the bombs sequentially and this was achieved through the use of a barbeque spit roast motor which was to turn a rotor which would fire the propulsion units in a controlled way, one at a time, in a manner similar to how a car's distributor fired spark plugs before the advent of electronic ignition. I knew from two separate witnesses that at least one salvo had flown, consisting of between 5 to 8 bombs flying simultaneously in a very tight formation. One witness was badly shocked as the bombs had gone directly over his head as he was in a sangar on the main mill roof, immediately under the flight path. The other witness was sited at the helipad next to the Buzzard hut. He was the Battalion's Intelligence Warrant Officer. He saw the bombs flying in close formation at the apogee of their flight and described them as resembling the black fingers of a giant hand. He was remarkably calm and lucid and gestured with his extended arm and hand in imitation of a grotesque claw. I felt the credibility factor of his information was high. This strongly suggested that the sequential firing circuit had malfunctioned. I could see there was a backup circuit in the firing pack which was capable of firing all of the bombs together in the (presumed) event of a failure of the primary sequencing circuit. If this had happened, the flatbed lorry would have been jolted by a massive recoil force which could have disrupted the whole baseplate. The motor in the firing pack was still running noisily. My heightened senses were overloaded, and I was getting even more irritated. After the briefest of safety checks, I disconnected the power supply to the whirring motor. The silence that ensued was almost gratifying. I then reasoned with the CATO, using logic and pointing out from the wiring evidence and the seven blinds, that this was likely a 16-tube attack. I could see he was too short to see the firing pack so I have no idea where his 8-tube theory originated, but you can call me an old cynic if you like. His initial reluctance started to mellow. I have never been a diplomat or sycophant, but I did try to be patient. He went quiet and sullen on me. We returned to the working area I had created earlier and, after a short chat, he was content for me to stick to my plan. He disappeared off and that pleased me as he was now 'out of my face'.

I have already explained why I now wanted to clear the bombs in the impact area as a priority. The flight path and impact areas were secure, but as the Bessbrook Mill base was so essential to operations in South Armagh, I wanted to restore normality as soon as I safely could. I started on the saw-tooth roof area with the bomb that was dangling through the broken roof. Although this building was single storey, it was built on split-level ground, so it was actually quite high up. At that time, I had borrowed a set of Vehicle Mechanic's coveralls to use as rudimentary protection over my uniform. My face was blackened with soot and my rank badge and ATO badge were now concealed. I was conducting a briefing near the unloading bay when a somewhat agitated major from the Resident Battalion arrived. He must have thought I was a very scruffy REME Mechanic. He reproached me for tampering with unexploded bombs and told me I would be in trouble big time if the ATO found out. He was normally a thoroughly nice gentleman and was dreadfully embarrassed when the others pointed out who I was. The group's laughter at the hilarity was uplifting amid an otherwise grim scenario.

I went back up on the roof and started to work on the dangling bomb. It was hanging nose- down on strands of chicken wire, the only means of support. The wire was wrapped around the bomb's tail unit. Mk 10

Mortar bombs are about 1.2 metres long and are very heavy at about 60 kgs (I weighed 75 kgs at the time). In the gloomy kitchen far below me, I could see that this bomb, silhouetted against the tiled floor below, had a lug welded to its side which indicated it was a Mark 10A and normally featured a percussion ignition system for the delay fuze, fitted in the nose. If the bomb suffered a fall from height, the fuze could be ignited, and the bomb would detonate. I could not believe my eyes that this slender piece of wire could take the weight. The bomb was swaying gently, and I realised it was only a matter of time before the bomb would break loose and fall onto its nose. There was one chance to get this right. The bomb was about a foot below my feet and I had to squat froglike on my haunches to reach downwards into the broken window frame to grab it. So I did; I soon realised I had a tiger by the tail. The inert bombs I had handled in training were clean and dry. This one was literally a greasy pole. Then the wire snapped. The bomb dropped and I tightened my grip. But then the bomb started to slide slowly out of my gloved hands. Just before it could plummet downwards, I regained my purchase with an adrenaline-fueled grip that made my knuckles pop. The weight was just about manageable, but my stance was off-balance, and the bomb was pulling me after it. The slimy black powder residue was lubricating my grip. The slide resumed but then mercifully stopped. The propulsion unit had two small bolts welded to the bottom, designed to prevent the firing cable from being severed by the bomb's tail. These bolts were now snagged on my glove and helped to stop the bomb's downward descent. I then tried to lift the bomb out onto the roof. Just on the cusp of success, the bomb started to slip from my grasp again. I squeezed harder and braced my thighs against the window frame for additional purchase. Then, as I got the bomb higher up, it changed my centre of gravity, which was now too far forward, and my boots slid backwards. I fell forwards and downwards with the bomb into the open window frame. In a reflex reaction, I spread my upper thighs against the window frame sides to stop my fall and my heels stopped against the back of the drainage gully behind me. I had only lurched down about a foot or so, but I imagined it felt like a condemned man on the hangman's trap going to hell. This stopped my fall and I now had two solid points of contact; the back face of the gully jammed against the heels of my boots and the window frame sides against my thighs. Every muscle I owned was now on fire or in spasm. I had to stop, control my breathing, regain best posture, re-balance, re-grip and try again. So I did, and then again. On the third go, I got the propulsion unit just above the window ledge and jammed it against the woodwork. I rested and then realised I had improved mechanical advantage. One good heave synchronised with straightening my legs resulted in me and the bomb gently toppling into the gully on the roof. Phew! If my Directing Staff at training had witnessed that, I would have been toast. I still remain convinced to this day that the biggest constant fear I had was the fear of the consequence of failure at selection and training. Dealing with real bombs was usually the easiest bit. To be fair, the very demanding training was probably about right: I am minded to recall the maxim 'Train Hard, Fight Easy'. But in harsh personal criticism of my perhaps impulsive attempt to retrieve the bomb before it could fall, I knew I had been very lucky, and was too embarrassed to tell anyone what really happened.

To move the bomb along the gully to where I could climb down, I elected to sit the bomb across my lap and then shuffle crablike on my bum along the five metres or so to the edge. My legs were shaking after the prolonged strain of that epic 'knee-trembler' and I was loathe to try and stand up. I tried the crab-shuffle once; it worked and then I took a short break.

Everything was very quiet. My legs stopped their shaking. By then, I had an audience. I could see civilians outside the base pointing at me. Far below, around the helipad, the Buzzard and Battalion RSM were watching. Aware now that my performance was being scrutinised, I looked around when I heard a droning noise some distance away. I looked towards the sound and eventually spotted an incoming fixed-wing aircraft at extreme low level; the penny dropped. It was an RAF Beaver photo reconnaissance aircraft, and it was getting even lower. I always thought these particular aircraft, which it was said could go backwards in a strong wind, operated at higher, safer altitudes when photographing suspect terrorist bombs. It got so low I felt like ducking! Assuming it snapped me as it went over my head, the picture would have been memorable. I did ask later if I could get a copy, but the answer was no. Having reached the edge of the roof, I placed my trust in the massive ironwork guttering. After a simple but careful weight test, I scrambled down the pipework, bomb across my shoulder. I was very pleased with myself as I was nearly at the bottom. Defeat was snatched from the jaws of victory when my clothing became hopelessly entangled in some chain-link fencing.

With my one free arm, I gestured to the RSM to come to my aid. He did, bless him, but he wouldn't touch anything. He asked me, "Is that thing safe?" I assured him it was as long as I didn't drop it. He cut me free, and I got the bomb into my working area.

On the second approach to the same roof, I picked up the next bomb and hoisted it across my shoulders and stood up as my legs were now doing as they were told. This was an easier method of carriage and enabled quicker movement. As I stepped off, I heard another aircraft approaching. I turned and looked up and was horrified to see a Wessex helicopter coming straight towards me. It went into a hover directly above me and then I saw someone's face peering at me over the side. This person was obviously lying on the floor of the load area. It wasn't the loadmaster because loadmasters are helmeted, tethered to the aircraft and are far more sensible. At this point, the down draft blew me off balance and I almost fell. I sat down hard and gesticulated to the helicopter (with two fingers) to go away. Well, how was I to know it was the Commander Land Forces on board? And who had overruled my request to cease any overflights? One of the last bombs I recovered was the only one to land on top of the original, high granite mill building. As I knelt beside it, I saw a vehicle approaching from the north. I paused what I was doing and crouched low behind the wall surrounding the roof. I watched as it passed below and out of sight and then I heard a loud cheer. It had come from Drumadd Barracks with rations and hot soup. Then I realised how hungry and thirsty I was and how welcoming it was when relief arrived whilst we were under an apparent 'siege'. I got this bomb down to my working area where it was dismantled. (The fruits of these labours are shown in the mortar attack photographs. There were seven bombs laid out on the corrugated steel sheet. Their explosive fillings had been extracted and decanted into vapour-proof bags on the ground behind them. The fuzes and exploders are out of shot, nearer the camera.)

After about 6 hours, I had recovered all of the bombs and had rendered them safe. The CATO turned up again and this time he was in patronising mode. By now, the adrenalin rush and whatever the Medical Officer had given me had worn off and was giving way to overwhelming tiredness. My skin, from fingertips to elbows, was stained yellow by the nitrobenzene and felt numb and prickly. My uniform was saturated in the same stuff, and I just wanted to get cleaned up, fed and rested. True to form, the CATO and me started bickering again about details. Now I was really starting to get mad. He looked at the seven empty bomb bodies lying in my work area and said he was pleased that I had at least had something to deal with. I thought that comment was grossly condescending. He showed no technical interest in the recovered bombs but seemed fascinated with the firing pack. Snapping point was reached when he asked in a loud voice (for the benefit of his entourage) if there was anything else he could do to help me. In the most succinct and direct way, I invited him to leave, and very promptly too, using very bad language on my part. My bad; he was, after all, my superior officer. That said, he and I were both very lucky I didn't punch him. I realised later that I was off my head with the effects of nitrobenzene and, at times, my mental state had been bordering on the irrational.

What criticism did come my way, and it was entirely justified and hurt me the most, was that I had forgotten to keep my team updated and involved in progress. There was little they could do directly as working at the sharp end is a one-man risk. I had single-mindedly and rapidly performed seven consecutive render-safes, hoping to restore normality so that normal operations could resume. When I got back to the Team Room, they were waiting for me and let fly. I was exhausted, frustrated and still incredulous at what had happened. I was so affronted at their anger that I would not back down and admit they were justified. I don't think they ever actually forgave me, but they were loyal and effective soldiers. My No 2 (Smudge) was magnificent and probably saved the day with his immediate reaction to the van fire. If the EOD device had burned to detonation, augmented by 40 litres of fuel in the jerricans next to it, it could have caused more casualties than the attack had. I heard later that he had calmed a hysterical young soldier who was caught but uninjured in the first blast. Taff, my lead Electronic Counter Measures (ECM) Operator (they were known as 'Bleeps'), was of small stature but huge heart. He was the Army's premier Rugby Regiment's Fly Half. In radio-controlled bomb scenarios, the Bleep is literally protecting the operator from the unseen radio command-detonated bomb. This was a massive responsibility on young soldiers, and, after meeting him when I arrived at Bessbrook, I rapidly developed an unshakable faith that my life was safe in his hands. But this made taking a right bollocking from him all the harder to bear. An illogical but massive guilt burden started to build in my head and I just wanted to go away and hide.

The next thing to happen was that Dutch, the RESA, and myself were invited by the Commanding Officer to join the officers in the officers' mess as their guests that evening. The CO explained he had arranged for us to be stood down so that we could drink. This was an unusual turn of events but then it had been a most unusual day. It was clear that a good session was planned but, to the CO's astonishment, I declared I was tee-total and only drank softies. I'm not sure this did my credibility any good, but he was very grateful at the way the attack was handled. At the beginning of the attack, he was on R & R Leave somewhere in England and had raced back as soon as he heard the news. I think he was genuinely distressed that it had happened whilst he was away.

The attack was over, but in my mind, the action replays started and continued relentlessly. I had pulled off one of the fastest ever clearances of a very large-scale mortar attack which started just after 11 am and the base was restored to normality by teatime. But I couldn't stop going over how I had handled things. I couldn't get down off the adrenaline rush. In those days, any suggestion of mental illness could see you forced out of the trade. It was regarded as a sign of weakness. Even one of my friends was critical and dismissive when I later mentioned the stress to him. For a laugh, some of the more mischievous soldiers in the mill would bang my door loudly to make me jump as they went past to the gym in the following days. I laughed with them but wished it would stop.

Over the next few days, I succumbed to the classic post-incident preoccupation of repeating and unrelenting mental action replays. I was trying to compile what was going to be a complicated technical report. MoD Scientists had interviewed me, and I was scathing in my condemnation over those aspects of the incident which I felt were down to intelligence failures. I was able to commend the way the CCTV system and tannoy helped me communicate both ways with the operations officer. The fact that the mortar attack alarm depended exclusively on mains electricity was woefully short-sighted and this issue bit twice. Firstly, the initial alarm tone only lasted a split second. Then, when the electrical power was restored midway through the clearance, the alarm went off again, albeit briefly; I think the panic button was still depressed. I remember being very angry. As they left, they thanked me for my 'incisive feedback'. A few days after I submitted the EOD report, which was routinely copied to MoD Technical Intelligence, in-house technical departments and the Royal Engineer Search Training Wing, I was flattered to receive a phone call from the QMSI (Quartermaster Sergeant Instructor) of the Search Training Wing. He was over the moon at the content of the report (I probably should have asked for a copy of that aerial photograph as I knew they had copies). Then I was to come down to earth (again) with a bump. A friend of mine phoned me to say that a technical officer in our EOD training centre had put my report on the branch notice board for all to see. He had highlighted the parts of the report he thought were wrong or unprofessional. One example was that I had listed the destruction of my contaminated clothing on the report which he ridiculed as irrelevant, but we were required to do that by HQ 321 EOD to support write-off and accounting action. This petty and factually incorrect criticism triggered a massive anger reaction in me. I should have recognised the signs and asked for help, but I didn't know who I could turn to. I certainly wasn't going to ask anyone at HQ 321 EOD Company. It seems I was up one moment and down the next. I still had the larger portion of my tour ahead of me with, as I would experience, some quite dangerous tasks to come.

Then a kindly word was had with me by the Royal Hampshire's RSM. He could see I was troubled and asked me why. I explained the criticism which had been coming in. He paused and then said that he had been taking phone calls himself about the mortar attack from his infantry peer group. These peers were envious of the Battalion's experience and lucky escape. He went on to say he thought those who were critical of me would have given their eye teeth to be in my shoes and it was jealousy. Right or wrong, I was uplifted by this pearl of wisdom until I remembered the plight of the seriously ill casualty.

One bomb I dealt with had partially detonated whilst still in its launch tube and the tube and bomb body were crimped together. I used an explosive device to cut the bomb loose which only partly succeeded. I thought there would be value in accessing the intact propulsion unit. I flooded the tube bottom with water and poured water into the circumferential groove I was cutting with a hacksaw. Eventually, I cut the tube loose and saw the propulsion unit. The hollow steel body contained an improvised propelling charge of very fine black powder with the consistency of talcum powder. I rated the quality as very high.

The black powder was sealed within by multiple wraps of light blue adhesive tape. Despite being immersed in water overnight, the black powder was perfectly dry. The igniter was a flash bulb. There was a number written on the tape in blue ballpoint ink. I believe it was the range in yards. When I compared the impact points of the bombs which flew, I could see immediately that several of them had been direct hits on reception, the main kitchen, the messes, the accommodation block, the sauna next to the EOD Team accommodation and the car park, which was also an evacuation muster point. The bombs which flew were anything but random in the way they fell into the busiest centres of activity in the 'softer' buildings. Only one bomb had landed on the solid granite mill building which contained a sacrificial layer under the roof to protect the soldiers' accommodation. The aiming point selected by the person who set the baseplate up was, I believe, a distinctive stainless steel boiler flue and not the main mill chimney stack which others had claimed. The lorry was not aligned with the main chimney at all. There was a final twist. I discovered a large dent in the flatbed's main chassis, inboard of the left-hand rear wheel station. It was well-defined and deep. I also found a shattered collar from a 7Lb CO_2 gas cylinder lying nearby. The collar exhibited classic brisance fracturing and high-temperature oxide colouring which I've seen many times in shrapnel from detonated thick-skinned artillery shells. It was my belief this was a secondary device which had been attached by a line to the universal joint where it would function and disable the vehicle if the vehicle was moved after arming. It could also kill or injure anyone trying to move it. As mentioned earlier, between 5 and 8 bombs had launched simultaneously and the high-energy recoil forces would have been more than sufficient to roll the lorry backwards, triggering this anti-movement device.

I was puzzled by the lack of follow-up to this major incident. I am clear about precisely why the mortar baseplate malfunctioned, and this is very sensitive information which cannot be disclosed. To this day, I harbour a suspicion that this attack was anticipated, and that the gang that delivered the lorry to the mill was under surveillance but that there was a major failure in that surveillance operation. Although not normally superstitious, I retained the split pin and ring used to start the firing pack timer which was discarded by the bomber when he armed the device. The forensic investigator declined to take it and it has been my lucky charm keyring ever since. The cover picture on this book shows the devastation in the reception area of the mill. I reiterate my opinion that this attack could have killed dozens. Also, that it was preventable and revealed what was a shameful lack of protective security. It transpired that just a few days before the attack, the military guard was removed from the carpet factory end of the mill and that civilian contract security replaced them. The lorry bearing the mortar baseplate was brought in and positioned perfectly to achieve the most lethal effect. It was not detected in the few minutes between delivery and firing. I heard that immediately before the first bomb launched, a phone call was received in the operations room from a covert agency to give warning, but that call was cut off and left no time to react. The demeanour of certain people belonging to covert agencies and unsolicited comments made in my presence convinced me there was more to this incident than has been disclosed. That is often the way of these things. When I eventually left the province, I felt the covert agencies were completely out of control and grossly uncoordinated. That is my unshakable opinion and if any member of the covert agencies who were present at the time reads this book, I hope they will reflect on how they let the troops in Bessbrook Mill down and how fortunate they are that truth and their failings will not likely be revealed.

Baseplate Vehicle destroyed after firing – note major structural damage to the building behind. An empty launch tube is on the ground behind the man in blue jeans.

7 of the 16 mortar bombs. The explosive fillings have been removed and bagged. From the left, bombs 4, 6 & 7 have the welded lug on the side which would normally indicate a bomb with a percussion-ignited fuze. Despite this feature, all bomb fuzes were ignited electrically on launch.

The Firing Pack. Crude but effective. The pack contained power supplies, switching, timers and BBQ spit motor to enable sequential launch through a ripple switch. A Perspex cover to the left of the timers into which the firing pins were inserted is barely visible. Attribution of photograph unknown.

On 25 April, I was assisting in a route clearance operation along a road in the rolling hills of South Armagh. It was fine and sunny. Dutch, the ARB Royal Engineer Search Advisor (RESA), was leading, and I was there only to resolve any potentially suspect items. We had two search teams and a Lilliput to provide electronic search. We were making good progress when I was called to investigate a twinflex cable that had been found running along the base of a hedge. It turned out the cable was innocent, it being the connection between a doorbell on a gate post some distance from the front door of a large house on a hillside. As I reached into the hedge, I could hear the search team banter on their local radio net. Someone was giving a running commentary on my actions, and I heard a voice say something like "ATO is reaching forward into the hedge towards the suspect cable". Then, a massive explosion from some distance away echoed over the hills. The two search teams were some distance apart and I could hear worried radio calls from the team furthest away asking if that was me that had triggered the blast. As this happened, a tall civilian man came striding towards me from the house. He demanded to know what I was doing, which, to be fair, was quite reasonable. I asked if he had heard the blast and he immediately responded by saying it "Was more Brits dead". With that, he turned and went back to his house. I promptly returned to RESA's location, and we requested a situation report from Bessbrook Operations Room. It turned out there had been a very large explosion about 11 km east of where we had been conducting the route clearance. The location was on the main A1 Road at Killeen, very close to the garage where Charles McIlmurray's body had been dumped. RESA and I were collected by an Army Gazelle and flown to the location, landing on the road where a temporary control point had been established by the first people to respond. On arrival, we were told there were two fatalities in a car that was nearest to a deeply incised bomb crater at the roadside and several injured persons had been evacuated from other cars, including members of the Irish National Rugby Team and two nuns. The identity of the deceased was given as Lord Chief Justice Maurice Gibson and his wife, Lady Cecily. Their bodies were still at the scene. Their car had caught fire and first responders had attempted a rescue which was impossible. They had been killed instantly in what was clearly a very powerful explosion, detonated very close to their car as they drove past.

We considered that an immediate recovery operation should be planned. We had the advantage of having already arrived at a location where we could work from. We now needed to comply with a number of mandatory operating procedures designed to keep us safe in case there were other bombs near us. The two search teams were urgently recalled by air and joined us. The Lilliput was brought in and then the remainder of my team from Bessbrook Mill. Our normal method of working was that RESA (Dutch) would be the liaison officer with the Reconnaissance Information Centre (RIC). After we had agreed our options, he would task aerial photography and would plan the search procedures. When the imagery was ready, he would usually fly to the RIC base at RAF Aldergrove and discuss the findings with a photographic interpreter. The imagery would then form the basis of a planning pack which could be used by all of the agencies needed to get the job done. This was likely to become a planned operation, involving hundreds of military, RUC and other emergency services. In planned operations, there was an established sequence of operational phases which had been developed through brutal lessons learned in the past. You would start with the primary objective, the most important of which was to save life. We knew the victims were deceased as this had been declared by the first responders. The wounded had already been evacuated, as had bystanders and the nearby garage. The aim of this operation was clear to us; we needed to recover the bodies in the safest possible way whilst preserving and recovering any evidence. The resources we had already tasked had been agreed and we now had to wait. I was crystal clear on my top personal objective at that point which was force protection. We were very close to the border and had been drawn in immediately after a huge explosion. The area was well known for its history of booby-trapping and command-initiated ambush bombs. We were still uncertain of how this attack had been executed. Given the high profile of the victims, we were assured of the fastest possible response by supporting agencies to get the operation under way.

Then the CATO arrived by road. He consulted the incident commander and then came over to see us. When he saw the two search teams at the side of the road, he demanded to know why they weren't already conducting a search operation. Dutch replied that we had tasked RIC to get overhead imagery and, until this was available, we couldn't plan the isolation search as we were blind to whatever might be out there. The CATO then insisted the search teams deploy immediately to complete an isolation search. Dutch protested politely that this was contrary to his standard operating procedures. The CATO then declared he was the senior EOD Commander in the Theatre (meaning Northern Ireland) and that he had the authority to overrule RE search procedures. Dutch then said he would need to refer up his own chain of command before he was prepared to commit his teams. CATO then changed tack and demanded that a final approach man carry out an immediate route clearance to the bomb crater to "Get his man in". This argument, with all of the aggressive rhetoric coming from the CATO, took place in front of onlookers who looked visibly bewildered. I was in the middle of all of this and felt the CATO was wrong. He had the authority to overrule procedures but there was no justification offered as to why we should now abandon caution. Frustrated by Dutch's unerring logic and polite but firm refusal to commit his teams, CATO turned to me and ordered me to conduct an immediate manual approach. He said he wanted me to clear the scene to enable the recovery of evidence before the crater filled with water. For me, the situation was rapidly deteriorating. Other than the Search and EOD phases, we had no opportunity to co-ordinate our activities with the other agencies. We were 'making it up as we went along'. We did next to nothing to seize the initiative back from the terrorists and now I was being ordered to put myself at considerable risk for no conceivable benefit. It was what you would call being between a rock and a hard place.

I got dressed in the bomb suit by my No 2. The usual team banter was absent, and I was surrounded by grim faces. Taff the Bleep handed me some man-portable electronic equipment and I started the approach, walking down the centre of the road. I had never felt so exposed in a manual approach, before or since, and I've done a few. As to fear, I felt none but my mental processes had been totally eclipsed in this regard by what I saw as an abuse of power. Normally, the prospect of failure was something which would prey on my mind, but I felt that we were now beyond failure. The terrorists had succeeded brutally, common sense had been usurped and now I was wandering around like a green version of Mr Blobby with no real plan except to react if I saw anything; it went against all of our established EOD doctrine. I had no prior awareness of the environment and couldn't even categorise what I was doing as a calculated risk. CATO didn't accompany me to the crater and waited at the control point for my signal to indicate it was safe for him to approach. I was focused totally on getting down

the road hoping I would see anything suspicious before I might come
to harm. I passed between the crater and the burned-out wreckage of
the victim's car. I could see the victims, cruelly mutilated, and the only
positive I could draw was that death would have been instant. That is
not to trivialise or mitigate the horror of what the terrorists had done.
I knew by then that the terrorists had wanted the judge dead and had
declared their intent in the media. This massive, radio-controlled bomb
was evidence of that and the outcome showed their only philosophy
was that the end would justify the means, even if it meant hurting
others like nuns and rugby heroes. I could see up to the border and
there were TV cameras pointed at the scene. I later saw that a live feed
was being broadcast as I approached. I knew a private ambulance was
back at the control point and that the media frenzy would continue
whilst the deceased's remains were present. After completing a survey
of the scene, I removed the bodies one at a time and got them up to the
waiting ambulance. After that, a detailed search for evidence under
CATO's direct supervision took place. I did not handle any of the re-
coveries nor was I involved in cataloguing what was found, if indeed
anything was found. We concluded the clearance and extracted back to
the mill. Just after getting back, the RESA's Troop Commander spoke to
me. He wanted to know if the ATO/RESA relationship was functional
and, if not, he would arrange to replace Dutch. For me, this was the
last straw. I got very angry at the suggestion that Dutch had allegedly
failed to support me, and I explained what I had witnessed. The young
officer looked uncomfortable and left. This incident marked the nadir
of my relationship with the CATO. In the South Armagh area, I needed
the reassurance of a competent senior officer who I might confide in
should the need arise. I concluded that CATO was a liability and that
I was under something of a cloud. For someone already selected for
promotion to WO1 at the age of 32, and shortlisted for a commission,

I should have been in a good place mentally but all I could feel was negativity.

The sharply incised crater at the roadside. The car containing the bomb was completely destroyed. The bomb was detonated by radio control as the victims drove past.

The remains of the victims' car. The attack was carried out in broad daylight and within sight of a nearby Army observation post. There was speculation that rogue members of the security forces had leaked the Gibsons' itinerary to terrorists. It turned out they had booked their journey with a travel agency in their own name.

One day, a phone call was received in the Team Room and the soldier who answered offered me the handset, saying it was my wife. As I answered, expecting it to be Christine, I was horrified to hear it was my ex-wife. Our marriage of about seven years was stormy, to say the least, and I would characterise our divorce as highly acrimonious. We had two children, and I was aware that my ex-wife had returned to her home city (Armagh) and therefore lived locally. What I didn't know, which I believe was deliberately concealed from me, was the lengths to which my ex-wife had gone to try and re-establish contact with me. I hung up on her immediately after telling her never to call me again. I had worked hard to make sure that all correspondence was conducted through my solicitor in Edinburgh, and it had been four years since our divorce. I then told the Team members that they should not accept any similar calls going forward. What happened next was profoundly shocking. The operator who I was originally to take over from (Jim) was short-toured and had left the province before I arrived. The operator I actually took over from was a temporary stand-in (Rob). It was explained to me that my ex-wife had joined the Ulster Defence Regiment and she was based in Drumadd Barracks in Armagh. Jim knew my ex-wife and knew I was scheduled to replace him. One way or another, the two had met up and my ex-wife found out I was on the way. The plot thickened when my ex-wife then allegedly made the acquaintance of a soldier based in Bessbrook whose duties involved making many journeys in Q Cars. I was told their relationship was intimate and was finally revealed to senior management when their Q Car became stranded near Forkhill, late at night, and they were obliged to abandon it. I was informed the journey was unauthorised and they were at very considerable risk of coming to harm as they were in a hostile area. This news suddenly made sense for me of the bizarre Q Car briefing at Lisburn when I first arrived; I hadn't imagined the body language at all and it was now clear that I was the last to find out. I was furious about this and I remember making a particularly irate call to the Senior Ammunition Technical Officer (SATO). Suspecting that senior management thought I was colluding in my ex-wife's behaviour, I declared my absolute repugnance for the way I was kept in the dark. In hindsight, I now believe this episode had 'poisoned the well' and that my integrity had been under a deep, dark cloud since well before I arrived. I couldn't understand the barely concealed hostility exhibited by the CATO towards me. He had never met me before and I was deeply disappointed in all the senior staff at HQ 321 EOD Company for not having the moral courage to advise me of what happened. It suddenly made sense as the dots joined up, but by then, the horse had bolted. My relationship with CATO had started badly and was to fall away even further after my tour in Bessbrook concluded.

I was always one to laugh at the dafter things that could happen in the direst of circumstances. On one occasion, we mounted a planned operation to deal with suspected bags of explosives which were thought to be an ambush device on the banks of a small river. We had gone to great lengths to follow our procedures. Dozens of people such as Infantry soldiers, RUC Policemen, Army and RAF aircrews, photographic interpreters and RE Search Teams had collaborated and we were finally ready for me to make a manual approach. The Final Approach man had cleared a route in for me. His job was to get in as close to the bomb as he could without actually touching it. We had worked all day in heavy rain to get to the climax of this job. As he briefed me on the approach route and what he had seen, I looked at the now heavily swollen river rushing past us. He described plastic bags with vivid markings on them and I said, nodding in the direction of the river, "What, like those?" It turned out that the suspect bomb was actually painting and decorating waste which had been fly-tipped upstream on the banks of the river and we saw them as the bags sailed by just feet away from us, heading for the south. It must have rated as the most expensive rubbish collection ever!

Vehicles could be a source of black humour. I knew from both training and personal experience that vehicles were capable of doing the weirdest things whenever they caught fire, which they often did during clearances. Lights would come on, the horn would sound, windscreen wipers would start working and engines could start up as the fire melted the insulation on the wiring. If the car had been left in gear, it could even move off and this equally horrific and hilarious outcome could result in the suspect car driving towards the team! We had a big vehicle clearance coming up and I pondered over what could possibly go wrong. The operations officer had briefed me that a vehicle abandoned on the access road to an observation tower near the border would have to be cleared and removed. This vehicle had history and he explained what was known about it. It was a 10-ton tipper truck. It had been hijacked by the IRA about a year earlier and then used to both transport and protect a team of terrorists who were heavily armed. The truck approached the tower and the terrorists, concealed in the back, opened fire. Fire was returned and, in the ensuing battle, the truck was hit by a burst of Army machine-gun fire and was disabled. The engine stalled and the terrorists then fled the scene. The side of the truck had gone into a soft earthen bank. It was not known why the truck wasn't cleared and removed at the time, but it was not uncommon for the Army to leave things alone if they weren't perceived to be a risk. As it had been left in the open for a year and not continuously watched, the truck and its immediate surrounds merited maximum caution. The troops in the tower above were at a safe distance from it and commuted by helicopter so its presence had been tolerated. The Army now needed vehicular access to the tower to carry out maintenance with heavy equipment. A track-laying excavator had been brought in and was now waiting nearby for the truck to be taken away.

A planned operation was conducted. After some hours, we reached the point where the search team final approach man was due to start his approach. I asked Dutch to nominate a Sapper who had a heavy goods vehicle licence. The reason for this sounded unlikely to the ever-sceptical Dutch but he agreed to indulge me. The final approach man went off and returned shortly, having established a safe route in for me to the side of the truck. I then approached and gained access to the cab.

I did a careful search and was then confident that the vehicle's gears could be checked to ensure it was in neutral. The bemused Dutch sent the final approach man with the HGV licence back to the truck and the gear stick was wobbled about and the truck was deemed to be in neutral with the handbrake off. One of the standard operating procedures for suspect vehicles was that we had to move them at least their own length before we could declare them to be clear. The track-laying excavator was called forward and I went forward again and connected the long tow chain to the truck. We were now ready to try and pull the truck out of the earth bank and at least its own length. I warned everyone to take precautionary cover as this could lead to an explosion. The excavator started up and moved off. The tow chain lying loose on the road straightened out and leapt into the air with a quiver. The excavator's engine note increased as it took the strain. I thought for a moment the truck wasn't going to budge but, as we watched, we saw part of the earth bank collapsing as the truck shifted position. Then it happened. As the truck lurched forward, big puffs of smoke emerged from its exhaust pipe above the cab. With a loud VROOM and under its own power, it then surged forward with a roar of seeming defiance. Cue panic and consternation in the ICP! Despite being up an incline, the truck started driving towards us! Dutch glared at me as though he suspected some trickery. As we urgently scanned the surrounding area looking for a safe refuge from the demon truck, it staggered to a halt and died on the road before us. It was hilarious because no harm was done. The final approach man was clearly a better searcher than an HGV driver it seemed and I left Dutch to deal with him.

Some weeks later, reports were received of unexplained explosions in the vicinity of a farm on the Concession Road south of Crossmaglen. This area had seen many dangerous come- on incidents in the past and we had every reason to be cautious. The local population remained tight-lipped. The area was earmarked for a future clearance operation. I performed two aerial reconnaissance flights in a Gazelle helicopter, several days apart, and took the opportunity to photograph the farm in some detail with a long lens camera. Remarkably, given the vibration and unstable helicopter platform, some of the photographs came out quite well and I could discern objects of interest such as the chain used to secure the main door which was looped through the door handles. This barn was a modern breeze-block structure. The main sliding door for machinery was closed and it had a smaller wicket door built into it for pedestrian access. There was no other conventional means of access into the barn. Then something really bizarre happened; I was summonsed to Crossmaglen to meet the farmer himself. He had reported his concerns about wrongdoing around his farm to the authorities and, by his own volition, he wanted to talk directly to the bomb disposal man. It was known that a member of his family was a convicted murderer serving a life sentence in prison. I was curious but felt out of my depth. It was inconceivable that a republican resident along the Concession Road would volunteer information to the Brits. I met with him in a room within the Crossmaglen Base. He was a sad-looking old man with watery eyes. Without wishing to be disrespectful, I was reminded of Wilfrid Brambell in the role of Albert Steptoe in the popular TV series Steptoe and Son. He professed concern for his property in the barn. I sensed he was trying to tempt me into entering the barn for nefarious reasons or, as the intelligence picture developed later, he was trying to distract my attention from something else in the vicinity. I took notes during our meeting and asked for detailed information about what was in the barn, where was it positioned, when had he last been inside it and was it locked and secured. He volunteered quite detailed information. He said the barn was locked and he hadn't been inside it for ages. I was able to create a diagram of where he claimed various bits of machinery, baled straw and a vehicle inspection pit just inside access door were located. It happened that my two aerial photography attempts demonstrated that the chains on the barn door had been moved between my overhead flights. Someone was telling porkies. I passed the information back to the ARB Operations Officer. I also called my technical HQ at 321 EOD Company. I reported my concerns and asked if they had any EOD intelligence resources that might be able to assist in assessing what was going on. They said they had no information. I expressed some disbelief that explosions had been heard in the area and these had not been reported or documented at the HQ which was normally an obligation on their part. This 'Doubting Thomas' episode on my part found its way to CATO's ears, and he phoned me afterwards and upbraided me. Typical of his chaotic style, the phone call started on a conventional phone which was capable of going into an encrypted mode. To do this, the initiator would issue a recognised code word, buttons would be pressed, and you were then permitted to discuss classified matters. Sadly, we couldn't get the encrypted mode to work. It turned out that new cryptographic key codes were issued every day. The key for that day hadn't been entered at the Lisburn end. In clear, over the phone I could hear the CATO yelling at one of his staff. Then he called out loud the crypto code over the phone as he entered it at his end. If I'd mentioned he had just compromised this secure communications facility, I would probably have been on a flight back to Germany the same day! The call was brief, entirely unhelpful and I was left wondering what the point of CATO was. We had clashed a couple of times already and I resolved to have as little to do with him as I could.

I spoke to the ARB Operations Officer. He didn't look like the stereo-typical officer. He didn't sound like an officer, but he was bright, had good listening skills and excellent judgement. He gave me unfettered access to some intelligence files containing information on the known terrorists in and around our area. One of them had a degree in elec-tronics and lived near Dundalk in the south. I went back to my office and started drawing together the confused intelligence picture which confronted me. My door was open into the corridor, and I sensed some-one was outside. Suddenly, a somewhat scruffy and unmilitary-looking person in combat dress appeared in front of me. He had long untidy hair and said he was from an organisation I had never heard of - the Northern Ireland Surveillance Section (NISS). I demanded he produce proof of identity which he did. He started to talk about the situation along the Concession Road. He spoke of something which was near the farm in question.

He already knew that a clearance operation was going to take place and said he had arranged to meet me there on the ground and he want-ed us to collaborate in dealing with a somewhat embarrassing situation. When I expressed my concern that this job was growing arms and legs by the minute and I still didn't have a clue about what was going on, but that I was expected to take all the risks, he mentioned that I should visit the office of another organisation. I followed him into the corridor, and he walked up to a large map which was pinned to the wall. Behind the map was a concealed door which opened into a small office complex. It turned out this was the Force Research Unit (FRU). In there, I was given more information. This included the suspicion that the IRA had concreted mortar baseplates into a trench system south of the border. The mortars had allegedly been registered (the process of test firing a weapon and zeroing it in onto a future target of opportu-nity) and it was believed they could accurately strike pre-determined targets in the north. The information made sense as it would explain the somewhat random explosions reported earlier but we still didn't know what the targets were.

Some days later, the CO sent for me. He expressed his concern that the forthcoming operation could result in many SF casualties. He had decided against using helicopters to insert his cordon troops and he had devised a quite unconventional method to deploy them into position. This reinforced my doubts about the whole situation. I planned that the EOD Phase would maximise explosive access to all areas of interest, especially the barn. I retrieved an old door and used it as a template to make an explosive access charge to breach the back wall of the barn; there was absolutely no way I was going in through the door. Final planning was conducted, and I elected to insert myself and the Team by helicopter quite close to a house containing a resident family. The rationale was that it was unlikely that a large explosive device would be sited near them. The planned operation was intended to take two days. We helicoptered into position, the Bleep and me initially alone as we used our electronic counter measures equipment to search for threats and we searched for physical threats. The full EOD Team, arms and explosive search dog and RE Search Team were then called in. We dug trenches and went firm. We had a planning pack of high- definition aerial photography and after the conventional all-round search for command wires and electronic counter measure procedures were completed, the final approach man cleared a route for me so I could approach the barn from the northwest direction in order to place the access charge against the barn wall. An infantry major accompanied me to my start point and then I approached the barn alone. I had attached two steel pickets (long steel poles with sharpened points) to the door by hinges giving me flexibility on where the charge would be placed against the wall and assuring the weight of this contraption would press it firmly into place. Satisfied with the placement, I rejoined the major and we sought cover behind an outbuilding some distance from the barn where we could see what was about to happen. I must point out that the explosive charge I had in place was 6 metres long and contained just over 1kg of explosive. The major asked if he could press the button. I told him how the exploder worked and what to do and we radioed a warning. The charge was detonated; even after years of conducting explosive demolitions and controlled explosions, I have to say the effect was dramatic. There was an immense thunderclap. The charge had been glued to the outer perimeter of the door. About two thirds of the door remained intact and flew towards us at great speed, passing by us whilst remaining perfectly vertical and falling to the ground.

Then we heard an odd creaking sound and turned our heads towards it. About another 50 metres from us was a single bay garage. It had an up and over door which had been rattled by the shock wave and had burst its lock. Under the force of the door's spring, the door opened upwards, revealing shrink-wrapped pallets of Tennent's Lager. We suspected some cross-border smuggling; I sensed my approval rating with the infantry had soared and the major was well impressed. As the smoke and dust subsided, I could see the aim had been achieved. The wall was breached, and I could get inside. On the first approach, I looked inside the hole, and I could see that the positions of the various items of farm equipment did not tally with the farmer's statement. More cause for suspicion. I got inside and cleared a route to the inside of the big door, past the inspection pit which was full of objects despite being supposedly empty. From the outside, the chains were given the explosive treatment and the doors were pulled open from a safe distance.

I turned my attention to the rest of the barn. I was now concerned with the inspection pit. I was told it was empty but now it was full of stuff like boxes, and large plastic containers. This phase of the operation was taking a little longer than I expected so I decided to expedite things by deploying a device we called Flatsword. This was a powerful explosive device capable of cutting through beer kegs and milk churns. It was positioned so that the projected blade would fly along the length of the pit taking out anything in its path. After firing it, the resultant smoke persisted longer than it should and we realised that a fire had broken out in the scattered straw piles. At this stage, I was frustrated by the lack of any results. I went back to my EOD Control Point to reassess the situation, checked my ammunition stock levels and told my number 2 to radio for a replenishment. A few minutes later, the SATO (Mark) called back wanting to know if we were trying to start World War 3! After the fire had self-extinguished, I was able to complete the clearance of the barn. Nothing of interest was found and I concluded the barn was a red herring; something else, so far unknown to us, lay behind what had brought us here. What I did know was that a wild goose chase along the border south of Crossmaglen was foolhardy; this place had a certain reputation and if you went looking for trouble, it would eventually find you. It was time to focus on what else was needing to be done and then leave.

The man from NISS had mentioned an interest in a derelict located east of the barn. So, on Day two, we switched our attentions to the derelict and its approaches. There was a stone wall built into an earth bank and route clearance along it was conducted by a young Sapper to clear a way in for me. When he came back, he briefed me on how the safe route was marked and that he had found nothing of significance. I then approached the derelict fully suited up, but as I neared the wall,

I saw a tell-tale soot deposit; it appeared to be gas wash from a small explosion. Some types of explosive, military and homemade, have what is called a negative oxygen balance. TNT is a classic example of this. What it means is there is insufficient oxygen in the explosive mixture to convert all the carbon in the detonation process into gas, for example, carbon monoxide or carbon dioxide. The carbon can then be deposited and, unlike soot from a fire, the deposit betrays the explosive nature of its formation. At the base of the deposit, there was no sign of impact or crater. There was no shrapnel or any other residue present. Someone had cleaned up but had missed the gas wash. I returned to the control point and conferred with the RESA and final approach man.

This was baffling. Then I was joined by the man from NISS. Together we went forward to sort out the object of his concern near the derelict. He was non-committal. I stood by as another phase of the operation was concluded and then we extracted. The whole operation concluded as mysteriously as it had started. I didn't expect the covert agencies to explain things to me as they would be classed as 'need to know'. However, what I did know was that the different covert agencies seemed incapable of presenting a cohesive incident context to me, to enable a robust threat assessment, when I felt I deserved better. I felt I couldn't trust them and they didn't seem to be accountable to anyone.

Late one evening, I was awakened and called to the operations room. Some electronic equipment at Crossmaglen had inexplicably detected a radio frequency signal which was exactly the same as an established terrorist bomb frequency and it was believed to be very close to the perimeter fence. No other information was to hand. The frequency detected had no legitimate purpose anywhere in the UK at the time and the reasonable conclusion was that a radio-controlled bomb had been positioned close to the base. I was sent to Crossmaglen in an

Army Lynx helicopter with some of my portable electronic equipment for the purpose of diagnosing what was going on. For those readers unaware of the precautions taken throughout South Armagh, I will explain what is entailed when a helicopter flies at night into a forward base like Crossmaglen. This Army base was located in the town, next to a Gaelic Athletic Association pitch and clubhouse. Crossmaglen was one of the most dangerous places in the province. Movement by road in marked Army vehicles was strictly limited and commuting was almost always by helicopter. It wasn't usual for helicopters to fly into that base in the hours of darkness. I had already been told that CCTV surveillance had noted that a great many windows in the town were open. It was a fine and mild evening; perhaps the locals needed fresh air? It was equally possible the locals were expecting a large explosion and they had opened their windows to reduce glass breakage. With some misgivings, I was on board the Lynx now heading for the base which might have a large bomb next to it waiting for a worthy target like this helicopter to arrive. The Lynx was crewed by two; the pilot was in the right-hand seat and his P2 co-pilot was in the left-hand seat. The aircraft was in complete darkness and not showing any navigation lights. The pilots were wearing night vision goggles. I was seated immediately behind the pilots on a bench seat. I was facing the left and my right shoulder was against the pilot's armoured seat back. In front to my left was the P2 and his SLR was slung over his armoured seat back. I was wearing my standard Mk 6 helmet and was not connected to the aircraft intercom system and did not have night vision goggles on. As we neared Crossmaglen, the aircraft orbited the base and started to transition from fast forward flight into a descent. Below, I could see the town's lights but the base below was mostly dark. There were very few visual references. I did notice the high communications towers in the base and the pilot was aware of these, and as we prepared to land,

I think they were on our right-hand side. As we neared the ground, the helicopter suddenly seemed to encounter turbulence. The aircrew were now shouting at each other and the pilot in control was the P1 in the right-hand seat. The aircraft seemed to be out of control; it was lunging in different directions. I was already strapped in with a lap belt. I grabbed the loose end and pulled it even tighter. Whilst it was obvious the aircraft had experienced a control loss and a crash might be imminent, I was drawn to the drama unfolding between the pilots and I watched for clues about what might be wrong. Then we struck the ground hard and the aircraft bounced. It twitched left and to the right. The P2's rifle swung with the bounces and whacked my helmet. It didn't hurt but it added to the sense of impending disaster. Outside the aircraft, the ground handlers were running away from us at each bounce and change of direction, it was as if the helicopter wanted to catch them! The emergency probably lasted only a few seconds, but it felt like ages. We hit the ground again and twitched some more. I had a sense it was like being on a roller coaster ride, complete with high G forces and plenty of bumps. The pilot managed to regain control and took the helicopter straight up. He then descended again and this time landed the Lynx on the pad. Then he shut the aircraft down. This confirmed there had been some kind of emergency. Helicopters do not linger in the forward operating bases like Crossmaglen and Forkhill. They fly in and fly out in the shortest possible time.

Now for the explanation. The Lynx was fitted with an autopilot called the computer acceleration control (CAC). This device was designed to reduce the pilot's workload when flying close to the ground, in ground effect. It worked by compensating automatically for any flight deviations not commanded by the pilot. Like any computer, the CAC could crash and this one did. The cut-out switch to allow the pilot to regain full authority was on the dashboard. In the violent throes of the impending crash, the pilot couldn't reach the switch to turn it off. This potential cause of disaster was already known about and the intended solution was to re-position the cut-out switch onto the cyclic control lever which the pilot almost invariably holds firmly all of the time. However, some bright spark had decided this Lynx fleet modification could wait until the aircraft was next in for scheduled servicing. I would liken the aircraft's several impacts with the ground to resemble the foot stamping and swagger of a huge Japanese sumo wrestler. The aircraft was deemed to be damaged and was unable to fly until it had been certified. The situation at Crossmaglen had now worsened significantly. There might be a radio-controlled bomb and there was now a stranded high- value target stuck on the helipad.

Anyway, back to the suspected bomb (which I had almost forgotten about). Using the pan and tilt controls of the CCTV system, I could see into the back yard of the GAA clubhouse. There was a large collection of beer kegs very close to the base perimeter. Beer kegs, along with milk churns, had been a bomb container of choice for many years. There were no other obvious potential threats near the perimeter so I positioned all the available counter-measure equipment optimally to protect us from that perceived threat. I was shown the evidence for the original signal and it looked very convincing. I called my HQ staff in Lisburn and requested technical assistance. The expert arrived fairly promptly and brought some even more specialised equipment, including one which had a good direction-finding (DF) capability. After a thorough sweep, the DF equipment indicated the suspect signal was coming from a service radio transmitter within the base. Now this was bizarre. The transmitter room was opened and thoroughly checked, and this found nothing untoward. It was decided to power the radio equipment down to eliminate it as the cause while we watched a monitor. When the main radio was turned off, the suspect signal vanished. The whole thing had been caused by a defect in the service radio transmitter. Inexplicably, a fault had developed and the transmitter was leaking radio frequency on the exact frequency of the known terrorist radio-controlled device. The whole thing was written off to experience. This had been my second near miss experience in a helicopter. I felt offended that a senior manager somewhere had decided the CAC cut-out switch replacement did not merit the MoD equivalent of an immediate product safety recall. Who are these faceless people that make these decisions and take what they might categorise as 'calculated risks'? Just like the covert intelligence agencies, who will ever hold them to account?

Towards the end of my tour, a job came in which seemed to be quite routine. The RUC at Newry had phoned to say a child had found a stray Army hand grenade and had handed it in. They had placed the grenade on the road outside the station but within the rocket fencing where it was screened by a small tower of old car tyres. I went alone by road to Newry and was treated to tea and biscuits on arrival. Then I needed to cease the pleasantries, collect the grenade and return to Bessbrook Mill. I looked inside the tower and this is what I saw:

A new improvised hand grenade incorporating
features copied from military grenades

I had never seen this type of grenade before. The usual action on discovering an improvised grenade was to document it and then destroy it. As this was a new discovery, it would need to be exploited and the details promulgated to the wider technical audience.

The dismantled grenade

After I had stripped it down, I could appreciate the potential lethality of this device. The filling was Semtex; lots of it. The method of ignition was similar in most respects to conventional military hand grenades. A striker, under pressure from a stout spring, was held back by a fly-off lever which was secured in place by a safety pin. Pulling the pin out and throwing it would release the striker which would hit the cap which, in turn, would ignite a short delay fuze. This was inserted into a plain detonator. In addition to the steel body, this grenade contained 19 pre-notched steel rings intended to produce shrapnel. The grenade did, however, contain a serious design defect. It was somewhat dishevelled,

302

and I attributed this to it having been concealed in a transit hide for some time. I reported the details and returned to base.

Sometime later, a terrorist tried to throw one of these grenades at a security force patrol and was killed as it detonated prematurely. We'll never know if the design defect caused his death or if he just failed to use it properly. The technical intelligence agency had just re- numbered their catalogue of terrorist grenade types and this new grenade was named the PIRA Mk 14. I don't think it was used again and it was soon superseded.

One of the last, large-scale air operations I conducted was the most directly frightening in terms of a personal threat to my life, a colleague and our equipment. We had information relating to a potentially significant find on the outskirts of Newtownhamilton. An object of interest in a derelict dwelling house had been seen and noted by a patrol. Part of the description was a match to a new type of radio-controlled bomb which we knew had been developed but it was yet to appear. This meant that there was a possibility that we didn't have any countermeasures against it. On the day of deployment, Taff (my Bleep) and myself were dropped by Gazelle helicopter in a field. An outer cordon of infantry was already in place. We carried out an immediate search of our surrounds and used our portable electronic equipment while we waited for the next aircraft. This was to be an RAF Wessex carrying a Heli-Lilli as an underslung load. Perhaps the insertion of the outer cordon was the giveaway, but we were suddenly rushed by a crowd of hysterical women. They piled into us, screaming, scratching and flailing. We were outnumbered by them and, for some reason, the cordon troops did not respond to our plight. The whole thing descended into a veritable scrummage and we were completely overwhelmed. Each of us was armed with a 9mm Browning pistol in a holster, and these were on lanyards attached to our belts for security. Grabbing hands started to pull at holsters and lanyards. The attack on us was being orchestrated by a man; the only man present in this large group of about 20 to 30 women. The very real fear was that through being overwhelmed, one of us might be disarmed and then the weapon turned against us. The women were completely hysterical, like a pack of dogs full of bloodlust. We could not draw our weapons as this would be an escalation and the women would likely ignore weapons being pointed at them. Our only options were to continue the physical struggle in the hope that the cordon troops would intervene or the potential use of lethal force which would be hard to justify; it was the classic 'between a rock and a hard place' situation which then got worse. An RAF Wessex hovered overhead and prepared to drop the underslung Heli-Lilli in the middle of this melee. Between slaps and punches from the women, I tried to wave the aircraft off. The Lilliput was a very valuable and highly-classified asset that we didn't want damaged or compromised.

Rescue came in the form of a solitary RUC Constable. The man orchestrating the attack against us was very close by me and a green blur flashed past and rugby-tackled him to the ground. The constable started shouting at him to see reason and, over the next minute or so, he persuaded the man, who he kept calling Jim, to get the women to go home and leave us to continue dealing with the suspect bomb which threatened their community. The helicopter with its precious cargo moved away and then the cordon troops arrived. Over their radio, we implemented a switch to an alternate landing zone and a few minutes later, we had been moved and the incident was over. I didn't get the name of the constable, but he told me the man orchestrating the women's attack was Jim McAlister, a local republican politician. We were relieved; the incident could have gone either way and we were probably very lucky and indebted to the powers of persuasion of that RUC Constable.

CHAPTER 12

Ammunition Inspectorate BAOR Herford 1987–1991

To introduce this chapter, I will clarify things as the chronology of my Herford tour might appear a little confusing in the telling of it. I was posted to Herford from August 1987 until October 1991 and, in that time, I was deployed to the Falkland Islands in 1989 and then the Gulf War in 1990 - 91. After the Gulf War, I returned to Herford, remaining there as a 'supernumerary' from March 1991 until November 1991. During this time, I was employed as the Administration Officer at 221 EOD Company.

After returning from Bessbrook to Rheindahlen, I was promoted to WO1 and received a posting order to the Ammunition Inspectorate BAOR, based at Herford, not far from Hannover. I finished the big staff project on the ammunition scaling for the Army and handed over a veritable 'book of books' to my successor. I already knew Herford, having lived nearby when my dad was serving at Bünde, and it was a lovely part of Germany. I was to be based in Hammersmith Barracks and became the SAT for 4 Armoured Division. I knew from experience in the UK that 11 EOD Regiment had a serious challenge in resourcing the competing workloads from the conventional inspectorate role and the burgeoning EOD role. In Germany, it was different and perhaps I will now draw some 'competitive fire' from colleagues when I say that inspectorate work in Germany was, in my view, 'real' inspectorate work. Our EOD role was significant but nowhere near as demanding as in the UK. The inspectorate work was, however, far more demanding. In Germany, most units had stocks of both operational and training ammunition. In the UK, most units only kept modest training stocks. The annual inspection of a teeth arms unit in Germany could easily last a week or more because they held so much stock and it all had to be exhaustively checked. All of the accounting was manual and, after returning from a major unit inspection, it could take weeks to generate the report. The bulk of the report took the form of the comprehensive listing of every single type of ammunition held and the list had to be in work-date order, so, if the typist missed a line or the inspecting AT drafted the manuscript list out of sequence, the whole report had to be redone.

One of my first duties on arriving at Herford almost involved a certain déjà vu. I was given a very limited briefing that the Intelligence Services believed that a Mk 10 Mortar attack against a large barracks in Germany was imminent. I was to be deployed in a two-man EOD Team to the barracks in order to provide an immediate response in the event that such an attack happened. Unbelievably, we were located right in the middle of the barracks. Despite my protestations, this not only placed us at risk of becoming casualties, but it also meant, assuming we survived, that we would be at the scene of the incident during the attack which would be far too early and I could see it might become the Bessbrook Mill mortar attack all over again. It is possible that other classified arrangements may have been in place, but I was not briefed on any of this, and it seemed we were just arbitrarily placed in harm's way. No attack materialised, which was just as well. It reinforced my view that 'Military Intelligence' was an oxymoron; again!

My experience of automating the procurement process in Oman then came to the fore. I was determined to automate the production of inspection reports and to capture the inventory held by each unit onto a computer record; this was, after all, 1987. In this task, I had an ally, a young corporal I will refer to as Mick. I think he was doing some kind of training in IT systems, and we were both deeply into IT as a hobby. For equipment, we had three Apricot personal computers in the office. Each one had an integral hard drive of 20 megabytes capacity, a 3.5 inch floppy disk drive and a dot matrix printer. For software, we had Ashton Tate's dBase 2 which was an early relational database. In those days, there wasn't the convenience of a command-centre or graphical interface. You had to learn the code and you worked in a text-based environment from the dot prompt. Mick did the bulk of the coding work and had the knack for it. I led on the design of the overall suite of databases which we integrated into a system we called the Ammunition Reporting and Management System (ARMS). Starting with designing the database of ammunition records, we moved on to include the details of units, personnel and inspection frequency. The finished ARMS programme could forecast inspections, generate inspection-related correspondence, including the all-important annual report, and you could even consolidate ammunition inventories across all of the units in Germany. The finished product was brilliant, if I say so myself, and on behalf of Mick. If you came back from a unit inspection with all your ducks in a row, it became our proud boast that you could put the kettle on and even the largest report would be sat in the printer's tray before your tea was ready. All you had to do was pull off the tractor ribbons on the prints and tear apart all the perforations and then staple the pages together. This informal programme became so popular that it spread by word of mouth and was exported around the world by floppy disk. At the time, the floppy disk was the only way to exchange information between our Apricot computers and this was something of an Achilles Heel. I will explain.

Mick was studying computers, and in those days, Microsoft DOS was the dominant operating system but it wasn't the only one. In MS-DOS, the prompt A:\ referred to the floppy disk and the prompt C:\ was the hard drive. To be fair, Mick was burning the midnight oil on both his computer course and moonlighting on developing ARMS. Disk storage capacity on both floppies and hard drives was minimal and he had to constantly delete obsolete data to make room for whatever he would work on next. The trouble was that in Apricot DOS, the prompts were the opposite of the convention in MS-DOS. Thus, one day, when Mick wanted to delete the contents of a floppy disk, he put the disk in an Apricot computer and typed in A:\ Del*.* and hit return. To the Apricot, this meant delete the entire contents of the hard drive; which included the sole copy of our prototype ARMS programme. He was absolutely beside himself when he realised what he'd done. I don't think I've ever seen a redder face. It set us back a while, but we bounced back and learned the value of keeping backups!

One day, a senior officer from our technical directorate visited and wanted to see a demonstration of ARMS in action. We pressed the start button to generate a report from a large unit and put the kettle on. True to form, the printout completed before the officer got his tea. He read through the pile of paper before turning to me and asking if it could track the mileage of vehicles used to move the inspection team between the units visited. ('Well of course it bloody didn't!!' thinks me.) He then declared that such an automated report generator would encourage idleness on the part of inspecting staff, and he didn't like it. The ARMS programme was therefore starved of official endorsement and was to wither on the vine. Ironically, it proved its worth in the 1990 deployment of troops and ammunition to the Gulf War. As the programme could 'see' where the stocks of war-winning' ammunition were being held in unit first-line accounts, it enabled the rapid detection and incorporation of these stocks onto the deployment. It fared better in this regard than the stores system, which had to resort to broadcasting teletext appeals on the Services Sound & Vision Corporation (SSVC) television channel for urgently needed spares. It seems to me, with the benefit of hindsight, that we depleted the entire BAOR to mobilise the single Desert Rats Brigade to Saudi Arabia. Then, when a second brigade was mobilized, we depleted the UK Base. Friends left behind in Germany told me of '56-tonne radio sets with no tracks or guns' left forlornly in tank parks. This was a dark-humour reference to the cannibalised hulks of main battle tanks, stripped to generate sufficient hardware for just four main battle tank regiments in a Light Division for Operation Granby; so much for the British Army supposedly having four armoured divisions on hand to deter the Warsaw Pact!

Shortly after reporting for duty, I learned that the CATO from my Bessbrook tour was to be the next commanding officer of the Ammunition Inspectorate. Although he was based in Rheindahlen, and didn't see us on a daily basis, he was to become the new CO. In a memorable visit from him, where he interviewed me about my commissioning application after I had been short-listed, he commented, "You're not charming enough to be a commissioned officer, Mr Robinson, but do apply again". But he nevertheless agreed to endorse my application. Months later, I learned that my application had been unsuccessful. I applied again and he offered similar insipid encouragement. I gained the distinct impression that I was perhaps being damned by faint praise. There are many reasons why a CO might do this, and I genuinely considered the possibility that I simply wasn't up to it. But I did wish that, would this be the case, he would grasp the nettle and tell me straight that he wasn't going to recommend me. This unhappy situation continued. I would apply, I would get shortlisted, and I would not be selected. This repeated in the years 1987-1988 and 1988-1989. In 1989, I looked at the prospects of commissioning outside my Corps. The Royal Army Pay Corps (RAPC) looked tempting. At that time, there was a second career path possibility with them. If you could commission as a Paymaster and complete a successful initial engagement, you could apply to go on the long finance course or the long information systems course and emerge with industry-standard qualifications in those areas. Another attraction was that the RAPC selected their late-entry officers through the so-called 'three-day event' process. This contrasted sharply with the RAOC process which was common throughout the Army. In the RAOC process, a candidate would be shortlisted based on a review of his last five annual reports. The selection board would then do a similar review which would include one more report completed by a brigadier. Thing was, most candidates were not well known to most brigadiers so the system relied on the candidate's CO writing a brief for the brigadier. Nepotism doesn't even cover it! The RAPC selection board was a far more objective process and, although my old friend fear of the consequence of failure was 'tapping me on the shoulder', my simple reconciliation with accepting the challenge was that if I didn't succeed, it would only be my lack of ability and not an ongoing personality conflict that was holding me back. To quote my old pal Brad: "If it is to be, it's up to me"! To be fair, I believe the quote originated with William H Johnsen but if we don't keep these motivational quotes in circulation, we will lose both them and the inspiration they provide.

In the spring of 1988, I was awarded the Long Service and Good Conduct Medal (LS&GC). The ceremony was informal and was conducted in the Pig & Stick unit social club. Brigadier Peter Forshaw did the business, and the event was also attended by my father who I had invited over as it seemed he was in remission from his cancer. There was some poignancy in this. Almost exactly 20 years before, I had watched on as he received his LS&GC at Donnington. He enjoyed himself whilst with us although I did notice that he would go to his bed very tired and would sleep in until late the next morning. My dad had always been an early riser, even if he'd had a few the night before. His tiredness was a portent that his cancer was back.

Shortly after that, we went home to Stirling on leave, and we were watching the news on TV on 19 March 1988 when the terrible pictures of the two corporals who had driven into a funeral procession on the Andersonstown Road were shown. They were dragged from their car and ultimately identified as soldiers before being murdered. I heard later that Corporal David Howes, who had only recently left us in Herford, was found to be in possession of a Herford Bowling Club membership card. It was theorised that terrorists may have misread this as Hereford, the regimental home of the SAS. Whatever, there can be no justification for their cruel beating and summary execution. The wild gestures on screen made by black cab taxi drivers left me with the opinion that their murderers were psychopaths. An enduring mystery for me since then was why there was no intervention by security forces, despite the presence of a helicopter immediately above the incident which would have been ideally placed to co-ordinate a rescue.

Later on, during that leave, Christine badgered me into accompanying her on a visit to a 'spookie' for a 'reading'. In other words, we were to visit a spiritualist to see what she might predict in our future. The spookie was an elderly widow and the reading was to be in her home. On arrival, we were welcomed, and I tried to conceal my scepticism from both Christine and the spookie. After a preamble talk about the spirits, we were seated on a couch and Christine was to go first. The spookie closed her eyes and started to talk about what she could see, speaking figuratively by saying things like she could see such and such a person in a top hat, which apparently meant that person would do well in life. Christine's reading took about ten minutes and was full of top hats. I sensed that the predictions were so vague that they would be difficult to prove or disprove. Then it was my turn. There were more top hats and I settled into an expectation that the reading was intended to be optimistic and positive. The spookie said I was a healer and then spoke of my father. Up until then, I believed Dad was in remission from his cancer. She said he was poorly. I replied that he was in remission and then she became quite emotional. She said he was desperately ill, and he needed me. I was quite taken aback by this revelation. In fact, I was shocked. I needed to get away from the spookie. Outside, I expressed surprise at what had transpired. I didn't expect to hear anything negative and thought the whole thing was meant to be a bit of harmless amusement. The logic I applied to explain her professed understanding was that she either had prior knowledge of Dad's condition, more than I had, or she did indeed see his parlous state in some mysterious way. I don't believe in this sort of thing at all. I'm not religious and simply do not buy into it. There have been times in my life when I thought I might have had a premonition but, on reflection, there were invariably subtle clues which had primed my instincts. I was so convinced the spookie was wrong that

I didn't phone my mother for several days. When I did, however, the news was grave. I asked her how my dad was, and she hedged her answer before changing the subject. This was exceptionally odd for my mother who was usually a straight talker. I contacted the Sailor's, Soldier's and Airman's Families' Association (SSAFA) and asked if they could obtain a report into my father's condition. Initially, the attending Clinician refused to disclose but, through SSAFA, I made it clear that I was serving overseas and had grounds to believe my father was very poorly; would they please ask again. The answer was quite profound; If I wanted to see my father again, I should get home as quickly as possible. I requested compassionate leave and travel and then visited the padre. I apologised for being blunt about my atheism and said I needed some pragmatic advice about what to do with a death in the family. The padre was very understanding and answered my questions. He also arranged for an Army padre near Birmingham to visit my father, for which I was grateful; it was, after all, me who was the atheist. Army compassionate travel arrangements are a well-oiled and effective system. I was escorted to the airfield, put on the aircraft last and in the front row. On landing, I was taken off first and escorted through Customs and Excise. My brother collected me for the journey home. When I got home, I understood my mother's emotional state instantly and she appeared to be drifting between reality and denial. My dad was in bed, and I went in to see him. My arrival on compassionate leave seemed to confirm in his mind that he was close to death. My mother and her best friend got him out of bed to take him for a bath and I was staggered at how emaciated he was. He was drifting in and out of delirium and brief periods of lucidity and was on morphine and oxygen. I arranged with my exhausted mother that I would tend to him throughout the night so she could rest properly. At his bedside, he insisted on having a fan blow into his face at a maximum setting. I discreetly checked his pulse and found it very rapid at 140 bpm but so weak it was almost imperceptible. I was to sit with him through several nights, getting the opportunity to have poignant but brief chats with him. When lucid, his mind was sharp, and he understood what was happening. I was shivering in the cold blast from the fan but needed to sit in front of it so as to hold his hand and periodically stroke his forehead. One morning, the local Methodist minister appeared, and Dad seemed overjoyed. Up until that point, I believed Dad was an atheist. Indeed, whilst growing up and attending so many schools, I was told by him to declare my religion as C of E on registration forms. That was when I first learned that Dad was a non-practising Methodist, but he had now returned to his church and then I learned that his dad had been a Methodist lay preacher. I discovered recently that I was actually baptised into the Methodist church as a baby, but I remain an atheist to this day. I must acknowledge, however, that my dad took great comfort from the minister's visits. My dad passed away in the early hours. I turned that bloody fan off and the silence left behind was like a vacuum. I could actually feel the heat radiating off my skin such was the fan's cooling effect. I cleaned him up and shaved him before tidying the bed and propping up his head and fetching mum to see him. I reflected then that life held a bewildering array of contradictions. My dad was far from perfect, but he was the best dad I had because he was the only dad I had.

On 21 December 1988, Christine's 27th birthday, we travelled home via North Sea Ferries to spend Christmas at Christine's family home in Stirling. We landed on the morning of 22 December, and we had heard news on the radio before boarding that a light aircraft had crashed into a garage near Lockerbie. Our route north would take us up the A74, and just after leaving Hull, the news on the radio was that the incident was far worse than announced on the radio the evening before. Pan Am Flight 103, a Jumbo Jet with 259 people on board, had crashed into the town with no survivors and had killed 11 people on the ground, a total of 270 victims. As we approached Lockerbie, it became obvious that something terrible had happened. The traffic slowed to a crawl, and I recall that it was misty around the town. It looked like the south-bound carriageway was blocked and we later saw on TV that it had been severed by a large part of the downed aircraft. To my left was a hedgerow and the top of it was sprinkled with small wriggly frag-ments of aircraft skin which seemed to glow an eerie yellowish green colour which was the aircraft's internal paint finish. Just beyond the hedge was a herd of cows, several of them with the same small pieces of aircraft skin on their backs which had been scattered like confetti. There was nothing else to see and we had no idea of the devastation visited upon the town the night before. The scale of the disaster was incomprehensible. My initial thoughts were that perhaps this was ret-ribution for the downing of the Iran Air Flight 655 on 3 July 1988 by the USS Vincennes, which killed 290 people. What was a certainty was how complex things were in the Middle East during the Iraq/Iran war. For me, it was a harbinger of yet more violence to come.

Meanwhile, back at the inspectorate, the busy day job continued apace. Unit ammunition inspections were the 'bread and butter'. These inspec-tions were often quite stressful for both the inspector and unit staff. In a bid to improve relationships, an innovation was brought about and, sad to say, I can't attribute it to any one person, but it helped solve a problem that can afflict any assurance process: The 'them and us' situa-tion. Every year, units would receive an annual ammunition inspection. All units had to receive several important annual inspections and it was important for a commanding officer to pass these inspections or it could affect his career. The potential consequences of a bad inspection outcome meant it could take a long time to build a mutual trust. In the Field Army, there isn't time to grow relationships due to the high turnover rate of personnel. The innovation was the creation of a social club known as the 'Wheelers and Dealers'. In my opinion, this really broke down barriers and helped to build trust between the inspectors and the inspected.

The way it worked was that Divisional and Brigade staff (the inspectors) would attend quarterly regimental dinners with unit personnel (the inspected). The units typically had the best messes with the most amazing traditions. The inspectors often belonged to large 'faceless' messes where there was little, if any, tradition and cohesion. As an example of how special these regimental dinners could be, I will describe one such dinner which was hosted by the 1st Battalion, The Royal Regiment of Wales (1RRW) in Lemgo. This unit has a proud history which includes the defence of Rorke's Drift, famously depicted, albeit with some inaccuracies, in the film Zulu. Guests were invited from the Divisional and Brigade HQ staffs, our unit and personnel from dozens of Army units based around that part of Germany. I seem to recall that we had over 40 different cap badges present. We were immersed in the 1RRW traditions and culture, including the bit where guests who had never previously been hosted by 1RRW had to eat a raw leek. We were lined up in the mess ante room and orderlies, accompanied by a drummer, brought in silver salvers stacked high with the raw leeks, piled up neatly like little green logs. Each of us had to eat a leek to a drum roll before being allowed to quench the consequential thirst with a foaming pint of beer. Sadly, being a teetotaller, I had to wait until I got back to my place before I could wash the hot, clinging leek down. Another aspect of our dinner, which was great fun, was that the band would play the Regimental quick march of each cap badge represented around the table. When your march was played, you were expected to stand up. Several guests didn't actually know what their Regimental quick march sounded like, and the dinner was plunged into hilarity when two such members were wrong-footed when they were prompted to stand at the wrong times. The presiding member of the mess was WO1 (RSM) Richard Heakin, who was an absolute gentleman. We had a great and memorable night, making new acquaintances and making copious notes of the many insurmountable problems the unit representatives had which was easily in our gift to resolve, and this promoted a harmonious and cohesive working relationship all round. Once home, Christine wouldn't let me into the bedroom until I had dispersed my now fiery breath with toothpaste and mouthwash! It made the next bit of dire news all the more unbearable.

Just a few weeks later, RSM Heakin was murdered in a close-quarter shooting by the IRA as he waited in traffic at a red light outside Ostend, on his way to get the ferry to the UK. The distinctive British Forces number plates we were obliged to display on our cars gave him away. Within months, the number plate policy changed, and we were to use plates identical to the UK system. This late change left a sour taste in the mouth. Those number plates might just as well have been targeting indicators.

The Wheelers & Dealers Tie

In the early summer of 1988, an incident occurred in Paderborn, and I was called to a suspect car in a car park outside an RMP Duty Room. When I arrived, the situation was well in hand, and I was given a competent initial briefing. The suspect car was a VW Beetle Cabriolet, and its four-way flashers were on. There was a somewhat convoluted history about the car, which was registered to British Forces Germany, and the witness seemed quite vague. My suspicions were not that the car could contain a bomb but that there was some kind of fiddle in progress which might be resolved if the car was destroyed by EOD action. I made my suspicions known to the RMP and they, in turn, were able to call the BFG car registration office to look at the car's history. I made it plain to the witness, who we were not sure was the registered keeper, that the car would likely only suffer minor damage and that vigorous police enquiries would take place after this emergency had been resolved. In the trade, it was common to encounter car owners who were ambivalent about what was going to happen to their cars. This was normally in Northern Ireland where our actions would often result in a car becoming burned out which could suit an unscrupulous owner who might want his vehicle 'disposed of'. The story the witness told was that he had purchased the car from his sister's boyfriend who was now overseas and couldn't be contacted. At this point, the RMP's 'waffle-detector' was triggered and the whole silly story started to unravel. The car was one of many VW Beetles being processed in a racket where they were purchased, registered and then converted into desirable cabriolets before being re-sold by an enterprising bunch of squaddies. They had gotten greedy, and this car had become an embarrassment to them. I handed the cleared and undamaged car back to the careful custody of the RMP and watched on as the hapless brother of an unknown car salesman's girlfriend was marched off to the nick. Suspect cars could be tricky and not just because there might be a bomb in them.

On 30th June 1989, I was on duty at M Range, at the Sennelager Training Centre (STC), providing technical cover to an infantry battalion during firings of the recently introduced anti-tank weapon, LAW 80. Each soldier would fire at least one rocket at a moving target several hundred metres away. The rocket would be fired from the shoulder and the firer was closely monitored by a Safety Supervisor standing next to him in the firing bay. I was standing in an adjacent bay, several metres to the left. The two soldiers in the firing bay wore full NBC suits and Service respirators. Additionally, because of the very loud launch signature of this recoilless weapon, everyone in close proximity was required to wear a double set of ear defenders. After an hour or so of firing, another couple entered the firing bay. After the firer had removed the hard protective covers from the weapon and had extended the telescopic launcher and erected the sight, the Safety Supervisor ordered the firer to engage the moving target with the shout "TANK - ACTION". The LAW 80 had an integral spotting rifle which could fire up to five 9mm spotter-tracer rounds which were ballistically matched to the rocket. If the firer saw a flash on his target, it confirmed his aim, and he could then switch over and fire the rocket. There would be a huge bang on launch, but there was no recoil. Having fired the weapon several times, I can vouch for that. The only feeling I recall was a slight sensation of movement as the rocket whizzed past your right ear, off your shoulder. The rocket was designed to be All Burnt On Launch (ABOL), so the huge bang was the sole source of propulsive energy and the rocket would coast towards the target after muzzle exit. You could easily follow the trajectory as the rocket arced towards the target. Typically, the rocket would strike with a tail-up attitude which was beneficial in reducing the relative thickness of sloped armour. After detonating, the aft section of the rocket would fly up into the air before tumbling to the ground down range. I was very impressed with the accuracy of the rocket and its effect on armour. I have fired a lot of recoilless anti-tank systems and in terms of target effect and accuracy, LAW 80 was comparable with the best, but sadly, and in my opinion, the weapon had design flaws. Logistically it was a potential nightmare. The exposed rocket was vulnerable to damage when being brought into action. Users were commonly unable to prepare the weapon and change over to the rocket from the spotting rifle. The spotting rifle magazine was pre-loaded with five rounds and if you didn't fire all five, the rifle would remain cocked and loaded which could be lethal. There was a special adapter which could be used to unload the rifle but there was only one included with each pallet of rockets which was woefully inadequate.

After engaging the target with spotter-tracer, the firer switched over and fired the rocket. This time, though, things were different. There was a double bang as the rocket warhead detonated just forward of the muzzle, well inside the 10-metre minimum arming distance. I looked at the two men in the firing bay and saw that they were injured, still standing upright but leaning heavily on the bay parapet. I ordered everyone down into cover and ran forward. I checked and grabbed the now empty launcher and placed it onto a bespoke rest before turning to the two casualties. Their respirators were still in place, and I was horrified to see what looked like the eye pieces of the first casualty filling up rapidly with blood, possibly indicating a catastrophic head wound but I couldn't see any perforations in the respirator. I removed his respirator and was relieved to see the source of blood was a small cut in his eyebrow which was spraying a thin drizzle of blood which was easily staunched. In a loud voice, I asked him his name and he replied competently despite being in some difficulty. I checked the second casualty who seemed to have fared better. I summoned the medics to take over before speaking to the officer in charge to cease the firing practice so I could start an immediate investigation.

The procedure was one I was well-practised in. Get the casualties away to medical care and freeze the scene to prevent the loss of evidence. Rain can be a problem, but it was a warm sunny day. In front of the firing bay, I noted that the ground was very sandy and was dry and crusty from having been wetted by rain some days earlier. This was important. There were witness marks in the sand directly below the point that I assessed was immediately below where the warhead detonated. It was crucial to record this evidence accurately in a way that would support scrutiny. After briefing the officer in charge to guard the firing point to prevent the evidence from being trampled, I ran over to the nearby 'Tin City' of the Northern Ireland Training and Advisory Team (NITAT). Their officer commanding was Bob, who had just been commissioned from the Ammunition Inspectorate, and I knew him well, having served with him at Kineton and Oman as well as Herford. I knew that NITAT used camcorders to record the way soldiers under training reacted to simulated incidents and if I could borrow a camcorder, I could record the ground conditions at the scene of the muzzle premature. Bob readily agreed the loan and I returned to film the scene.

An early consideration at the scene of an ammunition incident is whether it is safe to allow the continued firing of ammunition, both at local and global levels. Another aspect is whether there is a view that the fault leading to the incident was batch-specific to a small quantity of the ammunition or if it was generic and might mean all stocks of that ammunition were suspect. I prepared my brief to discuss the issue with a desk officer at our technical directorate in the UK. When I called him, I recommended a generic, world-wide ban on training firings as I could not identify the cause, but I did know for sure that LAW 80 had a very short arming distance, and the 1 kg warhead was powerful. It then occurred to me that I had just had a very near miss as I was only about 6 metres to the left of where the warhead detonated; however, no matter. The desk officer disagreed and wanted the training ban to be restricted to the specific batch of ammunition. I reminded him that I had witnessed the incident at close hand, the firer's drills were competent, the warhead detonated dangerously close to the firer and had caused injuries and there was another aspect. The batch technical records for LAW 80, it seemed to me, gave little evidence of homogeneity which meant that restricting the firing ban to a specific batch was illogical. He insisted on the imposition of a partial ban, to which

I replied that when I sent the notification signal, it would recommend an immediate global ban. The next day, at the office, I was gratified to see that my recommendation had been accepted and that a global ban on all training firings had been implemented.

The next part of the process was a joint investigation with the manufacturer which would start with a meeting in the UK. Before I went in, an officer from my technical directorate appeared to 'lean' on me. He suggested that my views might prejudice a £400M procurement project for the LAW80 System. I was unimpressed. By then, me and my colleagues had covered hundreds of firings and we had amassed considerable expertise and we understood well the nuances this system presented. This keenness for 'my side' to question my judgement went beyond the obligation to be impartial in my view. This was reinforced when we had the meeting with the manufacturer. My evidence was said to be questionable and subjective, and I couldn't possibly have determined the position of the warhead when it detonated. I countered by saying that I had excellent photographic evidence recording the striations in the ground from the fragmentation pattern. I had found the impact switch from the warhead with the tell-tale central perforation which demonstrated that the detonation originated from the fuze, and I had even found the copper warhead slug lying below the target. An adjournment of about a month was arranged to allow the MoD scientists to examine the evidence.

At the second meeting, the manufacturer turned up the ante by producing the computer-generated safety case which underpinned the Ordnance Board approval to bring the system into service. It was a massive pile of computer printouts, wheeled into the room on a sack trolley. After a joint review of the incident, the scientists were asked for their view on how close the warhead was to the firing point when it detonated. Their considered opinion coincided almost exactly with my observations. The warhead detonated at approximately two metres forward of the muzzle and well inside the designed fuze minimum arming distance. It then transpired that the manufacturer had experienced a premature during their own development trials. As the system was then under development, there was no obligation to notify the MoD, but I sensed a certain lack of credibility had just been exposed. We still didn't know why the warhead detonated prematurely and that was a problem. After some months, the ban was lifted, and training firings resumed. Sometime later, the cause was discovered, and it made interesting reading. At shot start, the accelerating rocket generates a prodigious amount of static electricity. This would usually discharge harmlessly through the forebody/aftbody joint which provided electrical continuity. But this was not 'designed-in' continuity, and it was discovered that in rare cases, the two halves of the rocket were not electrically conductive and that meant the warhead was at the mercy of a veritable lightning bolt of static. It was believed that this static could jump past the electrical safety features of the piezo-electric fuze and a current could be induced into the igniter circuit. Existing stocks of rockets then had a hot nickel wash applied to them to guarantee electrical continuity and this solved the problem. Throughout the whole investigation, I felt undermined by what I saw as unhelpful scepticism from my own side. In fact, I was furious. This abated somewhat when the senior officer at the technical directorate (LSA 4) wrote to my CO to say my work "Was of inestimable value to the investigation". The vindication was sweet, but the greater satisfaction was in seeing that a potentially dangerous munition design fault was rectified, and the firer was cleared of any suspicion of wrongdoing at the Board of Inquiry.

As 1989 wore on, I felt I was ready for a change. I had been in Germany for three years, I felt I was stagnating, and I wanted a move to another type of ammunition employment that might compliment my skill set and perhaps improve my prospects for commissioning. I think the reader may have heard the saying "Beware of what you wish for". I asked for and got an interview with the AT career Desk Officer at RAOC Manning & Records (the HR department in civvy-speak). I explained my situation and I was promised a posting. Christine and I then had a lovely holiday in Kenya and returned to Germany after two weeks away. As I unlocked the semi-glazed front door of our married quarter, I could see a large khaki envelope lying on the doormat inside. I remember saying to Christine that it could be the promised posting order; it was. I was posted to the Falkland Islands! Attached to the posting order was a second posting order which posted me straight back to Herford after I was done in the Falklands; you bastards, I thought! The Falkland Islands tour turned out to be eye-opening for me in many respects and, on the whole, I am happy that I got the chance to serve there. This tour is covered in the next chapter.

After returning from the Falkland Islands, I learned I had been successful in getting a place on the RAPC three-day event which would be held at their depot at Worthy Down. It did feel at that time that I was at the crossroads of potential change which I found unsettling but also strangely welcome. I realized there was added evidence of 'mindgames' at play. Later in that year would see me reaching the fourth year as a WO1 and I began to appreciate that I was no longer in the promotion 'rat-race'. I was more relaxed and enjoyed my work. Then it was time to go to Worthy Down. The prospect was both unnerving and exciting. In applying for a commission in the RAOC, I was largely involved in an annual performance report paper-chase, with a couple of important interviews. The three-day event, however, was far more demanding. We were constantly chaperoned by a major in the RAPC and, during the actual selection process, we were constantly watched by the five Board Members. It almost felt like test week after an advanced EOD Course because you weren't quite sure what was going to come next. Perhaps I had an advantage as I was well-practised in analysing situations, decision-making and formulating plans. The first day began with us carrying out the basic fitness test. Already dressed and ready in battle PT kit, we were briefed by the Board in a theatre about the conduct of the selection process. It was made crystal clear that we were not competing against each other and there was no quota. If everyone passed, all would be commissioned, and if we all failed, then so be it. We were issued coloured, numbered bibs and I was Blue 7; we would be addressed as such by Board Members. We then ran the test and the Board waited for us at the finish line, millboards and pens at the ready. The various tests and interviews were arranged to alternate the environment. You might do a physical test such as an assault course run featuring a command task, and this would be followed immediately by a classroom session but in a different uniform. There would be very little time to change between the various sessions and I sensed a subtle 'change parade'-induced stress level. Each of us had a one-on-one interview with Board Members and I was asked in the first interview about my birthplace, Gateshead. The interviewer then got stuck into me about the geo-political history of the town and region, seemingly expecting me to demonstrate awareness of this. I replied that I left aged just three months to go to Germany, where I was to spend the majority of my formative years. In these interviews, I sensed information-gathering was in progress and any 'porkies' would likely come back to haunt me.

We did a command task on the assault course, and I was to lead the Blue syndicate through it, negotiating imaginary crocodile-infested lagoons and various obstacles, all whilst carrying an empty oil drum to which was attached various rules of what you could do with it. The conditions underfoot were quite treacherous as it had just rained heavily. I got my syndicate into a briefing, outlined the task, allocated roles and then prepared to start. A Board Member then approached me and said he had bet a case of port on me to succeed. Undaunted, I specifically warned my syndicate not to take any foolish chances by trying to jump over obstacles as the chance of injury was high. One candidate then foolishly climbed a tree, intending to do a 'Buzz Lightyear' and 'fall with style' to the safety of an opposite imaginary riverbank. The Board rounded on him immediately for defying my safety briefing. We completed the task with success after the oil drum nearly fell from the top of a climbing frame. Leading from behind, I used my head, literally, to stop the drum from falling. Both my hands were committed to the frame and thankfully, the drum was empty and it only dropped a few inches but I did see stars.

On the last day, we were to be interviewed by the entire board in a formal setting. We were instructed to attend in business suits and were to remove the bibs. Our chaperone advised us that this interview was the 'big one' where those who might be lagging could pull it back and those who might be leading had it all to lose. We were kept together in a side room and entered the interview room individually. A chair, symbolically like the one in the TV quiz Mastermind, was sited in front of a long table. The board members were seated at it. The curtains were closed, and the room was illuminated in a way that made you feel under a spotlight. Behind where I was to sit were two additional staff who were from the officers' posting branch of the RAPC. To continue the comparison with TV shows, this setup could have become the template for the BBC series The Apprentice. The interview started and flew quickly, with board members randomly firing questions at me, leaving little time for me to consider my answers. It was clear the board had built their question set around the responses I had given during the earlier interviews. I also noticed that there was some kind of prompting with non-verbal signals being passed from the board to the anonymous pair sat behind me. After the interview concluded, I was ushered out. It felt like I had been in there for seconds, but it had been about 25 minutes. The shirt under my suit was drenched around the armpits. It had been a classic interrogation; fast, unrelenting, pressurized and disorientating. In fact, one member of the board was a psychologist. After this process, we were rested in a break room until all candidates had been grilled and we then had to await the adjudication.

We were then taken one by one to the same interview room and instructed to march in and halt in front of the table. It was like waiting for the verdict at a court martial. The senior board member read from one of two prepared statements in front of him. One was the script to say you had passed and the other was the fail script. I saw the lips moving but seemed not to hear what was said. I was marched out and the chaperone asked how I did. I said I didn't know. He laughed at my bewilderment and said, "Well done, you passed!" before shoving me into a side room. In there were a couple of candidates who had also passed. Over the next hour, we were joined by the other candidates who had passed. I think the candidates who failed were given the 'Apprentice taxi treatment' as we had been instructed to have our bags packed before this session. I think about a quarter of the course attendees had passed. We were then brought back into the interview room, quite informally. Inside, the curtains had been opened and the ambience had been switched from austere to welcoming. We were served champagne and welcomed into the RAPC. It was surreal. As we left, we were handed a briefing document about our new career. Up until then, perhaps because I had been far, far away in the Falklands, I didn't know anything about the future of the RAPC. The document informed us that we were destined for the new Adjutant General's Corps (AGC) and we were to become Regimental Administration Officers (RAO), not paymasters. This caught me out somewhat and I returned to Germany delighted at the outcome, but this was tempered by the news of the big shake-up to come. After returning to the ammunition Inspectorate BAOR, now renamed as 221 EOD Company, I learned that I had not been successful at my commissioning application with the RAOC. I believe it would be in context to say in German " Stellen meine überrashung" (imagine my surprise). At least I had one commission in the bag and, perhaps smugly, I felt I had been very thoroughly tested by the three-day event which was vastly different to what I viewed was the 'face-fit' process for commissioning in my own corps.

One evening, Christine and I went to a fancy dress party in our mess in Hammersmith Barracks. As I was the Duty EOD Operator, I didn't go in costume. The efforts of the mess members at their disguises were outstanding. One of our group was Alan, who attended with his wife, June. Alan had come along as a Ninja Turtle and had a cracking improvised costume complete with green tights and mask. We were seated close to the bar and two men disguised as Ku Klux Klan members suddenly swept in, wearing flowing white robes and full-face masks, topped off with conical tops. As the evening wore on, they remained seated at the bar, downing much beer which was heavily subsidised by a grant from the entertainments fund. The President of the Entertainments Committee (PEC) was a Royal Signals squadron sergeant major who circled around us all like a predatory shark to make sure we enjoyed ourselves (and that's an order). At each orbit, he would pause and talk with members, but we had noticed the two Klan members weren't saying very much and seemed quite determined to remain anonymous. At the penultimate orbit, I could see the PEC glaring at the Klan pair and his body language was all chary; he smelled a rat; in fact, two of them! He finally marched up to them and snatched away their masks. It was two of his own Signalmen who had enjoyed free drinks all night, right under his nose. He was furious and promptly marched the two malefactors off to the nick. He was raging when he got back. I talked to him and urged leniency; after all, any soldiers who could pull that off right under his nose showed outstanding nerve and panache and, in my view, were exactly the kind of soldiers we needed more of!

One day whilst Duty Operator, I was tasked by the RMP to deal with a suspect object in the nearby town of Bielefeld. The object was a beer keg which had been found in the street. It was unusual as the German Police had primacy outside of our barracks. When I got to the scene, I was met by a German Police Officer who had cordoned off the suspect device and it became clear the incident was a major disruption. I also noticed a very large RMP presence. When I asked why, it turned out they had been driving along the nearby autobahn (motorway), en-route to Berlin, when they heard of this incident on their radios and had diverted to give assistance; so, I had quite a crowd. When I was given a description of the device and looked at it with a swift scope, it seemed to me I had a beer keg and there was a pub nearby. I suspected the keg had been left behind innocently by the draymen, so I asked the policeman if the witnesses had noticed if the keg was sealed. He seemed to get annoyed at my approach and made it quite clear that all he wanted was for me to deal with the keg immediately and then disappear with it so he could get the town back to normal. To cut a long story short, I was able to see the keg was sealed and the brewery's details were available. I got the full keg into my control point, but the policeman was unwilling to contact the brewery, leaving me, a teetotaller, with a disposal problem. That was when I noticed a lot of RMP faces looking longingly at the keg; it was meadow beer, a premium beer brewed for Oktoberfest. I thought momentarily that I would leave the keg to them before my own team intervened. We had a planned social function later that day and evening and I was 'persuaded' to keep the keg and return to Herford. It was to be one of my better decisions…

One of the last significant Range Duties I performed was at the US Army Range Complex in Southern Germany, at Grafenwöhr. The natures I covered included 81mm Mortar, LAW 80 and Milan. An infantry battalion was firing live natures and the American range procedures in force were that the impact areas were out of bounds. If things went wrong, you couldn't enter the impact areas to recover evidence. The Milan firing point was on one side of a heavily wooded valley. The targets were on the other side, and we had used laser range-finding equipment to ensure the targets were within the Milan maximum range of 1860 metres. The Milan firing teams would be brought to the rear of the firing point in an AFV 432 which had been deliberately driven through rugged countryside to disorientate the firers. On exiting the vehicle, each with munition, they would sprint to the launch post, threading their way between small, smoky fires made from burning tyres. On reaching the launch post, they would load the missile on the firing post and take up a firing position. This was located between two adjacent walls of sandbags and there was a General Purpose Machine Gun (GPMG) mounted on a tripod to the left of the Milan launch post which was firing intermittently towards the target. Its purpose was to add simulated battle noise and distraction to provide more realistic firing conditions. On the command "Tank – Action", the firer would track the target and then fire. The Milan would launch with a characteristic bang, which was the pressure generator expelling it forward out of its launch tube, before the rocket motor ignited once the missile was far enough forward so as not to scorch to firer. Another characteristic was the 'chuffing' from the missile as it flew. The chuffing was the jet interrupter method of steering. The same team of two would then change roles and fire the second missile. After several firings had been conducted with success, a missile suddenly plunged into the wooded area and detonated, well short of the target. The manner of its failure was typical of a wire break. I knew the target was within the maximum range, so I initially attributed the failure to the missile but, in an isolated circumstance, was not unduly concerned. I noted the failure and told the safety supervisor that an additional entitlement to a replacement missile would be granted. I had also noted the failure occurred after the tracer from the GPMG had burned out, so it had to be just past 1100 metres. Several firings later, a similar failure occurred and then the same thing again. Something was wrong. I had the target range re-evaluated by laser. I stood back from the firing point and watched the next launch and that is when an intriguing possible cause occurred to me. The GPMG and the firing post were only about 5 metres apart. The GPMG was firing four ball, one tracer and it was firing directly at the target. I could see the tracer and the Milan were not only in the same arc but were converging as they approached the target. For every tracer I could see, there would be four other bullets, making that airspace quite crowded. Were the defective missiles being struck in flight by bullets from the GPMG? I put this point to the safety supervisor. At that time, the 33 Brigade Commander had just arrived and had been briefed on the failures. I found myself ringed by people seeking recourse for the errant missiles. By then, I had attended a lot of Milan firings and Milan was usually a very reliable system. The only common denominator between these failures was the use of the GPMG firing in the same arc. When I then asked for the GPMG to fire out of arc to eliminate the possibility that missiles were being shot down, the response was incredulous. I pointed out that engaging an armoured target with GPMG at 1800 metres was not essential to this training and there was nothing to be lost if the GPMG fired outside the arc. Reluctantly, the safety supervisor and attending officers agreed to my recommendation. The missile firings continued for the rest of the day with no further failures. On my firing report, I attributed the three failures to an 'error of drill' as the unit, in my opinion, had shot down their own missiles.

Along the way at Herford, I remember reading a report into the death of a soldier who was on armed duty in an ammunition compound. In summary, he and his colleagues were locked in an ammunition compound for a period of several days, during which they would provide an armed guard. They were accommodated in a bespoke guardroom which included living accommodation. They were issued rations and a welfare pack of video tapes to watch when stood down. A daily visit by a commissioned officer to check on them was part of the routine. In a colleague's statement, it was said that the soldier had watched a well-known film of the time which featured a potential suicide by the principal actor where he placed a gun in his mouth. The dead soldier had allegedly watched the film several times. Late one evening, as most of the guard force slept, one of them recalled thinking a door had been slammed. In the morning, the dead soldier was seen sitting upright, cross-legged on the floor with his head bowed. Someone thought he had vomited. Then they noticed his weapon was in his lap and the muzzle was in his face. He had somehow managed to discharge his weapon into his brain through his mouth. I read the report carefully and was struck by the tragedy of it and that it was so preventable in so many ways. The incident stayed with me as one of those I couldn't quite understand but there would be more of these tragedies in the years to come and I will return to this topic later.

While serving as the Administration Officer, as a supernumerary, I expected a posting order. Sure enough, one arrived. I was nominated as the next SAT of 11 EOD Regiment RLC. This was, and probably still is, the top job in the trade. SAT of 321 EOD Squadron was probably up there too but it largely depended on the levels of terrorist activity at the time. I was thrilled at the prospect of this posting and not a little daunted by it. This posting was one of those where an informal board would consider the available candidates and select the best available to them; it was no random posting 'raffle win'. Some weeks later, I was working late in the office. The OC was in the office next door to me. My phone rang. It was an officer I had known well in the 1970s, but I hadn't served with him since then; he was now a lieutenant colo-nel. He seemed surprised that I had answered, and so I explained my stopgap appointment as the Administration Officer. He asked to speak to the OC, and I put him through. Between our two offices there was a doorway which was no longer in use, but it meant you could hear conversations without trying. I tried to ignore the voice from next door but then my name was mentioned. I dismissed the thought that I was the subject and tried to focus on the pile of annual confidential reports in front of me, which would become overdue if I didn't get them fin-ished soon. Then I got that odd realisation that dawns on you when what you can hear intrudes into your inner mind. The conversation lasted about ten minutes and I was now totally convinced it was about me. Common sense suggested I had only heard part of one half of the conversation, but I had picked up on negative intones and challenged the OC as soon as the call ceased with the question "That was about me, wasn't it, Sir?" The OC looked somewhat uncomfortable. It turned out the caller was the CO designate of 11 EOD Regiment and he was apparently lobbying to have my selection as his next SAT changed. I was vehemently against it. I suggested that if the new CO had issues with me, a meeting between us to discuss whatever lay behind this be thrashed out. Then Manning and Records Office got involved. And so did other agencies who, whilst not overtly taking my side, pointed out that my selection was appropriate and should stand. Finally, I spoke to my Desk Officer at Manning and Records, and he said the final choice would be mine. Appreciating that I was now well and truly on the horns of a dilemma, I considered my options. I was told that if I volunteered to change my posting, RMCS Shrivenham was an option. I then volunteered, reluctantly, to change my posting. The grounds for my decision were brutally simple. A tour as the SAT at 11 EOD Regiment was going to be very demanding and it seemed to me to be a plain truth that the CO and the SAT had to be 'joined at the hip' to ensure success. If I insisted on going to 11 EOD Regiment, I was going to come a cropper and nobody I consulted was prepared to contradict that view.

Before leaving Germany, I was called to a farewell interview by the Commander Supply BAOR who was the late Brigadier David Harris. I have written about this interview and what transpired in the chapter titled 'Reflections'. It seemed my penchant for making enemies had caught up with me and, in the minds of the now senior officers I had previously 'crossed' years beforehand, I was clearly mortgaged to their chagrin.

CHAPTER 13

The Falkland Islands 1989

At the time I deployed, the Falkland Islands were deemed to be immune from the terrorism that plagued the UK and Europe because of their remoteness and that travel to and from the islands was mostly by RAF aircraft. When you arrived, you were given a briefing about minefields. This was seven years after the 1982 war, such had been the reckless wantonness of Argentine soldiers who scattered mines all over the place but failed to keep records. The flight was in two legs: Brize Norton to Ascension Island and then onto RAF Mount Pleasant. I was struck by the raw beauty of the volcanic Ascension Island. As we were about to land at RAF Mount Pleasant, I heard a bang from the side of the aircraft and noticed a black object streak past, below the window. I called a steward. I told him what I'd seen. I got a bit of a lecture about it being "Perfectly alright, Sir" and he walked down the aisle with an exaggerated air of calm. He went through a mid-aisle galley and closed the curtain behind him before sprinting towards the cockpit! He re-appeared quickly with someone from the flight deck. I described what I had heard and seen. I think it had been a chunk of rubber strip, possibly from within the wing, which had broken free as the flaps were extended. It was deemed to be alright to continue with the landing, which was routine, but I did notice the Rapier anti-aircraft missile launcher with missiles 'on-beam' as we went past, just before touching down. The wind when you stepped out of the aircraft was awesome; you had to lean into it like a ski-jumper. The Falklands' climate was about the same as the UK in terms of cold temperatures, but the wind chill and incredibly changeable weather were what impressed me the most. You could get weather from all four seasons in one day.

A stark warning on the main road
between Port Stanley and RAF Mount Pleasant

The first thing I appreciated at RAF Mount Pleasant was the infrastructure. It had been built from scratch and was far better than I'd experienced elsewhere... with one exception - the bloody tannoy system! There was a speaker mounted on the wall directly outside my room in the sergeants' mess and spurious messages about this and that with no relevance to myself constantly disturbed the peace. Funny old thing, that speaker stopped working just after I arrived. My job in the Falkland Islands was as Ammunition Platoon commander, within the Falkland Islands Logistic Battalion (FILOG). The role had two aspects: Management of the ammunition depot and the Ammunition Inspectorate. Although the Falklands War was seven years behind us, the Islands were still on a form of standby called 'Military Vigilance'. As I mentioned, RAF Mount Pleasant had Rapier Missile protection, with Rapier Missiles 'on-beam' on their launchers. The very high wind speeds would often blow articles into the missiles and cause dents in them especially around the soft warhead crush switch. The missile was very vulnerable to damage and, in the photograph below, you can see the protective covers, secured with string. There was a 6-month beam-life on the deployed missiles and this meant missiles had to be turned over with new ones regularly. Missiles just 'off-beam' would then be fired at training.

Four Rapier Missiles 'on-beam' providing point defence around Mount Pleasant. The protective covers are fitted around the impact switch area to prevent wind-blown articles from denting the crush switch.

I was based at RAF Mount Pleasant and the job entailed managing about 20 soldiers. There were no officers below the Company Commander level, and I enjoyed considerable autonomy. In the office next to mine was the clerk who managed the depot ammunition account. Within a few days, I sensed that he was somewhat uncertain of depot accountancy procedures. Each year, the depot would receive replenishment stock issued from the UK and the stock would arrive by sea. The clerk had been entering the anticipated replenishment stock on the computerised account in what was termed the 'Dues-In Process". Somehow, after the new ammunition stock had been received, the Receipts Procedures were not cancelling out the Dues-In Procedures and so the ammunition stock on account was double that which had been physically received. The problem was so severe, according to the account, that what we were theoretically holding couldn't possibly fit in the explosive storehouses! I asked the clerk to print me a stocktake sheet for the storehouse nearest my office. Print in hand, I went to the storehouse and started to check the contents. Within minutes, I realised I could not reconcile anything. I wondered if he had printed the wrong sheet. I went back up to the office, did some checks and then returned mob-handed. With the help of several other staff, I confirmed that the stocks actually held were substantially less than what the account suggested but that was not all. I couldn't get any stock lines to reconcile. I extended the checks to progressively more storehouses before calling off the stocktake and investigating what was going on. It turned out there were two causes. The first one was that the computer accounting programme had become corrupted. The second cause was more systemic. Some years earlier, a training needs analysis for Technical Clerks had identified that ammunition depot accounting procedures were not sufficiently in demand as a core skill to warrant them being retained in the syllabus. The topic would henceforth be dropped and only offered on a needs basis. Problem was we had a need, but nobody had informed the trainers! I briefed the Company Commander who simply couldn't get his head around the scale of the problem. I invited him into the depot and demonstrated the issue. The only way out was to conduct an urgent 100% stock check and then reconcile the account. As an aside, the computer account bug needed to be identified and resolved. I knew the subject matter expert (Bill) on the programme, which was known as Microfix, and so I phoned him at Didcot. He grasped the problem immediately and I was reasonably competent with the coding as I had already developed the ARMS programme in Herford using the same software. Between us, we were able to replace the lines of corrupt code and the programme started to work properly. However, we couldn't retrieve the correct stock state so I would still need to manually reconcile the account after the stocktake.

At Mount Pleasant, buildings were in clusters connected by fully enclosed walkways, probably the nearest I'll come to working in something like a spaceship. The ammunition depot was located near the runway. My office window faced the direction that landing aircraft mostly approached from, and you would see them on approach as they turned on their landing lights. The larger aircraft would often be escorted in by the combat air patrol F4 Phantoms. They would usually take off shortly before the incoming aircraft arrived and then do a very steep climb-out before disappearing into the cloud ceiling; it was a game they liked to play; I imagined their vertical track would light up Argentine radars on the mainland. The distance between the westernmost end of the runway and the ammunition depot was remarkably short and too close for my liking. One day, whilst standing outside with a colleague, we watched the Phantoms take off, but this time, the one nearest the depot had a problem. A short black streak of smoke came out of one of his engines and he started to turn towards the depot. He passed overhead and we thought we saw a tiny object fall to the ground inside the depot, Over the ubiquitous tannoy, an emergency was declared, and the aircraft went around and landed safely. We were concerned with whatever had fallen into the depot, which had been built on peat and, if this object was hot, it could start a fire. It didn't and we were OK.

Heavy drinking was part of the routine at RAF Mount Pleasant. In our mess at the end of the bar was a large bottle of 400mg strength Brufen tablets, and at closing time, the heaviest drinkers would take one or more as they left. One of my staff in the depot had recurring back pain and reported to the medical officer. When he came back, he was pretty annoyed with the diagnosis. The young female RAF medical officer had asked a few lifestyle questions and it emerged she considered he was drinking too much. She had taken a urine sample and had recommended a reduction in his alcohol consumption and would review his condition the following week. Whilst I commiserated with him, I had noticed he would often consume between eight and ten cans of cider most evenings. I was still teetotal but was always conscious of not being seen as a prudish. I wasn't; my cessation of drinking suited me and my circumstances at that time. I did have a 'live and let live' philosophy and was happy to leave others well alone unless I perceived their actions were having an impact. When the soldier with the sore back returned to work after his follow-up, he was jubilant. He had been seen by an older, male medical officer who was a squadron leader. The squadron leader allegedly apologised for his zealous junior practice partner, explaining that she had perhaps been somewhat messianic and didn't fully appreciate that soldiers in the Falklands were thousands of miles away from home and loved ones and that excessive drinking was tolerable as a measure to relieve boredom, provided, on return to home, that the drinking habit was reduced. I was taken aback by that view and my perception increasingly turned to the view that binge-drinking was tacitly tolerated by the entire chain of command.

To be fair, the chain of command had tried hard to grip the unsatisfactory morale situation. Efforts were made to reduce the amount of leisure time through working on Saturdays, the inference being that boredom was a factor. The RAF had an active programme of welfare trips and excursions, often referred to as 'MINJOs' (Men In Need of Jolly Outings). The infantry company was well positioned to conduct field training and there was plenty of resource for range firings and patrols activity. Although it was never officially acknowledged in my time, some of the accommodation areas became 'no-go' areas for outsiders. Violence after bar closures was common and, during my tour, a party of senior officers and their wives was accosted by drunk soldiers as they walked along the covered walkway to the church to attend Christmas Mass. In short, discipline was a mess. Drunkenness, drink-driving and injuries suffered through drunken horseplay were commonplace and seemingly accepted. I had noticed a sickness absence trend in my own soldiers, and they were coming to work after Sick Parade with signs of injury such as bruising. I asked for the cause, but my soldiers brushed off the suggestion that they had been assaulted. I knew the buck stopped with me; I was responsible for my soldiers, and they were suffering. I took one of them aside and prised the truth out of him. It seemed there was a soldier in the accommodation who was regularly violent and would attack soldiers as they slept in their beds. I committed the details to a written record and asked the Service Police for assistance. My intervention led to the arrest of the culprit.

The reaction of my Company Commander was interesting. I was called to interview with him and asked to justify my actions. I was incredulous at his attitude. I listed the injuries suffered, time lost to sickness absence and the need to impose normal discipline. We were at loggerheads and our voices became raised. The office door was slightly ajar and the FILOG Commanding Officer had overheard our conversation. He intervened directly and asked for an explanation. Having listened to the somewhat vacuous reason for inaction compared to my own concerns, he declared on my side; or perhaps I should re-phrase that. It was less about my side and more about doing the right thing which is as close to the definition of integrity as you can get. The disciplinary case against the violent drunk was continued and he was eventually sentenced to 56 days detention which, by coincidence, matched the number of days left of his tour. I requested that he be released into my custody during working hours, and this was approved. Once his drinking was taken out of the equation, he became a conscientious 'guest' worker in my platoon and came to be well-liked by the end of his tour.

About the same time, tragedy struck, as if to underpin the consequences of chain of command indifference to heavy drinking, a topic I return to in several places under the title of 'Attrition by Alcohol'. In the NAAFI bar, it was common for soldiers to indulge in bets and dares where the typical win was a so-called 'slab' of beer; a shrink-wrapped cardboard box of canned beer, typically containing a dozen 440ml cans of beer. Most of the buildings at RAF Mount Pleasant had very high-pitched roofs and internally, the ceilings were exposed with steels joists and tie beams open to view. A bet was laid in the NAAFI bar that a soldier, who was already worse for wear through drink, couldn't climb up into the roof space to retrieve a slab of beer that one of his colleagues had jammed into the exposed metalwork. The soldier climbed up but at about the highest extent of his climb, he fell, landing on the solid floor several metres below him, face and knee impacting first. He suffered devastating neurological injuries and was evacuated to the hospital in Port Stanley in critical condition. Unaware of this, at work the following morning, one of my junior ammunition technicians (I'll call him Andy) impulsively hitched a ride to tea break on the forks of a fork-lift truck. He had wrapped his arms through the telescopic mast to secure himself and then, prior to moving off, the operator tilted the forks slightly backwards. Sadly, this brought into play some moving parts which then trapped Andy's upper arm in a scissor-like grip, inflicting what appeared to be a very serious upper arm injury. He was taken to the same hospital as the soldier from the previous night's incident. I felt dreadfully upset at Andy's injury, which I feared could be life-changing. I phoned the hospital and asked if I could visit. They agreed and I was told to report to reception.

When I arrived at the hospital, the staff appeared to be waiting especially for me. I heard someone say something like "His RSM's here now". I was taken into a small room and ,through some curtains, I could see an obviously very sick patient with all sorts of tubes and monitoring devices attached to him. I turned to the nurse and asked how a possibly broken upper arm could have deteriorated in such a short time. It was mistaken identity! They thought I had come to visit the soldier injured in the bar. Massively relieved, I was taken to see Andy who was suspected of suffering a soft-tissue injury to his upper arm, not to mention the ear-ache he would get from me when he came back to work! The episode served me up a graphic illustration of attrition by alcohol. I was told that surgeons battled through the night to save the soldier injured in the bar. He was stabilised long enough for relatives from the UK to arrive and spend some time with him before the end.

To mix my metaphors, I felt that the inaction by a few good men had led to this wholly preventable waste of a man's life.

I had already mentioned that the remoteness of the Falkland Islands allowed for a relaxed approach to security related to Northern Ireland terrorism. In September 1989, a bomb in Deal Barracks had killed 11 Royal Marines and then in November 1989, an undercar booby trap very seriously injured a serving soldier near Colchester. Within the headquarters of the Army in the Falkland Islands, a concern was expressed that soldiers serving here might become complacent over their personal security and it was considered that mandatory awareness training be delivered to all personnel immediately before they returned to the UK. Thus, it came to be that my signature on an attendance certificate was a prerequisite to boarding the 'Gozome Bird'!

In those days, you were given four days Rest and Recuperation (R&R) during your tour, which had to be taken in the Falkland Islands. I elected to take my leave at Pebble Island, the location there made famous by the SAS raid to destroy Argentine Pucara ground attack aircraft during the Falklands War. I was flown to Pebble Island in an Islander aircraft, and we 'hopped' into several isolated communities on the way, using grass and beach landing strips. The Pebble Island Hotel Manager was also the nature reserve manager, and we spent much time together exploring the scenery and wildlife. The hotel had a wind generator which was broken but a limited power supply from a diesel generator was available. I greatly enjoyed my time there, visiting penguin colonies containing hundreds of thousands of birds with absolutely no fear of man. Around the periphery of the colony, Sea Skuas dived in trying to take vulnerable chicks. I climbed down a vertical cliff face, where the rocks were fractured in a pattern, providing a ladder-like climbing aid. At the top were Peregrine Falcons with their now-fledged chicks dispersed nearby. As I descended, I went past cormorants and shags in their cliff-face nests who were not in the least bit concerned by my presence. At the bottom in the tussock grass was a Turkey Vulture and flying about were Striated Caracaras which the Islanders nick-named 'Johnny Rook'. A few metres out, basking on exposed rocks, we had sea lions. About 400 metres further out were hundreds of Brown Albatross gliding among the white tops whilst below them, dozens of penguins continued their feeding commute. It was hard to believe how fertile the environment there was. Cupped hands of sea water would reveal hundreds of beasties wriggling about and the sky was so blindingly clear you could see forever. Having learned of the vast distances over which penguins ranged in their hunt for food, I reflected on how cruel it was to confine them in zoos in small concrete enclosures and anthropomorphise them. Penguins, like polar bears at the other end of the world, are best seen in their own habitat.

Me, watching Rockhoppers, watching me. These birds are quite pugnacious and if you obstruct their route to the sea, you are likely to get a vicious pecking, which I did!

I mentioned we would turn over stocks of Rapier Guided Missiles after they had been on-beam for six months. This was done at firing camps which took place next to the sea. I would film each launch which was invaluable in diagnosing any in-flight problems. I always liked to be close in whenever monitoring firings and this was no exception. The missiles would be mounted on their launcher, and I was able to stand in a small gully behind the launcher, at an appropriate minimum safety distance. The targets were drones which would fly in an arc several kilometres out over the sea. When the drone was in position within the safety arc, the instructor would issue the command to engage and within seconds, the selected Rapier would issue a rapid zip-like sound as the gyroscope de-caged and spun up before the missile roared away. To film each missile, I had a camcorder and the only drawback to this was the very small black and white viewfinder. The sky was brilliant in the sunshine, and it made tracking a missile quite challenging. The firings were going smoothly, and we had gotten into something of a routine. I watched the next firer preparing to engage and I could see the drone in the far distance beginning a run from the right-hand edge of the arc. I screwed up my left eyelid to close it and peered at the view through my right eye. At launch, I would be in wide-angle, and I would zoom the camera as I tracked the flight to impact. The order to engage was given but nothing seemed to happen. The window of opportunity to fire was relatively short as the arc was narrow and the student would not be allowed to fire unless the anticipated impact happened within the arc. The instructor shouted "out of arc" but this coincided with the student firing the missile which took off. The instructor shouted "Cut" which meant he would trigger the self-destruct mechanism. He did and I heard the bang as it went but I couldn't quite see it. In my right eye, I could see the missile and, although it had been cut, it continued to fly and was now climbing quite steeply. As it went, I could hear the rocket

350

motor sound diminish as it flew further away but then a sense in me detected that the sound was increasing in volume and rapidly too. In the viewfinder, my vision was basically two-dimensional. I moved my head to one side and opened my left eye. In a heart-stopping moment, I realised that this now rogue missile had climbed up into a loop and was coming back on itself; directly towards me! Before I could even start to move, I saw the missile yaw wildly and then it started to drop vertically downwards. It dropped into the sea, a few metres out from the high-water mark with a decent splash and then there was a stream of bubbles breaking the surface. Apart from the sound of the generator, it was dead quiet. That was fun, nearly, but I got it on film!

Missile being inspected prior to being mounted on-beam by Ozzie, the Ammunition Inspectorate sergeant AT.

The view down-range out to sea. The taped-off area was to protect a ground-nesting Nightjar

This is the bird. I think it was a Nightjar; perhaps any twitcher readers could confirm?

Missile away!

My boss called me in one day and said the National Audit Office was going to visit. It seemed they were concerned about ammunition accountancy in the depot. A previous review had exposed some issues and they were coming back to investigate in greater detail. By the time this came to light, we had already completed the depot stocktake, repaired the corrupt accountancy programme and reconciled the account. To support the reconciliation, I had generated a prodigious pile of issue and receipt vouchers. I had signed off each voucher and was now confident that we had an accurate account. Prior to the NAO visit, we had the depot annual technical inspection which was to be performed by a lieutenant colonel from our technical directorate in the UK. Just after entering my office and settling down to a cup of tea, he broached the matter of the NAO visit. I took him through the whole sorry saga of what had happened. The one point he was already aware of was a multi-million-pound discrepancy in Rapier missile stocks.

The NAO were concerned this stock had been lost. As the colonel and I exchanged our views on the issue, it became obvious that there had been no physical loss. The problem was that the missing missiles had been fired at training over the seven years since the Falklands War and post-conflict accounting action had not restored the account sufficiently to prove this. I showed the colonel the two piles of vouchers which were raised to reconcile the account. He was happy at one level (perhaps a tactical level) that we had sorted out the mess but was rightly concerned at the strategic level that I did not have the financial authority to be signing off millions of pounds worth of ammunition. After the inspection, he left happier than he had been on arrival, however, he was somewhat concerned that the vouchers would need to go to the Treasury for formal authentication. At that point, I disengaged. The issue was now well above my pay grade. At the tactical level, we now knew exactly what was in the depot and that was really all I needed to know. As ever, there was to be a sting in the tail. In FILOG, we had two computer systems for accounting. One was in the ammunition depot and the other was in the Rations Platoon. The Rations Platoon had an additional task of providing food for the small number of residences of the married accompanied senior officers in the Falklands. The raising of all transactions was done on the Rations Platoon computer system and as this affected these senior officers directly, the Rations Platoon computer system was seen as too important to fail. Perhaps the fundamental problem was that these essential information systems were not sustained by any form of backup; software or hardware. After I left the Falkland Islands, I got word that the Rations Platoon computer had broken down. The ammunition depot computer was taken away and used to replace the one in the Rations Platoon. It was all too silly for words; even today, I don't know if this news was a wind-up, or if it was true.

In the Falklands, it was easy to lose contact with current affairs in the rest of the world. We didn't have a live TV service and what TV news we saw would arrive by tape and so we would be typically two to five days 'behind the curve'. The collapse of the Berlin Wall was played out to us on taped TV broadcasts. It was mind-boggling to see those pictures which contrasted vividly with my memories of watching refugees on TV, fleeing the east when the wall was first erected.

In the Falklands, we had a command headquarters which was located in a bespoke building some distance from the ammunition depot. As with all military headquarters, there were stereotypical characters at large who seemed to be relics from a bygone age. There was one officer who I occasionally dealt with who fitted that description precisely. He would have 'weird ideas in the bath' about enhancing training realism and I was constantly having to reign him in to keep soldiers safe. One day, I decided he needed to have his leg pulled. A constant source of envy was the matter of telephones and transport. If you had a telephone in your own office, you were constantly being asked to relinquish it in favour of some higher-ranking chap who thought he was more important. I had telephones because of my role. I also had my own vehicles and that would really wind people up. This particular officer seemed to have his finger in every pie and seemed to enjoy pedalling influence for favours. He needed taking down! I had with me a Psion Organiser which, for those that don't know, was the world's first practical, compact, hand-held, portable, pocket computer. It was a nerd's dream (that's me) and I liked to write simple code on it and have the built-in speaker produce sound effects. One I had already done was a Trim Phone ringing tone. One day, knowing I was to meet this officer in his office, I set a delay loop to have the Organiser start ringing while I was in his office. The Organiser was in my inside pocket and just as we were reaching the climax to yet another 'why can't we do this' conversation, the 'phone' rang. I got the Organiser out, pulled it out of its casing and answered it, simulating a telephone conversation. As I announced to him that I had been called away to an urgent task, the look of disbelief and envy on his face was world-class! To the sound of multiple buts coming from his office, I hurried away to the depot to hide for a while. In the next two hours, heaven and earth were apparently moved in a bid for the headquarters to reach a communications par with EOD. You absolutely know when a wind-up totally works when the victim never, ever, mentions it after!

The remoteness of the Falkland Islands is more than eclipsed by that of South Georgia. I never got to visit this place, about 800 miles away, but knew of it. The infantry would conduct training there and, one day, near the Fortuna Glacier, an infantry section set up a machine gun (GPMG) to do some live firing. As this was being prepared, a reindeer in desperate physical condition appeared. Reindeer had been introduced in 1911 in yet another 'species introduction' bad idea. Initially, the reindeer thrived and multiplied, however, eventually, they exhausted the available food supplies, and they were trampling nesting grounds and affecting native bird species. Things got so bad that many reindeer would starve to death, and it was even said the strongest were cannibalising the weakest. The NCO in charge decided to euthanise the wretched animal and did so with his GPMG. Trouble was that the incident was witnessed by a somewhat vocal naturalist who briefed the outside world. Whatever the actual truth of the matter, it was stated that the standard British Army L2A2 7.62mm round was not appropriate for euthanising such a large animal humanely. It was decided to procure a round in the same calibre that was designed to kill humanely. This resulted in one of the fastest ever ammunition re-supply missions

I had ever seen. Firstly, the experts had to identify the bullet characteristics that would do the job. Then, the MoD Procurement Executive
and various other bodies had to agree if the proposed round could
actually be fired through Service weapons. Then the ammunition had
to be procured in the UK and flown to the Falkland Islands. On receipt,
we packaged the boxes in buoyancy aids and the ammunition was air-
dropped into the sea from a C-130 and soldiers in a rigid raider then
recovered it. I suppose this episode was resolved in a way that would
appease those with empathy for the hapless reindeer. To compare and
contrast it with another dilemma, we didn't pay for our food in the
Falkland Islands because the supply of fresh food depended critically
on re-supply twice weekly by air from the UK. The F4 Phantoms based
in the Islands then needed a lot of spares to keep them serviceable and
so these spares got priority for air freight over the food and, on occasion, even our mail. We actually fed quite well in the circumstances,
but we couldn't use locally produced fresh food as it didn't comply
with EU regulations. The Falkland Islands were an odd place but, in
many ways, I am grateful for the experience of having been there and
having witnessed so much irony.

CHAPTER 14

Saudi Arabia and Kuwait Gulf War 1990–1991

On 2nd August 1990, I was attending an Open University Summer School at York University. I was doing a 'Living With Technology' foundation course. When we started the Materials lectures, the tutor asked us if we wanted the spoken introduction or the singing version. We opted for the song, and this entailed him placing a somewhat wobbly plank between two laboratory benches and then singing as he walked the gap pretending to be an elephant and the plank sank predictably as he reached the middle. This was our introduction to materials and stress. It broke the ice (but not the plank), made the point about stress and then we launched into a practical, designing and then constructing model bridges from ABS plastic. The session concluded with destructive testing which was great fun; we had bits of plastic flying all over the lab and loud bangings as the weights used to test our designs crashed to the floor. My point is that I was about as far from the Army environment as you could get.

What could possibly go wrong? At lunchtime, we ate whilst watching the news. The invasion of Kuwait was the headline. I was shocked at what I saw; two friends and their families were in Kuwait with the British Army, serving with the Kuwait Liaison Team.

As the invasion continued, and international fury looked to be turning into a possible popular coalition response to eject the invaders, I pondered on what it could mean for me. The Iraqis were suspected of having weapons of mass destruction, especially the chemical agents Mustard Gas, Tabun, Sarin and VX, which were alleged to have been used against the internal opposition populations of the Kurds. This culminated in the chemical attack launched against Halabja. Later analysis by the CIA refuted the use of nerve agents but I had learned long ago to take intelligence estimates with more than a pinch of salt. I suspected there would be British Army involvement in a military solution if the diplomats couldn't sort things. Having recently completed a Loan Service tour in the desert Sultanate of Oman and recently qualified on the Biological and Chemical Munitions Disposal (BCMD) Course, I thought I might be deployed or otherwise involved in the pre-operational training of the military who might be sent. After a very enjoyable summer school, I returned to Herford.

As the weeks went by, British Army involvement was confirmed. It took some time before the deployable formation was identified; it was to be the 7th Armoured Brigade – The Desert Rats.

With one exception, the promises of getting us desert clothing and equipment came to naught, but they did tell us to take a spare empty kit bag for the kit we would get in theatre. The one exception to pre-deployment promise failures was the Desert Rats' arm badge.

Armed with one of these, I could probably trade it for a tank from an American! Seriously though, the Desert Rat badge was a powerful symbol, and our American allies revered it; I hoped we would be able to deliver as well as our famous forebears. This sense of belonging was to be snatched away later in the deployment when we were re-badged with a black snake as we were logistics. To make it worse, one of our senior officers was deeply into all things Blackadder and started naming things after the various characters. It was so embarrassing. I wished ill on the 'bag-carrier' who must have been telling him the troops liked it!

The Ammunition Inspectorate had already been re-designated as 221 EOD Company. A new sub-unit was spawned: Detachment (Gulf) 221 EOD Company RAOC, abbreviated to Det(G) 221 EOD Coy. Our existing Officer Commanding was Major Nick Bell RAOC who was due to be posted. It was decided he would lead the new detachment which would be manned primarily by ammunition technicians. Our role was initially to be bomb disposal in a Force Protection setting. We also assumed a BCMD role but lacked the equipment for this to be anything more than a reconnaissance or diagnostic capability. On 11th October 1990, myself and another WO1 flew to Al Jubayl on the east coast of Saudi Arabia as the Advance Party. Our departure bordered on farce. We were 'fully tooled up' with weapons and ammunition but we still had to go through security! As we boarded the aircraft to fly from RAF Gütersloh, an Army general bade us farewell, shaking our hands and wishing us luck (I remember thinking what's luck got to do with it?). When I saw that we were boarding an RAF VC10, which was really showing its age, I could see why we might need some luck; I had flown to Singapore by VC10 in 1968, 22 years earlier.

During the flight, we had two happy moments and one not so happy. Firstly, we were directed to seats situated over the wing. The VC10 was not a wide-bodied jet and is very cramped. But, since the Manchester Airport fire disaster, passenger aircraft were forced to create more space around emergency exits and to install exits over the wing if there weren't any. As a result, me and Taff found ourselves with sheds of legroom. We were instructed to place our SA80 weapons on the floor between our feet. The unhappy event took place later on the descent into Al Jubayl airport. As the aircraft's nose went down, a large amount of condensed water, which had accumulated on the tops of the overhead luggage bins, ran down above us. The modification to add the extra exit meant the overhead bins had a gap between them, right above my head. A cold slug of water went down my neck! However, as if to compensate, the next event was hilarious. As the aircraft came to a halt, an Air Movements Controller boarded the aircraft and took up position at the front exit. Out of the window, I could see our baggage was being ground-dumped. Whist the military are in transit, Movements Controllers become omnipotent. As this flight was an Advance Party flight, there were a lot of ranking officers on board and they were seated up front. The Movements Controller nominated the first 6 rows of passengers to be baggage handlers and they were unceremoniously ordered off to hump our hold baggage onto the waiting lorries; oh, happy days!

The US forces were already well-established in Al Jubayl and, to be frank, our force reception arrangements looked quite amateurish by comparison. By this, I mean the overall British deployment. For our part, as specialists in EOD, we were welcomed by the Americans as we could help protect key points. Our British Commanders coveted our vehicles. When the main body of the Detachment flew in on 13th October, we were immediately operational, and a bit of a bun fight ensued when the Supply Regiment wanted to utilise our manpower and transport. I recall one occasion when the Supply Regiment wanted our accommodation for themselves. I was told this whilst on a joint reconnaissance with one of their officers: His smug comment was, "We can't have you languishing in air-conditioned comfort". We spoke to the J3 operations officer and immediately after that dispersed our three teams into key point protection duties with the US Marine Expeditionary Force. We rotated the teams through Al Jubayl port, the airport and also provided technical cover at range-firings on Jerboa Ranges. Each rotation concluded with teams spending time in training, equipment maintenance and rest. We had moved into Camp 4 on the outskirts of Al Jubayl. This was originally a transit camp for pilgrims journeying to Mecca. It was comfortable and the portacabin accommodation was air-conditioned. Whilst this was going on, our own forces were gradually getting their act together. The Royal Engineers had done a great job already in constructing temporary accommodation under canvas. Their next significant project was to resurrect defunct accommodation in Al Jubayl port called Old Port Barracks (OPB). When ready, we moved in. The facilities were far safer as the buildings were bricks and mortar. At that time, Major Bell elected to live alone in a 12-foot by 12-foot tent at the end of the commercial pier. This was not good for command and control and left him exposed to risk if there had been a missile impact. This was a very real threat but, true to form, the intelligence analysts had assessed the risk as low.

When we first arrived, we had been herded into a huge warehouse on the commercial pier. An RSM was strutting his stuff shouting at people and generally being obnoxious. I remember him complaining about the American Meals Ready To Eat (MRE) rations being disgusting. Well, these rations were far superior to ours at the time; we had none! Personally, I enjoyed MREs, especially if I was able to heat them and add some Tabasco Sauce. The missile threat was all but dismissed by the hierarchy. We were told that before any Scud launch, the Iraqi gunners would launch meteorological balloons to assess high-altitude weather conditions, especially wind speed and direction. The weather data would then be used in the aiming of Scuds to improve their accuracy. Our Intelligence Staff believed this data would be collected up to 12 hours in advance of a launch and that radar, codenamed 'End Tray', would monitor the balloons. This radar activity could be detected so we would have a warning well in advance. This misplaced trust in Iraqi methods, and our intelligence estimates, almost led to what would have been the biggest disaster to befall the Coalition. (More about this later).

Once we got into the rhythm of rotating through Key Point protection and technical cover on Jerboa Ranges, life became more orderly, and we enjoyed the stability and activity. On my first stint in a US Marine tented camp in the desert, near the airport, I found myself immersed in a Vietnam War-era environment. The large tents we lived in had sandbag walls between them for protection against 'incoming'. Each large tent had been modified by the US Construction Battalion (the CBs) through the installation of a stout wooden internal frame, solid wooden floor and electrical power. I was reminded of scenes from the popular TV sitcom about the 4077th MASH in the Korean War. But we didn't have a Margaret 'Hotlips' Houlihan! At that time, Coalition Forces were very much in a defensive posture and there was a concern the Iraqis would launch a major pre-emptive strike into Saudi Arabia before the Coalition Forces were ready for it.

As I was fully embedded with the US Marines, I was expected to participate in general camp duties and I was allocated a fire position on the camp perimeter defences which I was to man if we came under attack. It was quite sobering. The position was an entrenchment with hard-packed sandbag overhead cover. Standing at the fire position underneath all of this, I was shown my allocated M60 machine gun.

It was pintle-mounted and pre-loaded with linked ball and tracer ammunition, about 10,000 rounds, with the belts already linked to enable continuous high rates of fire. In front of me was a fire step so I could look out of the slit towards any approaching enemy. On the step, you could see wooden stakes bracketing the M60 muzzle with high visibility markers on their rearward- facing sides. The stakes marked the left and right arcs of fire and could be used as hard stops if you were firing whilst ducking-down for cover off the fire step. If you sighted enemy troops, you were expected to open fire, step back, duck down and maintain sustained fire whilst traversing the gun between the stakes, almost like hosing down the lathered side of a vehicle in a car wash. Some distance beyond, in front in a hollow, were large rolls of razor wire, still packaged as they came from the stores. Running back from each of them was a buried firing cable. This cable came into the trench and down onto a shelf just below the gun. On the shelf were recycled firing devices from Claymore Mines, each one connected to a firing cable. Inside each roll of razor wire was a demolition charge of C4 explosive and an electric detonator. The briefing was that if the position was over-run, someone would declare loudly "FINAL DEFENSIVE FIRE" and the improvised Claymores would be triggered. Unlike Claymores, the improvised versions up top would spread lethal splinters through the full 360 degrees. The ghosts of Korean and Vietnam war experiences of being over-run clearly still haunted the American psyche.

Our whaleback tented accommodation with the US Marines

Between rotations through key point EOD duties, we were also conducting investigations into ammunition accidents. In one especially tragic incident, a soldier had shot himself dead in his accommodation. Suicide was mentioned but I have never bought that as a cause before seeing the evidence first. I examined the scene and listened to what witnesses said when the body was discovered. He had been sitting cross-legged and the weapon, an SA80, had fired from under his chin, either touching the skin or extremely close to it, but there was no evidence of tattooing or an exit wound. My role was to examine the incident to see if the ammunition was in any way at fault. A simple declaration of suicide would make my life very easy as the ammunition would have performed as designed. What I saw convinced me that the incident was complex, and I felt the ammunition could have been at fault. I ensured the weapon was recovered and subjected to a detailed armourer's inspection. I then closed the door and blinds in the room and switched off the lights. I was looking for the bright sunshine outside to reveal a 5.56mm hole through the wall or ceiling which would give some important clues. There was no bullet hole. There was a very small, almost insignificant entry wound. This was quite bizarre. The SA80 ammunition at the time was powerful and the ball contained a steel tip. On the right eyebrow of the dead soldier was a tiny sliver of what looked like a yellow piece of matchstick. I examined the ammunition. It was dirty but not to the extent that would cause problems. From memory, there were about 29 live rounds and one empty casing, and they had been mostly found scattered on the linoleum floor around the body. Interestingly, all of the percussion caps showed evidence of what is known as 'cap piling'. This is a phenomenon which can arise when ammunition is chambered in a weapon with a floating firing pin. It is possible for the floating pin to leave a small graze mark or dent on the cap and repeated chambering of the same round can cause the graze mark to worsen into a small lump. This can then get worse to the point where the piled metal on the cap leaves an insufficient gap between itself and the firing pin and when this happens, the act of cocking the weapon can result in the round firing, even if the safety catch is applied. I had previously encountered floating firing pins with all their potential nuances in the Sultanate of Oman where mismatched ammunition and the Steyr Army Universal Gun (AUG) nearly resulted in disaster (See Chapter 9). I spoke to the military police personnel and asked them to re-interview the witness about the events leading up to the incident. My concerns were that the deceased's personnel weapon was a pistol, so, why was he in possession of an SA80 and was he qualified to use it? The answer came back that he was fanatical about small arms and was a qualified instructor. The next revelation was both shocking and saddening. He believed the weapon he had borrowed had an intermittent fault in that it would suffer stoppages (jamming). Witnesses had seen him repeatedly filling the magazine, loading it and then cocking the weapon rapidly until the magazine was empty and then doing it all over again. This explained the cap piling I had seen. When asked why this grossly dangerous activity had been tolerated in the accommodation occupied by dozens of service personnel, the reply was that he must have known what he was doing because he was a qualified weapons instructor. This posed a worrying problem. If the death was caused by cap piling, it could indicate a potentially lethal defect with the weapon, the ammunition, or both. I hurriedly arranged ad hoc trials where I repeated the dead soldier's alleged actions, using his own cap-piled ammunition and a fresh batch and also several weapons, including the one which fired the fatal shot. The Armourer's report had cleared the weapon of any defects. With due regard for safety and keeping the weapons pointed down range at all times, I cycled weapons and ammunition umpteen times and found that the repeated chambering did not make the cap piling significantly worse after about a dozen cycles. But I did notice that my hand blistered at the repeated contact with the cocking lever. Cocking the weapon like this in the prone position was very tiring and I then appreciated why the deceased might have resorted to cocking the weapon with it standing on its butt, between his crossed legs, in a vertical position. The position of the ejected ammunition in his room corroborated this and then I put together the most likely scenario which may have led to his death. Firstly, there was no evidence of suicidal intent, and he was said to be in good spirits. Secondly, I was told that there was an illicit still for fermenting alcohol in use in the accommodation. Thirdly, I was shown a radiograph of his head. This clearly showed the bullet track. It had entered through the front of his neck and had arced upwards to the rear base of the skull. The track showed the bullet had been gradually deflected by the curvature of the inside of the skull until it struck the prominent bony ridge that underlies the brow. It came to rest at that point and in the picture, I could see the unravelled guilding metal jacket, lumps of the lead antimony core and the steel core was in direct contact with the brow ridge. This corroborated the finding on the eyebrow, which was identified as a tiny bone fragment, expelled by the internal impact as the bullet remnants came to rest. My explanation of how he died could not be proved but there was no other explanation that came anywhere near to besting it.

Thinking the weapon was defective, he had decided to 'dry-test' his weapon's functioning with live ammunition. He did this by repeatedly cocking live ammunition through it, releasing the cocking handle each time he used it to allow the working parts to close as designed. Through fatigue, and possibly the influence of alcohol, he may have fouled the cocking handle as it went forward. This would slow down the breech block to the extent that it would not then rotate to lock the breech shut which would bring the safety interlock into play. This was a device to prevent the gun from being fired before the breech was positively locked. He would likely perceive this as a stoppage. The safety catch was released, and the trigger was likely pulled. If this happened whilst he was pushing the cocking handle forward, he would inadvertently bring out what is known as a 'forward assist'. If trigger pressure is applied, this can cause the weapon to fire. There are a lot of 'ifs' in that explanation, not to mention the possibility of intoxication, either in him or his colleagues in the accommodation who knew what he was doing. There was no forensic pathologist available in theatre and I believe his body was repatriated without being tested. This aspect of the investigation was deemed too politically sensitive to pursue and was not reported on as there was no evidence that alcohol played a part in the events and there was no post-mortem alcohol test result available. I was convinced his death was accidental and that both weapon and ammunition were fit for purpose. I was called to give evidence at his inquest, which was conducted by the Oxford Coroner, as that was the jurisdiction covering repatriated remains landing at Brize Norton. The bereaved parents were sitting directly opposite me as I gave my opinion that his death was not due to a defect in the ammunition or weapon but was most likely a handling accident. This outcome was upheld by the coroner, and I was gratified on behalf of the parents that suicide was not the verdict. I did, however, put a lot of thought into why it was that an NCO, with weapons training, broke several cardinal rules on weapon safety and then I remembered that someone had said he closed the door to his room so his 'morbid risk-taking' would not be witnessed. I will return to what I have termed 'morbid risk-taking' in Chapter 19.

Another task I was allocated was nightly visits to the British Army part of a large ammunition supply point (ASP). The ammunition technical soldiers there were employed on de-plugging 155mm smoke shells and replacing them with role-specific fuzes. It turned out that our stocks of this ammunition had not been cleared for storage and movement if the actual fuzes were already fitted. This meant they had arrived in-theatre but were unfit for purpose. The ammunition technicians were not members of Det(G) 221 EOD. They were few in number and were not that experienced. They were conducting the fuzing task in the shelter of a large tent and it was a round-the-clock activity. Their numbers had been made up with gunners from Royal Artillery units. On my first visit, I was horrified to discover evidence of cigarettes being stubbed out on the shells themselves and that the workforce appeared completely indifferent to the stringent safety standards that normally apply whenever ammunition is being processed. The senior technician present appeared to be the only one with any prowess but it was clear that he had no overhead cover. There was a young captain ATO but I formed the view that his priority was in trying to impress Army nurses who he would invite to the improvised demolition ground where he could show off by conducting demolitions. This breakdown in both military and technical discipline was appalling. I probably then made myself very unpopular with the troops when I demanded better of them but I wasn't there to be popular.

Whilst providing technical cover at Jerboa Ranges, I was alerted to three issues with the 155mm M109 Self Propelled Gun. These gun systems were firing in close dispersal in the somewhat cramped facilities on the Jerboa Ranges. Their target was actually very close, being about 6 kilometres away and so close that the shells could be seen impacting in and around a collection of derelict buildings labelled on the map as Goat Farm. I overheard a soldier extolling the virtues of "the new stainless-steel reusable 155mm shell" and that dozens of them were scattered around Goat Farm. We had to observe many breaks in firing as the airport was nearby so in one of these breaks, I went over to Goat Farm to investigate. We found a large number of shells lying on the surface. They had been fired as the driving bands were fully engraved. I could see why a casual observer would think they were stainless steel. The shells had plunged into the deep sand from a very high angle and would have been spinning at about 20,000 RPM; they had been sand-blasted! A minority of these shells showed signs of a partial explosion, short of being a high-order detonation. The large number of shells discovered, coupled with the likely higher number of shells lying unseen below the surface, indicated a very serious problem which merited an urgent investigation. We recovered a few shells and examined them. At first, we didn't spot the cause; it was one of those 'hidden in plain sight' scenarios. Then we realised that the fuzes fitted to the blind shells did not reach the bottom of the fuze cavity. This meant there was a substantial air gap between the base of the fuze and the bottom end of the cavity. Detonating explosives do not like air gaps. Another aspect was that the air gap meant that design measures to prevent the sensitive Tetryl exploders in the cavity from being shocked or heated through spin friction were ineffective. There was a distinct risk of a bore or muzzle premature which would likely be fatal. Now that we could see why the shells were not detonating reliably, we needed to ascertain what was going on.

Partially exploded M107 Shell caused by incompatible M577 Fuze

The history of these M107 shells gave us the first clue. They had been sent to Saudi Arabia from the UK without fuzes fitted. The fuze cavities were closed off with threaded plugs. About 5,000 of these shells had been issued from the UK to be fired at training. A bulk stock of matching suitable fuzes had not been issued. Somebody in the supply chain had asked the US Logisticians if they had any suitable fuzes we could use. As NATO members, it is desirable that our ammunition be interchangeable with that of other NATO members, but this is not always possible. We discovered that the fuze fitted to the blind shells was the US M577 fuze. This fuze was not capable of detonating. It would instead ignite a gunpowder ejection charge which would expel and ignite the contents of a carrier shell, such as smoke or illuminating canisters. There was a publication known as the NATO Interoperability Handbook and this handbook appeared to show that the M577 fuze was compatible with the 155mm M107 shell. However, compatible did not always mean full interoperability. In this case, an extra component would have to be attached to the M577 fuze to convert it into a detonating fuze. One of the fuzes which would definitely work with the 155mm shell was the fuze M557 and you can probably see how confusion could arise. We spoke to some of the Gunners who had been inserting the fuzes into the plugged shell immediately before they were fired. Some of them admitted they could see that the M577 fuze was physically too short to reach the base of the cavity but they didn't raise a concern. We returned to the HQ to investigate who might have authorised the use of these incompatible fuzes. Nobody seemed to know but we did find that the handbook page giving the compatibility details had been torn out and disposed of. One of the possible organisational causes of this disaster-waiting-to-happen was that the HQ FMA Supply Branch did not have an ATO or AT embedded in it. This lack of technical expertise in the supply management of ammunition was only corrected after the ceasefire was declared and Det(G) 221 EOD Coy returned home.

Another embarrassing supply failure occurred when the Gun Regiment was given an allocation of ammunition packed in the new Unitised Load Container (ULC) configuration, the idea being that the Gunners needed to familiarise themselves with this new method of pack. Several ULCs were issued from the ammunition supply point but when the Gunners opened them, they were found to be empty. This was primarily due to a complete lack of experience by the Issues Team in the ammunition supply point. Firstly, they failed to notice the lack of seals on the empty ULCs and the forklift truck drivers didn't notice the ULCs they were handling were substantially lighter than they should have been. In depots, returned empties are almost invariably stored well away from filled containers and usually not even kept in the explosives area. The bottom line was that we had become a 'peacetime' army and this mobilisation was exposing our weaknesses.

The last tale of woe about the SP M109 Gun concerned an ammunition upgrade from the 'short and dumpy' M107 HE Shell to the long and sleek L15 HE Shell. The newer shell, manufactured from a vastly stronger steel alloy than the old one, didn't require the massively thick shell walls to withstand the shock of acceleration at shot-start in the breech of the gun. As the shell walls were thinner and the shell was longer, the new shell had almost double the explosive capacity of its predecessor and ballistic improvements increased the range substantially. The new ammunition was compatible with the old gun but an oversight occurred when it came to storing the new shell in the ammunition carousel inside the gun.

An additional issue was that the length increase was made worse when the newly issued Electronic Multi-Role Fuze was fitted. After the Gunners had loaded the ammunition into the carousel, they managed to guillotine several fuzes the first time they rotated the turret. The new shells wouldn't fit and protruded above the turret ring.

The MLRS rocket pods we received in theatre had been moved around on flatracks but, sadly, not enough strapping was sent out with the flatracks. The 'movers and shakers' had to make do and mend and use fewer straps than the tie-down scheme required. Flatracks are dis-mountable load platforms which are tilted significantly when they are lifted onto the flatrack vehicle and then ground-dumped at their desti-nation. We had to sentence a number of rocket pods as unserviceable as they had fallen off the flatracks during unloading operations when the few straps that were used were over-stressed and snapped.

Hand grenades have always been a source of black humour, ironically because they are so potentially dangerous and lethal when things go wrong. Despite belonging to the so-called 'Common User' category of ammunition, knowledge of the grenade, its safety precautions, how to prepare and throw it and how to deal with a blind was not common. Tragedy struck when a soldier, working on an armoured vehicle with a large wrench, accidentally caused the wrench to strike his chest. In a pocket, he had a fuzed grenade. The impact of the wrench displaced the safety pin and, four seconds later, he was killed. In another example of ignorance, a corporal was clearing the effects of a soldier who had died of natural causes. The dead soldier's possessions included his issued ammunition which would be retrieved. The ammunition included an L2 hand grenade and an L25 fuze. The very sad tale repeated to me was that the corporal did not understand how the grenade fuze worked, so, whilst holding the shiny, bright cylinder at the bottom (the detonator) between thumb and forefinger, he pulled out the pin to see what would happen. He suffered serious and permanent life-changing injuries.

Let me once again mix in some humour. We were already 'leaning forward' (Army speak for being pro-active) in being available to in-

vestigate and destroy blinds (duds) on the ranges. Normally, destroying blinds was a unit responsibility but if we did it for them, there
would be less disruption to training. Military training is absolutely
essential, and you would have thought that was a given; well, not so.
Training is expensive and, in peacetime, all armies are tempted to take
shortcuts. Sometimes, the temptation to save in peacetime is emboldened by the assurance that catch-up training before deploying to war
would be given. Promises, promises, I say. An example of this was
with one of the main battle tank regiments. They belong to the Royal
Armoured Corps (RAC). Training policy for the various parts of the
Army is predicated quite rightly on what the war role is to be. In the
RAC, each soldier should be trained on hand grenades to a level up
to and including the advanced stage. The most basic stage teaches a
soldier how to put the fuze in a grenade and how to throw it. The advanced stage would follow on where the soldier would be taught how
to get a grenade into a hardened enemy bunker, perhaps a so-called
'pill-box'. The act of getting the grenade inside through a window or
firing slit is known as 'posting'. It was realised, late in the day, that
the majority of RAC soldiers had only been trained to the basic level.
They would all have to be taught and tested to the advanced level.
I was sent to the grenade range to provide technical support to this
training. It is a fact that throwing a live hand grenade can be stressful.
Once the pin is out of the fuze, fumbling or dropping the grenade can
result in tragedy. To boost confidence, between the queuing soldiers
and the grenade-throwing point, the regiment had positioned their
Padre. Dressed in combats, topped off with his trappings of office, he
would accost each would-be grenade thrower as they went forward.
Words would be had, a blessing would be administered and the hapless grenade 'postie' would go around a large berm to the throwing
point where he was out of sight of the rest of us but we could hear the

safety supervisor giving instructions. There was a rhythm. Shouted instructions, shout of "GRENADE", pause of 4 seconds, BANG! Soldier reappears completely covered in white dusty sand, looking ghostlike and often visibly shocked. Padre steps forwards, soldier is re-blessed and step forward the next thrower.

Now, I am an atheist and, at every opportunity, I would wriggle out of church parades and Padre's hour. I respect those who believe but I don't, especially in the matter of divine intervention. As I watched, I formed the opinion that the Padre's intervention was often making the occasional nervous soldier even more nervous. After about an hour of bangs, a nervous would-be thrower gets the Padre's blessing and disappears around the other side of the berm. The rhythm resumed but after 4 seconds, there was no bang. 5, 6 , 7...... "BLIND!" came the shout. The soldiers started laughing and shouting for the ATO (me). I picked up my demolition box and headed for the throwing point only to see the Padre striding forwards to intercept me, intent on issuing moral and religious guidance. To the roar of laughter from the audience, I legged it around the corner to where even the Padre couldn't go.

It was my opinion, based on direct observation (and joking aside), that ignorance, poor preparation and changes to equipment and ammunition created systemic failings which, for the most part, emerged during training and could be remedied before battle. My old friend LAW 80 proved too fragile and vulnerable to the ingress of sand and tactical handling. I witnessed a firing where sand contamination impeded a rocket as it was launched. I did a rapid investigation and got a report off to our technical directorate. To be fair, the response from them and the manufacturer was impressive. In short order, they replicated the failure on a range in the UK and issued frangible protective caps which could protect the launcher from the ingress of sand whilst the weapon was tactically deployed, without its protective hard restraints during so-called 'tank stalks'. There were several other incidents where ignorance, peacetime training cost reduction measures and a simple but gross lack of experience of living in the field with live ammunition contributed to avoidable injuries and equipment losses. I personally intervened when I found a Warrior AFV and crew on Desert Dog Dragoon Ranges resting up and making a meal. They had placed a camouflage net over the vehicle and had a large bonfire burning at the end of the net. At the Warrior end of the net, the open back door revealed a full vehicle allocation of both Milan Anti-Tank HEAT Guided Missiles and LAW 80 Anti-Tank Rockets. In other cases, smoking was the direct cause of two very significant fires where gun charges were ignited by carelessly discarded cigarettes.

The retention of obsolete armoured vehicles was also a bone of contention. Despite the known and very dangerous hazard presented by a petrol-engined armoured vehicle, we had armoured bridge-layers on old tank bodies fuelled by petrol and we had retro-fitted explosive reactive armour (ERA) to them. One caught fire and burned out. I recall seeing how the explosive fillings of the ERA had melted and poured out onto the tank's body, which now looked like it had a caramel coating! There was a vast amount of ignorance, inexperience and, frankly, indifference to well-established field army conventions relating to the husbandry of ammunition. There were deaths and many injuries caused by this and I have detailed the more serious incidents and near misses within this Chapter.

On 16th February 1991, our indifference to the Scud missile threat nearly cost us dear. For some reason, the Patriot missile battery providing cover for the port had come out of action; in effect, the goalie had gone to sleep. Next thing we knew, we were subjected to a missile attack and the promised early warning of 'END TRAY' radar activity had not materialised. In the early hours, the civil defence air raid sirens sounded while we were sleeping. That night, I was in-camp but Ian Rimmel, who was permanently based in camp, told me to disregard the civil defence alarms as these didn't discriminate which area was being attacked. He said we should only react if the OPB air raid sirens started. No sooner had he said that than the OPB sirens started to wail and the dulcet (not) tones of the Watchkeeper boomed out on the tannoy "AIR RAID WARNING RED", etc., etc. We got out of bed and started to slowly but methodically dress and then got into our NBC suits (so-called Noddy suits). False alarms were frequent, and our now tardy drills reflected our jaundiced responses. As we fussed over getting the kit on, there was a huge bang which sounded very close. The effect on our NBC drills was electric and we immediately dressed at best speed. However, for some obscure reason, I couldn't get the hood of my NBC suit over my head. Then I heard the respirator-muffled guffaws from Ian when he saw that I still had my combat helmet on! I had put it on at the sound of the bang. We did the 'buddy-buddy' thing and, once we were dressed, we switched on our portable chemical reconnaissance kit and started sampling around the windows and door. All was negative and we emerged from our room into the darkened corridor outside. There we found the remaining occupants from the block, some from upstairs. As the ambient temperature was high and NBC kit was hot, many of the troops were lying flat on their backs on the cold concrete floor to keep cool. We progressed down the corridor, waving our humming monitors about (probably looking as outlandish as something from Ghostbusters) and as we approached the end, we saw a person in a Noddy suit frantically struggling and shouting and his voice was strangely loud (the service respirator tended to muffle voices). It turned out he had abused his equipment and had knocked an eyepiece out of place. He had tried to improve the protection from his broken respirator by putting his hand over the missing eyepiece but then totally lost the plot when the 'Ghostbusters duo' approached him! After a while, the warning was cancelled, and we went back to bed, mystified by what had just happened. In the morning, it was business as usual. I decided on impulse to visit the US Navy EOD Team who were located in tentage just inside the breakwater of the commercial pier. Their commander was a Chief Warrant Officer 2 called Mick who was quite amiable. As they were 'under the stars' in their tents, I asked if they had seen or heard anything the previous night. At first, Mick's denial was polite and plausible, but I did sense some reticence on his part. I suspected there was a chance he or his team could have seen or heard at least something, and our conversation moved to a discussion about the general Scud missile threat. I spoke of that system's capability and the two variants the Iraqis had improvised which put us well inside range. Mick was immediately quite curious and seemed to be hanging on every word I said. More's the point, I started to wonder why Mick was so curious. He asked if I would keep his confidence as he had something to show me which was operationally secret at that time.

[*I am bound to point out that I have done a literature survey about this missile attack and the whole thing is already in the public domain, having been revealed by a US Freedom of Information request some years ago.*]

Mick invited me into a more secluded part of his tented accommodation which appeared to be a briefing space. At its heart was a large screen rear-projection TV unit and next to it was video player. He then said that he and his team had seen an incoming object plunging down from high altitude, emitting some flames and sparks and, as it drew closer, they could see it was glowing a dull red colour. The object struck the water within the pier's breakwater with a large splash and much hissing. It submerged and resurfaced a few times, eventually sinking in what was about 50 feet of water. An acrid smell was noted. A small boat performed an immediate reconnaissance, and a buoy was placed to mark the impact site. At first light, an underwater team dived the location and Mick's preamble became the introduction to the video film he then played on the large TV. I found myself looking at a Scud missile, lying on the seabed, which appeared to be in three pieces. These were the warhead section, main missile assemblage and the rocket engine. This missile had narrowly missed a very large US Marine Expeditionary Force logistics vessel and the adjacent quayside upon which had been disembarked hundreds of M26 Multi-Launch Rocket System pods, stacked two-high. If the Scud missile had struck these, the resultant potentially massive conflagration could easily have denied much of the commercial pier to the allies' logistic efforts and would have been a major setback. Each M26 rocket carried a payload of 644 bomblets so with 6 rockets to a pod, there was a total of 3,864 bomblets. If any of the MLRS M26 rockets had ignited and become propulsive and airborne, their potential maximum range of 32,000 metres could have seen devastation over a huge area. In simple EOD threat assessment terms, the worst thing that could have happened was a large loss of life and loss of the commercial pier, not to mention a strategic impact on the forthcoming Liberation of Kuwait. The most likely thing that could have happened would have been a more localised outcome with perhaps the loss of about half of the pier's capacity as a logistics base and the attendant loss of life. The best thing that could have happened did. It was now essential to maintain operational secrecy and Mick was rightly anxious that I didn't tell anyone. My potential part in this and the reason for his frankness was that he needed to access a 'render safe' procedure so that he and his team could safely deal with the missile and recover it. I offered to contact the UK MoD Technical Intelligence staff using an appropriately classified communications system to request 'render safe' documentation. I also asked if I could inform our Force Maintenance Area (FMA) Commander which Mick agreed to.

I returned promptly to the UK FMA and requested an urgent meeting with the FMA Commander, a brigadier. His staff said no but they would pass on any message they considered warranted his attention. I said the matter was OPSEC (operationally secure) for his ears only on the authority of the US Port Commander, but the stonewalling persisted. These 'bag-carriers' were young officers and I had promised to keep the matter on limited distribution; in fact, I didn't even tell my own boss. As he was living alone in a 12ft X 12ft tent quite close to the impact area, perhaps I should have mentioned it, but a promise is a promise. I started to get annoyed, and our voices became raised. We were in a large open-plan area which had been set up as an operations room and the brigadier was nearby. The raised voices attracted his attention and he asked for an explanation. I asked for a private meeting with him, and this took place, and I got access to secure communications equipment. I then needed to send a signal to the Technical Intelligence staff in the MoD requesting the documents needed. The next piece of drama involved a real Walter Mitty character who flew out from the UK and then vanished on his own sight-seeing trip up-country, seemingly oblivious to the threat, and there would be enough material to write another book, but I will save you all the ordeal. We got the documents and Mick and his team eventually rendered the missile safe whilst I was deployed away to Kuwait City. On return, Mick showed me the hardware on the quayside. It looked like one of the two known Scud variants, and I noted the missile had broken up at the two main joints between the warhead and main body and the rocket engine and main body. I wanted to check the integrity of the welding in the tankage sections, so I climbed inside the tanks and photographed the welds; they were very high quality. The official reports state that the US had already got the 'render safe' documents and there is no mention of the UK role in acquiring these. The errant Walter Mitty was rounded up and sent packing which is just as well because Mick confided in me yet again to explain what he and his team wanted to do with him; it's not worth my liberty to print it!

Meanwhile, back on the ranges, we agreed to maximise what limited time was available for live firing on the ranges by agreeing to deal with ammunition blinds immediately. This would allow the firing units to continue their shooting or live fire manoeuvres uninterrupted. Normally, units would deal with their own blinds and so our exposure to how units operated was enlightening to say the least. We saw examples of live LAW 80 munitions being abandoned because user firing drills were sometimes incompetent. I was called to deal with a 51mm Mortar HE bomb blind and, when I exposed the body to place a demolition charge, I could see the safety pin had been left in the fuze. In perhaps the best example of user inexperience, I was present near a Giant Viper assembly point at Devil Dog Dragoon Ranges. A large-scale all-arms live fire and manoeuvre exercise was about to commence. A large rectangular berm had been erected by Sappers and this was covered in camouflage nets. Inside were most of the senior field commanders and well-known members of the press. I was standing just inside the entrance when an anxious-looking Sapper came over from the Giant Viper assembly point where several box trailers were parked up, side by side. He was holding up an object and shouted something to the effect that there would be an explosion in 7 seconds. That wasn't logical as the soft sand between the parked Giant Vipers and the berm, not to mention the distance being about 60 metres, meant the 7 seconds must have already expired. The assembled VIPs looked somewhat alarmed, so I went over and asked what the problem was. If there had indeed been an explosion, all of the Giant Vipers would have detonated en masse, and this would have killed most, if not all of the senior staff and journalists standing inside the berm.

I now need to describe the Giant Viper for the benefit of readers who might not know what it is. It was one of the most spectacular pieces of ammunition in our inventory. The Giant Viper was a very long and flexible hose pipe. It contained over 1,000 kg of plastic explosive and its job was to clear a path through minefields. The hose was over 200 metres long and in order to work, it would be towed in a large box trailer to the edge of a minefield. The box contained the coiled hose and rocket motor assembly. The rockets would fire and pull the hose out of the box. The coils would impart a snake-like wriggle to the hose which flew upwards and forwards until the rear end of the hose was pulled clear of the box. As the end was pulled clear, a lanyard attached to the trailer would start the initiation sequence. At the same time, a parachute would deploy from each end of the hose to stabilise it and pull it straight. The hose would then fall to the ground. After a delay, the hose would detonate from rear to front end and the resulting blast was intended to clear a lane about six metres wide and 200 metres long. It sounds simple but it was anything but. Each Giant Viper had to be put through a series of preparatory assembly stages. The 8-rocket motors mounted on a ring had to be assembled onto a launch spigot. Then the rocket motor igniters had to be circuit-tested. After the top side was readied, a Sapper would need to get underneath the box trailer and open a small access hatch to enable the preparation of the anchored L3 striker mechanism. This was fiddly work which had to be done carefully and with the right tools. If all went as planned, the launch sequence would start with an explosive bolt being fired to bring the rocket motor spigot post up into its elevated position. The rockets motors would then be fired but the hose could not fly until the combined thrust of all motors exceeded the minimum needed for a full flight. When the correct thrust was achieved, the pull was sufficient to snap a shear bar, allowing the motors to take off and drag the hose behind them. The last action as the hose left the box trailer was that a lazy line release block would be pulled clear of the striker mechanism, allowing a 7-second clockwork delay mechanism to run down. This would then allow the striker mechanism to function and ignite a short delay fuze attached to a detonator. The delay was sufficient to allow the hose to fall where intended.

In summary, to get through all the preparatory phases required careful supervision with all phases carried out in the right sequence. I took the lazy line release block off the Sapper and ran over to the Giant Viper. I got underneath and accessed the striker mechanism through the hatch. I made the Viper safe and then tried to see what had gone wrong. The lazy line release block was attached to the striker mechanism with some very fine hexagonal nuts. I knew from what the Sapper had told me that the block detached whilst he was tightening these nuts with a spanner. I saw that the bolts along one side were sheared off. I looked at the spanner he had used. It was an open-ended spanner. In the very tight working space, I could see it was possible for the open ends of the spanner's jaws to collide with neighbouring bolts whilst one of them was being tightened. This was sufficient to shear the retaining nuts and bolts, allowing the block to fall clear and release the delay escapement.

The whirring noise as it came away must have been terrifying but there were other safety features in the striker mechanism to prevent disaster. Problem solved, situation safe, move on.

One of the last major equipment firings scheduled to take place before the Division was to depart for its assembly area, prior to battle, was of the Multi-Launch Rocket System (MLRS). We knew that Operation Desert Sabre, the land attack against the Iraqis, was imminent. We also knew the outline plan for the attack which was highly classified. The plan had already been briefed to us in the Operations Room where the Chief of Staff emphasised the importance of secrecy and what would become of us if we divulged the plan or even speculated about it. In the middle of an historic and fascinating briefing of an audacious plan, the Chief of staff suddenly noticed the presence of a locally employed cleaner in blue overalls, complete with mop and bucket, who was listening avidly; cue yet more apoplexy! The Iraqis had hopefully been deceived to expect both a head-on attack into southern Kuwait and also a major landing by US Marines from the sea at the head of the Gulf. The actual plan involved what had been called the 'left hook'. The coalition Land Forces' main effort was to move out to the west to outflank the Iraqis and then move inland to cut off their escape from Kuwait. To reinforce the deception plan, we heard that the range radio nets had been recorded over recent days and immediately prior to the attack, these recordings would be re-broadcast to swamp any listening Iraqi monitoring efforts to confuse them. For this to work, there was to be radio silence after the range activity ceased. We didn't have any radio equipment of our own and we used that of Infantry Range Control who had been located about 150 metres from our position. Trouble is, as soon as the MLRS firing finished, everyone cleared off.

Then I got a message that there was a problem on the MLRS firing point. Kris and I drove over to see what was up. When we got to the firing point, we found two MLRS pods ground- dumped. Each pod held 6 rockets before firing but there was only one rocket in each of these two pods. In those days, MLRS did have an Achille's Heel. When one of these rockets launches, it generates a powerful shockwave and a lot of high-energy efflux as it bursts forth from the launcher. The crew are safe in the armoured cab, but I had by then attended quite a lot of firings where I was very close to the launcher. Sometimes, a rocket would launch and, as it took off, the blast could suck the forward protective cap off a neighbouring tube. If the next rocket to fire was close to the now-exposed tube, the rocket efflux could stray into the now-unprotected tube. The Achille's Heel I spoke of was the gold dot connector which provided the communications link between the rocket and fire control computer. If the gold dot connector was damaged, it would result in an error message on the fire control computer, or, if the connector was severed, the computer would assume that the rocket had already been fired. The launch sequence was automatic once it had started and then, when complete, the launcher would move rapidly away to a replenishment point and reload. Looking down the tubes containing misfired rockets, I could see one connector was severed and the other was damaged.

MLRS had not been in service with the Royal Artillery for very long and our Technical Directorate had written a 'render safe' procedure (RSP) for us to follow in the event of misfires. The RSP made certain assumptions: Firstly, the misfire would happen in established permanent ranges in the UK or Germany. Secondly, there would be manpower and equipment resources to enable the RSP. Thirdly, we were supposed to refer these problems to the Directorate immediately. Well, what can I say? These misfires were on a deserted range complex in Saudi Arabia. Apart from Kris and me, there was a bemused Infantry Major present. Other than a Land Rover and a mostly depleted demolition box, we had no equipment and communications were prohibited for operational security (OPSEC) reasons. The range was not secure. Local Arabs were already wandering in, and it would be wrong to abandon these rockets as the locals would almost certainly assume they had found some scrap metal.

Now for a word about the RSP. After a safe waiting period, the ATO in charge was to arrange to have a 12-man party seconded to him from the firing unit. A forklift truck and artillery staff (a big stick) were also required. The ATO would already be equipped with an enhanced 400-metre-long hook and line. The caps at each end of the launch tube would have to be blown off (unless they had already come off as described earlier). A hook and line would then have to be attached to the rocket's fin restraint system in order to pull it clear. The fin restraints were explosive and would release the folded fins as the rocket left the tube going forwards. If it came backwards, however, the ATO could suffer severe injury if he was too close, so the 400-metre hook and line was pretty essential. After the fin restraint system had been dealt with, the forklift truck would be positioned in such a way that, as the rocket was pushed out, it would land on the forks. The rocket would be pushed out with the stick (I mean Artillery Staff) by the work party. The rocket would then be moved to a suitable demolition area for destruction. The RSP would be concluded with a voluminous report.

We had two choices; stay and guard these misfires for God only knows how long or destroy them in situ with a 'make do and mend' revised RSP. Staying was not an option. I asked Kris to see what was left in the demolition box. His face as he looked back at me was a picture. We only had several plain detonators, one reel of safety fuze, matches fuzee, a small amount of plastic explosive, a length of detonating cord and, quite useful as it happened, some SX2 sheet explosive. The SX2 could be shaped into diamonds and, if detonated from each end, the converging detonating waves would collide and act as improvised linear cutting charges. This was ideal if you wanted to render a rocket motor non-propulsive by cutting both ends off at the same time but, if things went wrong, you could have a very energetic rocket motor, capable of flying 32,000 metres, completely spoil your day (and some-one else's). And we had two of them!

I planned the positioning of charges and calculated what would be needed. We had just enough if we were able to move the rocket pods and turn one over so as to position the two misfired rockets next to each other. The major joined in and, with a bit of help from the Land Rover, we had the pods side by side and, happily, facing the impact area in case anything went wrong. I cut out the diamonds and made SX2 strips to create two-point initiation. I had more plain detonators than I needed so I used these with small lumps of left-over sheet and plastic explosive to make small boosters as detonating cord doesn't always detonate PE4 unless you've got lots of it. After about an hour of messing about, I stood back to admire my work. Kris put on his best brave face. The major wasn't sure about what was going to happen next. In the trade, we had an abbreviated risk assessment; something like: What's the worst thing that could happen? What's the best thing that could happen? And what's the most likely thing to happen? I sensed it was time to take a leaf from a past SAT's book of optimism. For those readers who might know him, this was the late, great WO1 Ron Little, probably the funniest AT in Christendom!

Crunch time approached. We selected a safe viewing point uphill and about 1,500 metres away in the safest arc from the rockets. The plan was I would leave Kris and the major up there and then return in the Land Rover which I was going to leave in dead ground about 200 metres from the rockets. I would signal the lighting of the fuze with a wave which would start the timing process with Kris. I rehearsed the walk between the rockets and the dead ground. The stern lectures from my basic EOD training rang in my head: Scarf the fuze. Secure the fuze to prevent it rolling back on itself to cause a premature. Keep the match fuzee in your hand as you retire and, most of all, don't run on the demolition ground! Anyway, it was now 'shit or bust' time. With Ron Little's ghostly chuckles now drowning out the demolition ground mantras in my head, I lit the fuze. Making sure it was securely pinned down, I waved to Kris and then walked (quickly) to the waiting Land Rover. After churning through the soft sand, I joined them and watched the deserted terrain in front of us. Fuze was usually not a first choice for a demolition as it lacks the precise control of electrical initiation, but I had no choice. I scoured the horizon for any interlopers who might enter the danger area. Kris was counting down and reached zero; nothing happened. EOD Operators will be very familiar with that sinking feeling when fuze overruns. However, fuze burns at 40 seconds per foot plus or minus a 10% margin, so I clung to this marginal sliver of optimism.

Then there was a brilliant flash to our front and the most beautiful demolition I have ever conducted erupted like a massive Genie getting out of his bottle. It was almost a perfect but miniature replica of the ball-shaped white Wilson Cloud seen at the Operation Crossroads (Baker) nuclear test at Bikini Atoll in 1946. Bright red shards of burning high-energy propellant shot up into the air and then the bang rolled in sharp and crisp. The wind blew the cloud away and I glanced at the other two. Kris was mesmerised and I swear the major looked like he wanted to have my babies!! Aping my old TV favourite, the late Fred Dibnah, I asked, "Did yer like that?" I went down to do a safety check. The demolition was complete. The sand at the centre had melted in the heat and had solidified into crude glass. All that was left was bits of harmless rocket pod. Declining all requests for an encore from the Infantry, we departed; job done.

RAOC EOD support to Special Forces in recovering the British Embassy was in planning for some time before the Coalition Land Forces switched from Desert Storm to Desert Sabre. The land invasion launched (G Day) on Sunday 24 February 1991. Various options for EOD Support had been considered and ranged from a heavy, vehicle-mounted capability complete with electronic support, to a lightweight 2-man team with limited equipment on foot (i.e. no vehicles). The lightweight option was chosen, and the two-man team was nominated and was to consist of myself and Boo as the No 2. Our time of deployment would clearly depend on how Operation Desert Sabre progressed. We were re-deployed to a Special Forces Mounting Base where we joined the other personnel in tented accommodation. Our first briefing by the designated full colonel Commander of British Forces Forward (Kuwait) was somewhat unsettling. We were brought together quite informally in a tent. The group consisted of a member of the Kuwaiti royal family, Special Forces personnel and a Royal Signals Satellite Communications Detachment (SATCOMDET). The Commander, Colonel Talbot, introduced the aims of the operation and then spoke of administration. He said we were all volunteers and that, upon being nominated, those of us based at Al Jubayl had our personal records uplifted and these had been sent elsewhere. He spoke of us being henceforth on a very short notice to move and that this was a reflection of the rapidly unfolding situation in the ground war. On being called forward, all of us would board a C-130 Hercules and we would be flown directly into Kuwait City Airport. And that was that. We slept and ate and waited. I think there was at least one false start before we eventually boarded the aircraft.

You always knew when a flight was going to be unconventional by watching the Loadmaster. Typically (and with good reason), Loadmasters could be pretty anal, especially if you brought explosives onto their aircraft. On this flight, the Loadmaster was quite sanguine which added to the air of irregularity. Boo and I boarded last, behind the other passengers, who were up forward. The royal stood out like a beacon, being dressed in a spotless dish-dash. We heaved our 'lightweight' equipment on to the top of other cargo which was secured under a cargo net. I thought for a nanosecond about telling the Loadmaster how much explosives and detonators we were carrying but the body language didn't seem right somehow. There was nowhere to sit so we elected to plonk ourselves down on the cargo. We taxied out to the runway and took off. At first, the flight was uneventful. Then the aircraft started to fly as though it was taking evasive action, going from a terrain-following path and then climbing up and down. I think it was the black smoke from the burning oil wells which was making a normal flight impossible. It was also possible the pilot had been given an air corridor to comply with and needed to fly tactically which can be great fun, provided you can see where you're going. Down below, we started to see some signs of the chaos of war. The flight was quite short and, after a few minutes, we were clustered around the nearest window. Inside, the cabin was dark. Suddenly, the cabin lit up with a brilliant flash. It was surreal; I tried to wrestle with my hyper-vigilant mind. There was utterly no point in getting wound up as our fate was locked into that of this aircraft. Then I realised the flash was defensive flares from our aircraft; Crab Air 1, RAOC EOD Nil! Then we were landing. The aircraft taxied in quite close to the main terminal. The ramp came down and we peered outside. The usual well-ordered state of an airport was not expected but what we saw was, all the same, awesome. Right next to the terminal building was the burned-out skeleton of a British Airways Boeing 747. We got into the terminal building which had been completely trashed. Anything glass had been smashed; anything attractive and portable had been nicked by the Iraqis. We created a space for ourselves on the first floor. A short while later, a Loadmaster came looking for me, looking a little unhappy. I followed him back to his aircraft and, on the left side of the lowered ramp was a Rockeye Submunition. The explanation was that someone had picked it up and carried it on board intending to keep it. On the basis it had been moved already by some oh-so-lucky, lucky souvenir hunter, I removed it carefully to a safer environment behind a concrete wall. I dealt with it later, with a destructor incendiary in the bottom of a pit. I was surprised as most of the explosive filling burned away before the fuze detonated with a loud pop! Then it started to rain heavily and the sky darkened. Overhead was a massive, low-level black cloud of smoke from the burning oil wells. Day became night and even the raindrops were black. We went back inside, preferring the man-eating mosquitos to the apocalyptic exterior. As we looked for somewhere to adopt as a temporary home, we went into an office. There on the desk was a big rubber stamp. I picked it up and read the inverted lettering. It was a customs stamp dated 2 August 1991. This was priceless! I bagged it and later franked all my Blueys to send to the family. If you didn't know, Blueys were the officially issued mail forms we could send home for free. At some point, someone found the stamp where we left it in our accommodation, and we lost it. The memory of it was preserved, however, as my wife Christine kept all of my wartime Blueys, which I still have today, and the ones from after this airport saga all bear this historic date stamp.

Later on, Colonel Talbot asked me if I would go over to a nearby American base as they had reported 'a problem'. By now, it was nighttime and naturally dark. When I got to the base, I found it was in a large compound, mostly comprising sand with an internal network of asphalt roads. There were several box-body trailers, connected by cabling and what looked like a satellite earth station. I reported to an American officer who asked me to investigate a number of objects they had discovered with parachutes attached to them. I walked amongst the trailers and soon realised what had happened. On taking over this compound, they had unwittingly entered an area containing unexploded French Beluga Cluster Bomb Sub-munitions. The danger level to everyone present was very high. These submunitions could be of 3 types - a general-purpose anti-personnel/anti-material bomb, an anti-tank bomb or an interdiction bomb with a variable delay and we had no way of telling what the delay was. The cluster bomb would contain 151 munitions. The armed devices should never be moved by hand. I returned to the senior officer to tell him what I had found. I explained I could destroy them in situ and mitigate collateral damage with sandbags or other improvised tamping. I would, however, have to evacuate personnel before initiating any charges. His reaction was astonishing; he refused point-blank to evacuate any personnel as this would adversely affect his mission. I could have my controlled explosions, but his equipment must not, under any circumstances, be damaged. In other words, the equipment was more important than the personnel.

I took time out to think through what he had just said. As I was pondering what to do next, the warrant officer in charge of the Royal Signals SATCOMDET approached. He asked what was up. I said I was puzzled at the notion that hurting troops was apparently preferable to damaging their equipment. He asked if I understood what was going on. I clearly didn't and asked for an explanation. It turned out this base was the American Forces' Forward Headquarters Army Central (HQ ARCENT) and the bit I was in was their satellite earth station providing real-time communications with the Pentagon. Their immediate concern was in organising a meeting with the Iraqi leaders to arrange the cease-fire at Safwan. Buggar! I had nobody to refer up to and, under EOD task categorisation policy, this task was almost certainly right up there with the most critical. Controlled explosions were out of the question and I would have to use manual methods to make the place safe. I did a more organised sweep of the area. Daylight was now upon us and I could see a number of clues that made me suspect that the parent cluster bomb may have been dropped from too low an altitude or could even have struck terrain before the bomblets could be dispensed properly from the cluster bomb. In other words, these bomblets might not have armed before coming to rest; well, I hoped so, anyway. I also found a bomb which had been driven over by a Humvee; this added credence to my suspicions. As I searched for bomblets, a flapping cloth in the breeze drew my attention. It was a small parachute which gave away the presence of a bomblet. This bomblet was immediately behind a typical US Army field latrine. It had been run over and squashed into the sand. Please bear with me as I describe the scene to you. The latrine was made of wood. From memory, I think it had five toilet seats inside. There were no windows, but all openings were screened by a fly-proof mesh. To use the latrine, you stepped up into it as it was split-level. The seats were nothing more than bum-holes and your business would fall about a metre into an oil drum positioned immediately below. The drum would usually be primed with Loo-blue. When you used the latrine, you could see your neighbours, they could see you and we could all see what was going on below. These latrines were functional, but you left your dignity outside! The Americans are big on field hygiene; I almost wrote 'anal' which would be an unforgivable pun but I think you get the picture. When the drums were full, the command "Police the Heads" would be issued. At the rear of the latrine, each bay had a large, hinged flap. If the flap was raised, the person nominated to police the heads could hook the drum and pull it out. If it was safe, a common method of cleaning the drum was to pour a jerrican of diesel fuel in it and then set fire to it. It worked but you learned not to stand down-wind! The aforementioned bomblet was at the right, rear end of the latrine. Part of it was under the wooden framework and I needed to inspect it from inside the bay. I approached carefully, knelt down behind the end bay, unhooked the hinged flap and raised it, securing it with the top hook. As my head entered the bay, there was a loud PLOP! I looked up; a very large American was mooning me from above and was now staring disbelievingly at the apparition below him. His eyes moved to the flapping parachute next to me and widened like great white porcelain saucers. He screamed "HOLY SHIT!" and fled. For me, something about bombs and toilets was developing into a pattern. Anyway, enough of that and back to the serious bit.

I elected to move the bomblets over to the other side of a solid compound wall. Nine bomblets were moved in this way. Whilst the bomblets were still potentially dangerous, they were now well away from personnel and equipment. I left the scene and returned to the airport. On reflection, I now appreciated a number of things. We were apparently the only EOD asset in Kuwait City at that time, there was no HQ staff EOD expertise available, we were expected by US Forces to conduct all aspects of EOD (which was permitted in general war), we had no Force Protection and we had no transport of our own. In light of this, it was bemusing some days later to be reproached by a Royal Engineer officer for 'poaching' tasks normally conducted by his own Corps. What did he expect I do at HQ ARCENT whilst ceasefire negotiation arrangements were being finalised? How lame might it have sounded if I had responded to their Chief of Staff's cry for help if I had said, "Sorry, I can't deal with this because I'm in the RAOC"?

Beluga sub-munitions in HQ ARCENT

And so onto the embassy clearance. I will now do the Public Relations equivalent of 'farting in church' over what actually happened, as opposed to what news viewers saw on the TV screens. Having scrounged a vehicle, we approached the British Embassy. We were alone and sporadic small-arms fire was erupting all over the place. It could have been celebratory gunfire, but we had heard that isolated pockets of Iraqi troops had been left behind in their panic-stricken retreat and that Kuwaiti resistance fighters were mopping them up without necessarily taking prisoners. I have no idea if this was true but it was all we had to go on.

Some force protection would have been nice but there was a general level of disorder and when we first arrived, I didn't recall seeing any friendly forces. I remember telling Boo to be alert and ready to return fire if we were attacked. We didn't know where or when the SF troops we were to support were due. To the south of the embassy was a large dirt football pitch. This was surrounded by a solid concrete dwarf wall. We could see an abandoned enemy entrenchment near the road so I went over to check it. What I found was what appeared to be an enemy medium mortar pit. The weapons were gone but ammunition was stacked haphazardly, and local children were playing amongst it. I decided it would be prudent to check the entrenchment and all of the ammunition and ensure everything was as safe as practicable. I had assumed that SF troops might be landed by helicopter on the pitch and so loose ammunition and any other potential hazards needed to be sorted to ensure this potential landing zone was safe. We managed to recover about half a ton of ammunition and got it stacked. Then I noticed the mortar trench appeared to conceal an entrance into a tunnel. Taking well-established precautions, I gained access and discovered the tunnel concealed a cache of looted private property; some of it valuable. Disturbingly, I also discovered a lot of female underwear. With it all were two leather-bound Holy Korans. I had already noticed a couple of people standing in the open gates of the embassy. I believe one of them was a British member of staff and the other was a locally employed civilian who I took to be a caretaker or janitor. I asked the official if he could take temporary charge of the valuables, including the Korans. He refused; in fact, he wanted to use some of the earth-moving equipment I had requisitioned to clean up the embassy grounds. I looked inside to see an open-air swimming pool which now resembled a cesspit due to lack of maintenance. I was told the Ambassador wanted to have the embassy re-opened and functional ASAP. I asked the Janitor if he knew if any Iraqis had entered the embassy after it was evacuated.

He said he had remained there for the duration and the Iraqis didn't go inside. He had a bunch of keys with him which he offered to me. I asked him to remain available and we would await the arrival of the SF Troops.

Fancy dress and guns outside the embassy. It was surreal. Kids were running about, firing automatic weapons into the sky but unable to control the muzzle so the last few rounds would fly over your head.

The concealed loot after recovery and sorting

Concealed entrance to the tunnel where the loot was cached.

I returned to the mortar position and noticed that crowds were gathering, mostly young people. The extraordinary thing was that many of them were in Disney fancy dress costumes. They were celebrating their liberation and were very excited. Some of them had found abandoned Iraqi weapons and were firing them into the air above our heads. Being of small stature and unused to automatic weapons, it was alarming to see children discharging a full magazine of ammunition whilst holding the weapons in one hand. The weapons would arc out of control, and you could see the tracer streams starting to become almost horizontal. When someone only about four feet tall, dressed as Mickey Mouse, does that right behind you, it gets even more dangerous than EOD! Then another type of danger arrived in the form of one of my pet hates; a souvenir hunter. A British Army Land Rover approached. It was towing a single-barrelled 23mm ZSU anti-aircraft gun. The vehicle drew up next to me and a Royal Artillery warrant officer dismounted and asked if I would make the gun safe and certify it as 'free from explosive' (FFE) so they could take it back as a 'gate guard'. If you ever saw Rod Hull's Emu when it got mad and was about to attack someone, you can probably picture the look on my face. "Seriously?" I asked, incredulous at the childishly grinning person before me showing a complete disregard for safety. Now, I've known a few Royal Artillery Sergeant Major Instructors Gunnery (SMIG) and I've always respected their approach to gun safety; this guy must have been in admin! I immediately pointed out the obvious dangers with the gun. It was loaded with 23mm HE ammunition. The gun was being towed with the horizontal muzzle pointing directly at anything behind it. You could see the working parts had seized and that the next round to fire was half-chambered. Any sudden bump or jolt could dislodge the obstruction, releasing the stoppage and the gun could then fire. He was completely unperturbed by my concern and declared his intent to drive off and find someone who would clear his gun for him, despite my admonition for his recklessness and the danger he posed to all around him. It was clear he was not going to listen. This situation could only be resolved if I cleared his weapon. I unhooked the gun and elevated the barrel, pointing it out to sea. The harbour area was believed to be empty of manned vessels and this seemed to be the safest arc in which to point the gun. I was not a weapons specialist; I could only work from general principles. I jammed the breech to prevent it from moving forwards. I couldn't work out how to unload the weapon, which was filthy and coated with matted, greasy sand. The next best thing would be to cut the ammunition belt so that if the gun fired, it would limit the number of rounds discharged. With the belt cut and the ammunition supply removed, I returned to trying to unload the weapon but to no avail. I elected to fire the gun at high angle to clear it. At the back of the receiver, I found a prominent cam protruding and suspected this might release the mechanism. Warning all present to stand back, I pressed the cam. BA-BANG! Two rounds fired and I saw their tracers go up high into the air. The embassy man ducked for cover watched by the bemused Janitor. The uncontrite Gunner left with his spoils.

Another surprise was imminent. As I walked around the embassy compound walls, I noticed a sheet of wood over a hole in the ground on the western perimeter. I stooped to look into the hole just in case something untoward was lurking. Something was indeed lurking. The wood flew to one side and the hairiest and smelliest hermit known to man shot out and ran at me. He embraced me asking to be kissed and declaring that Margaret Thatcher was his saviour, and did I have a Union Jack (sic) for him? It turned out he had spent much of the occupation living in this hole in the ground, emerging only at night to scavenge for scraps.

He danced about excited, exalting the virtues of the British Prime Minister. I didn't have the heart to tell him she had been ousted so I left him to his joy and search for a Union flag.

Just then, a vehicle pulled up. It was of a type known to be used in the desert by Special Forces. A tall officer dismounted and greeted me. He wasn't SF and I had met him weeks earlier; it was the officer who had triggered the blind hand grenade; I groaned internally and wondered what else could possibly go wrong. He announced that the embassy would shortly be recaptured, and SF Troops would be helicoptered in and fast-rope down onto the roof as soon as the TV cameras were in position. When I pointed out the Janitor watching from the gate and that he had the keys and that no Iraqis had gone inside the embassy, my protests were dismissed with a wave of his arm and off he went. Just after this, the Press started to appear. Nothing else was going on, so one of them came over and asked what I was up to; it was Mr Ben Fenton of the Telegraph. I showed him the looted property and the now-empty mortar fire position. He did an article on it which was published in his paper.

After a while, the unmistakable sound of an approaching Chinook helicopter announced the arrival of the SF Team who were to re-take the embassy. As their Chinook hovered above the embassy, they roped down onto the roof. They used explosives to breach the doors and gain entry. I heard later that the Ambassador was not best pleased about the damage. The TV images of something that looked almost as good as the ending of the 1980 Iranian Embassy Siege were compelling but, I'm afraid, I must spoil this good story with the truth; it was all theatre.

Within a day or so of the ceasefire, the Forward British Headquarters increased in size and a more organised Joint EOD capability developed. I recall being in the EOD Operations room one day and seeing the two world-famous oil industry trouble-shooters, Red Adair and Boots Hansen. At the time, we had an estimated one thousand burning oil wells and, having worked in the Al Ahmadi field in very close proximity to a burning well head, I can vouch for the sheer ferocity and intimidating presence of these fires. The noise is incredible, the vertical flame-thrower effect is often the sole source of light, with the wind switching day into night and vice versa as the swirling black clouds overhead trade places. On the 4th of March 1991, we were teamed up with two US Army EOD Operators and sent out to a large reservoir on the Mutla Ridge. Our task was to clear some unexploded ordnance which contaminated the site. A quick survey revealed that the site had been bombed by both conventional general-purpose high-explosive bombs and also the American MK-20 Rockeye cluster bomb. After destroying one obvious Rockeye, we then did a more detailed search. The American Team went up to what might have been a tactical Iraqi headquarter location where they found a field telephone. They cut the wires from this HQ, which appeared to run downhill towards the main water outlet valves. As they were returning, Boo and I were looking at a large concrete slab which had been moved from its normal position where it sealed an underground chamber. This slab probably weighed several tons and I felt it had either been lifted and forced to one side by the effects of blast from a large bomb or moved by heavy plant equipment. Whatever moved it revealed something I would characterise as a war crime. The following photographs show what was found.

Access into the valve chamber

First view inside. The dangling grey lead is a firing cable and the red lines are detonating cord. The sandbags concealed 10 electric detonators, 2 canned primers for safety fuze initiation and 175 kgs of plastic explosives in 2 linked charges. This was vastly more than what was needed. The execution was amateurish but would have done the job.

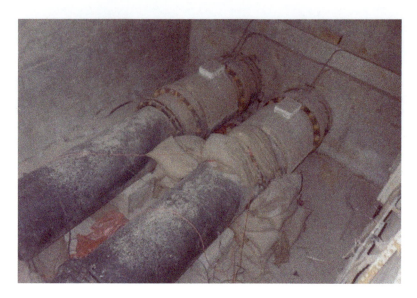

Other end of the chamber showing the concealed second charge and interlinked twinflex electric cable and detonating red cord.

Close-up showing the exposed explosive charge (the white material). The detonators with red/yellow leads were underneath and inserted directly into the charge. The knotted detonating cord had also been inserted into the charge.

As Boo and I peered into the gloomy underground chamber, we saw that a prepared demolition had been laid by Iraqi military personnel with the intention of destroying the outlet valves. We then checked another similar chamber and found that this, too, had been prepared for demolition. We all appreciated the importance of this site to Kuwait City. Most national infrastructure was badly damaged or completely destroyed. We had previously surveyed water desalinisation plants and found that deliberate demolitions had taken place and those plants would take weeks to bring back into production. This huge reservoir was uphill of the city and water could naturally flow downhill, however, if the main outlet valves were destroyed, the precious water would be rapidly lost. These demolitions needed to be cleared with no margin for carelessness. We had two teams and there were two chambers. We agreed to tackle the chambers concurrently. The chamber the American Team had was very clean and tidy. The one we had was partially filled with wind-blown sand. The two underground chambers had been linked with a double length of detonating cord. This was cut to isolate them.

Boo and I discussed the clearance procedure plan. Although we could see the detonating cord lines between the alternative safety fuze initiation point and electric detonator leg wires, we couldn't see anything else. The Iraqis had used sandbags to both contain and tamp their charges and sand obscured almost everything. We set up an EOD control point some distance away and I elected to work under 'one-man risk' rules. I was especially concerned that the sand and sandbags could conceal a booby trap or anti-personnel mine so my progress was very slow but methodical. I climbed down the steel access ladder and hung off it as I started a systematic prod and reveal process from above. Eventually, I cleared a safe working spot in the corner nearest the larger of the two charges. I could see two canned exploders but there was no sign of any plain detonators. Above me, on a ledge, was an abandoned respirator, presumably for a 'stay-behind' Iraqi sapper who would initiate the fuze if the electric initiation failed.

I went back up on the surface to find the weather conditions had deteriorated. We had an overhead electrical storm which fizzled away but the conditions were freezing. I had no severe weather clothing, so I was soaking wet and shivering. I donned a lightweight plastic chemical suit which helped. I went back down and, using semi-manual clearance procedures, exposed two rows of electric detonators with red/yellow leg wires, five in each row, inserted directly into military-grade plastic explosive. Now I could see the entire layout and electric circuitry, I could cut out all ten detonators. Time for a pee!!

The two demolition charges were then removed and taken up to the surface. We didn't have scales, so the all-up explosive content was conservatively estimated to be about 175kgs, vastly more than was needed. As I extracted the hand-moulded plastic explosive, I could see the handprints of the Iraqi sappers who had laid the charges; it reminded me of a bunch of kids having a Playdough session. In my opinion, the execution by the Iraqis had been amateurish but effective. The American Team completed their end of the job and I must confess that as we left (teeth still chattering with the cold), I was almost overwhelmed with the satisfaction of knowing that we had completed a vital clearance operation and we had prevented Saddam from achieving yet another act of gross vandalism.

After things had started to settle, Boo and I found ourselves accommodated with hundreds of US troops in what had been the Kuwaiti

Ministry of Education Supply Depot. We were in a large warehouse, sleeping on the shelves, somewhat bizarrely between rows of bagpipes!

After a few days, we even had a treat in the form of an American Laundry and Bath unit visit. By the time we got clean again, we had been working outdoors exposed to the elements and crude oil pollution. Crude oil there was a brown colour. Superficially, it looked black but tiny beads of crude would form on your hair. Everything stunk of crude; it was on your food, in your mouth, up your nose and everything was slimy. The scalding hot shower we had was heavenly. Our uniforms got laundered and returned whilst a trusty Yank took care of your personal weapon. I remember the separation anxiety when I handed it over; I had slept with that bloody rifle for months! That evening, after we had eaten and were feeling mellow and relaxed, more 'shit' happened. Isn't it always that way when you let your guard down and start thinking about going home? An American Captain carrying a cylinder in his arms appeared in front of us. "Are you guys Brit EOD?" he asked. (Cue yet another inward groan). "Yes, Sir, what can we do for you?" was the mouthed reply, but our eyes were already focused on that cylinder. He held up a Polaroid radiograph transparency. The image was almost entirely burned out as he had over-exposed it. He went on to explain that his troops had found the cylinder in a heavy engineering workshop area of the Al Ahmadi oilfield. They thought it was suspicious. Someone told him that there was a British EOD Team who were experts in improvised explosive devices (IEDs). He decided he would consult us; good decision. He brought the device to show us into accommodation filled with hundreds of troops; bad decision; no, I mean really bad. I took the radiograph off him and looked at it. The image was almost completely useless. At the time, we used Polaroid radiograph film but we didn't use transparencies. Instead, we used a conventional photographic positive. However, back in the early '70s,

I had been trained in the use of our first-generation X-ray equipment. These included the Andrex equipment and also the so-called Gamma Bomb. They both used X-ray plates in conventional cassettes, similar to those used in hospitals at the time. More relevant to this anecdote was that the plates were wet-developed and were transparencies. Because of that, we knew of a simple technique to reveal some burned-out features in a radiographic transparency. To the astonishment of the officer, I was able to discern power sources, circuitry, two electric detonators and a probable explosive filling. When I showed him the technique of turning the plate edge-on to a good light source, he was really made up but the ending wasn't happy when his new-found knowledge was eclipsed by my more fundamental concern with why any rational person would bring a suspect bomb into a barracks? We agreed to store it safely elsewhere and visit the scene of the find in the morning.

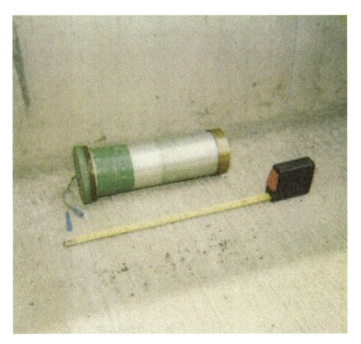

The suspect cylinder brought into the accommodation

I took a lot of photographs to record the dismantling of this device and its exploitation. What we didn't know from the outset was that we were looking at a sophisticated initiator for a much larger device. The officer took us to the Al Ahmadi oil field where we were shown the ISO container store where 40 of these devices had been found. I noted there were also other objects made up of bicycle wheel rims with steel disks inside them. At the centre of each rim was a steel collar with securing bolts. This hub was double-walled and the gap between the inner and outer rings was filled with what looked like hardened, epoxy-based car body filler. These objects were in well-made but im-provised bespoke packaging. There were coloured-coded symbols on the packaging which I assumed were likely to be role-related mark-ings. I set about dismantling the first cylinder. As I worked, progress was somewhat hampered by the alternating bright sunshine and pitch blackness as the overhead dense black clouds swirled about in the wind. The roaring noise from nearby burning wellheads was the only constant, something like standing next to a jet engine on take-off pow-er. I got the cylinder top off and eventually dismantled it to the point of being empty. The contents turned out to be the most sophisticated IED I had ever personally encountered or even heard of. Inside, at the bottom, there were indeed two electric detonators. Their leg wires were twisted pairs coloured red and yellow and had been cut to length to suit the internal layout of the device. They, in turn, were within a 225 gm cast block of explosive which was similar in all respects to a re-cast TNT-based explosive filler, perhaps scavenged from a conventional munition such as an artillery shell. I discovered a nearby cache of Ital-ian VS 1.6 anti-tank mines. Some had been broken open with a ball pein hammer. The main filling of this mine is Composition B which is a 60/40 mixture of RDX/TNT. If this assessment was correct, it could be corroborated by the presence of ball pein hammer witness marks on the VS Mine's internal plastic components and that the explosive I recovered exhibited a visible and tactile lack of homogeneity, probably caused by the different melting and setting temperatures of the two explosive types. Composition B will melt at the same temperature as pure TNT but the RDX remains solid unless the mixture is heated to a higher temperature. This solid explosive casting incorporated two parallel recesses to accommodate the detonators. The explosive filler was contained within its own aluminium alloy cylinder, closed off at the base with a brass screw-threaded cap. At the upper internal end of this cylinder was a small hole allowing the leg wires to pass through to the next component.

Working conditions in the Al Ahmadi oilfield. Photo taken at midday

The next component was truly an eye-opener. It was a British-manufactured, long-delay electronic timer designed to initiate explosive charges and was capable of a range of settings from one minute up to 99 days, 99 hours and 99 minutes. It had an integral power supply and the casing was robust and watertight and could be sealed against the ingress of moisture with a combined screw thread and rubber O ring. I could see who the manufacturer was but this detail is very sensitive and I will not disclose it in this book. I have included photographs of the timer because they reflect exactly what I found and are beyond dispute.

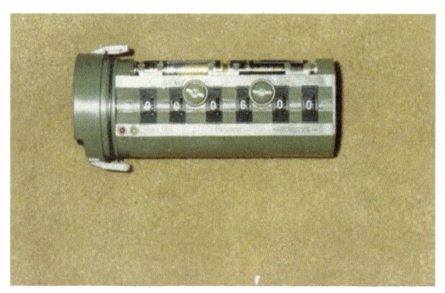

Commercially manufactured electronic long-delay timer

225 gm cast explosive filling in the base of the cylinder. This was assessed as an RDX/TNT mixture. Note the double detonator cavity. It was believed the explosive filler was scavenged from VS 1.6 anti-tank mines. Empty mine casings were found nearby with tool marks from a ball pein hammer used to dismantle them.

On top of this commercially made timer was another component which puzzled me as to its purpose. It had wires coming out of each end and was enclosed within a pod of heat-shrink tubing. I cut this open and inside there was a plastic circuit board with several electronic components, including an integrated circuit (IC), a programmable timer marked as MC14536BCP and a fairly large electrolytic capacitor. This puppy was capable of initiating an IED on its own so why did the device contain two timer initiators? At the time, this was not a rhetorical question; I simply didn't know. My primary concern was that this was highly sophisticated. I had already noted that the wheel rim component had an incorporated electric circuit and moving the (disconnected) rim produced a discernible clicking; almost certainly concealed microswitches. I began to suspect this might be a denial weapon. More to follow. Now, the swirling black clouds were to prove helpful. As I opened the black pod with a knife, in relative darkness, the first thing I saw was the upper face of the programmable IC timer. As I rotated the opened pod between thumb and forefinger, a shaft of brilliant sunlight shone through a parting in the clouds. The light reflected off the shiny black plastic of the heat-shrink pod and I thought I saw a ginger hair on the back of the timer. I blinked a few times as my eyes were affected by the crude oil and smoke, and there it was again. But it wasn't a ginger hair. It was a single strand of thin copper wire. On closer examination, I could see it had been soldered to the IC to connect two legs, one on each side. I had already separated this component from the detonator so the only probable hazard was I could get a belt off the capacitor if I shorted it. At the time I did not understand the purpose of the ad hoc wire connection, but it was an improvised device and sometimes you don't need to know why as long as you stick to well-established IEDD principles. I was careful to document and photograph all of the components to allow exploitation by Technical Intelligence staff.

Secondary timer with a programmable integrated circuit modified by a thin strand of copper wire soldered between legs 7 and 13. As the sun penetrated the overhead black clouds, the presence of the wire was revealed as it glinted. This modification would reverse the outputs from these legs.

Above this component was the screw-threaded top closure cap. This had a small central hole through which two connecting wires protruded. These were about 10cm long and were finished with blue-coloured torpedo connectors. I moved next to examine the bicycle rim component. Two things were obvious. There were matching torpedo connectors for the cylinder device. The hub of the bicycle rim contained a collar fitted with clamping bolts. The cylinder was a good fit inside the hub. As this was an oilfield, there were oil drums all over the place. A quick comparison with a drum showed that the bicycle rim could be fitted on top of a standard, but modified oil drum. I now started to believe that an oil drum could be used to house a main charge. I was trying to join the dots but my technical knowledge did not include an understanding of marine weapon dynamics. I was eventually proved right that I was dealing with a complex initiator for a very large, improvised explosive device. I could see the bicycle rim device contained hidden moving parts and the hollow steel collar was filled and sealed with a hardened epoxy body filler. I needed to get inside; for this, I turned to the .50in De-Armer. This was a violent weapon, and I knew I would need a very safe down-range corridor as the projectile was almost certainly going to keep going after doing its job. We contrived a backstop and set the thing up. On firing, the projectile penetrated the device beautifully and also cracked open the epoxy filler. It was the best possible result but we never saw the projectile again! Inside the filler were two Lycon microswitches which were connected to the external leads. This was obviously the trigger but what I didn't get was that the trigger could only work in one direction. Why would such a sophisticated IED have such a limitation incorporated in its design?

All the bits after being dismantled. The cylinder was a good fit in the centre of the hub. One of the Lycon microswitches can be seen at the 7 O'clock position on the disk. The disk could be moved side to side which would actuate the microswitches. The shiny round objects roughly top and bottom on the disk are there to keep the disk horizontal and contain greased bearings. The detonators are laid on top of the disk and were originally inside the cylinder, connected to the two timing devices.

The assembled cylinder and bicycle wheel components are here shown offered to the top of an oil drum to evaluate potential applications. The drum theory was accurate and I was later told that a very large, cruciform-shaped cast TNT was the main filling contained in an oil drum which gave a crude but effective shaped charge effect. The air gap provided both buoyancy and the space for the shaped charge jet to develop.

I reported my findings to the EOD Operations Centre and offered an assessment that there could be a large number of highly sophisticated and very powerful IEDs dispersed in the oil field with the possible aim of hampering fire-fighting operations. It was my best guess; I was wrong but not in the least embarrassed. Royal Navy Clearance Divers (amazing people but you generally don't meet them in the desert) will tell you that when a moving ship strikes a sea mine, the mine is forced against the hull and the mine then rotates. After my exploitation report was reviewed, the whole picture emerged. The combination of cylinder, bicycle wheel rim and an oil drum with a cruciform explosive filling made up an improvised but advanced sea mine. The two separate timers, each capable of detonating the mine, were to enable a 'safe to arm' period as the mine was laid and then the long delay timer was apparently a self-sterilising device to ensure these mines would detonate eventually and not become a persistent hazard to shipping in the post-conflict era. The cruciform shape of the cast explosive filler gave a crudely shaped charge effect capable of breaching a ship's hull. The rim was aligned on top of the drum so that as the mine rotated against the hull, the Lycon microswitches would close when they were perpendicular to the hull and the mine would detonate. "WHOOSH BANG, OH NASTY!" as my erstwhile instructor at the Army School of Ammunition would say. This was the late, great Major Ron Cooper, known as the avuncular 'Uncle Ron' to generations of young technicians in the trade. He sadly passed away in the late 90s following major surgery after an outstanding career.

I gather there was some debate well above my head about whether this was an improvised explosive device (IED). I am crystal clear that it was. The definition of an IED at the time included the possibility that a device could contain military components. Someone else discounted my theory that the cylinder's explosive filling was derived from the VS-1.6 mines I found nearby. One of my regrets about the whole EOD/ IEDD 'thing' was the lack of post-tour operator de-briefing. And perhaps one of the ironies is I understand they named the bicycle-wheel device after the chap who first found it and brought the bomb into barracks. As my No2 at the time (Boo) would later comment, "It is the way these things go – either named after somebody heroic or stupid, and occasionally heroically stupid". After these jobs, we sensed the end was coming. We spent the last few days clearing and destroying unexpended ammunition from Iraqi armoured fighting vehicles.

Above and below: De-bombing enemy armoured vehicles

We returned to Al Jubayl by road in mid-March. What we found when we got back was absolutely disgraceful and I point the finger at the chain of command for their negligence. The Prime Minister had set an urgent priority that troops were to be repatriated as quickly as possible. The effect of this was that our Teeth Arms withdrew rapidly from Iraq and Kuwait, back to Saudi Arabia and Al Jubayl. The fighting vehicles and personnel were routed through ammunition collection areas near to the main ammunition supply point. The withdrawing troops quite literally dumped their ammunition on the ground and legged it; no other way to put it. As we surveyed the huge mounds of ammunition, our hearts sank. There were two extremely dangerous situations I became aware of. In one, there was a stack of mixed ammunition piled high. The stack included bulk explosives and bar mines. On the top of the stack was a bar mine which was found to be armed. Nearby were approximately ten thousand L2 hand grenades with their L25 fuzes still fitted. Kris and I spent days removing the fuzes. In some cases, users had splayed the pins completely open and back to prevent accidents. If they had needed to use them in anger, they would have needed a pair of mole wrenches to get the pins out! Worse still, many of the pins had been closed fully and were capable of falling free from the fuze body if picked up carelessly. Photographs of what we encountered are included below. Amongst the ammunition dumped on the ground were Swingfire anti-tank guided missiles minus the safety feature of a Smart and Brown Connector and L26 APFSDS DU long rod penetrators worth a fortune. What this sorry tale illustrated, which has happened after every armed conflict and was repeated in the Balkans later, was that the British Army's ammunition management was primarily a peacetime occupation. War is a messy business. In the few days remaining, we did the best we could before we were repatriated on 25th March 1991.

Swingfire missles

120mm APFSDS (DU)

30mm APDS

30mm HE

It would be remiss of me not to mention what it is like to emerge from a male-dominated military war-fighting environment where the norms of polite society and home comforts have been absent for a long time. Our evenings were then very much our own, and one night, the majority of us in the now reconstituted unit got the opportunity to watch a video in Old Port Barracks, in one of the larger rooms. We sat ourselves down wherever we could, the light went off and the film started. It was the uncut version of Nine and a Half Weeks!! You could have heard a pin drop as about two dozen blokes struggled to maintain their composure. It was one of those awkward moments that will stay with me forever.

The flight back was something else! The MoD had chartered commercial aircraft to cope with the demand. Our flight was on a British Airways Boeing 747. As we boarded, we saw the cabin was bedecked with yellow ribbons. As we taxied for take-off, the Captain announced that his crew was proud to be taking us home... and the drinks were free! Me and a friend (Bob W) were seated next to each other, already plugged into our linked Gameboys playing golf. I was a teetotaller then so when a steward asked what I wanted and I replied that I wanted a softie, we were immediately surrounded by dozens of new-found infantry friends eager to have my share of the booze. The flight was uneventful, but the landing wasn't. We landed at Hannover and the aircraft taxied to a makeshift stand, well away from the busier part of the terminal. Trucks were waiting to load our baggage (with proper baggage handlers this time!) and we watched from the cabin as we waited to disembark and saw soldiers being carried away on stretchers. They weren't war casualties. Drinking at altitude is not a good idea, especially if you've had no alcohol for months. Some were so bad they were out cold!

Another aspect of the return was, in my opinion, a sad reflection on the abuse of freedom of expression enjoyed in democracies. As we boarded a coach to return to Herford, it was explained to us that the journey would be slower than normal. We were told anti-war protestors were lining the main roads and to avoid trouble, we were taking a scenic route.

What was touching, however, was that these back roads would pass isolated farms and very small hamlets where the older generations were at the roadside waving Union Flags as we went by. That was special but what was even more special was the reception waiting for us at Herford. As we approached the main entrance into Hammersmith Barracks, we could see over the perimeter fence and hedgerows from our elevated seating positions. From our seats, we glimpsed yellow ribbons and excited children on the lawn in front of our unit social club, the Pig & Stick. The coach turned into the barracks and arrived at the unit HQ. I've come home a few times from operational tours but never to such an overwhelming tsunami of emotions. There wasn't a dry eye in the house. What made it different was that our unit had deployed as a formed-up unit and had returned safely, all together. Previously, all of my operational tours were alone as an individual with no sense of unit cohesion and togetherness. To be fair, one of our number was missing; this was 'Cammy' who had suffered a blast injury to his hand whilst he was handling an MUV 3 igniter. There was an immediate concern that he could have sustained a life-changing injury and he had been evacuated by the US Forces in early March. It was sad he was not there, but we knew he was OK, wherever he was, and he eventually passed through rehab, and I believe the injury had no long-term consequences, or should I say, I sincerely hope so.

Post-conflict, there was speculation in the media about campaign medals. In amongst this, the Saudis decided they would award medals to all coalition military personnel for the liberation of Kuwait. Our government let it be known that any such medal could not be worn in uniform, but they were prepared to allow us to accept the medal. After we were repatriated, I learned from my brother, who was a toolmaker in a firm of contract toolmakers in the West Midlands, that they had been contracted to make a medal for a middle eastern country. They were only going to fabricate the metal pieces; the medal ribbons would be made by another contractor. When I eventually received my Kuwaiti Liberation medal, I showed it to David, and it turned out that this was the medal he had made. He and his colleagues had never seen the finished product, so I loaned him the medal in its presentation case so he could show it to them. What an amazing coincidence that turned out to be; shame we were never allowed to wear it.

The finished medal in its presentation case, complete with medal ribbon. To the left is a strip of metal showing the outline of the webbing press tool run. To the right is the main stamping. Look out for this on the Antiques Roadshow in 100 years' time. I dare say the provenance might add some value to what a grateful nation intended as a medal that HMG downgraded to a bauble.

CHAPTER 15

The Royal Military College of Science Shrivenham 1991–1994

I reported for duty at Shrivenham in November 1991. Immediately prior to the move over from Germany, our car suffered a cylinder head gasket failure, so we replaced it, very much last minute. With us was our African Grey parrot, Grumpy. He had been a little sod; risking the loss of a finger in taking him to the vet to arrange his import into the UK, I had warned the vet that he hated being handled and I had brought heavy leather gauntlets along; I expected mayhem but the vet didn't seem daunted in the least. She slowly lifted the cover on his cage, talking to him softly. Expecting a trap, I held my breath as the unprotected hand went into the cage. The little sod rolled over on his back and totally submitted. Grumpy was clearly a ladies' man.

We had sailed over on the ferry to Hull and stayed a while at Christine's mother's until we drove down to take over our married quarter at Highworth. Our quarter was in a quiet street in Highworth and was embedded in the local community. It was very different to being behind barbed wire in Germany with RMP patrols. Highworth was a short drive from the campus. I was to work normal hours. I did wear uniform, or I would have thought I was a civilian. In terms of the job, it was a geek's paradise, and I was the consummate geek.

The RMCS Shrivenham was a Defence University. It was a military unit but the academic side was contracted out to Cranfield University. My primary role was to be the Senior Ammunition Technician (SAT) in Ammunition Branch which was part of the Weapons and Vehicles Division. There were three of us in Ammunition Branch which was located in Wellington Hall. The boss was an RAOC Lt Col. His appointment title was Director of Studies (Ammunition) 2, abbreviated to DS (Ammo) 2. There was a Royal Engineer WO1 and me. Between us, we had a museum, a tearoom, two offices and two classrooms. Our main bread and butter was in hosting the annual Ammunition Technical Officer's Course and the Ammunition Technician's courses of varying frequency. The ATO course started in January and finished in June. The AT courses were of shorter duration, typically about 6 weeks, and we ran up to three of them per year. We also ran smaller courses, arranged to suit demand, to provide technical briefings to senior officers and civil servants who had been given managerial roles involving ammunition. We were also involved in the delivery of training and range supervision to students attending the three divisions of the Army Command and Staff courses. Division three was the shortest and most frequent. There could be up to 120 students on this course and the young officers attending it ranged in abilities from mundane to sheer genius. This made pitching lectures to them somewhat challenging. The spread of ability was so diverse that you could never be sure you had achieved your training objectives with all of the students without either being condescending or over the top. Division Two of Staff College was longer and was for officers selected for higher things. These officers were academically brighter and generally more imaginative than the average Division Three punter. I enjoyed teaching this course the most. Division One was your future generals. They were very bright, and you generally couldn't cuff your way through the various subjects with them.

I'm sure my first boss at Shrivenham wouldn't mind if I put it out there that he could be hilariously accident prone, he didn't like teaching, he had great ambition and drive to improve our Branch and especially the ATO course content. He provided all of the above in quantity.

My boss had often found formality and rules to be somewhat tedious. One day, he rode his bike to work from his quarter to Wellington Hall. He rode the bike on the pavement and was promptly captured by an MoD Policeman. He was sternly rebuked for this transgression and warned not to do it again. An endearing habit he had was whenever 'stuff' happened to him, he would confess all to me and Graham. We would listen patiently and sympathetically until he left and then we would totally split our sides! There was nothing spiteful about this, he was just hugely entertaining. True to form, we were treated to the 'full SP' about the injustice of this jobsworth copper who had lectured him on road safety. A few days later, the boss came into our office, tripping over his bottom lip. We waited patiently for the explanation and when it came it was brilliant. He had repeated the offence of riding his bike on the pavement. He had been looking out for the jobsworth, who, it seemed, was looking out for him. In fact jobsworth was hiding behind a tree in ambush and he emerged from it last minute, with a shout of "HALT!" The boss crashed into him. Jobsworth filed a report which went to the boss's boss and he was now awaiting his summons. He left the office and we collapsed into side-aching spasms of laughter.

To balance this account, it would only be fair to mention the very positive contributions my boss made to Ammunition Branch and our students. The first change he brought about was to ask Graham and me to share an office. His rationale was that our ATO students didn't have their own bespoke recreational facility complete with a phone so they could do some administration during their breaks. Graham's erstwhile office became the students' rest room. Another aspect was that we needed to steward our young officers along the right path and a rest room gave us the chance to mingle, listen and support them. The next major change was that we set out to completely re-write the ATO Course Syllabus. The old one was defunct, difficult to plan and resource and didn't identify learning objectives. This was a laborious task of painstaking detail, but the end result was awesome.

One of his earliest and most effective improvements concerned the ATO Course Projects. The course traditionally carried out development projects after being split up into 4-man syndicates. The projects would run through the whole course and would conclude with formal project presentations to an invited audience. The major downside with the current project philosophy was that the projects were very narrowly defined and were, frankly, uninspiring and boring. A recent example had been a project to re-design a packing piece in an ammunition container. The boss wanted the ATOs to design, build and market whole new weapon systems. Some of the academic supervisors were furious. They protested that the new approach to projects was completely un-achievable. I must say, with great respect, that the boss stuck to his guns. In fact, he stuck his neck out and took a huge personal risk. Any failure to deliver would be very damaging to his reputation. The ATO Course Projects results were formally presented to an invited audience of very senior officers and captains of industry. I would liken these formal presentations to a cross between the Dragon's Den and the final of The Apprentice; only with a room full of cynical sugar!

In the first round of new projects, the boss called for help from his old nemesis from his boarding school days; the Reverend Lancaster. He had massive respect for this man and not a small amount of trepidation. He would tell me of his school days with the omnipotent Reverend, dressed in a cassock, sternly circulating and meting out discipline to the non- conformists. The Reverend had an interesting side-line; pyrotechnics. Apparently, what this man didn't know about gunpowder simply wasn't worth knowing. He had established a successful pyrotechnic manufacturing company and the boss's idea for the first tranche of projects was right up his street. When the Academic Head of the Ammunition Science and Explosive Technology Unit at Shrivenham found out, he was vehement that failure would be the only outcome. The course would form only two syndicates and their project brief was to design, manufacture and test-fire a multi-launch rocket system (MLRS) simulator. WOW! Now that was ambitious. For those who don't know, the MLRS was used to great effect during the Gulf War. It was deadly accurate, and each launcher carried 12 rockets with a maximum range of 32 kilometres. In turn, each rocket had a payload of 644 dual-role bomblets. The bomblets would be ejected from the rocket when over the target. Any person or equipment caught in the open was guaranteed to be shredded. A single launcher could fire 12 rockets in one minute and saturate an area of one square kilometre with lethal effect. The Royal Artillery MLRS Regiment was christened the 'Grid Square Removal Service'. The Iraqis nicknamed the effect as 'Steel Rain'. The boss's proposal sought to address a perceived deficiency. There was no way to simulate the effect of an MLRS attack safely and effectively at the receiving end during training. The students would have to create pyrotechnic bomblets capable of producing noise and flash on a par with the real thing and they would also need to design and build some kind of launcher and dispersal burster.

This was a massive undertaking and, at the project briefing, I could see the awestruck faces of the students as they took in their task. This was more than compensated for with the enthusiasm and zeal they brought to their seemingly insurmountable task. An academic supervisor was nominated for each syndicate and Graham and I supervised their practical efforts. Over the next five months, we watched the students grow their tiny acorns into mighty oaks. The first few practical experiments could take place on the Explosive Range and Demonstration Area (ERDA) at Shrivenham. Each syndicate managed to produce effective working submunitions, but the real challenge was in developing a launching method which incorporated a lifting charge, a bursting charge and then an individual delay to allow the submunitions to fall back to earth, evenly distributed, before exploding. This could be very tricky and the margins between success and failure were very narrow. A balloon method of raising submunitions to the right height was devised but this presented a risk of disaster if the bursting charge failed and the balloon kept going! To mitigate this risk, the boss brought his shotgun in, and any failure would be shot down. Our academic critics laughed out loud. One day, the students managed to build a prototype launcher with submunitions where the delay fuzes seemed ideal. The experiment failed when the carrier burst charge was so powerful that all of the submunitions exploded in the air with a mighty bang that set off all the car alarms in the main car park!

The students managed to overcome this difficulty and we reached the point where we were ready to conduct the final proof firings. These were going to be filmed and there would be firings in daylight and darkness. We needed somewhere really big and not too far away. RAF Kemble fitted the bill and we set off with jangling nerves, hopeful of success but dreading failure. To be succinct, the outcome was spectacular. The night-time firings were the most dramatic and the film work looked awesome. The students brushed up their project notes and prepared their speaking parts for the formal project presentation. Both presentations went extremely well. I had never presided over anything like this before and was overwhelmed with a sense of pride in what our students had achieved. Even the academics were obliged to express their admiration at how well the projects had gone. The real aim was never to create an MLRS simulator for the Army. It was to challenge a group of potential ATOs, getting them to collaborate and use their newly acquired knowledge of explosives to maximum effect. I was so pleased the boss had moved them on from designing packing pieces! It did, however, leave us with an impossible dilemma; how the hell were we going to better that with the next course?

For the remaining months of 1992, we racked our brains to come up with topical design projects and the boss did it again. He came up with the idea of four separate design projects, one per syndicate, where the students would weaponise fuel air explosives, otherwise known as FAE. The advantage FAE could bring to a weapon designer was primarily one of payload. A significant portion of conventional explosive warheads was the oxidiser needed to enable an explosion. If your warhead only needed to include fuel, you could, in theory, get more bang for your buck by using atmospheric oxygen. The downside was in achieving an efficient detonation. To do this, the fuel would have to be dispersed in a cloud and mixed with exactly the right amount of air. This is what happens in an internal combustion engine but replicating this in the open air was fraught with difficulty. Besides that, we didn't want a controllable fuel burn; we wanted complete detonation. It was known that the Russians had FAE munitions which they had turned on the Mujahadin in Afghanistan. It was ideal for defeating the enemy hiding in the extensive cave networks in the Afghan mountains. There was nothing like this in the NATO inventory, so this was good enough for the boss to be more innovative than the first projects. The scope of this project set was going to be more complex than making a pyrotechnic simulator so it was decided that the four syndicates would each develop variations of FAE weapons from a common origin. The fuel would be a mixture of propylene oxide and ethylene oxide and each weapon would use similar methods of cloud dispersal and detonation.

The FAE munitions to be made would be an offensive (blast) hand grenade, a building demolition charge, a jumping anti-aircraft mine to combat enemy air mobile brigades and a nuclear bomb simulator. The students experimented with different mixture ratios of the two fuels and methods of detonation and the results were outstanding. Large-scale FAE bombs are sometimes known as the poor man's nuclear bomb. An FAE bomb can, in theory, generate a very large cloud of fuel and, when this is allowed to mix with atmospheric oxygen, the results can be devastating when the cloud detonates. Interestingly, it can devastate built-up areas without making huge craters. A more sinister characteristic is that the bomb consumes atmospheric oxygen, and this can lead to asphyxiation, especially in confined spaces.

We contacted the ammunition technical officer at Shoeburyness ranges on the east coast and requested range time and facilities. This officer was Jim, and he didn't let us down.

Range staff constructed targets for us. The grenade target was a small simulated sangar made of breeze blocks. The building for the large demolition charge was immense. It was constructed of Pendine blocks. These are solid reinforced blocks commonly seen when being used as lane dividers on motorway repair jobs, to separate vehicle flows. The target building was bigger than a detached house and even had a roof to simulate how a building would confine the pressure wave which would enhance the effect. We had been given a Lynx helicopter airframe to model how a helicopter would fare when targeted with an FAE mine and the nuclear bomb simulator was set up on a concrete pan. We had the use of range instrumentation which included high-speed video and pressure sensors. As we prepared to run the live tests, anticipation ran high that the videos, to be shown at the formal project presentation, would be spectacular; provided the experimental FAE munitions worked.

The first munition to be tested was the grenade. The enthusiastic syndicate leader volunteered to be videoed carrying out a classic grenade posting into the simulated enemy sangar. He would hurl the grenade inside and crouch down to await the bang before bayonetting the mannequins inside, just for good measure. It was almost a shame to reign him in and he was reminded that this was a trial, and the munition would be triggered using the much safer remote firing option. He was disappointed but we set the grenade up and retired to the safety of a splinter-proof shelter some distance away. The countdown took place and the grenade was fired. The bang was incredible, and the breeze block sanger immediately collapsed, and the heavy blocks were cast aside like expanded polystyrene. If the syndicate leader had been granted his wish, he would not have survived. Pressure gauges showed the blast over-pressures in and around the sangar were at lethal levels. All of this from a device about the size of a coke tin!

The next firing was to be the building demolition charge. After final preparations, we retired to the safety of the shelter and awaiting the firing. The bang was immense. We stared at the target which was still standing. The improvised roof had vanished. As we cautiously approached to inspect the result, we could see that all of the extremely heavy Pendine blocks had been pushed outwards. The test demonstrated that a conventional building would have been destroyed. The device was constructed from two pineapple tins the students had found in the officers' mess kitchen waste. Day one concluded with the students in very high spirits and Day two was expected to be even better. For the test of the aerial mine, the range staff had used a crane to position the Lynx airframe on a high concrete plinth. We were very lucky indeed to enjoy such support.

I will deviate now to explain the working area where we were to try and destroy the helicopter. Shoeburyness is on the coast and we were working on tidal mud flats. When the tide was right out, the wet sand was firm. As the tide came in, it would move in fast. Consequently, we spent much of the time in wellington boots when the water was at a modest height. The window of opportunity to conduct demolitions and controlled explosions was therefore limited and we could not risk the consequences of the experiment being flooded as live explosives could be swept out to sea. In the time available, we had only one opportunity to attempt a firing. If anything went wrong, such as a misfire, we wouldn't have time to observe a safe waiting period, diagnose and fix and then attempt to fire again. I had already explained to the students that saltwater conducts electricity. The upshot of this was that the lengthy firing cable needed to be completely intact. If there were any junctions, they would have to be insulated and attached to a picquet to keep the junction out of the water. From a safe distance, with the tidal flow lapping our legs at mid-calf level, we started the countdown. The Shrike exploder was used to fire the aerial mine. Nothing happened. The student was instructed to take the immediate action drill on misfire. He did and got the same result. We would now have to wait the safe period before anyone could approach the experiment. We were already out of time. As heads bowed with disappointment, my gaze followed the D10 firing cable as it entered the briny water. As the water lapped up and down, I thought I could see something on the firing cable. I lifted the first few metres out of the water and there it was; a taped junction which had been immersed in the sea water. I admonished the young officer who was incredulous and disbelieving. When I demonstrated a positive continuity test with the Shrike using a short length of cable in an open circuit held below the water, he got it. It might not have been him that did it but he was the syndicate leader and he should have checked. If Lord Sugar had been presiding, he would have been fired. He wasn't. Despite the disappointing outcome, all of the syndicate had just re-learned a valuable lesson; one they would never forget. Their FAE mine, designed to disrupt enemy airborne forces during landings, was effective in blast terms but we didn't have a shredded airframe to demonstrate the point.

Inland, on a dry concrete pad, was the final experiment. This was the nuclear simulator and was by far the biggest device we were going to test. From the safety of the shelter, the device was fired. It cut the mustard, as they say. We went outside to see the massive mushroom cloud as it climbed ever higher into the sky. It kept getting higher and bigger... and higher and bigger. The wind had caught it and it was now heading towards Belgium!! You could say it was an embarrassing success. The project presentations were amazing. It turned out that the students had actually exceeded the known maximum explosive efficiency expected to be achieved with the basic fuels we were using. A senior officer questioned the syndicate about what he saw as the overly sophisticated construction of the building demolition charge. The swift riposte detailed the simple two-pineapple-can construction, much to the amusement of many in the audience. The second set of projects in the new era had proved successful, demonstrating what can be done if you take risks, set ambitious targets and unleash imaginations.

One of my responsibilities was in booking resources for the ATO course and this included visiting lecturers. In 1992, a retired Royal Engineer Bomb Disposal Officer was to deliver a lecture to the potential ATOs about his experiences in the Second World War. The students and I were in for a treat. It would be far more than a talk about this or that fuze; it was to be a lesson in fortitude and resilience and the critical part information management played in warfare; it would be memorable.

Captain Ken Revis MBE RE joined the Army at the outbreak of the Second War and became a Bomb Disposal Officer in the Royal Engineers. He dealt with hundreds of enemy bombs before being detailed to 'delouse' the two piers at Brighton in 1943. Canadian Engineers had mined the two piers to prevent their use by the enemy when the threat of invasion was high. Ken cleared the mines on the Palace Pier before rowing over to the West Pier. He declined to use the normal access and climbed up onto the pier on a rope. After he had cleared the first batch of mines, which he thought was going well, he returned to work and was then very seriously injured when 13 mines detonated. He was to lose his sight and suffered many operations in the fight to get fit again. Ken had already made many visits as a visiting lecturer, but this was the first time I had met him. Any thought I had that I was hosting a man of limited abilities were put aside the moment we met. He was immaculately dressed and was aided by his wife, Jo. All he wanted of me was to put various bomb bodies and fuzes on the bench in front of his teaching post. I took his hands in mine and placed them on each exhibit which he identified as we went along the row. When the time was right, the ATO students were brought in and sat before him. They already knew he was blind and any misconceptions they might have harboured about being sympathetic and understanding soon turned to admiration.

Ken started to speak, moving between and holding up the exhibits he located unerringly from his mental memory map. A stranger would not have realised he was completely blind. His style was modest, inform-ative and, at times, dramatic. He spoke of the sacrifice of friends who perished whilst trying to dismantle booby-trapped fuzes in the effort to exploit these mechanisms and make the process safer. Towards the end of his talk, he delivered the 'irony of ironies'. At the time when these fuzes proved so effective during the blitz and so lethal to unwary operators, the precise details of how these fuzes worked were filed in the London Branch of the Patents Office. In his own words, he said that a messenger could have been sent across London on a bike and could have returned with the details so essential to him and others in staying alive. Even in 1943, Information Management was still a dark art practised by few.

Whilst all of this was going on, I had five other concurrent big deals running. Christine was expecting our first child, I had been appointed a Conductor RAOC, I had been shortlisted for a commission in the RAOC, I was continuing with a second-level Open University course and I had started an academic project of my own. When I first arrived at Shrivenham, I thought as a senior WO1 that I knew a thing or two about ammunition. Within a few days, I realised how superficial my trade knowledge was. As an Ammunition Technician, the training I underwent was largely vocational. The training for Ammunition Technical Officers was structured differently. In 1972, it was explained to me that the officers would spend most of their career time employed away from ammunition duties. Between ammunition postings, there were likely to be many changes in Land Service Ammunition, with new natures coming in, other natures undergoing mid-life development and other natures being phased out. The ATOs were said to need to be trained more in the general principles of ammunition design and the scientific background to explosive technology. I don't know if this was actually true, but in the trade humour of the day, the difference in our qualification badges was jokingly explained thus - that the AT badge had an A in it to show they knew about ammunition, where the ATO badge only featured a black hole! The actual explanation was less flippant. Historically, the ATOs did not have a badge. ATs, on the other hand, were A-Class Tradesman. The flame part of the badge came from the Board of Ordnance. The ATOs, as commissioned officers, could not be tradesmen so an A on their badge would be inappropriate. The current badges evolved as the former Ammunition Examiners were retitled Ammunition Technicians and the officer's title changed from Inspecting Ordnance Officer to Ammunition Technical Officer. Commissioned ATs were titled Ammunition Executive Officers and eventually the difference was eradicated.

Mindful as I was of my limited understanding of the science behind ammunition design, I started using the facilities at Shrivenham to catch up. I was already aware that the vocational bandwidth of AT knowledge was largely restricted to what ammunition was in service in the British Army. My tour in Oman had involved Soviet and Chinese communist ammunition which was an eye-opener. Professionally, I felt motivated to expand my knowledge and understanding. As a Conductor RAOC, I was now the most senior warrant officer at Shrivenham. This anomaly could cause issues as traditionally, the Regimental Sergeant Major was the Presiding Officer in the Warrant Officers' and Sergeants' Mess. The Queen's Regulations of the time allowed a work-around. A Conductor was permitted to elect to become an Honorary Mess Member which prevented the RSM being usurped in his own mess. On appointment, I had elected to become an Honorary Member. At the Mess Christmas Ball in 1992, I found myself seated at the 'top table' with the RSM and guest of honour who was the Commandant of the RMCS. As we chatted between courses, he asked if I had any ideas on how to improve the throughput of students attending the college. At the time, the MoD was seeking to rationalise the numbers of training venues it had. It seemed we were in competition with another high-profile institution and the winner would expand whilst the loser was exactly that. We had already taken on a large number of civilian undergraduates to boost our numbers, but it seemed we needed a more convincing raison d'être. I had an idea based on my own ambitions and the Commandant had another.

I suggested to the Commandant that Shrivenham could expand its student body and value to the MoD by opening the 12 available MSc courses to senior warrant officers from all three services. I went on to say that such warrant officers usually retired after completing their career engagement, which was wasteful in my view, but if the best of them could attend RMCS for a full-time six-month MSc course, followed by a remotely conducted project phase, they could then become senior instructors in their own centres of excellence and their careers could be extended, possibly through commissioning. My boss was already aware of my MSc ambition and the Commandant spoke to him the following day. My boss then wrote back to the Commandant outlining the detail. What then took me by pleasant surprise was that the Commandant wrote about this proposal to the Director Army Training (DAT), another major general. In the meantime, I had asked the RMCS Registrar if it was possible for me to be admitted to the Explosive Ordnance Engineering (EOE) course, perhaps privately, at my own expense. Her advice was interesting. There was indeed a direct route available to a second degree. If, on seeking admission, the applicant could demonstrate a minimum of 12 year's heuristic experience in a technical trade, it was possible for this to negate the requirement for a first degree. She advised me to speak to the Head of the Ammunition Science and Explosive Technology Unit (ASETU). I did, and he laughed at me. When I then pointed out that I currently delivered several of the modules in the EOE course, supervised the practicals and set many of the exams, he relented and agreed to consider it. I was much encouraged by all of this and looked forward to what the DAT's view would be. The result, when it came, was disappointing. He rejected the proposal and I felt his reasoning was perverse. He opined that since regular officers were not at the time routinely offered a study opportunity to achieve the MSc, it would be iniquitous to offer this to non-commissioned officers. To me, this argument was banal and conservative to say the least. This outcome led me to consider other ways that I might improve my academic standing. I was already about halfway through an OU first degree. I was also employed as a military supervisor on several projects being run at the time. My own ATO students could apply for the Graduateship of the City & Guilds Institute qualification (GCGI) off the back of their ATO Course project achievements, so I spoke to my boss about me completing a City & Guilds project and he was supportive.

I had already shortlisted several topics that I wanted to pursue. I chose to do a project with the aim of researching the feasibility of creating a high-explosive disruptor, capable of disrupting even sensitive bombs at speeds of 2 to 3 magnitudes faster than was possible with the disrupters in service at that time. After conducting some simple trials, I demonstrated a warhead design which could be reliably used against sensitive explosive fillings without them exploding. Further, I then discovered that I could scale up the design so that it could be used on a device as large as a lorry bomb. There was also a clear indication that the disrupter could be effective against weapons of mass destruction. There was a problem; it was security. This development would have to be classified as it was highly sensitive and intellectual copyright was also an issue. Shrivenham was something of a Mecca for explosive entrepreneurs, so I decided to keep the matter very much in-house.

The project received some very welcome support from an MoD scientist based at Fort Halstead. I had already made his acquaintance as he was a visiting lecturer. He had a reputation as one of the foremost warhead designers in the business! After consulting him, I was invited to Fort Halstead to meet him and look at how computer simulation might help me. The velocities achieved by my experimental warheads were already too fast for the instrumentation available at the RMCS. At Fort Halstead, they had a Cray Supercomputer, and I was invited to try it out to see if it could model the many design parameters I was working with. On the first visit, I presented my project proposals and was both delighted and encouraged to find strong support. I was expecting to load some simulations on the Cray but the limitations of that technology won the day. The cooling system for the Cray was managed by a well-known and popular brand of personal computer which had broken down! Even the mighty Cray had an Achille's Heel. I was to make several visits over the next few months which proved fruitful. The project was to conclude with me doing a viva (oral presentation) with an engineering professor from Cranfield University. I had written an extensive dissertation and I made a formal project presentation. I gained the GCGI out of it which was, at the time, said to be the equivalent of an honours degree. The classified project report was handed over and put on a shelf somewhere in a classified library and I was to hear nothing more about it. It would be nice to know if the project ever came to anything, but it achieved for me what I wanted it to and anything else would have been a bonus.

I think I have already alluded to my frustrations towards ammunition souvenir hunting in the Army with the tendency by even senior people to overlook the presence of live explosives. As a staff sergeant, I had investigated a 17-year-old souvenir hunter's actions after he succeeded in blowing off both of his hands with only about 1.5 grams of explosive when he was trying to dismantle a wartime 2-inch mortar HE bomb fuze (Fuze Percussion No 151) in his digs. Scrap yards and range areas were a common source of explosive souvenirs. One (thankfully) near-miss was at Barry Buddon Ranges in Scotland in 1983 when a gang of children were seen playing with matches on the beach by one of the range staff. They ran away as he approached, and he was shocked to discover that they had found several pounds of plastic explosive and a very short length of fuze and a plain detonator. They had assembled these into a viable explosive charge and, not realizing how little time was available had they lit the fuze, they repeatedly tried to light it with ordinary matches. To their good fortune, the blustery onshore wind extinguished their first attempts until they were discovered. That could have been six young lives cut short. So, I'll say it again - I do not like ammunition souvenir hunters.

There was a shameful repeat episode of souvenir hunting which could have resulted in disaster. This came to light at Shrivenham when the Weapons and Vehicles Division acquired a new exhibit. This was a self-propelled, radar-guided anti-aircraft gun known as the ZSU-23-4 Shilka. It is entirely legitimate for a place like Shrivenham to acquire this kind of hardware but that wasn't the issue. The staff, expecting the Shilka to arrive on a low-loader, had asked me to look it over to ensure it was free from explosives. It is very common for small items of ammunition to fall into confined spaces on armoured fighting vehicles and a check like this is prudent. The Shilka had allegedly been recovered from the Gulf War and I was told it had been a 'gate guard' at the Army Air Corps Centre, Middle Wallop, thus its provenance was as a souvenir. There was no 'freedom from explosive' certificate with the vehicle, so a careful check was in order. The Shilka duly arrived and was offloaded. I looked it over quite thoroughly to make sure there was no ammunition present. After a few minutes, I was nearly done but I didn't like what I saw with one of the four 23mm guns. All of the breech areas were heavily contaminated with sand and muck and the breech of one gun was still partially open. I thought the chances of there being a live round partially chambered were probably nil, but I wanted to make sure. The building was having some renovation work done and I found a long slender offcut of a composite material which was long enough and thin enough to allow me to depth-gauge the barrel from muzzle to breech face. Before doing this, I wedged a piece of steel bar into a position where it would prevent the breech from closing as this could cause the gun to fire unexpectedly. The ammunition, if present, was likely to be a high explosive 23mm shell and then I noticed the barrel was pointing towards the Uffington White Horse several miles away. It turned out that a comparison of dimensions showed there was indeed something in the breech approximating the known length of a live round. I alerted the officer in charge as a matter of urgency, and he simply expected me to remove the shell. If it was that easy, I would have done so but the working parts were corroded and caked with a solid patina of muck. Now, this was one of those situations where a clumsy attempt to remove the round could result in disaster. I was unfamiliar with the ZSU and was, frankly, out of my depth. If anything went wrong, it would come back on me. I declined the instruction to remove the round and then called my own boss to explain the situation. Over the next hour or so, there were repeated requests for me to make the ZSU safe. I dug my heels in. Eventually, management got the message and the task of removing the round was passed to a colleague in 11 EOD Regiment. This outcome was, I think, a victory for common sense. As the 11 EOD Regiment response was now a formal task, it made everything above board. I'm quite sure that management were dismayed at this outcome as they probably wanted this embarrassing problem to just 'go away'. With the technical assistance of the Artificer Weapons, my colleague was able to extract the round safely and we destroyed it on the Shrivenham explosive range. Once again, I had shown I was not the Shrivenham Detachment of 11 EOD Regiment, and I was not about to start doing informal favours to spare the blushes of people who should have known better.

As my time at Shrivenham came to an end, I had to attend a medical examination prior to commissioning. This was to be conducted through a Standing Commissions Medical Board at the Cambridge Military Hospital. When I got there, I was shown into a consulting room occupied by a relic of a bygone era. This was Colonel Blimp personified, in civilian dress as he was a retired Brigadier. I wondered if it was the same 'old git' that reviewed me in the field hospital in Al Jubayl after my reaction to three vaccinations I had the night before for Pertussis,

Plague and Anthrax. If not, they were cut from the same cloth. He called me in quite gruffly and instructed me to sit. He was smoking a cheroot and it seemed to me everything in the room was yellow. My eyes started to smart immediately I walked in, and this affected my soft contact lens. Within a couple of minutes, I sensed that I would have to take the lens out and wear my glasses. He insisted on putting me through an eye test before this, however. His reaction when I couldn't read down to the line worthy of a commissioned officer, was to angrily denounce me as 'effin' blind. I explained that his smoking had affected my contact lens, which he took as an affront, but he allowed me to remove the lens and then wanted a delay to allow my eyes to settle which was seemingly the only reasonable thing he said. The delay was achieved by sending me down the corridor for a hearing test. This test produced the remarkable result that my high-tone hearing had improved over the years! I returned to the smoker's den, and he proceeded. My eyes were fine and then I had to strip. As he studied my posture, he announced "Good God, man, your tits are squint". He didn't say any more about my posture, but I believe it was symptomatic of an unresolved lower back injury which was to plague me for years to come. The medical concluded and he seemed to reluctantly agree to my fitness for commissioning. I returned to Shrivenham, pleased to have the 'tick in the box', but, oh so grateful that a prostate exam wasn't needed!!

The one thing that Shrivenham had going for it, as distinct from our competitors, was the Explosive Range and Demonstration Area (ERDA). The explosive limit was one pound of plastic explosive which was more than enough for the typical small-scale explosive projects that we supervised almost every working day. In a typical year, we would conduct an average of 2,000 controlled explosions. The range was so busy, in fact, that the pheasants bred on site for the shooting club were completely battle-inoculated! For the non-technical, battle inoculation is the deliberate exposure of trainee soldiers to battle noise, such as gunfire and explosions, to get them used to it. Stories from the shooting club commonly reported that the beaters couldn't get the pheasants to take flight as they advanced, and the birds wouldn't even take off when the guns fired. In one case, a beater was said to have actually picked a bird up and thrown it into the air to be shot. One morning, I was surprised to get a direct phone call from the Commandant. He asked if we were using the ERDA that day and it happened that we were. He asked if I would kindly detonate the maximum amount of explosive permitted at precisely 1235 hours. I agreed I would detonate one pound of explosive in the open air at the appointed time and this was done. Later in the day, a very pleased Commandant phoned again. He explained that he had hosted a ministerial visit which was part of the review into which training establishment would go forward as the preferred venue for the proposed Defence Academy. He had been hosting the minister to lunch in the mess, when, at 1235 hours, a loud bang rang out, causing a small flake of plaster to fall from the ceiling into the minister's soup. As a replacement bowl was arranged, he used the contrived cue of the bang to underscore the trump card Shrivenham enjoyed over the opposition - our explosives range, the ERDA!

So, after a very shaky start, my three years at Shrivenham were fruitful and enjoyable, not least because of the two inspiring colonels I worked for and the amazingly organised RE WO1 I worked with (Graham). The first colonel was hilarious but ambitious, was prepared to take risks and was dedicated to his calling. His replacement was a different character. He was an exemplary leader, worked very hard at rehearsing all of his lectures and espoused the recently issued Army Values and Standards.

The first colonel had plotted my 'gotcha' moment when my Conductor's appointment was announced and the second set me up for the news about my commissioning application. I had been sent to DLSA Didcot on the day the Commission Board's announcement was due. He phoned me in the office where he knew I would be and asked if I would call at his house before going home. Colonel Mike (actually they were both called Mike) had already invited Christine around and, when I knocked the door, I was confronted by grinning faces and champagne. What a pleasant set of memories those endearing guys have left me with! In that short space of time, I had two big achievements at work, three if I count the success of my GCGI project - our first son was born, and I got through that year's OU course. Next stop commissioning!

I would finish with a note about Graham, the Sapper WO1 with whom I worked for three years at Shrivenham. He was incredibly well organised all of the time. His administration was superb, and he had applied for a commission in his own corps. I fully believed he would succeed; in fact, I thought he was more likely to commission than me. Sadly, he didn't, and it was probably due to a personality conflict with a colonel in his own corps. I was very much a specialist and Graham was more generalist with a wider skill set. To this day, I still believe he would have made a far better officer than me, but he was denied. Personality conflicts can have a huge opportunity cost. When will people ever learn?

CHAPTER 16

HQ 621 EOD Squadron RAF Northolt 1994–1997

At the end of March 1994, I joined 621 EOD Squadron as second-in-command. We moved into a lovely house just outside RAF Northolt, a five-minute walk from work. Now, as a commissioned officer, I joined the Officers' Mess and had a pleasant surprise. I had never previously been able to empathise fully with officers. A turning point for me, after 19 years of mistrust, started at Shrivenham where I saw first-hand how much pressure there was on young officers to work towards their career goals and, indeed, how many of them were dedicated to this end. Membership of the Officers' Mess now started to sway the social aspects of my views. These views may well be anathema to warrant officers and sergeants, but they reflect my own experiences, prejudices and earlier environment as an Army child. To openly compare and contrast the differences between officers and soldiers is to flirt with certain condemnation from all sides, but I would emphasise the differences are exactly that. One side is not necessarily better, superior or more worthy; they're just different from each other. As a child enjoying the occasional Sunday roast dinner in the Sergeants' Mess, I was browbeaten into being meticulously well behaved. The hated Brylcreem would be slapped on my head and my hair combed into glossy submission. I wore my best clothes and table manners had to be perfect. Afterwards, when we got home, my parents would exchange comments about this or that child and how disgraceful this or that behaviour was, and how it showed their parents up. A classic and oft-repeated one-liner from both parents concerned the way they characterised the forms of address in the messes whenever officers and soldiers were at the same function; It would be "Officers and ladies and Sergeants and their wives are invited to dance or dine" or whatever. It was a form of inverted snobbery. This was most apparent whenever a mess invited the other mess to a function, traditionally at Christmas. It seemed to me that the Sergeants' Mess invariably sought to out-do the hosting generosity of the Officers' Mess. From the moment I first attended an Officers' Mess social function as a member, I was made to feel hugely welcome. It was not that I was in the company of posher people but more that I was in the company of professional people, capable of polite informality. There was, however, an air of mischief in the Officers' Mess which could eclipse the Sergeants' Mess; after-dinner games. We did have a few in the Sergeants' Mess at Paderborn. We would play cabbage rugby or put all the long dining tables together to form a racing circuit where the German cook's stolen bike would be ridden in time trials. One such race ended (mercifully) without tragedy when a table was moved at the last minute to an open window as the hapless racer was on the last leg. The tabletop was awash with spilt beer and both rider and bike disappeared into the night sky from the first floor. We voted to pay for the cook's damaged bike at the next mess meeting! At Kineton, we once catapulted female officers off long tables to be caught in sheets in a drunken parody of Royal Artillery gun drills. However, the officers took after-dinner games one stage further.

On one of my first nights at Northolt, when I was temporarily accommodated in a room in the mess, I entered the main bar having thought I could hear the sounds of raucous laughter from a large crowd. The bar was completely empty when I got there, and the steward nodded towards the anteroom as he poured me a softie; I was still teetotal at the time. I walked around to the anteroom and could see through the gap between the double doors that there was a crowd of people with their backs to me, facing the large fireplace. That Officers' Mess was a lovely old Edwardian building with high ceilings, tall sash windows, chandeliers and grand fireplaces. Fascinated, I peeped through this gap wondering what was going on. Out of my sight, between the crowd and fireplace, were two young RAF pilots. One was affectionately known as Beaker after the Muppet Show's Lab assistant and the other was nicknamed Bozo. Each had a powerful display rocket and they had snapped off most of each rocket's shaft. They were both pyromaniacs. The game they played consisted of igniting the rocket's fuze and the winner would be the one who held onto his rocket the longest before releasing it. Hopefully, there would be sufficient time between throwing the rocket up the chimney and the rocket motor bursting into life. As I said, I couldn't see what was happening. The crowd alternated between fits of giggles and shouts of encouragement. Then I could hear fizzing. The crowd's excitement peaked, and I heard first one whoosh and then another. The first rocket had been thrown up the chimney. It had ignited and roared off into the sky. A few seconds later, through the open sash window, I saw a brilliant flash from the night sky as the maroon burst above the mess, lighting up the runway outside. By now, the second rocket's whooshing seemed to get louder. What nobody realised was that too much of the shaft had been left attached and the rocket was too long to negotiate the 'dog leg' in the chimney's climb to the roof outside. Then the maroon portion exploded with a huge bang inside the chimney. Oddly, there was no flash. Instead, everything went pitch black and deathly silent. The corridor lights were still on, so it wasn't a power cut. As I continued to peer through the gap in the door, I could see a dim chandelier above the cowering, murmuring crowd getting brighter. The exploding rocket had blown a huge soot-fall back into the ante- room. Everyone was coated!

On another evening after a dinner, we were treated to the RAF tradition of blowing up a piano. While we were dining, a condemned piano had been placed outside the main entrance to the mess. At the appointed time, we were invited outside to watch. The piano had been primed with bangers and petrol. As we watched, the piano was explosively dismembered, and bits fell to the ground. A fiery mushroom climbed up into the air. There was much chanting and revelry and then the fire died back. The recently arrived Northolt Troop Commander, possibly seeking recognition as a fellow pyromaniac, dashed forward with a can of petrol to restore the spectacle. As the petrol showered onto the piano, some fell on the leg of his mess kit and up he went. Fortunately, the flames were doused promptly and only his pride and trouser leg were singed. We went back inside and Paul, the Squadron OC, had to duck when a powerful rocket was fired towards where we were standing. It passed through a door behind the bar before screaming between us to crash into the wall opposite the bar.

As hosts to our wives, the RAF Officers were second to none. We had a dinner to celebrate the anniversary of the Battle of Britain. The one criticism I have about RAF Officers is concerning their mess kit. It was just about the drabbest, most banal uniform you could imagine. The RLC mess kit, however, was a riot of colour, almost verging on gaudy, but the ladies loved it. A feature of mess dinners was that a photographer would be hired to take posed pictures for posterity. The RAF wives kept stealing me to pose with them, much to the chagrin of their husbands. My uniform sported all manner of colours and stripes, my ATO badge, miniature medals, stripey trousers and silver spurs in my George Boots. I might add these were bloody dangerous when coming down the stairs. Just at the point of becoming blasé with all of this flattering attention from the RAF ladies, I realised I had been spotted by an honorary member in a dinner jacket. He sported a monocle and had an ebony black cane with a silver ball handle. He was seated at the bar on a stool and was bracketed by two young barmaids who appeared to be totally under his spell. Then I saw the miniature medals, rows of them. I had five, four of which were what we would euphemistically call NAAFI queue medals. One was a Northern Ireland GSM, one was the LS&GC and two were for service with the Sultan of Oman's forces. The fifth medal, with rosette, was for the Gulf War. This elderly campaigner was now rising to his feet and coming towards me. I was reminded of the comedian Professor Jimmy Edwards. The medals on his jacket instantly eclipsed mine. As he approached, the black cane rose and pointed at my medals. He demanded to know what I got them for, before launching into how he earned his most memorable decoration. He was piloting a Lancaster Bomber on a raid deep inside Germany; it may have been Berlin. He was carrying a full bomb load and some of them had delayed-action fuzes. The crews were not told of the delays set in case they were captured. The aircraft was damaged by fire as it flew over Holland. It lagged behind the main concentration and at a lower altitude. They reached the target and dropped their bombs but one was hung up due to icing. They returned to base but were damaged again. As the aircraft descended into warmer air, the hung-up bomb fell and was caught in the bomb bay doors. They believed the bomb fuze was now armed and as they approached the Lincolnshire coast, the weight of the bomb started to prise the bomb bay doors open. There was a risk the bomb might fall clear as the doors separated so, despite serious battle damage, the aircraft was turned around and headed back out over the North Sea where the bomb bay doors were opened allowing the bomb to fall harmlessly. They then returned and managed to land safely, albeit heavily damaged and with casualties. It was fascinating to listen to this story; a story where the crew's gallantry and devotion to duty lasted many hours, not the span of mere minutes you might associate with ground battles, and that kind of gallantry is often the most demanding.

RAF Northolt had been a swamp which was drained, and the original airfield dated from the Great War. The airfield and surrounding houses were bombed in the Second War and the Home Guard had a base there too; more to follow about their legacy. 621 EOD Squadron had previously been located at Beaver's Lane Camp, Hounslow. There had been a rationalisation study concerning surplus MoD bases around northwest London and the outcome was that a number of bases were deemed surplus and that they could be sold and the displaced units located elsewhere. The income from the sale of land would provide the investment to rebuild. This all made sense and it was certainly the case that MoD infrastructure in many of the old bases was aging and in a poor state of repair. Before I arrived, the Squadron had relocated to a disused runway at RAF Northolt and was accommodated in portacabin offices and the EOD vehicles were kept in what is called a Rubb Hangar (big rubber tent, for those not in the know). The IRA managed to pull off a spectacular attack against Heathrow Airport as I arrived although we weren't directly involved in this as our colleagues in the Metropolitan Police Bomb Squad covered the area of London inside the M25. When I had settled in, I started to study the plans for our new buildings.

We were to get a new combined squadron headquarters and Northolt Troop building, an EOD vehicle garage and an ammunition store. All of this was to be erected next to the perimeter road which led from the so-called White House Gate to the VIP Building. As RAF Northolt acted as a hub for air-commuting by royalty and a plethora of other celebrities, it meant that we regularly had passers-by who merited fear, respect or adulation. Before I arrived, there had been two spontaneous meetings between the great and the good and squadron personnel. The first was when the Queen and Prince Philip were being driven past our somewhat tatty portacabins. Prince Philip allegedly asked his driver to stop, and he questioned a startled squadron member about what was going on. The soldier explained the squadron's role and the move from Hounslow into proposed new real estate here. Prince Philip was reported to have replied with a cynical quip that the squadron was likely to be disbanded as soon as the accommodation was completed! Another impromptu meeting was between one of my predecessors and the Spice Girls as they passed by each other through the White House Gate. I might explain that we were late-entry officers, and we were in our forties, seemingly ancient to our young soldiers. When the Spice Girls saw my predecessor's adorable dog, their limousine was halted and Spice Girl adoration poured forth; for the dog, I mean! The next morning, name-dropping started about this memorable encounter. Quick as a flash, our sharp-witted Royal Signals Bleeps christened him as the sixth Spice Girl-'Grumpy Spice'!

Another crossing of paths proved less salubrious and led to possibly one of the fastest Works Services I have ever seen completed. The Queen had been going past on her way to the Royal Building and had glanced at our temporary accommodation. Behind the portacabins, we had single portaloo toilets of the kind you might see at pop concerts

461

and other outdoor events. As she looked on from her limousine, one of our portlier soldiers was exiting the loo nearest the road. In the very tight space of the loo, he found it easier to open the door a little to give him more space to hoist his trousers up. A gust of wind had flung the door wide open, and he allegedly mooned Her Majesty who was most definitely not amused! Within minutes, workmen arrived and constructed a stout wooden screening wall betwixt loo and road.

On another occasion, the corporal who managed our road transport was ordered to get a temporary hire vehicle to replace the Squadron's command car which needed servicing. The command car was a 3-litre Omega Police Special used as an emergency response vehicle. Our emergency response drivers were all fully trained and qualified by the police in the dark but exciting art of high-speed response driving. It's a dark art because, other than the driver, occupants would close their eyes as lamp posts on the M25 flashed by at 120 mph! The job-worth on the other end of the phone at HQ London District, responsible for arranging hire cars, laconically declared that a car for a mere major could only be something like a Ford Fiesta. Didn't our man know that even the General Officer Commanding London District couldn't get anything that powerful? The task of liaison was passed to me, and I called the reticent corporal to brief him on the squadron's role and that we were regularly required to travel in police convoys at speeds well in excess of the national speed limit. He promised to call back but he didn't. His even more anal boss did. He unleashed a torrent of rhetoric about the dreadful sin of speeding. As I listened with the phone at arm's length, Mr 'Foghorn Leghorn' droned on and on. He did have a speech impediment; he needed to pause for breath, at which point I said I needed to talk to his boss. We did speak and the upshot was that Mr 'Foghorn Leghorn' was invited to attend one of our periodic training drives around the M25 with the Metropolitan Police. The day arrived, bright and sunny. The convoy was to consist of about six fast movers with our command car in the middle. The police cars were all in police livery with blues and twos. Our car was unmarked except we had more discreet blues and twos. Our driver had graduated in first place from his police driving course and was no shrinking violet. Mr 'Foghorn Leghorn' arrived in his Ford Fiesta, dressed smartly in his barrack dress, looking for all the world like he was embarking on a genteel sight-seeing tour around the London Orbital Motorway. I chuckled as he was strapped in; he wasn't going to see much! The White House Gate was alerted and the barrier lifted. Motorcycle outriders went on ahead to stop the traffic on the Ruislip Road. The convoy would exit right at the gate and then head towards the Polish War Memorial before joining the motorway via the A40. They took off and went out of sight. We heard their wailing progress as they shot down the Ruislip Road. Then it was quiet. I went back into the office, amused to see the look on 'Foghorn Leghorn's' face as the accelerating car snapped his head back. As the 'real' Foghorn Leghorn would say of him, "Son, ah say, Son, he wuz about as sharp as a bowlin' ball!" They returned a short while later. The white-faced passenger struggled to find his land legs as he returned to his pedestrian Ford Fiesta. After that, future requests for high-performance cars were honoured without question.

As I pored over the plans for the squadron's new buildings, I realised something was drastically wrong. Whenever the Army designs new infrastructure, the process usually starts with a Quartering Brief; in other words, what is actually needed in the new build? Once this has been thrashed out, the result goes to architects, and they design what the builders will construct. You get what you asked for and no more. The references in the design drawing related to documents in

the Quartering Brief that were 15 years old. In the 1980s, our EOD vehicles were Ford Transits. The vehicles we were now equipped with
were DAF 45s; considerably bigger than a Transit. I ran outside with
a tape measure and checked the difference between plan and reality.
The DAF 45s would not fit in the new garage; the bays were too small!
The garage had to be a secure weathertight structure with reinforced
steel security fittings on the inside. Changing the plans would not be a
matter of adding a couple of courses of bricks. Looking further, I could
see the office plans did not reflect modern requirements. The typists in
the headquarters and Troop had been allocated their own office as, in
the old days, typists were noisy and could be distracting. Open-plan
offices with networked word-processing facilities were now standard
practice. To make it worse, each office had only two electrical sockets
and there was no provision for IT network conduits. The entrances on
the ground floor did not incorporate disabled access ramps and even
the Troop General Store didn't have a ramp. A lot of expensive and
major changes would be needed. It was to get worse. The VIP Building
next door was often referred to as the 'Royal Building'. It was very
smart and had been finished with very plush (and expensive) cladding.
The local authority scrutiny of the plans had noted that our buildings
were to have a standard engineering brick finish. A yellow card was
shown, and our plan had to be upgraded so that we too would have the
same swanky exterior, including the ammunition store! I phoned the
project officer at Aldershot and arranged to meet him. My 'emperor's
clothes' moment had not gone down well; it was apparently my fault.
I can only assume that an old Quartering Brief had languished in the
'filing cabinets of indifference' until the new funding stream from the
sale of northwest London bases was suddenly granted. No systematic
review appeared to have been carried out. You might say the chickens
had been counted before...(you know the rest).

As time went by, the prospect of building a folly to incompetence was not lost on the MoD planners. The Quartering Brief was re-visited, and the plans were modified. The build contract was awarded to John Sisk and Sons. The estimated cost was in the region of about £2.5 million. The building site was immediately outside my office window, and, in a rare example of proactivity, the MoD Project Officer allowed me to attend monthly site meetings as an observer and that any issues were to be quietly noted by me and referred directly to him and definitely not directly to the builder. As mentioned, RAF Northolt was built on a drained swamp. Our main building was to be a two-storey steel-framed building with Bison- Block flooring on the first floor. Piles had to be driven down to the firmer strata well below the surface. Atop each pile was to be a reinforced concrete pile cap. A sub-contractor excavated around the piles to make holes for these quite large pile caps. Cages of rebar were constructed on top of each pile and preparations to pour the concrete were completed but here another mismatch between new and old intervened. I was at liberty to walk around the site and observe as long as the supervisor knew I was there, and I was wearing my PPE. As I went past a couple of contractors standing by one of these piles, I heard them discussing the merits of shuttering the boxes used to confine the concrete to its designed form as it hardened. Instead of wood, they were going to use polystyrene. It didn't seem to be an issue to me at the time. The concrete mixers turned up with those elevating pipes and from my office, I watched as much concrete was poured. About two or three days later, I found myself looking into a hole at one of these now-hardened pile caps. There were chunks of polystyrene blowing about in the wind, too many chunks for my liking; in fact, FOD on an Air Station. On closer examination, I was mortified to see the polystyrene shuttering had collapsed outwards for want of rigid supports whilst the concrete was still soft. Instead of nice symmetrical caps with square sides, the sides of the holes themselves had provided the poured concrete with a more random shape to conform to, and the concrete had mostly flowed away from the rebar. Around the site, contractors were looking into other holes. Heads were being scratched. The upshot was that the abortive pile caps had to be grubbed up and then the piles had to be extracted. Huge spaghetti piles of rusted rebar soon littered the site. I think the project was delayed by about a month and there was a massive cost overrun.

I was able to get the numbers of electrical sockets greatly increased and the typists' offices consolidated into open-plan orderly rooms. The extra space resulted in the OC's office being quite palatial and we were able to incorporate a conferencing suite in his office. I got the contractors to build in conduits so a computer network could be installed. I did the wiring myself based on the BNC format of that time and we were eventually using Windows for Workgroups. Our HQ was so swanky that when he could, the CO would hold meetings in our HQ rather than in his own tired real estate at Didcot.

I had already mentioned that RAF Northolt was a commuting hub for those travelling by air. The RAF charged a landing fee which I think was cheaper than Heathrow's, hence we saw a lot of this business. On the 13th of August 1996, a Spanish Learjet attempted to land at RAF Northolt but crashed after passing off the end of the runway and exiting through the southern perimeter fence onto the A40 dual carriageway. From the official accident report, it appeared it came in too fast, the spoilers had not been deployed and there was a plethora of other issues contributing to the cause. Ever being one not wishing to spoil a good story with the truth, the version of events we heard was that one of the pilots spoke limited English and there was some kind of kerfuffle in the cockpit when it dawned on the pilots that they were going to over-run. Their sole passenger was a comedienne who was flying in to join John Cleese in the making of a film. Fortunately, all three on board only suffered slight injuries. The aircraft ended up on the dual carriageway and a van then collided with it, becoming embedded in the side of the aircraft and trapping the driver. The saving grace was that there was no fire. We heard later that the hapless van driver lost his job because he was allegedly doing a 'homer' and his unknowing boss saw the incident on TV News. I hope that bit is untrue but what a tale for his grandchildren!

It was about this time that I went to see the medical officer about getting a vasectomy. The RAF doctor was on leave, so I was seen by a civilian locum. He reached behind him, grabbed the form that would start the process and signed it. I expected to be summoned to a pre-vasectomy counselling session and that the whole thing would take about a year.

Unbeknownst to me, he filled in the wrong form; the form he used was to book the actual procedure after counselling. Two days later, my phone rang and it was Hillingdon Hospital. The Chief Clerk transferred the call to me in my office; I assumed it might be about families' welfare but the woman said, "Do you want this vasectomy or not?" Ever being one that liked to get things like this over and done with, I agreed to the proposal. I had been booked into a slot made vacant by a late cancellation... for the next afternoon! I had elected to have a local anaesthetic. A traumatic childhood experience when I was four, undergoing a tonsillectomy, had left me with an illogical but unnerving fear of general anaesthetics. The Bleeps took me to the hospital in a DAF 45 after lunchtime. I had been told to bring a book. By bizarre coincidence for a man facing the chop, it was titled The Edge of the Sword. It was General Sir Anthony Farrar-Hockley's biography. A nurse escorted me to a battered old, winged armchair at the end of the day ward. The beds were all full of grim-looking men. As she put screens around my chair and passed me two gowns to change into, she explained the men all wanted a general anaesthetic for the same procedure I was to have. I wondered what they knew that I didn't. The nurse complimented me for bringing a book to read while I waited and thought it was hilarious when she heard the title.

After what seemed an eternity, and saw me make deep inroads into the book, I was summoned. I followed a nurse to the operating theatre hub. Outside were several tearful women. The nurse explained it was the day for paediatric surgery. I felt slightly embarrassed at my sense of anticipation about getting the chop, not to mention the cold draught up my arse where the tying tapes were missing from the gown. She ushered me into a small room with a flickering overhead fluorescent light. Sitting on a surgical trolley was a jovial Asian doctor who talked me through the consent form after checking my identity. As he spoke, I looked around. I seemed to be in a store cupboard. There was barely room for the three of us. To my left was a pile of boxes and there was a rack of drawers against the wall. It was a little claustrophobic. I re-assured myself that the door at the other end would lead to a spotless theatre where the deed would be done. I signed the consent and was asked to lie down on the trolley. The nurse was a gregarious Geordie. I noticed she now had a big wet swab in forceps in her right hand. With her left hand, she lifted my gown. As she said, "This will feel cold", she swabbed my nether regions. I swear my laughing tackle tried to retreat and she laughed. The doctor then produced a syringe seemingly big enough to tranquilise a bull elephant. Mercifully, the banter with Geordie started. After a few minutes, the doctor stood upright with something grasped in self-locking forceps. It was a length of my vas deferens which he had snipped out. It was his belief I should see this to be convinced that the procedure was effective. Before he could start the other side, the door flew open, and a porter asked Geordie if she could pass him a box from the pile on my left-hand side. The box was passed over me, the door closed, and an apology was muttered as the doctor resumed work. When done, I walked back to the chair. The ward was empty. As I walked, the sharp ends of the sutures were scratching my inner thighs annoyingly. With a sense of anticlimax, I dressed wondering what all the fuss was about. I would find out later. Outside, my Bleep driver, now with a knowing grin a mile wide, promised to take it easy on the drive back before bouncing off every bloody traffic-calming hump he could find between Hillingdon and Ruislip. I went straight back to work, but about an hour later, the ache started. I went home to sleep it off.

I was now in my final year at 621 EOD Squadron. By now, we had moved into the newly completed accommodation and this was when I started to experience personality conflicts. I simply did not get on with the CO. I had conducted a Board of Officers' audit on another squadron and a lot of people were unhappy with my findings. I had discovered that two rifles were missing. They had gone with soldiers deployed to the Balkans but there was no accounting action taken to confirm this. In an ammunition store, I found a sealed package which had been repackaged and sealed by one of their own ammunition technician sergeants. It was a small box which, if the markings were to be believed, contained several Charge Assembly Maxi Candles. The box was manifestly too small to contain these so I opened the box and found the quantity was wrong, and therefore, there was a deficiency. The staff were aggrieved that I had opened a sealed box for a stock check, but since the box was sealed by one of their own ATs and was too small, it was quite proper to open it. One of my own senior NCOs had been caught misappropriating a vehicle and was remanded for court martial. All in all, I was not Mr Popular at the time and plenty of people in the squadron had a motive to try and get even. Or what I am about to describe was a practical joke gone wrong or just bad stores husbandry.

We had just returned from a squadron licensing exercise at Longmoor. We had taken three 9mm Browning pistols with us to fire our annual classification whilst there, as a concurrent activity. Just after we got back, I saw the squadron's stores officer walk past my door to the OC's office at the end of the corridor. I was quite busy and thought nothing more of it. Later on, in the early evening, there was a knock at my front door. It was the Squadron OC who lived in the house opposite mine. He started talking about missing pistols, but I was completely unaware of what he was talking about. Then I asked if that was why the stores officer had gone to see him earlier. He said it was. Feeling annoyed at being passed over in that way, I asked why, as the Squadrons Security Officer, I had not been immediately informed. The reply was that it was now too late as the matter had been reported to the Royal Military Police. This elicited another point from me. Although weapon and ammunition losses were a very serious matter, most of such losses were usually quickly resolved through a thorough search. I was told I could not do any searches as it was now a police matter. The subsequent kerfuffle lasted about three months. Our Squadron's good name was trashed. As ever, someone had to be blamed. An allegedly inadequate arrangement for weapon accounting was identified as the cause, which came back to me, despite the existing system having been in place for some years and well before my time. I was verbally admonished by the CO who was angry that his efforts to deliver favourable outcomes for the Regiment had been usurped by this alleged act of negligence. It could have been the inspiration for sackings in the popular TV reality series, The Apprentice.

A few days later, I was called in and ordered to conduct a 100% arms check in the armoury at the West London Administration Staff

HQ. The armoury had been out of bounds to us since the RMP had conducted a 'forensic search' of it after the loss was reported. As a commissioned officer, I was especially irritated that I had to be accompanied by an MoD Policeman. I went to the armoury with our store's lance corporal. On gaining entry, with the MoD Policeman watching, I started the check. The corporal pointed at the rifle rack which appeared to be full and so was considered to be correct. I put him right that we were to conduct a full check by serial number. I then asked to see the rifle magazines, bayonets and cleaning kits to which he replied that these didn't need to be checked. I put him right on that score too and he opened a five-foot by two-foot steel locker where there were boxes of magazines for the rifles. The top shelf of this cupboard, where the pistols were normally kept, was empty. I lifted out all the magazine boxes and stacked them in a pile. The first one I opened contained 11 magazines. The next one had 9 in it. I pointed out to the storeman the common-sense approach of having the same quantity (10) in each box. Then I took the lid off the next box and thought I was seeing things; three pistols were lying flat in the box. I alerted the policeman who looked like he'd been caught napping. I phoned the retired Colonel who was in charge of the armoury. He came running down from his office and smothered me in a bear hug, he was so pleased. I called the squadron HQ and passed the news to them. Then a shadow went past the outside of the armoury door. A vehicle braked firmly to a halt and a tall man in civilian dress ran in; he had just been told. He was the RMP RSM who had been involved in the investigation and he seemed very angry and demanded to know how I had gotten the three pistols. I explained how I had just discovered them. He countered by saying his sergeant had conducted a thorough search of the armoury and they hadn't been there, so I must have replaced them. It felt like I was being set up for some kind of conspiracy connected with the illegal possession of firearms. The cloud over me didn't lift and things felt even worse. It felt like finding the weapons was even worse than their supposed loss. When questioned by my own bosses, I probably ruined the chance of getting back on their Christmas card lists when I repeated my earlier comment that an immediate and thorough search at the time of the suspected loss would have reconciled the matter and our reputations would still be intact.

With hindsight, it could be that the weapons were accidentally mixed up with the rifle magazines, but somehow, I don't think so. It was another example in a litany of things that went wrong, and kept going wrong, in the last year of my tour. Perhaps I presented the impression of being quixotic to my superiors but in response to such a charge, I would label most of them as being 'short-termist' and perhaps too inclined to submit to the latest fashionable trends in military thinking, if not to use the term high-brow in the way that personnel were managed.

In two examples of what I considered to be the perverse application of 'rules is rules', in personnel management, I saw two good men thrown on the heap because they couldn't pass the BFT and the Army couldn't, or wouldn't, rehabilitate them. The first example was a Lance Corporal, a driver by trade, who was modestly overweight. He could do his job as an EOD No 2 and driver competently. In addition to his weight issue, he suffered from gastric reflux. Just after starting a fitness test, he would collapse in a coughing and choking fit. I asked the station medics to observe him on a run, but they refused. In his last unit, this soldier was commended for his actions in the Balkans but now it counted for naught. He left the Army prematurely. The second example was even more extreme. An ammunition technician sergeant was in my unit. He was in a minority that had passed his high-risk EOD training. He completed an EOD tour in Northern Ireland and was pulling more duties than his physically fit peers because he could pass his EOD assessments whereas they could not. On one occasion, he had rendered safe a terrorist bomb in a very public place, despite the local authorities trying to play things down and send him away. He persisted and saved their bacon. The unit even received a letter of gratitude from on high. I ran with him on tests and could see all he needed was more routine physical training. In my opinion, he had moral courage and physical courage in buckets and was a competent EOD Operator with a proven track record. Despite my protests, the CO applied for and got his discharge because he failed to pass the BFT. I felt ashamed of the shabby way he was treated. We threw out a man who could do his job in favour of retaining 'racing snakes' who were unemployable on EOD because they couldn't pass their assessments. It seems the lessons of the Falklands War were ignored. 'Racing snake' men with low body mass indices (BMIs) were more likely to succumb to hypothermia. Heavier built men could withstand severe cold better and carry more kit. With some irony, I was told of how daft our fixation on BMI had become in a lecture from recruiting staff on my commissioning course. They quoted the example of the BMI threshold being so low that most of the current England Rugby Union squad would be deemed unfit to join the Army.

My frustration with the wasteful personnel management of soldiers, where my instinct was to rehabilitate and reintegrate (extreme cases excepted), did, on occasion, extend to more technical matters. On 24th April 1996, two powerful bombs were placed under Hammersmith Bridge in London. They failed to detonate. A few days later, I learned that an intelligence agency had classified these bombs as time and power units (TPUs) which I profoundly disagreed with. TPUs are discrete components of a bomb containing a power supply and timing mechanism, designed to detonate a bomb. They were not at that time complete bombs in their own right. These two bombs, however, had integrated TPUs and to classify them as just TPUs was wrong in my view. This was discussed in our headquarters during a Metropolitan Police Counter Terrorism Branch visit, and I expressed the view that these were, in fact, improvised versions of military-prepared rapid demolition charges, designed to cause the bridge to collapse. The two devices, one each side of the bridge on the southern end, were linked with cord detonating. The technical opinion was that this was 'redundancy' (belt and braces) to ensure that should there be a failure in either bomb, The other would detonate and destroy any evidence of failure. My logic was that the bombs were linked to ensure the maximum destructive effect on the bridge. I could see the hallmarks of a classic rapid bridge demolition technique, a topic which I had covered many times when lecturing at Shrivenham. I advised the police that in the group responsible, there would likely be someone trained in combat engineering. The attack on the bridge would have been preceded by a close target reconnaissance. One member of the Police team appeared to take my opinion seriously. The Army (RLC) technical staff present were politely but firmly sceptical. This was a time when the RLC experts needed to have a Royal Engineer on board to give a more balanced expert opinion. I heard nothing more about this case, but it was interesting to note years later, that there was, at the time, a committed terrorist in the ranks of the IRA who had the requisite qualifications. He was already known to the authorities; he was a dual nationality Irish American who was also a US Marine veteran with combat engineer training. From the perspective of my own vanity, I would love to know if my contribution was helpful, but the truth will be forever lost in the 'neither confirm nor deny' policy relating to the murky world of intelligence.

Towards the end of my tour at 621 EOD Squadron, my relationship with the CO was at rock- bottom. In my opinion, he was a control freak. This became obvious when he took command of the Regiment and he wrote us all a very blunt and harshly worded letter, warning us that he expected the utmost loyalty from us all... or else. His control freakery was confirmed during the time when I was hoping to negotiate my next posting with the senior staff officer who managed our career desk. In a complete reversal of the way things were managed, he ordered all of us Late-Entry officers in the Regiment not to contact the career desk directly; we were to go through him first. Eventually, I got a posting order. I had wanted to go next to a demanding technical staff job to balance my career profile to improve my chances of converting my short service commission to enable a full career. It was not to be; I was posted to Longtown as the Officer in charge of accounts. Longtown was a wonderful place, but it was a quiet backwater; I felt I was 'put out to pasture'. I was greatly disillusioned by this. As a consequence, when I arrived at Longtown, I was already intent on resigning my commission.

CHAPTER 17

Base Ammunition Depot Longtown 1977–1999

arrived at Longtown in late March 1997. I had two years remaining of my Short Service Commission. Not long after arriving, all of us Late-Entry officers still in the first five years of commissioned service were offered an extension of 12 months. I understood this was a manning expedient. I was interviewed by the Commandant, and I declined the extension, saying that I was now committed to putting my family first and leaving the Army. At the time, promotion to major for us was primarily contingent on serving long enough to get into the promotion zone for selection. I was going to retire at five years, before I would be eligible for promotion. I could have hung on, but my heart wasn't in it. I had gotten this far in my career despite vindictive treatment by previous superiors. There are almost invariably two sides to every story, but more than one confidante had revealed to me that some of the officers I had clashed with allegedly had form when it came to trashing the careers of officers and men they disliked. Their words had some resonance for me, and to paraphrase them, their views were similar: "In their ascending wake, as they clawed to the top, there was a debris field of wrecked careers behind them". Another very disturbing revelation concerned Freemasonry, and I had very good reason to deem this credible, but I will not disclose the source lest he be blackballed! In preparation for the move to Longtown, Christine and I had bought a new family home in Dunblane, as we had sold the first home when I got commissioned. Our quarter at RAF Northolt was our last and this signalled an end to the very stressful business of 'marching out' of married quarters. It also meant a departure from the ubiquitous magnolia-coloured walls that seemed to be mandatory in married quarters, however, I must confess that many years after retiring, I still have magnolia-coloured walls in my own home! My spare time in the week gave me the opportunity to indulge in a favourite hobby of radio-controlled model-building and flying. One of my models was a powered paraglider. It featured a fairly realistic gondola, when viewed at height, containing a dummy pilot, and I learned to extend its limited flight duration by catching thermals. I could launch and recover this model by hand, so I didn't need a take-off strip. One day outside the mess, I heard the approaching sound of the SATO's wife's Citroen 2CV as she drove through the back gate. However, the sound didn't get louder and I realised she was driving around in circles. Eventually, she appeared from behind a large windbreak of Leylandii trees and I saw that she was looking up at the sky through the driver's side window. Then she saw me with the tell-tale transmitter in my hand and the penny dropped. "JOHN ROBINSON, it's you! I thought it was a parachutist falling into the depot!"

I built several large models whilst I was there and I specialised in quarter-scale WW1 fighters, one of which is still flying today, 25 years after being built, as a trainer in a model aircraft club. My boss at the time was quite absorbed by my hobby, and on one occasion, he scrambled up the mess chimney to recover the paraglider where I had got it stuck. June, the mess Chief Steward, gave him a right telling-off. My hobby was even reported in detail in my annual confidential report with my bedroom in the mess being described as "An aircraft factory". I didn't mind; I didn't need any more 'ticks in boxes'.

Having resolved to leave the Army, I focused on what was left of my time. There had been a lot of re-organisation since the formation of the Royal Logistic Corps. Much of it was essential and quite proper but I sensed the drive to efficiency, on a par with car manufacturers, was being over-played and a lot of proposed efficiencies were, in my opinion, driving us towards some potentially unsafe practices. I found myself to be a part of the Army Base Storage and Distribution Agency (ABSDA). I was sent to attend a Total Quality Management (TQM) course. On this course, I was openly derided for not allowing soldiers to address me by my first name. This was indeed a clash of cultures! I thought the tenets of TQM were sound, if perhaps derived from basic common sense. On returning to Longtown after the course, I presided over several 'Quality Circles' where the workers themselves would consider how to solve problems. I was impressed by the way the staff in the Control Office collaborated; they were loyal, knowledgeable and fully committed to the units who we issued ammunition to; or should I say customers?

There was a sad occasion whereby redundancies were being planned. In the Control Office we had several E1 Administrative Officers, each managing a discrete part of the inventory of ammunition in the depot; at that time 80,000 tons, valued at about £2billion. The people conducting a review of our staffing levels made a simple assumption. As there were several E1s, there must be duplication. Future employment was threatened. When the announcement on job cuts was to be made to Depot staff, industrials and non-industrials alike, attendance was restricted to trade union members only. The staff in the Control

Office not in a recognised TU would have to ask for this very relevant information second-hand. I was affronted by this; they were good people and deserved better.

The drive to enhanced efficiency caused me many misgivings. A number of our safety- conservative ammunition processes were deemed to be too conservative, and the outcome was to reduce ammunition inspection activity, including in the case of ammunition which had been returned unfired. It was easy for the commercially minded to persuade the policy-makers to change our procedures to save money. It looked good on paper but my lifetime of experience on how potentially unsafe this could be was largely ignored as 'Luddite'. Perhaps there was some truth in this. An interesting problem arose in ammunition accounting for stock that had been deployed to support operations in the Balkan theatre. There were two streams of accounting in force at the time: Ammunition was either on the depot account or it was on a unit account. The trouble was that there was an intermediary stage of ammunition holding. Ammunition could be held on ships at sea or in land-based compounds. There was a complicated interface between operational ammunition and training ammunition. The upshot was that a huge discrepancy arose which attracted the attention of the National Audit Office (NAO). I had seen this happen before in the Falkland Islands, after the 1982 conflict and also after the First Gulf War. Peacetime accounting lacked the flexibility to manage ammunition accounting during operations. It was said that large amounts of ammunition had been lost; this conclusion was drawn by the NAO as we could not prove what had happened to the stock we had issued. I can only hope matters have improved.

At Longtown, we had a thriving officers' mess, and I was the sole occupant during the week, commuting home to Dunblane at weekends. The staff in the mess were all civil servants, not contractors, and they took massive pride in all they did. The mess enjoyed a well-deserved reputation for hospitality, and we regularly hosted MoD guests on official business who preferred to stay with us rather than at nearby hotels. The viability of our mess was questioned by anonymous budget staff high-up in ABSDA. Its operating cost was deemed wasteful, and its closure was recommended. I understood that the review of operating costs ignored its utility and income as a guest venue and that Longtown was also the headquarters of Cumbria Garrison. The breakfast the staff would provide for guests was legendary and, having stayed in the officers' mess at Stirling Lines in Herford, I can vouch for their breakfast being marginally superior to an SAS breakfast! The faceless ones on high got their wish and the mess was to close. They were allowed to ignore the requirement in Queen's Regulations for the provision of a mess to serving officers and I was offered alternative accommodation for my last three months of service in a 5-star hotel at Gretna. So much for progress. The mess was demolished almost immediately after I departed, and I was left wondering what had happened to the Visitor's Book. This book contained an amazing entry from VE Night in 1945, and all the officers present had signed their names. I finished my time and left. Our family home in Dunblane was now well-established and our planning for my resettlement had at least solved one half of the double-whammy of leaving the Army; avoiding homelessness. All I had to do now was find a job!

As Longtown was also the headquarters of Cumbria Garrison, we were responsible for delivering certain aspects of administration in that county and this included casualty notification to the next of kin of soldiers who had died in service. I performed this important duty twice during my final tour and, to the best of my ability, as I believed this was a noble duty. One afternoon, I was contacted by the divisional headquarters and given very patchy information about the next of kin of a soldier who had died. The mother was next of kin, and it turned out for all sorts of reasons that the information was grossly misleading, and the only reliable fact was the town where she lived. I believed the MoD was to issue a press release on the early evening news and the last thing I wanted was for the mother to find out that way; she deserved better. I went to the town and asked the local police. I was put in touch with a protestant church minister who was also an Armed Forces Chaplain in the Reserves. After some enquiries, we tracked her down and broke the news with due solemnity and just before she was to go to the bingo. The family requested the funeral be conducted in a Roman Catholic chapel, close to the family home, despite the family being Protestant. I left that in the hands of the Chaplain who had accompanied me. The next morning, the divisional headquarters staff phoned me to say thanks, relieved that the mother had been found and notified appropriately. The caller then said the Senior Chaplain in the division wanted to speak to me and handed him the phone. The pompous git chewed me out for arranging a funeral in an RC chapel for a Protestant soldier. I put him straight on that one in very short order; so much for Christian compassion.

Whist at Longtown, there was a politically driven influence campaign in progress about the so-called Gulf War Syndrome. The new Government sent me a letter saying they were committed to getting to the bottom of it. I was sent a questionnaire by the Gulf Veteran's Illness Unit (GVIU). One question concerned my possible proximity to Scud missile incidents and the answer format was multi-choice, where the options related to how close I might have been to a missile. I think the nearest distance offered was about 1 km, but I wrote in clear terms 'none of the above – I was inside one'. I knew that would wrinkle some brows and, sure enough, I ended up being interviewed twice about it. In Chapter 14, I have described my involvement in the Scud missile impact in Al Jubayl. When I returned to Al Jubayl in mid-March, the US Navy EOD Team had recovered virtually the whole missile and the empty tankage section was lying on the quayside. It had been immersed in sea water for the best part of a month, there was no obvious hazardous fuel or oxidiser and I wanted to examine the weld used to extend the tankage section to increase the missile's range. So, I climbed inside and took several photographs. The quality of the circumferential weld was impressive. It looked as though it had been done by a machine as the consistency was too good for it to have been done manually. With hindsight, the GVIU questionnaire had apparently been designed for Mr Average Squaddie in average conditions and there were several questions where the multi-choice answers offered were not appropriate to EOD personnel. No matter: I personally did not subscribe to the view that there was a Gulf War Syndrome. In expressing that view, I am not denying that a lot of people got very sick after the conflict but, having been intimately involved with depleted uranium ammunition, exposed to large volumes of high-energy propellant smoke, work in the burning oilfields, vaccinated against anthrax and plague and on Nerve Agent Pre-treatment System (NAPS) for several weeks, not to mention all the insecticides, if anyone was likely to get it, it would likely be me and my EOD colleagues.

In the depot, we had long-serving civilian staff who had a great pride in the history of the region. One man was a respected local historian and has appeared in a least one TV documentary speaking about the shell shortage crisis in the Great War and how this resulted in the development of His Majesty's Factory Gretna on the Solway Firth coast in southwest Scotland. Mention of Gretna might evoke recollections of young couples from England eloping there to marry but the bigger concern was the manufacture of cordite to resolve the shell crisis. The undertaking was huge, and the government undertook measures to improve efficiency by, for example, reducing the strength of beer and the use of licensing laws to restrict pub opening hours. The whole project greatly assisted the war effort, but the unseen cost was the health of the workers. Gun cotton was manufactured in vast quantities and contemporary photographs show the largely female work force mixing the explosive with their bare hands in the nitrating pans where the pasty mixture became known as the 'Devil's Porridge', a sobriquet credited to Sir Arthur Conan Doyle after one of his visits there. The local history of Gretna is worthy of many published works, but this is my story, so what I have included here is sufficient, I hope, to give a sense of how special Longtown was and is to this day. The local historian's interests even extended to the Roman occupation of Britain, and he was actively researching the remains of their infrastructure whilst I was there. He spoke passionately about the local Roman roads, forts and their use of the prominent Burnswark Hill, several miles north to the east of the present A74(M). To this day, as I commute along that road, I make a point of looking over at the hill, imagining its fascinating history from Iron Age hill fort to its capture by the Romans. When I left Longtown, Gordon Routledge was researching the possibility that a Roman road led directly from the site of a suspected camp in the Longtown depot to Burnswark and I also heard the remains of a Roman road were found after the officers' mess was demolished. After the Romans and then the contribution made to winning the Great War, I suspect fate isn't quite finished with that area yet.

CHAPTER 18

Christine

As I planned this book, I started with the notion of leaving a record of my life for my family. This notion expanded into possibly publishing my biography, assuming I could find a way to publish, with two charities benefitting from any profits. It was going to be by me and about me. As I approached the end of the first draft, I started to realise that I couldn't finish without writing about Christine. I probably came close to mental illness twice during my life. I'll now talk about those times briefly because it builds context and shows how important it is to have the love and support of a loyal partner.

At the age of 19, I was put through psychometric testing. I was already a qualified class 2 Ammunition Technician in the rank of corporal but failing this test could have resulted in my having to leave the trade. This happened to a friend of mine, and I recently learned of his story, directly from him. After failing the test, he was whisked away like a bad smell. Although he retained his rank, he was ordered to remove his trade badge, the 'Flaming A', as he arrived at the guardroom of his new barracks and, for me, it was reminiscent of the public shaming and cashiering of Alfred Dreyfuss in 1895. Whilst this action was administrative, it felt more like punishment. I knew John quite well and he was a loyal friend and good company. From the outset of this testing policy, I was sceptical about its value and I still am. There is a parallel between mental and physical fitness testing. My view is that the authorities wanted a cheap and simple Go/No Go test and, to be blunt, I thought they were trying to 'cover their arses' because of the high casualty rate in N Ireland. I thought the most likely cause of high casualties was due to a poor or immature EOD doctrine in the early days and this was to improve as time went by. My point is that my mental capacity for avoiding killing myself in a career in bomb disposal, was assessed in a one-day paper test and that test was adapted from one used to see if submariners were stable enough to cope with long periods of time submerged at sea. Then I had to re-sit the test after I was over 25 because that age was deemed to be a watershed in the mental development of young men. The parallel I mention was with another test of capacity, this time, physical fitness. As a recruit, I experienced an all-round approach to physical development and fitness. Regular sessions in the gymnasium, confidence courses, assault courses and the litmus test was the 'March and Shoot'. In a squad, carrying a weapon and a standard load of equipment, you did a route march of 7 miles. Immediately on completion, you did a test-shoot on a range. In those days, our recruits and soldiers were fat, thin, tall and short. As you marched, you would be urged on by instructors. The Army has a saying that you can only march as fast as the slowest man. The slow people would be moved forward to the front of the marching squad. If they floundered, they would be 'encouraged', not just by a possibly heavy-handed instructor, but by the rest of the squad. It wasn't about being an individual. The squad had to complete the test together. The fitter men would carry the slowest man's equipment. In some cases, the exhausted would be physically assisted to the finish line. There was group cohesion and inclusion in this, even before the term inclusion came into popular use.

Army policy for fitness testing, certainly in my corps, changed in the early 1970s to the Basic Fitness Test (BFT). This test would take less than 30 minutes. Without equipment or weapon, a squad would march and jog 1.5 miles together, timed to take 15 minutes. When this distance was reached, the squad would immediately run a further 1.5 miles, but this time, as best effort as individuals. Your age dictated how much time you were allowed. This test was taken annually. In many cases, despite other testing techniques being applied inconsistently, this was the only test, especially in working units where productivity at work was a higher priority. The bottom line was that my mental fitness was tested at 19 and 25, both times with a written test. My physical fitness for most of my career was tested annually for half an hour. With mental fitness, if an ammunition technician had an issue, you were toast; gone. There may have been exceptions but I'm talking about me and my experiences. If you couldn't pass the BFT, you could be discharged; gone. What was missing was a consistent approach to maintaining fitness of both kinds, between or after any testing regime. Some units, depending on their role, could programme physical fitness training into working time but official policy was that fitness was an individual and personal responsibility.

I said I would speak of two occasions when my mental health suffered. These occasions should not be confused with short-term confidence crises. I would characterise these two occasions as periods of extreme and prolonged mental anguish where there was no support and I felt isolated. Since this chapter is about Christine, I will describe the difference it made to have her in my life.

The first example of extreme mental anguish arose in 1982. My first marriage had been rocky from the outset to say the least. With two small children to cope with, my first wife needed welfare support from the authorities at Kineton. I returned from my 1979 EOD tour in Belfast to find myself marched in front of the CO to be reproached about my wife being a burden on them while I was away. I took this on the chin and promised to try and do better in future (as if). What was completely overlooked was the total lack of organised support for the wives and families of the very small numbers of ammunition technicians deployed to N Ireland.

There were hundreds of troops and families based at Kineton. Out of this large number, only two ammunition technicians were away on operations at that time. To contrast with this lack of care, in the formed-up units deploying to N Ireland, there were organised rear parties with specific welfare resources to support families. Our unhappy marriage had a history of temporary separations but, each time, the service authorities' focus seemed to be on achieving reconciliation at any cost. In 1980, I applied for a tour of duty in Hong Kong and was subsequently posted there. In Hong Kong, our relationship worsened and, on a memorable occasion, an officer I knew very well pleaded with me not to separate from my wife for the good of the unit and other wives and families. Eventually, I asked permission to move into the Sergeants' Mess to remove myself from the marital home. This was flatly refused. I had been drinking heavily throughout this period and deliberately working long hours to avoid being at home because it had become a toxic environment.

Throughout this time, I was accused of being a wife-beater and a latent homosexual. I was placed on a warning order which would result in my discharge from the Army if my alleged misconduct did not improve. I was ordered to attend an appointment with a medical officer to have my sexual orientation established. All of this came to a climax as I was alone in the ammunition depot on Stonecutter's Island, waiting for a ferry to go over to Kowloon and then Hong Kong Island to face the music. I expected to be disciplined, possibly discharged from the Army and maybe even court-martialled; I was quite paranoid. I felt completely isolated and trapped. I stood behind an ammunition store in the shade and turned things over in my head. I then realised I was shaking, quite violently, and gasping. I didn't know what a panic attack was at the time, but this was one. As I desperately reached for a solution, it came to me. I needed to stick to my guns, press for a permanent separation leading to divorce and accept that the cost of getting this done would be that I would probably never see my children, then aged three and one, ever again. I don't really do emotions, but the logic of this solution was unassailable. As I resolved to do this, the shaking reduced, and I immediately started to feel calmer.

I boarded the ferry to Kowloon where I was to be interviewed by the commanding officer. As I was already on a warning order, I thought something else was going to be raised which would worsen things. When I was marched in, I was informed that the warning order had been rescinded on the instructions of RAOC Manning and Records Office in the UK (in civilian-speak, this was the corporate HR department). I left puzzled at this turn of events and then went to see the Medical Officer at HMS Tamar on Hong Kong Island. He was in the Royal Navy, and I'd never seen him before. He was kindly and sympathetic. He listened as I told him of the panic attack and how I'd resolved to sort things out. As to my alleged homosexuality, I sensed he was appalled at the way this had been handled and that he was somehow expected to make a judgement on it. He gave me some pertinent lifestyle advice, assured me he did not think I was a homosexual and wished me well for my future. The rest is history, as they say, and I was not to see my children again until they were adults. As all of this was happening, a warrant officer phoned me from the Army Pay and Documentation Office (APDO) at Kowloon (this was another HR department). He had seen the paperwork going to and from the UK. He said he could not intervene but did say my superiors were acting outside normal manning procedures in their apparent haste to get rid of me. He urged me to take heart and soldier on despite what my own officers were saying and doing which he characterised as an 'abuse of power' over me. This kindly intervention meant a lot to me.

This crisis was well before I met Christine. I was sent back to the UK a month after my first wife left Hong Kong, as my separation was said to be incompatible with continued service there. I sensed this was a 'symbolic sacking' and still feel this way today, over 40 years later. To be fair, society was different then and military society, ever more lagging behind general society, more so. When I reported for duty at HQ 521 EOD Company in Catterick, the officer commanding assured me that he was in my court and would protect me from any further flak arising out of the acrimonious separation. What really made it high profile was that my first wife's twin brother, an RUC Constable, was murdered by terrorists just after she left Hong Kong. Some of the service authorities were pressing for me to apply for a married quarter for her at my new posting but I stuck to my guns and refused. My new boss was supportive of this but many others, more senior, were not.

After arriving at Edinburgh, I was based at Craigiehall. A financial settlement for maintenance was brokered through the courts process and, in the days before the Child Support Agency (CSA), a court order was issued. The payment was a very large portion of my disposable income. I arranged to pay the maintenance through the Army Pay

Order Book (APOB) system. For the first nine months at Edinburgh, my pay account was in arrears, and I received no salary. On the back of my pay statement was a reconciliation sheet and this showed big numbers on it, owed by me to them. Encouragingly, however, this number got smaller as the months progressed. I lived in the Sergeants' Mess, I had already given up drinking alcohol, I hadn't smoked since being a teenager and it was possible to get by on next to nothing and my meals were provided for me in the Mess. As I was regularly driving all over Scotland, dealing mostly with wartime unexploded objects, I was able to get some money from travel and subsistence claims and so life was not too bad. The shadow of what had happened in Hong Kong hung over my head. The thought of another relationship was far from my mind; anyway, what woman in her right mind would mix it with a nearly divorced father of two children up to his neck in maintenance payments? I started to suffer from insomnia over concerns for the welfare of my children, which I knew was affecting me at work. I consulted the civilian medical practitioner who was our medical officer (the equivalent of a GP). I reported the symptoms of insomnia and asked if I could be prescribed anything that might improve my sleep. His reply, noting that I was a bomb disposal operator, was that if he did diagnose stress-induced insomnia, that I would be immediately relieved of my duties. He gave me a stark choice: I could walk out of the consultation and there would be no record made, or I could continue with medical intervention with the consequences he had outlined. Nowadays, we might refer to this as being 'between a rock and a hard place'. There was nobody to turn to. I considered applying for the custody of my children and discussed this with Army Legal Services. The advice was blunt; this arrangement would likely render me incapable of operational duties and was incompatible with continued military service.

One day in mid-1983, a friend of mine, another ammunition technician who lived in the mess, suggested I go out with him and his new girl-friend on a blind date. He was persistent and I was initially reluctant. I had become something of a recluse, I still had very little money and almost no civilian clothing. My only leisure activity, duties allowing, was that I would catch a bus to Edinburgh on the weekend and walk for miles around the city and up and around Arthur's Seat. I found these trips to be immensely calming. At work, I was somewhat prick-ly and overly sensitive, so I kept myself to myself. Another welcome distraction was running. I joined the Hash House Harriers, and I also took to running long distances. A favourite route was out of Craigiehall and up the A90 towards Fife. I would run over the bridge and a few miles into Fife before turning back. The wind could be awesome on the bridge. Depending on its direction, the wind at my back would make me soar huge paces but, in the opposite direction, the wind in my face would have me lean forwards like a ski-jumper and my face would go numb with the wind-chill-driven cold. I recall one such run where I had a nasty fright. I was running along the A90 on the grassy verge. On the TV news had been coverage of the disappearance of five-year-old Caroline Hogg. The wind was in my face and was affecting my vision. About 100 metres in front of me was a bundle of clothing on the grass. For some reason, I suspected something sinister and wiped my eyes to get a better look. With about 20 metres to go, I had convinced myself the bundle was a child. As I drew closer, I was mightily relieved to see it was just a discarded coat. Your eyes can play tricks on you, and this was unpleasant but at least it wasn't the body of an innocent child.

Despite my protests, I agreed to the blind date. My mystery date was to be the cousin of Ron's girlfriend. Problem was, I had very little to wear on a night out. This excuse was dismissed by Ron who borrowed some items of clothing for me to wear. I felt a right Wally. I had utterly no self-confidence and felt like running away. I would have found a manual approach to a suspect bomb far less challenging! The venue for the date was the Crammond Brig pub, just over the road from Craigie-hall. I knew of it as I would regularly walk from the camp and pass the pub on the way down to the sea, along the river on one of my many walking routes. The date itself was not memorable. There were polite introductions, small talk and then we all parted. My recollection was that the girl was very young, very quiet and I would probably never see her again. The girl was Christine. She was 21, I was 28 and I thought the age difference too wide for us to have anything in common. She managed the Lennards Shoe Shop in the St James Centre in the city. Ron's girlfriend was called Anna. She was the chef in our Mess, so I saw her most days. She lived nearby in Winchburgh with her parents and Christine lodged with them. Christine's actual home was in the Cornton at Stirling, and she lived in Winchburgh to be closer to work. The match-making persisted and there were a few more dates. One evening, I realised that something was developing between Christine and me. I panicked. I didn't feel ready even for a casual relationship. However, I went with the flow. I said it before: What woman in her right mind would mix it with a nearly divorced father of two children?

The frequency of dating increased, and it reached the point where we had both realised we were 'an item'. One night, we were in the Tally Ho pub in Winchburgh and we had been joined by two of Anna's girlfriends. As the conversation about another couple developed, one of girlfriends exclaimed, "And it turns out, she's going with a married man with two kids". My divorce hadn't yet come through at that point and, although I wasn't the subject of the conversation, I felt quite humiliated and the ensuing, embarrassed silence was painful.

Christine made it abundantly clear that my immediate past history did not concern her. We drew ever closer in just three months. I went on a 10-day inspection tour of the British Army Training and Liaison Unit Kenya (BATLUSK) and the separation angst from being away from her was very telling. We decided to get married at some time in the future. We went looking for an engagement ring in Prince's Street Edinburgh and Christine picked out a modestly priced but nice-looking ring. We didn't notice that my Troop Commander was nearby. The following Monday morning, at our scheduled Troop Briefing, he reproached me in front of the whole Troop for not seeking his permission to marry first. This was to be the beginning of a bad relationship with that particular officer which persisted until 1997.

Christine became a both a loyal companion and a mentor. Just before we met, I had applied to go on an unaccompanied Loan Service tour in the Sultanate of Oman. In late 1983, I got a posting order. We faced the prospect of almost two years apart. We decided to marry and I applied for a surplus married quarter in Edinburgh. Two weeks after marrying her in St Margaret's Chapel in Edinburgh Castle, I flew to Oman. Christine continued her work with Lennards, commuting from our Army house at Dreghorn. My tour in Oman was very busy but was great fun. I missed Christine dreadfully, but we got through it. We saved enough money during that time to put a deposit on our first home in Dunblane. We were never able to live in this home as I was to spend the rest of my time in the Army too far from Dunblane. With the unconditional love and support of Christine, and the stability she gifted me, I was able to put this first bout of extreme mental anguish behind me and move on.

21 April 1984 – Just married and posing with Christine's parents. The day was cold, windy and bleak but the weather turned sunny later.

The second extreme mental anguish happened in 2015. I might start by explaining why I use this phrase 'extreme mental anguish'. I am not qualified to make objective statements about the many mental health issues we are all susceptible to. All I can say is that my two bouts were extreme but I remained 'high-functioning' despite them. I never experienced a total loss of self-control which might be classed as a breakdown, but the events of 2015 onwards came very close to it.

In late 2014, Christine had found a lump in her breast. She went straight to her GP and was fast-tracked to a triple test. The test was negative but the quality of communication between consultant and patient was poor. Her doubts continued and she was re-referred two more times. It was clear from the outset that there were cultural issues that played a part in the consultation. The consultant was an Asian man but he didn't have a reassuring rapport with Christine; perhaps this could be re-phrased as a lack of 'bedside manner'. Throughout all of these three consultations, I was present in the same room and there was also a nurse chaperone present. I was always very sensitive to the question of my being racially biased and this held me back from being perhaps a little more pro-active as things progressed. It started as soon as we entered the consulting room. The consultant turned his back on me and completely ignored me. As he spoke to Christine, he identified the wrong breast.

Christine was so anxious that she didn't correct his error. I politely intervened but the look on the consultant's face was disparaging. The consultation continued but the rapport between them remained remote and distant. We eventually departed after a day of clinical examination, ultrasound and radiographic imagery and a biopsy by needle aspiration. His clinical techniques seemed perfectly fine but his eventual decision of 'negative' sounded totally unconvincing. I have rarely been so studiously ignored as I was in that room. A few weeks later, we were back. The outcome was the same as before and I was completely ignored. I formed the opinion that the consultant had some kind of profound social disability. On the third visit, one thing was different; there was a female student present as well as the nurse. As we were ushered in, I noted that she had put two chairs together in front of the consultant. Previously, my chair had been in the corner behind the door, rendering me completely incommunicado. The consultation started and I noted the consultant avoided eye contact with me. To be fair to him, I could see he was very concerned with Christine's anxiety. He reviewed the previous results and then the third triple test session started. Later on, we returned to his office. The chairs were in the same place. I sensed the next conversation could be awkward. He announced today's test results were negative and then offered Christine an elective mastectomy of the breast affected by the lump on the grounds of her anxiety. I was mortified. I then intervened, politely, and tried to act as Christine's advocate. I then noticed that his computer monitor could only be seen by him. He kept pointing at it but we could not see what he was pointing at. I asked him to explain the results of the imagery. He said the suspicious lump was diffuse and that the biopsy could not be guaranteed to have sampled in the right place. I then asked why an ultrasound-guided biopsy couldn't be done and, with some exasperation, he swivelled the screen around to face us and said, "There's nothing to see". And he was right. And then the penny dropped. For a reason lost in the world of conversational nuances, he had never previously made it clear that the diffuse lump could not be seen on any of the imagery. These things happen but this outcome was bitter-sweet. Christine didn't have breast cancer, but we had both been through a hellish period of worry. Outside, we spoke to the nurse who said she was not surprised; this consultant was known to have communications issues with his patients.

As a mother of two children and now being in her early 50s, Christine did have a small issue with piles. Nothing serious but she saw a GP in September 2014. The GP re-assured her that it was probably OK and these things can flare up. I think there was some advice about increasing fibre in her diet and that was that. Christine did not seem concerned at all. She would go on regular walks with her friend and had a healthy lifestyle. In late February 2015, she saw a GP again about the same issue but this was a different GP. She gave her an examination and said she was going to fast track her for a sigmoidoscopy. Two weeks later, I took her for the procedure at the local district hospital. When she emerged, she was very distressed and couldn't speak. The procedure had been extremely painful and she had panicked. A biopsy had been taken. I got her home and she eventually calmed down. I had my own health concerns and was due to undergo a shoulder distension procedure for a frozen shoulder. This was done and when I got home, I erected a system of ropes and pulleys I could use to give the shoulder non-loadbearing exercise. I set this up on the upstairs landing, using the attic hatch. In a spare bedroom we used as a study, Christine was working on her Doctorate thesis when I heard the phone ring. I got on with my exercises but about a minute later, I heard Christine say in an anxious voice, "But you're making me worried now and I don't want to wait". I instantly knew she was in trouble. I went into the room and Christine said to the caller, "So you're saying I have cancer". At that point, I only had one half of the conversation. The call was from a clinical nurse specialist (CNS) at the hospital who wanted her to come in for MRI and CT scans following her sigmoidoscopy.

Christine rightly knew these scans were expensive and not undertaken lightly. The nurse explained it was against protocols to give news of a diagnosis on the phone but, as Christine was now very worried, she explained the biopsy had disclosed an anal cancer. Instead of arranging appointments for a scan, the call concluded with an arrangement to meet a consultant the following day. Overnight, we googled 'anal cancer' to death. We were both upset but it looked like the cancer had been caught early and could be curable.

We reported to Outpatients the next day and sat in the usual waiting room. After a short wait, a tall lady appeared and spoke to the Receptionist who nodded in our direction. She came over, introduced herself and asked us to follow her. Strikingly, she wasn't wearing scrubs and was very smartly dressed. Something seemed odd. We were familiar with the layout of this outpatients from the previous year's breast cancer appointments but, instead of taking us to a consulting room, we were ushered into a small room to one side that I hadn't previously noticed. There was nothing clinical about this room. It had subdued lighting, paintings on the walls, three comfortable armchairs and flowers on an occasional table. Without saying anything to Christine, I suspected this was a 'bad news' room. The well-dressed lady was the CNS who had called the day before. She left and returned a minute later to say the consultant was ready. We went in and were welcomed and he introduced himself. After a quick review of Christine's initial symptoms and that a sigmoidoscopy had been carried out, he suddenly became more intense. I noticed that he had positioned his chair directly in front of Christine. I was very much a part of the meeting, but he had leaned forward and started to talk in deliberate and careful tones. He told Christine that the biopsy result had disclosed the presence of mucosal melanoma. From a photograph, they knew the tumour was 11mm long, it was black and was positioned over the anal sphincter. He outlined potential courses of action. The simplest one was to simply excise the tumour, but he would have to ensure a margin of tissue around the tumour was taken too. That would almost certainly result in permanent anal incontinence and there was a greater chance of spread. The more complex surgery was called Abdominal Perineal Resection (APR). This would entail the removal of the lower bowel and the entire anus. The remaining bowel would be attached to the stomach wall and would terminate outside the body in a colostomy bag. We were both too shocked to speak. The consultant concluded his briefing with what seemed to be a carefully prepared and rehearsed statement. "The best you can hope for is a colostomy for the rest of your life". There was a brutal ambiguity in what he said. Inside my head, I heard 'the best you can hope for is a colostomy for <u>what's left</u> of your life'. He went on to mention that recent advances in immunotherapy were increasing survival rates for this cancer. He hoped the operation would be curative, but he had to await the scan results to see if there had already been any spread.

The next few days were weird. We were both up and down. We hoped the scans would be good. It turned out they were, or so we were initially told. Christine was scheduled for exploratory surgery the following week with the big APR operation a week later. I would complement the majority of NHS staff, clinical and non-clinical, who we met, but there were horrible exceptions, and I will detail what happened with them as we entered the ordeal of cancer treatment.

For the exploratory surgery, she was admitted as a day case, which was right. What wasn't right was that we waited for hours after she had changed into a gown in a crowded waiting room. In itself, perhaps of no consequence, but it was like Piccadilly Circus. The staff kept losing track of their patients and there was a classic waiting-room stress environment. The worst part was that an elderly gentleman was sat in a wheelchair next to us and it was apparent he had moderate dementia. He kept moaning as he was obviously in pain. This went on for ages. We were no different to anyone else and didn't merit any special treatment and didn't expect it but we didn't expect this 'cattle-truck' treatment either.

A week later, we were back. Christine's surgery was expected to take at least six hours, so she was first on the list. She was quite distressed and the staff wanted me to leave. But I accompanied her to a large open-plan ward where there were about a dozen cubicles, separated by curtains. The stoma nurses came in to mark her abdomen where the stoma was to be sited. Stoma nurses have some of the best empathy and patient care skills I have ever seen. Christine was quite disgusted by the prospect of pooing uncontrollably in a bag but the Stoma nurses understand that. Then came time for her to walk to the anaesthetic room. I accompanied her to the door. The consultant saw me and as I left with her dressing gown and slippers, he walked with me towards the exit. He said carefully that I should trust him; I did, but my Christine was not going to walk alone; anywhere.

I wandered around the hospital's open areas in a complete daze. I went into the chapel to be alone. I am an atheist but I am basically a spiritual person. I sat quietly in there for about an hour. As I left to go home, the news on one of the waiting room televisions spoke of a crashed Germanwings airliner. I got home and sat in a chair. I didn't move until the phone rang hours later in the afternoon. The surgeon explained the operation had gone well and Christine was in recovery and I could come in to see her once she had been transferred to a ward. This puzzled me somewhat. I had understood she would spend some time in the high-dependency unit. Instead, she was to be placed in a single room at the end of a large ward. When I got to the hospital, I found her in a single room. The nurse said she was doing alright and that they were short-staffed. I went into her room where she was lying on a bed, propped up, with oxygen, drips and monitors attached to her. She acknowledged my presence but was well out of it. Then two nurses came in and said she was to stand up and then spend a while seated in the patient chair next to the bed. I understood the merit of mobilising patients quickly and was greatly encouraged as Christine got off the bed and moved to the chair. After half an hour or so, the Stoma nurses appeared to carry out the first post-operative change of her colostomy bag. I asked if I could do it under their supervision. They readily agreed and I got on with it. I was emotionally overwhelmed to care for Christine in this way and it filled me with a new optimism that things would turn out alright. I also felt I was contributing to her care instead of just being a useless spare wheel.

Now for some of the bad bits. There was an air-conditioning unit somewhere above her bed, above the suspended ceiling. It was powerful and very noisy. There was a perpetual whistling sound of rushing air coming through the door. I stayed with her after she got back into bed. She was very tired and thirsty. I gave her sips of water and noticed her saline drip was empty. I went out to the nurse's station and told them it had gone dry. They said they were short-staffed, but someone would attend to it soon. Christine always had quite low blood pressure and, although it was normal for her, it kept tripping the alarm on the monitor. She was on a morphine pump but reacted badly to the drug becoming mildly angry but confused. She wanted me to stay with her. Nobody said I was to leave, which I would have respected. I ended up sitting with her all night. I had gone out again to tell the new shift of nurses that Christine's saline drip was still dry, but nobody came to replenish it. I kept giving her sips of water and talking to her each time she woke, usually because the blood pressure alarm had disturbed her. At about 2 am, a student nurse came in and asked if I would like a cup of tea. I hadn't eaten or drunk anything since 7 am the previous morning. I couldn't get the words out in answer to her and felt embarrassed as I broke down, trying to stifle the sobs in case Christine heard me. The nurse returned a few minutes later with tea and sandwiches. I was still there in the morning when a doctor swept in with a different nurse right behind him. This one had the bedside manner of Atilla The Hun. He checked Christine and declared she was febrile and dehydrated.

Then he asked who I was. I explained and said I had repeatedly asked for her saline drip to be replenished. He seemed more cross about me being there rather than with the apparent neglect over the saline drip. Then the nurse turned on the charm (not). She was, by accent, a Glaswegian. She kept addressing me as 'Pal' loudly and in a manner which felt aggressive. I asked her to use my name, but she persisted with 'Pal'. I was asked to wait outside whilst nursing things were conducted. As I went out, I said I knew the Stoma nurses were due back and that I was to change her colostomy bag. When I was allowed back in, all of that had been done and Christine was sitting in the chair. She was upset and as I was talking to her, another doctor came in, did a quick check of her and then reproved me for staying with Christine. He accused me of having an infantile insecurity for not leaving after visiting the previous night and that when his wife had a recent surgery, he was man enough to leave her in the ward alone, so why didn't I? All this happened in front of Christine. I asked for the opportunity to address his criticisms, but he said he had to go. Later in the morning, the surgeon came in to see Christine. We both complained of the brusque manner of the two doctors and although he didn't respond, he was clearly not pleased. I left to go home just after that. Christine had to discontinue the morphine because of the way she reacted. Unbelievably, the only pain relief she had needed after that was paracetamol tablets. Day by day, she got better and was ready for discharge earlier than expected. After I got her home, she was recalled for another operation. Pathology results showed that they hadn't achieved cancer-clear margins around where her bottom used to be. This third operation troubled her the most and the new scar wouldn't heal. I took over changing her dressings and could see why things weren't working out. The dressings being applied were cut from bigger dressings and the wound wasn't being protected. I modified the way the dressing was shaped and the difference that made was dramatic. Christine couldn't yet face changing her colostomy bag so I did it for her; it was the least I could do.

Her referral to the Beatson Oncology Hospital in Glasgow was scheduled for about six weeks after her operation. As the day approached, it was clear she couldn't sit upright in my car for a journey of that length. We requested patient transport, explaining that she would need to be laid down in transit. The booking was accepted but only on the basis that I didn't accompany her in the ambulance because I wasn't entitled. The way this was put to me on the phone was quite confrontational. The only option was that I should follow the ambulance in my car. Then I explained she had a new colostomy which was still behaving unpredictably, and could they assure us that a competent person would be there in case things got bad. I was asked who her carer was and I said it was me. That still posed a problem as I was not entitled. I spoke to the Stoma Nurses and one of them saw red. Stoma nurses tend to be capable of very straight talking when it comes to 'jobsworths'. Another phone call was made and when the ambulance crew turned up, they couldn't have been nicer.

At Christine's first meeting with her Oncologist, we asked about scans and the likely prognosis. We were told bluntly that the scans would see little because of scar tissue. Scans would also expose her to the risk of excessive radiation and she could find herself upstairs on the ward with end-stage leukaemia. The prognosis was declared to be that the operation had been curative. The Oncologist was not prepared to discuss anything else until after the next scheduled scans due in about 6 months. In the intervening period, she got used to walking again with a Zimmer frame and although I am not a celebrity watcher, Christine wanted me to walk her the few hundred yards from our house in Dunblane down to the Perth Road. Andy Murray was getting married that day in Dunblane Cathedral. His expected route to the reception at Cromlix House was along the Perth road. As we arrived at the Kippendavie crossroads, the cathedral bells pealed for the end of the ceremony. Minutes later, the wedding car approached us. Christine perked up immediately. Then her day was made when an impish youth pressed the button on the pedestrian crossing lights. They switched to red and the newlywed's car had to stop, right in front of where we were standing. Christine waved at them, and they smiled and waved back. She was overjoyed; I was too because she was.

The time came for the first post-operative scans at the Beatson. When we attended for the results, the news was not good and this is where I really started to lose the plot with the oncologist. Whether he was trying too hard to be optimistic is my preferred theory but, from the get-go, he seemed quite flippant. He had already dismissed the notion that Christine's cancer was rare. Well, trust me, it was. The statistics at the time were a little inconsistent but they showed the incidence of anal mucosal melanoma to be between one and two persons in a million. I asked the MacMillan organisation for information. They had plenty for skin cancer melanoma but nothing on mucosal melanoma. We were told that the latest scans had revealed lesions in both of her lungs. In short, we went from curative to advanced cancer with a very bleak prognosis. This wasn't anyone's fault but when the options for further investigation and treatment were discussed, there was a disclosure which I felt belonged to the obsolete world of 'doctor knows best'. The oncologist explained that he was confident that the newly discovered lesions were metastatic melanoma because they were in exactly the same place as lesions seen in her pre-operative scans. At

that time, we were told the scans were clear. The oncologist then explained that lesions of a small size were probably not cancer and were
deemed to be 'not of clinical significance'. We asked about getting a
second opinion. He replied there was no point as he claimed he was
the acknowledged UK lead on melanoma and anyone else being asked
for an opinion would come back to him for his views. Our hopes were
then pinned on an immunotherapy drug called pembrolizumab. At
that time, this wasn't available on normal prescription, but he submitted a special application which was approved. Whilst this was
going on, Christine was completing her PhD. An external examiner
had done a demolition job on her at her viva and had recommended
major changes to her dissertation. She was now at an all-time low.
The pembrolizumab treatment involved infusions and, on the first
attempt, her low blood pressure caused big problems in inserting the
cannula. She needed to have a venal access device fitted. Of the three,
we opted for the so-called Hickman line. The ideal device to enable
her to continue swimming would have been a port device under the
skin but that wasn't available on the NHS. The Hickman line would
need to be cleaned, flushed and the protective dressing changed every
week. It was said the District Nurse could do this for her at home
but I volunteered to do this and I was given training in how to do it.
Christine would giggle as I appeared in our bedroom to perform the
weekly Hickman maintenance, dressed in a white disposable apron,
wearing a mask and pushing a surgical trolley I had borrowed. This
arrangement suited us both as she didn't need to wait in all day for
the ever-busy District Nurse and I felt I was supporting her in the
best possible way. The pembrolizumab didn't work. Next up she
participated in a clinical trial. In an apheresis session over several
hours, a large portion of her white cells were harvested, sent to a lab,
modified and then infused back into her over a period of 6 weeks.

This didn't work for her but we both hoped the outcome of the trial would be meaningful for the future of cancer treatment.

It was decided to try another monoclonal antibody treatment called Ipilimumab. The 'mab' suffix in the name indicates a monoclonal antibody but why these drugs have otherwise unpronounceable names is beyond my ken. It was common to shorten the name so this was 'Ipi'. Ipi could be a miracle drug in a very small sample of patients but carried a high likelihood of dangerous side effects, in particular, hepatitis and colitis. Within a few days, Christine presented worrying symptoms of both. I had to take her to the Forth Valley Royal Hospital in Larbert for assessment. The Beatson staff had advised that she be promptly started on steroids by IV, not by mouth as the colitis would make tablets ineffective. It was recommended that she be admitted to the Gastro ward but that was full, so she was put in a general ward. Five days later, I complained that she hadn't yet been put on steroids. There had been some sort of misunderstanding because she was not on the Gastro ward. I asked if a Gastro specialist could see her in the general ward instead of her waiting for a vacancy there before being seen. This happened and she was prescribed steroids by mouth. This was ineffective because her colitis meant anything she swallowed was going straight through her. In desperation, I phoned the Beatson. In some ways, their hands were tied because they were a so-called 'dry' hospital. Apart from radiography and some other specialist cancer treatments, they couldn't treat patients suffering from co-morbidities. Christine's hepatitis resolved but the colitis worsened. I was instructed to bring her to the Beatson. There, she was admitted for five weeks and treated more appropriately. I was becoming increasingly frustrated by the lack of a holistic approach in the care of patients with cancer. Scans were done at Larbert or the Beatson. Some procedures were done at

Gartnavel, next door to the Beatson. Routine visits to the Beatson could be nightmarish.

Most staff were incredibly dedicated but, despite the Beatson being very recently built, it was overwhelmed. On our first visit, there was nowhere for patients to sit, let alone family. Sickly cancer patients were queuing in the corridor. The appointment system couldn't cope with the numbers. Typically, Christine would be seen on Tuesdays. We would arrive in the morning, she would get a blood sample taken, and then she would be weighed. In the afternoon, she would see the oncologist but sometimes the blood results weren't ready. Sometimes we would wait so long that it got dark outside. Everybody would be seen because the department didn't close until the session was completed. I got fined twice by the Glasgow local authority for very marginal bus lane infringements. I didn't know I'd been caught twice, two weeks apart, and both fines arrived by post together. I developed a huge dread of commuting there, hanging around waiting rooms and trying to stay calm for Christine. It wasn't about me. Matters weren't helped when she had to have a colonoscopy after her colitis had been controlled. This had to be done in the Gartnavel. She was still an in-patient in the Beatson and a porter pushed her around, using the access tunnel. In the colonoscopy pre-treatment room, I was asked to leave and wait in the general waiting room. I explained Christine had a colostomy and offered the nurse her colostomy accessory bag. This was dismissed as unnecessary and, after a very patronising and condescending admonition, I was sent to the waiting room with the all-important bag. After about ten minutes of me working through some of my coping strategies to control my stress, the nurse appeared. She asked if I would come back and remove Christine's colostomy bag as they didn't know how to do it. The irony seemed to be completely lost on her. I said I should be called when the procedure was over to re-fit a new bag, but she said a Stoma Nurse would do that. I explained I was Christine's carer and I was trained by the Stoma Nurses to look after her colostomy but the same condescending face was pulled at me. I returned to the waiting room with the bag.

For those that don't know, colostomy bags are amazing. Bespoke bags with tailor-made holes to fit each patient's stoma are available. These bags even incorporate stealth technology! Stomas can be trouble-free but if things go wrong, it can get bad. About half an hour later, the nurse returned and asked me to do the honours as a Stoma Nurse was not available. I went back to find Christine very upset and what she needed was some TLC. After the procedure, the doctor had just put a plain dressing over her stoma. She was terrified the stoma might become active and soil everything. I fitted the replacement bag, and we went back to her ward in the Beatson. The colonoscopy result was satisfactory. By then, what I would describe as my extreme mental anguish was peaking. She came home but the colitis persisted. Without warning, her stoma could become active and completely overwhelm the colostomy bag. This happened several times. When it did, we're talking messy; really messy. Christine would become very distressed. I was deeply upset too but I was able to say calm, deal with the awful disaster zone our bedroom had just become and calm her. To her credit, after each of these episodes, she was able to regain her composure. Her three best friends were very supportive of her and she greatly enjoyed their company.

One of the early triggers for my anguished state was that Christine had said I should find another partner after she passed. I was now in a pretty bad way mentally. One of my coping strategies for stress had always been to keep busy and not dwell on negatives. Despite the anxiety, I remained high-functioning. I continued to work full-time as the Estates Manager at a nearby boarding school and, when I could, I would dive into my many hobbies, one of which was building steam engines and model aircraft. In my workshop, connected by intercom to the house, I could totally lose myself and would emerge later, tired but relaxed.

One day, when Christine and I were talking about something, I noticed that she was occasionally using the wrong word and seemed to be unaware of it. I believe this is a condition known as Aphasia but I didn't know that then. I reported my concerns to her clinical nurse specialist at the Beatson. At her next routine scan, they included her brain. Christine noted this but if she was suspicious, she didn't show it. Some cancers are known for spreading to the brain, but oncologists do not routinely scan the brain for metastatic cancer unless the patient is symptomatic. This episode was stressful. When a loved one in these circumstances might be deteriorating, do you keep quiet? Do you tell them? Do you tell the clinicians? There is no completely right answer. When we met to review the scan results, the room was crowded. Christine's anxiety levels rose. The nurse introduced a Neurologist Oncologist Radiologist person. That's a lot of 'ologies'. He asked Christine specifically if she was aware of any neurological symptoms and she said she wasn't. He turned to me, saying words to the effect, "But your husband is". I described what I had noticed as Christine glared angrily at my apparent betrayal of her. I apologised and explained I didn't want to worry her if it turned out to be nothing.

Then the chap with all the 'ologies' spoke. He said the conversational difficulties were corroborated by the brain scan and lesions had been found in her brain with one near the part responsible for language. He went on to say she would be a candidate for stereotactic radio surgery.

Although the word surgery was included, the treatment was purely radiographic. She had to be fitted with a bespoke facial mask to ensure her head was orientated correctly. The treatment was administered and then we had to wait several weeks to see if the lesions had shrunk. If they had, the 'ologist' explained that, if the lesions returned, the treatment could be repeated and would be life-extending. The scan result was devastating. The lesions were bigger. We had known from the outset that Christine would not survive this cancer, unless the immunotherapy had been effective. When it was effective in a tiny minority of patients, the results were miraculous. The lesions in her lungs had not grown rapidly but the spread to the brain was ominous. The stereotactic radioactive surgery was deemed pointless and discontinued. All that was left was a version of a 40-year-old melanoma chemotherapy drug called dacarbazine. This version was called Temozolomide. It was a drug which could get through the brain's blood barrier.

As time went by, more treatments were tried but the cancer proved to be refractory in medical terms which means it was treatment-resistant. My frozen shoulder had worsened and I was told the cartilage was badly worn. I saw an osteopath and when he examined me, he reported crepitus, the crunching sound of bone on bone. I had now had this condition for several years. It was painful and would ache, especially when I was in bed. When I was busy, I didn't notice it so much. I lost a lot of weight through sleep deprivation. I was taking prescription-strength co-codamol at the maximum dose. This went on for five years. The codeine played havoc with my bowel habit. I was fast-tracked for a colonoscopy. This amused Christine somewhat; she did have a wicked sense of humour. The pain in my shoulder and weight loss caused another GP to fast-track me in case I had lung cancer. Then, in November 2017, disaster struck when Christine's mother, Sadie, herself frail from cancer, fell down the stairs at home and suffered a catastrophic head injury. She didn't awaken and passed away. At the time, I had started seeing black spots in my left eye. This was very distracting, and I saw an optician. Assured it would probably be OK and that it was floaters, I dismissed it from my mind. The only positive I could draw from Sadie's passing that was that she wouldn't see her eldest daughter predecease her. After her funeral, we attended a wake in the afternoon and something odd happened. I looked out of a window and saw a black object in my left eye. It was moving up and down and filled the lower one third of my vision in that eye. When we got home, I phoned the optician and she told me to come straight in. She examined my eye and said a portion of my retina had become detached; this would require immediate medical attention. To cut a long story short, I had the detachment re-attached under a local anaesthetic. This worked and I spent a weird couple of weeks looking at the world through what was like a spirit level in my left eye. The procedure involved putting a medical gas in the eyeball which would gradually be absorbed as the eye healed. Three months later, I returned to have the consequential cataract removed and replaced with an artificial lens.

Just before Sadie passed, we got a dog. He was a very large black Labrador called Buck, aged 6 months. He was brilliant. I was able to take him to work and the school had over 50 acres of grounds for him to play in. As I was the Estates Manager, I was constantly outside so, it was a win/win situation. Everybody loved Buck, especially Christine. Since the failure of the stereotactic radio surgery, Christine had been on oral doses of chemotherapy. She was stable most of the time, enjoying long walks, going out and she was working with charities in the area of homelessness affecting Service Veterans. She had become involved with Melanoma Action and Support Scotland (MASScot) and had made new friends there; so- called 'Melomates'. She had been appointed a Research Fellow at Stirling University and had a business card announcing her as Dr Christine Robinson. Notwithstanding her cancer, it looked like her huge academic investment was starting to pay off. She had attracted a very large research grant from a mental health charity for the university and the cancer had slipped into the back of both our minds.

In late November 2018, we went to a supermarket in Stirling. Christine had the ability to keep a very accurate tally of prices as she filled her trolley and could almost invariably predict the bill before we checked out. On this day, we entered and I got a trolley. I noticed that she seemed a little unsteady on her feet so I suggested she push the trolley for support and I hold on to it in case it rolled away. She went over to the dairy counter and was looking at the shelves. I then realised she had become transfixed. I nudged her and asked if she was OK. She tried to reply but it was plain to see she had become unwell. We abandoned the trolley and I guided her back to the car and we went home. Over the next few days, Christine became increasingly unsteady on her feet. She also spent increasingly longer periods sitting in a chair looking at the TV but not actually watching it. She had a couple of falls, none too serious, but like a tortoise on its back, she needed to be physically rescued each time and I insisted she always ask for help when she wanted to move about. Her deterioration was rapid. I spoke to her GP and likened her symptoms to those of a dementia sufferer. She could no longer count and when looking at the tablets she took, she asked every time what they were for and how many she should take. A typical exchange would be, "What's the wee white ones for?" "Those are steroids," I would reply. "How many do I take?" "Four". "Oh, and what are they for?" She would giggle girlishly as she started to realize she was struggling to communicate. As she was going downhill at an alarming rate, I worried that she might forget who I was and that would be the end of my caring for her.

Christmas came and went. Christine was relaxed and happy but was sometimes zombie-like. At Hogmanay, we were invited as usual to a party at her friend's house. By then, I had gotten a wheelchair for her as she could only manage a few steps and then only with support. She wasn't sure what was going on and wasn't able to pick what she would wear. She was normally quite fastidious in choosing what to wear and I had the dress sense of a plant pot. I picked out an outfit and off we went. As we arrived at the friend's house, her face lit up as she realized where she was. As the evening wore on, she managed short snippets of conversation. Since the colitis episode, she could only manage a small amount of alcohol, so she had a small glass of Prosecco. We saw The Bells in, exchanged the usual greetings and wishes for the new year and I took her home. As we left, I ran as I pushed her wheelchair up the road and she loved it, squealing with laughter. Over the next two weeks, she gradually became less responsive and needed more care. Buck sensed something was wrong and would lie quietly beside her. She had been given a onesie for Christmas. It was soft and fluffy with pom poms on the collar. She liked it and wore it constantly. She had an appointment on 15 January, and I phoned the Beatson to say she was too unwell to attend. The Clinical Nurse Specialist returned my call on 14 January to confirm how she was and could she attend. By then, Christine had slipped into a coma and was completely unresponsive. I asked for the necessary certification of her condition to trigger a Power of Attorney. The outreach nurse from the Strathcarron Hospice came out and did the necessary to keep her comfortable while she slept. That evening, quite late on, there was a knock at the door. It was the GP Christine liked the most. She asked to see her and I took her to the bedside. I had attended my father in his last hours when he died in 1988 and I was familiar with the symptoms at end of life; I knew Christine was very close to passing. The GP said there wasn't long to go and then did something spontaneous but hugely touching. She laid down beside her and stroked her hair whilst talking softly to her. I believed the last sense to lose close to death was hearing and I had Christine's favourite singer's songs playing continuously in background; it was Rod Stewart.

The GP arose, wished the best and left. At five past two in the morning, Christine passed away. The sense of loss was overwhelming but knowing that she was now beyond any more suffering helped. Christine was a giving person all of her life, never selfish and always caring. She deserved better out of life and had much more to give but was taken from us. This second period of extreme anguish was over, but the grief was enduring. Early on, just after her diagnosis in 2015, Christine had voiced her anxiety about my mental health. I was invited to a GP appointment. I was in a very bad way, and I was struggling. The GP prescribed beta blockers. After a few days, I was invited back and asked how I was managing on the tablets. Throughout most of my life, my resting pulse was typically 52. I reported that my pulse rate had lowered. The GP asked what it was. It was 32. The prescription was hurriedly changed to sertraline. The first few days on this drug were a nightmare as I couldn't sleep. After a week, I noticed that I was sleeping better and felt calmer. I think the sertraline was very effective and probably stopped my anxiety from worsening. My frozen shoulder was very painful but my focus on Christine distracted me from it and I postponed any more radical treatment for it whilst I was caring for Christine. After she passed away, I returned to the orthopaedic clinic and was told I needed a total shoulder replacement. This was done and proved successful. Within a week, I stopped taking the co-codamol which wasn't easy, but I did it. I then spoke to the GP and arranged to come off the sertraline.

In September 2021, I retired from my post at the boarding school. I now appreciate that widowhood is isolating, and the isolation increased when I retired. I live alone with Buck and my African Grey parrot, Maverick. I've grown used to my new way of life and have started to resume old friendships with the people I served with in the Army. I also travel more which is great fun. My modest success in life is due in no small part to Christine. I miss her dreadfully but count my blessings. She is gone but is still here; if you know what I mean.

Addendum: A few weeks ago, my youngest son asked if he could have his mother's engagement ring as he intended to pop the question to his long-standing and very patient partner. He asked, she said yes, and now that ring means something amazing again.

CHAPTER 19

Reflections

Almost unbelievably, I now find myself retired. Later this year, I will turn 69. Where did all that time go? I spent the first half of my life wishing I was older or, at least, that I looked older. I was frustrated at the many times I was told I looked too young for my rank. Now I am comfortable in my skin. I don't want to turn the clock back and I don't hanker after having my time again. I certainly don't believe in the good old times; what on Earth was so good about them? In this chapter, I will reflect and ponder on the changes affecting society and my own attitudes during my life. Over the years, I remember watching TV in disbelief and awe as: JFK was assassinated, Winston Churchill died, the first manned moon landing took place and then there was that day the world changed forever when the twin towers of the World Trade Centre were destroyed by terrorists. As an Army child in Germany, I had watched the evening news on German TV, showing graphic pictures of people fleeing the east over the embryonic Berlin Wall. In 1989, from the Falklands, I watched the Berlin Wall come down. In the middle east and far east, I had enjoyed privilege as a child over the locals in the post-colonial period without pausing to reflect on the immorality of it all. The British Empire, once taught to me at school from a large map covered in red and pink, is gone. The Commonwealth seems to be in decline. Why is a major part of our honours and awards system still based on God and empire? The way ahead must be grasped and, whilst the past must not be forgotten, there are bits which belong only in the history books. Statues must not be torn down, but their real historical context should be clear for all to see. I do believe in the self-determination of people. Thus, I have no issue with populations in the Falklands and Gibraltar wishing to retain their British identity. If they wanted otherwise, then so be it. If the democratic will of the majority in N Ireland sought to join the Irish Republic, I would expect the minority to acquiesce and with grace. I fear that my adoptive country of Scotland may achieve independence in my lifetime as, in my opinion, this is a bad time for small countries to go alone. Even bigger countries can be vulnerable, as we see today with the Russian invasion of Ukraine. The irony is they gave up their large nuclear inventory in exchange for Russia guaranteeing their security. If Scotland became independent, our UK independent nuclear deterrent would need a new home and the Iceland Gap could become easier access for Russia into the Atlantic. The war in Ukraine has exposed the parlous state of our national defence.

When I reviewed the ammunition state of the British Army in 1986, I was dismayed at what I found in what I would describe as an 'emperor's new clothes' moment but keeping official secrets obliged me to stay silent. My superiors could see what I could see when the project ended but their careers were more important to them in the short term than our nation's security in the longer term. Successive Defence Reviews have decimated our Armed Forces, each cut being justified by a review which was too short-term and was politically expedient. Only recently has the Government reiterated their policy that Defence is a priority for spending. Even if we had immediate and limitless funding, it would take a generation and more to repair the damage caused by political expedience.

On the social side of life, I grew up in the Army surrounded by a great many uncles and aunts who were friends of my father. Rank, gender, religion and race didn't come into it. We lived in a world where a soldier would often be identified by his physical appearance. Thus, if you were left-handed, you might be known as 'Leftie'. Many of Dad's friends were single; many were of different or mixed race. I had Uncle Darkies and Uncle Chalkies; nobody questioned their sexual orientation or discriminated against them. Overseas, at Christmas, bachelor uncles would stay at our home as welcome guests. The only obvious expectation was that their loyalty was to the unit and comrades. As to homosexuality, I think we had a 'don't ask, don't tell' policy long before that phrase was even thought of. In the 1970s and onwards, a spotlight shone on inequality within the Armed Forces, but it shone through the lens of conservative Christian ideas of morality based on ancient scriptures. Gay people have always punched above their weight in the military, the arts and the sciences; in fact in every walk of life. Imagine a world without Alan Turing, Elton John and my mother's favourite, Liberace, to mention but a few. And in the 1990s, as a commissioned officer, I was taught, and was expected to believe, that gay people were a threat to operational efficacy. In the face of increasing opprobrium, the military even held a survey to ask us what our opinions were. I saw gay people hunted down like vermin in the Army. I also witnessed the behaviour of some of the most highly motivated anti-gays in seeking to 'out' gays. Bizarrely, some of these people were gay themselves as they ducked and dived to deflect suspicion, which is shocking.

On the heterosexual front, I remember being on duty in the guard-room at Kineton when a minibus would pick up female WRAC soldiers and take them off camp. I was shocked to hear the explanation when I asked if the girls were enjoying privileges the men didn't get. They weren't getting a free lift home, as I thought. They were being taken to a military hospital down south to have abortions. In those days, if a girl got pregnant, the choice was stark - leave the Army or have an abortion. That was how society was at the time. I don't excuse it but that was the reality then. I wonder how many of these unfortunate girls are now wracked with guilt in their dotage.

As my career was drawing to an end in the late 1990s, I was increasingly involved in providing welfare support to my soldiers. Whilst on deployment overseas, I had one soldier who wasn't thriving. I struggled to understand what was wrong with him. I was deeply saddened to learn he was illiterate, as was his wife. It ended up that I would write his letters home where the Padre would read them to her and then reply for her. I would reciprocate at our end. I've ever felt so humbled in my life that something I entirely took for granted could be so debilitating for another person. The look on his face when I read to him the details of how his new-born son was thriving was overwhelming. My late wife Christine had a hand in moderating my modestly right-wing attitude. It was inevitable that someone born and brought up in the Army, and then serving until the age 45, would harbour conservative social views. But I hadn't just acquired these views through 'familial osmosis'. On an Army educational course in 1976 in Germany, I was actually taught that married men were a safer bet than allegedly feckless single men in positions of responsibility. Academic 'collateral value' was added when the instructor (a female captain) lectured us on Maslow's Hierarchy of Needs which she felt justified this view. In military man management, it was said to be desirable for the Army culture of heavy drinking be condoned but confined to barracks, out of sight of the public. A local unit at the time was causing absolute havoc with drinking and violence in and around Paderborn which resulted in the German Mayor petitioning for and getting the unit transferred away.

We were taught that women were preferably employed in industry at repetitive tasks, as exampled by the Japanese industrial model of that time; I think we would label this as misogyny today. As our instructor was an officer, decorum limited just how robust we might be if we disagreed with this diet of nonsense. I absolutely nailed her when we were being taught the now obsolete planning process then known as 'Appreciating a Situation'. Typically, you would be given an unsatisfactory scenario which had to be resolved urgently. You would harvest all the salient factors from the written narrative. These would be ranked, and you would then consider relevance and importance to the situation. This would result in the next order of filtering of the information which would be your deductions. These should lead to an 'options available' summary. You were expected to pick two or three options and list the pros and cons before recommending a firm plan of action. A common sub-set of factors could include simple arithmetic considerations of time and distance or fuel consumption versus range questions. In the example we had been set, we were in a car that had gone off the road into a very deep snow drift in sub-zero temperatures and we were completely entombed. We couldn't escape and it was known that it would be so many hours before a search party could locate and rescue us. At the heart of the nest of factors lay a fuel consumption question. At fast tick-over, the engine would keep us warm for a projected time but there wasn't much fuel left. In the hypothetical scenario, it was presented as fact that we would freeze to death rapidly if the engine stopped. She went around the class asking for solutions after we had been given half an hour to plan how we would stay alive. I was last up. When I explained that imminent death was inevitable due to carbon monoxide poisoning, the class erupted. We got sent home early.

Perhaps the most difficult time in the Army for me was in reconciling my treatment at the hands of the lieutenant colonel who was my CATO in N Ireland in 1987. This man had almost unlimited power over me and was apparently accountable to nobody. His disdain for me did not cease at the end of my 1987 EOD tour. By unhappy coincidence, his next posting was to Germany where he would become my commanding officer. As if his behaviour in Northern Ireland wasn't enough, he was to twist the knife two further times. The first occasion was when he presented one of our corporals with a GOC N Ireland Commendation. The whole unit, including wives and children, were gathered in the unit social club. We were wearing Service Dress as this was a formal occasion albeit not being celebrated with a formal parade. The colonel started his award speech by explaining that the corporal had allegedly gotten off to a bad start on his EOD tour and was nearly sacked. He then changed tack and finished the story by saying the corporal had turned his performance around and had done so well he merited the award of a formal GOC's commendation. I felt embarrassed for the corporal; in my view, up to that point, the colonel's award speech had been cringingly condescending, but it got worse. He then went on to say how hard it could be to receive an award for service in N Ireland before looking at me and passing what I took as a disparaging remark about my recent performance in the province. It had apparently fallen short of the threshold for consideration of an award. This was said in front of Christine, who was upset by this callous indiscretion. As if this slight was not enough, his retribution for our awful relationship was to continue. I can only assume that his public spat with my RESA, after the assassination of Lord Chief Justice Gibson, had resulted in some embarrassment for him from higher up the chain of command.

The second occasion was when I had been shortlisted for a commission and part of the process required that a candidate have an unqualified recommendation from his commanding officer. This was documented in the annual confidential report. This report had four parts. Only the first two parts were seen by the candidate in those days, but all four parts had to contain an unreserved recommendation. When I was called to interview, the colonel was quite jovial and said he would recommend me for a commission but then tempered the recommendation by saying, "You're not charming enough to be a commissioned officer, Mr Robinson". Needless to say, I did not get selected. I applied a further two times whilst the colonel was my CO. I was shortlisted but not selected, so, in 1990, having just returned from a tour of duty in the Falkland Islands, I applied for a commission in the then Royal Army Pay Corps (RAPC). At the time, there was a potential career path in that a good tour as a Paymaster would permit me to apply for a long course which would result in either becoming a Management Consultant or Data Consultant. At that time, I was conscious that my 22-year engagement would finish in 1994, we hadn't yet started a family and I needed to be thinking about long-term career continuity. I also applied for a commission in my own corps, and this resulted in me being shortlisted for both commissions. The same colonel then presided over the paperwork for my RAOC commission. The RAPC commissioning process was radically different, however. I would have to attend a so-called 'Three Day Event' at the RAPC Depot at Worthy Down. The appeal to me for this particular process was that it did not depend on my 'face being a fit' with my RAOC CO. I remember feeling very apprehensive about the RAPC Board beforehand but reconciled myself to it being a fundamentally fairer and more searching test of my abilities. If I failed it, I couldn't moan about it. If I passed it, I would be given the result immediately, before I left. When I got there, I was given a coloured

bib to wear; I was to be 'Blue 7'. The three days involved a wide range
of physical and mental challenges, debates on current affairs, IQ test,
maths test and five one-on-one interviews with each board member.
The different activities were deliberately mixed, so you did a mental
test whilst still panting with exertion from a physical test. You would
be given very little time to change between tests, so the pressure was on
you all of the time. The final day involved a crunch interview with all
five board members firing questions at you, all at once. After that, you
were kept in a room until all the interviews had concluded. One-by-
one, we were then ushered back into the interview room. The Chair of
the Board then read from one of two prepared scripts which announced
your result. I was marched in, ever conscious of the continuing scrutiny; we had been told to wear a business suit on the last day. Christine
picked my outfit; I thought it looked good. One of my peers had turned
up in pillar box red socks and was openly criticised. I saw the Chair's
lips moving as he announced my result; the declaration was very brief
before I was marched out the door. Outside, the officer who was our
usher asked my what my result was. I was so wound up I couldn't
remember! He laughed out loud and shoved me into a room and said
I had passed. Over the next half-hour, I was joined by about six more
successful candidates. I was quite numb with the shock of success that
I didn't expect. I was already regretting the thought of leaving the
trade I loved, in which I had invested so much. I returned to Germany.
On reflecting that I might now become a commissioned officer, I was
almost paralysed with stage fright. During my career, there had been
several instances where an officer had suggested directly that I should
apply for a commission. It happened when I was a recruit and again
when I was a sergeant and I had intervened in a serious welfare case
and prevented a soldier from coming to harm. It happened again in
1979 when the CATO N Ireland, the late Lt Col Peter Forshaw (later

brigadier), insisted I should apply for a Middle Entry Commission and not waste my time waiting to become old enough to apply for a Late Entry Commission. This was at my end-of-tour interview in Belfast. On each occasion when I was asked, I remember with crystal clear clarity the sinking feeling in my stomach that I was not good enough. From the outset, I had believed the aspiration to a commission to be far beyond my reach. Officers to me were like a different species. My primary reflection now is that what held me back, time and time again, was fear of the consequence of failure.

In the event, as told in a preceding chapter, I deployed to the Gulf War in October 1990. My call forward for commissioning and transfer to the RAPC (soon to be AGC) arrived in December 1990, complete with my new officer's regimental number but I turned it down. This time it wasn't fear of the consequence of failure but loyalty to my trade and unit. A war was coming, and I wasn't going to dodge it. As I had declined a commission, which was apparently worse than farting in church, I had to have the inevitable 'interview without coffee' with a senior officer which, to quote the late Denis Healey, was like being savaged by a dead sheep. I thought the officer concerned was a buffoon so the pathetic attempt at changing my mind was never going to work and was soon replaced with an admonition for having the temerity to decline a commission. Sometime later, I received another letter confirming I had not been selected for a commission in the RAOC which came as no surprise. After repatriation, I spent about six months at 221 EOD in Germany employed as the 221 EOD Company Administration Officer. I was then selected for a posting to 11 EOD Regiment as the SAT, a truly prestigious post, but I was 'face-gauged' by the CO designate. He lobbied behind the scenes for my posting to be changed. I was given the final say by Manning and Records and I elected to be posted to RMCS

Shrivenham instead, fearful that I might have another spat with another colonel which could only result in misery. Before going, I had to have a farewell interview with the Commander Supply at Rheindahlen. This was the late Brigadier David Harris who was a very sharp cookie and was a man to be respected and who I did respect. During the interview, he asked if I had applied for a commission. In the intervening year since the Gulf War, I hadn't. He insisted on asking why. I explained that I had four unsuccessful applications in the RAOC behind me and had little confidence in succeeding. He insisted on asking why, again. I said my face didn't fit and this irritated him, and he insisted on asking why (an insistent chap, this). I had nothing to lose, so I gave personality conflict as an excuse; "What? Four bloody times?" He pressed the call button on his intercom and asked his PA to get the Officer In Charge of RAOC Manning and Records on the phone immediately. A couple of minutes later, the phone rang. I shifted uncomfortably on my seat as the brigadier quizzed a full colonel about my lack of success. My personnel file had been pulled. The annual confidential reports were read out to the brigadier, audible on the phone's speaker. The conversation was brief; the all-important Parts three and four of my last four confidential reports were either blank or contained nothing about my commissioning prospects. By default, this meant my name would not go forward to the Selection Board. This was completely at odds with the now-evident tongue-in-cheek recommendations in each of the first two parts. The brigadier was upset, and it wasn't for show. He insisted I apply for a commission for the next year. I was gratified by his candid concern.

When I arrived at Shrivenham, my boss and work colleague must have had serious misgivings about my motivation and possibly even my mental health. I was all-consumed by anger and frustration that, despite being recommended by a panel of officers for the post of SAT at 11 EOD Regiment, I had been rejected by the CO designate without any explanation. I felt humiliated and struggled to keep myself effective. I had a massive chip on my shoulder and couldn't let go of the disappointment. I give credit to two officers who I found myself working for, who were to restore my faith, albeit in entirely different ways. My first boss had huge imagination and ambition for the ATO Course. He had arrived shortly before me and the Branch needed modernising in almost every way, as explained in Chapter 15, and he achieved this. His replacement was a very different character who gave me every encouragement to seek a commission.

A totally unexpected event happened several months after arrival to put me back on the rails. Danny, the RSM, phoned me early one morning and asked me to check out a suspect parcel he had received. Since my arrival, I had been asked several times to deal with suspect parcel bombs at RMCS and I had asked the administration staff to stop doing this and told them to follow the same procedures as all other military units, eventually declaring to them that I was "Not the Shrivenham Detachment of 11 EOD Regiment". I hung up on Danny and the phone rang again. This time it was Ron, my old mate from Edinburgh, who started to say something complimentary, but I cut him short, saying I needed to sort out an urgent issue, but I would call him back. I strode up the path to Danny's office. I could see him standing behind his desk. I prepared to upbraid him about the stupidity of bringing suspect parcels back to his office but, as I entered, I sensed something was wrong. Firstly, partly concealed behind a large steel locker to my left, I could see shiny brown shoes on the floor. Looking up, I saw outstretched hands holding a silver salver. The lower arms were clothed in Service Dress with the tell-tale cuffs of a commissioned officer. On the salver was a parchment warrant and the badge of a Conductor RAOC. It was a 'GOTCHA!' moment and I had fallen for it; probably the only come-on I ever actually fell for! The owner of the shoes stepped out and it was the Commandant, Major General Edmund Burton. He announced my appointment to Conductor and then said he had won a case of port from his opposite number, the Commandant of the Royal Military Academy Sandhurst. In a conversation with him, he had let it be known that he was about to appoint one of his warrant officers to Conductor RAOC and this appointment was senior to all other warrant officers in the Army, including the Academy Sergeant Major at Sandhurst. A wager was placed and a copy of the rank and precedence page from the Queen's Regulations was faxed over to Sandhurst. The Commandant then invited me to become the Presiding Member of the Sergeant's Mess and Danny' face fell as he looked about to be usurped in his own mess. The alternative was for me to elect to become an Honorary Member of the Mess which would preserve Danny's status. I chose the latter and became an Honorary Member. When I called Ron back, he offered his congratulations. He called earlier about this as he had just seen the announcement in his own unit. That call almost compromised the Commandant's ambush. I had an afterthought: This was the last Conductor's Board of the RAOC. Was I the last Conductor to be appointed in the RAOC?

Addendum: The Ron I referred to here and in Chapter 8 was Ron Dean, my partner in mischief, the man who introduced me to my wife Christine in a blind date and who was to become my Best Man at our wedding. On the cusp of sending this manuscript to the publisher, I learned that Ron had passed away suddenly, so I pay tribute to him here for his friendship, loyalty and company in the darker days of my time at Edinburgh.

During that year, I applied for a commission in the RAOC. It was unsuccessful. In 1993, my last window of opportunity, I applied again. I didn't expect to get it, having been awarded the honorary appointment of Conductor RAOC in 1992, the last year of the RAOC, prior to amalgamation into the RLC. It was a soldier's tale that the award of Conductor to a senior WO1 (I served 7 years as a WO1) was a tacit acknowledgement for meritorious service where a commission was not considered to be merited. As already mentioned, my posting to 11 EOD Regiment had been effectively vetoed by another lieutenant colonel I didn't get on with, so my expectations were not high. However, my new bosses at Shrivenham were both inspiring in their own ways and I enjoyed my tour there. I was sufficiently ambitious to seek a commission but there was another conflict; this time, nothing to do with personalities. I was in my last year of service. It was due to end in March 1994 for sure, unless I got a commission. I should have focused all my attention on Resettlement Training. So, which path to take? Do I invest in my future as a civilian and do my resettlement training (not to mention our first child was on the way), or do I put 100% into working towards a commission? Fear of the consequence of failure did it for me again. I didn't want to be a civilian; I couldn't remain a soldier, so I had to succeed and get a commission! All the eggs went into the one basket and this time I didn't fail; it had only taken six attempts!

After I retired from the Active List in 1999, I was mindful of some unfinished business. I had previously investigated or come across reports into the deaths of service personnel at their own hand and was unhappy with the way these awful deaths were being considered as suicide or even subjected to some fanciful conspiracy theories without there being, so far as I could tell, any evidence of an intent to end life. My experience with weapons (the Steyr AUG in 5.56mm calibre and the SA80) was that chambering a pristine round would result in a faint witness mark being left on the percussion cap by the floating firing pin. This mark was faint but easily discernible if you knew what to look for. Whenever I checked ready-use ammunition in guard rooms, I would examine the ammunition carefully and was concerned to discover that a large proportion of ammunition bore witness marks from being chambered; in fact, far more than could be credibly explained. In most cases, I knew the ammunition issued to the guard room was brand new training stock which would be turned over after several weeks as the excessive handling would degrade it. The mark on the percussion cap was so characteristic of being chambered that it could not have been caused by anything else. This established in my mind the likelihood that soldiers were cocking their rifles when alone on guard duty far more than was fully appreciated. That in itself increases the risk of accidental or negligent discharge. Further, the SA80 being of Bullpup design, was much shorter than the 7.62mm SLR and its predecessor which meant the weapon could easily be turned in towards the head or torso by the handler. The death of the soldier I described in Chapter 12 was preceded by him repeatedly watching a potential suicide sequence in a popular film of the day. In his case, the weapon was a folded Sterling sub machine gun, but his placing of the muzzle was similar to the film scene. The soldier who shot himself just prior to the outbreak of the Gulf War (see Chapter 14) was clearly contravening safety regulations and had closed the door to his room meaning his actions could not be observed and yet his colleagues were aware of what he was doing. I had coined a phrase to describe these disturbing circumstances. It was 'morbid curiosity'. The common denominators were: Apparent defiance of strict safety regulations, the lack of direct supervision and the ease with which these weapons could be turned on the handler, but that still left the matter too vague. Just after I retired, I became aware through media reports of the research work done by an Irish A&E Consultant. He had been involved in the care of very many young people who had succumbed to serious injuries brought about in circumstances which resembled suicide. One case I recall from the literature concerned a young man who repeatedly drove a car, alone, around a very sharp bend, increasing the speed until he crashed. I seem to recall the Consultant reviewed about 100 cases and he had the post-mortem serotonin levels checked. In a statistically relevant portion of deaths, he found the serotonin level to be abnormal. He was also able to draw attention to a link between serotonin and cholesterol levels. By now, there was a substantial media campaign by the families of the young soldiers known as the 'Deepcut Four'. I felt that the vacuum of real evidence was being filled by fanciful theories. It seemed to me that each of those deaths had similarities with the deaths I was aware of from my service. I contacted the detectives conducting the investigation and gave a statement. I also wrote of my concerns to a serving senior officer. I informed both parties of my concerns and also that I was aware that live rounds were very commonly being chambered when young soldiers were unsupervised. I added that a simple inspection of ammunition would detect evidence of chambering and if the soldiers knew their inappropriate actions would be detected, it could have deterrence value. Since then, I've heard nothing. The cap marking following chambering may still be evident unless the modification to the SA80 to upgrade it to the A2 model has changed that characteristic. When soldiers are issued live ammunition with weapons, it becomes a potent mix, especially when those soldiers might then be unsupervised and alone. Checking those percussion caps after duty could save a life and spare the distraught families the ongoing pain of bereavement followed by endless speculation and inquiries.

When I retired from the Army, I wanted a clean break and a fresh start in civilian life in a permanent home and a stable family life for my two sons, who were five and three years old respectively. This was largely successful and, as one of my sons was to develop a disability which could not be forecast, it was fortuitous that I wasn't in the Army any longer with all the attendant turbulence that would entail. I lost touch with my cohort but despaired as I saw the mounting casualty lists from Afghanistan and Iraq. I got into social media in a passive way and kept up with some of the trade's current affairs. We never really had what I would term an ammunition technician's veteran's forum, with the exception of the Association of Ammunition Technicians. I have admired the way Scottish Infantry battalion veterans seem to coalesce into family groups with a strong identity and powerful cohesion. Through social media, I saw the appearance of emerging trends of ill health in retired ATs and ATOs. Various types of cancer and mental illness seemed prominent, but it is tempting to become alarmed without the presence of factual evidence to give a proper perspective. As an occupational group, we were probably too small to raise any red flags at the national level and the sad fact is that cancer is very common. Through social media, a former colleague expressed concerns at what he saw as excessive levels of terminal illness, and especially the rates of bladder cancer. He campaigned quite vigorously, and this included raising the matter with politicians and eminent clinicians. The campaign has yet to deliver a positive outcome and, to be fair, how could you define what that positive outcome might be? The simple answer would be some form of health screening. To this end, I would highlight my own experiences with carcinogens. In 1979 I had a significant occupational exposure to mercury. From that time, I suffered continuously from severe mouth ulcers. Dentists would say it was a medical problem and the medics would say it was a dental issue. When I retired in 1999, I had the freedom to refuse dental amalgam in fillings. Since then, mouth ulcers are a rarity for me. However, so-called white fillings are expensive. So I pay for them privately. The dentists consistently refuse to accept that my prior exposure to mercury is sufficient justification for me to be prescribed non-amalgam fillings for free. In the next week, I am to have a root-canal procedure and I don't want amalgam to be used. Under NHS treatment policy is a so-called 'same tooth policy' which proscribes the mixing of private and free treatment on the same tooth so the estimate for my treatment is just short of £1,000.

In 1987, I had a severe occupational exposure to nitrobenzene (NB) by inhalation and absorption. This was completely unavoidable for operational reasons and in the hierarchy of risk, NB exposure was a factor, but it was near the bottom of the risk ladder. Following symptoms of acute exposure, oxygen was administered at the scene by a medical officer along with pain relief for the severe headache. There was no medical follow up. NB is an acknowledged carcinogen and, like many of my colleagues, I have also had exposures to a variety of heavy metals and other explosive compounds. I am not paranoid about my health, but I do feel it would be prudent for us all to be passively screened through blood and urine tests. Bladder cancer seems to be a common cancer in my former cohort and by the time blood is seen in the urine, it can already be too late. Perhaps the real issue is the lack of epidemiological statistics; there may be an occupational health issue or there might not be. To paraphrase the HIV/AIDS awareness campaign, I wouldn't want to die of ignorance.

In July 2022, I attended the very first event that might be classed as a reunion since I left the Army; it was the 'Kineton AT100', an open day to celebrate 100 years of ammunition technical training. It felt like coming home again. I met people I hadn't seen or heard of for almost 50 years. On the back of this, a 321 EOD reunion was proposed and then organised by the indefatigable Brad of 'spirit in the sky' fame from 1974. This is to be in early May, and I note His Majesty has chosen the same weekend for a party of his own. I am very much looking forward to going and, perhaps wisely, have booked an extra night's accommodation to ensure my drive back home is unimpaired. I am hoping to have this book ready for publishing about then but, if it gets out before the reunion, I might need flak jacket, ear defenders and helmet again for the critique.

To conclude, it seems that fear of the consequence of failure has followed me around all of my life. Another piece of 'baggage not required on journey' is likely to have been my turbulent upbringing which may have affected my ability to forge sustainable relationships with peers and superiors alike. An 'also-ran' is the possibility that I have autism as I seem to 'tick all of the boxes'. If this is borne out, it would help me make sense of some of the less salubrious episodes I had, especially with the personality conflicts and awkward social interactions. Fear of the consequence of failure is not what I would describe as a 'direct fear'. I have known a few situations which were frightening, such as two forced helicopter landings, described in the Oman and Bessbrook chapters. In those circumstances, I seemed to become detached, and the worst aspect was brought about by my inability to personally affect the outcome because I wasn't actually in control. In the first aircraft incident in Oman, as we plummeted towards the ground from several thousand feet with an engine failure, I had calmly devised a plan to jettison the door immediately before impact and throw the explosives in my lap clear in case a fire developed. This was me trying to regain some control over the possible outcome. And I thought of how angry

Christine might get. It was only a day or so after that that the 'lucky escape' thought intruded into my usually logical thought process. When it comes to dealing with a bomb, my fears would not coalesce around the thought of coming to harm but rather that others might see I had responded incompetently; after all, I wouldn't want some 'Peter Perfect' telling future generations of EOD Operators that my demise arose because I might have been drunk, emotionally unstable, downright stupid, ignored the obvious, took a silly shortcut or even cut the wrong wire. And even if I didn't come to harm, would my EOD report pass scrutiny? Fear of the consequence of failure became my 'guide rails' quite early on in life. It kept me focused and orientated and I learned to rely on it but were there times when I should have jumped off those rails? Could I have been more successful in life? Or could I have overreached and messed up? I'll never know.

I'll finish off with some wishes. These are not related to a desire to change the events in my life and there may yet be time for these wishes to come true. These wishes share the common theme of 'asymmetry' where the balances of political, legal and moral aspects of life in the UK need tweaking.

The first would be for a genuine and enduring commitment by the Government and MoD to provide medical screening for veterans for illnesses such as cancer where the risk of illness may be linked to occupational risk. The Armed Forces Covenant seemed to be a good start in this respect, but it feels like the initial enthusiasm for it and political will to finish what was started has stalled. The fact is that we were employed on a legally binding contract to be prepared to give up our lives in service to the state. The latent effects of this asymmetric contract do not cease on discharge and can continue for a veteran's life, or what's left of it. Several of my erstwhile colleagues have led on this topic and I am a follower.

The second would be a desire to know and understand the perspective and actions of terrorist bombers, perhaps through a process similar to the South African Truth and Reconciliation Commission. It seems to me that the balance of 'amnesty' for past crimes in Northern Ireland is distorted in favour of convicted terrorists and the legal pursuit of ageing veterans is sickening to observe. I would like to hear from the terrorists about the devices I dealt with; perhaps not face to face but in a way that would fill in the many blanks in my understanding of what went on. We were engaged in asymmetric warfare and that asymmetry has persisted.

The third wish concerns what I see as the demise of our Armed Forces. It is shocking to consider how small our conventional forces have become. NATO planning for war anticipates a nuclear exchange at some point in a future major conflict. It is generally accepted that the threshold for a nuclear exchange reduces as conventional force structures reduce, as does the real value of deterrence. I am not a war monger but as Sun Tzu said, "The art of war teaches us to rely not on the likelihood of the enemy's not coming, but on our own readiness to receive him; not on the chance of his not attacking, but rather on the fact that we have made our position unassailable". Political expedience and broken promises must give way to preparedness. The decline in our conventional forces, in number and capability must be reversed.

NEVER LET FEAR OF THE CONSEQUENCES OF FAILURE HOLD YOU BACK

Jargon Buster

Please note that definitions are contemporary to my service and may now be obsolete.

ABSDA	Army Base Storage & Distribution Agency
A&ERs	Ammo & Explosives Regulations – Haynes manual for ammunition
ACR	Annual Confidential Report
ANFO	Ammonium Nitrate & Fuel Oil
ANNIE	Ammonium Nitrate & Nitrobenzene homemade explosive
APA	Ammunition Process Area
APC	Armoured Personnel Carrier
Aphasia	Difficulty with language or speech
Apheresis	Collection of blood cells by filtering the whole body blood volume
APR	Abdominal Peroneal Resection
ARB	Armagh Roulement Battalion
ARCENT	US Army Central HQ
AS of A	Army School of Ammunition
ASD	Ammunition Sub Depot
ASGM	Air to Surface Guided Missile
AT	Ammunition Technician
AT4	Swedish anti-tank rocket
ATO	Ammunition Technical Officer
AWOL	Absent Without Official Leave
Azimuth	Direction of compass bearing where a weapon is pointed
Back-squadded	Moved back to a more junior training platoon to repeat training

BAD	Base Ammunition Depot
Barmine	Bar-shaped plastic anti-tank mine containing 8kg of RDX/TNT
BAS	Battle Attrition Study
BATLSK	British Army Training & Liaison Staff Kenya
Batman	Officer's valet or 'dogs body'
Battalion	A formed unit of soldiers several hundred strong
BBK	Bessbrook
BCMD	Biological & Chemical Munition Disposal
Beaver	Light, fixed-wing aircraft used by the RAF for aerial photography
Beluga	Cluster bomb sub-munition
BFES	British Forces Education Service
BFPO	British Forces Post Office
BFT	Basic Fitness Test
BI	Blast Incendiary – explosive device containing accelerant
Bore Premature	Premature functioning of ammunition within the bore of the weapon
Buddy-buddy	Mutual assistance & checking each other when donning equipment
CAD	Central Ammunition Depot
Cdr	Conductor – The senior British Army warrant officer appointment
CE	Composition Exploding or Tetryl
CFT	Combat Fitness Test
Chinook	Twin-rotor medium-lift helicopter used by the RAF
CILSA	Chief Inspector Land Service Ammunition
CLA	Conventional Land Ammunition
Company	A formed unit of soldiers about one hundred strong
Composition B	Castable mixture of RDX & TNT
Concession Road	Short-cut between adjacent parts of Eire, south of Crossmaglen
CSM	Company Sergeant Major
Delta Day	Fourth day of duty cycle in Belfast with 12-hour notice to move
DEMS	Defence Explosives & Munitions School (see AS of A)

Dhobi	Laundry
DI	Destructor Incendiary – military munition containing thermite
DLSA	Directorate of Land Service Ammunition – superseded CILSA
DMS	Boots with Directly Moulded Soles
Duncairn Gardens Fund	Large bag of 50 pence pieces – proceeds of fines for cockups
EDI	Explanation, Demonstration, Imitation – monkey see, monkey do
EOD	Explosive Ordnance Disposal
Escapement Mechanism	Clockwork delay mechanism found in mechanical fuzes
Fast Roping	Exiting hovering helicopter on a rope
Felix	Call sign for EOD operator or EOD Team
Fiddlers Three	Sergeants' Mess in Salalah, Oman, named after bribe-takers
FKL	Forkhill
Flight Premature	Premature functioning of ammunition in flight after muzzle exit
FOD	Foreign Object Damage – Detritus that can damage aircraft
Frangex	Commercial explosive
GCGI	Graduate of the City & Guilds Institute
GM	Guided Missile (referring to the bit that flies)
Gozome Bird	The aeroplane that takes you home
GP	General Purpose
GP	Gunpowder
Grid Square removal service	See MLRS below
Grim Reaper	The staff officer at Didcot who nominated personnel for EOD tours
GW	Guided Weapon (referring to the whole system including launcher)
HME	Home Made Explosives
IEDD	Improvised Explosive Device Disposal
INLA	Irish National Liberation Army
IPLO	Irish People's Liberation Organisation

IRA	Irish Republican Army
IRFNA	Inhibited Red Fuming Nitric Acid
IRI	Inspection & Repair Instruction
JNCO	Junior NCO
Khaki	Brown colour
L15	Sleek, long artillery shell – see M107 below
Land Shark	Man-eating dog
LAW 80	94mm anti-tank rocket system
LE Commission	Commissioned from the ranks
Licensing	6-monthly testing of EOD Operator's competence
Lynx	Army Air Corps helicopter
M107	Short, fat & dumpy 155mm artillery shell
M109	Self-propelled gun able to fire the M107 shell
M60	7.62mm US Army machine gun
Meadow Beer	Premium German beer
Mercury Fulminate	Primary detonating explosive
MILAN	Missile d'Infanterie Léger Antichar – an anti-tank missile
MLRS	Multi Launch Rocket System
MoD 90	Service Identity Card
Mucosal Melanoma	Very rare & aggressive melanoma variant arising internally
Muzzle Premature	Premature functioning of ammunition on exiting the muzzle
NAO	National Audit Office (Government bean counters)
NBC	Nuclear, Biological & Chemical (clothing, equipment or warfare)
NCO	Non-Commissioned Officer
NTH	Newtownhamilton
OIRA	Official IRA
OPB	Old Port Barracks in Al Jubayl (renovated for us by the RE).
PE	Plastic Explosive
Pig	Humber APC
Pipe Range	A gun range inside a large concrete pipe, ideal for confined areas
PIRA	Provisional IRA

Platoon	A formed unit of soldiers up to 30 strong
POP	Passing Out Parade
Q Car	Covert car
R&R	Rest & Recuperation
RAOC	Royal Army Ordnance Corps
RARS	Revised Ammunition Rates & Scales
RDX	Research & Development Explosive
RE	Royal Engineers
RESA	RE Search Advisor
REST	RE Search Team
RIC	Reconnaissance Information Centre
RLC	Royal Logistic Corps
RMCS	Royal Military College of Science
Rockeye	Cluster bomb sub-munition
RPC	Regimental Proficiency Certificate
RPC	Royal Pioneer Corps
RSM	Regimental Sergeant Major
RSP	Render Safe Procedure
SA80	5.56mm Rifle
SACLOS	Semi-Automatic Command Line of Sight – missile guidance type
SAGM	Surface to Air Guided Missile
Saracen	Alvis 6-wheeled APC
SATO	Senior Ammunition Technical Officer in rank of major
Schadenfreude	Pleasure derived by an individual at another's misfortune
Scout	Light Helicopter used by the Army Air Corps
Sea King	RN Helicopter
Section	A formed unit of soldiers about 10 strong
SI	Statutory Instrument
Sioux	Light helicopter used by the Army Air Corps
SLR	7.62mm Self Loading Rifle derived from the Belgian FN
SNCO	Senior NCO
SOAF	Sultan of Oman's Armed Forces
SOAPAT	Surveillance of Ammunition Performance At Training

SOXMIS	Soviet Military Mission
Squadron	Numerically similar to a company
SSC	Short Service Commission
SSGM	Surface to Surface Guided Missile
Stickies	Nickname for OIRA
STT	Special To Theatre training course
Swingfire	SACLOS anti-tank guided missile
SX2	Sheet Explosive 2
TNT	Tri Nitro Toluene
TOW	Tube-launched Optically-guided wire-controlled anti-tank missile
TPU	Time & Power Unit
TTW	Transition To War
UDMH	Unsymmetrical Di-Methyl Hydrazine
UFF	Ulster Freedom Fighters
UVF	Ulster Volunteer Force
Weegie	Of or pertaining to Glasgow. A Glaswegian
Wessex	RAF Helicopter
Woka	See Chinook
WSIT	Weapon System Integration Test
XMG	Crossmaglen

Milton Keynes UK
Ingram Content Group UK Ltd.
UKHW022318081123
432208UK00001B/2